SEA HARRIER OVER THE FALKLANDS

SEA HARRIER OVER THE FALKLANDS
A Maverick at War

by
Commander 'Sharkey' Ward, DSC, AFC, RN

LEO COOPER

London

First published in Great Britain in 1992 by
LEO COOPER
an imprint of
Pen & Sword Books Ltd,
47 Church Street, Barnsley, South Yorkshire S70 2AS

Reprinted November 1992

ISBN 0 85052 305 2

A CIP catalogue record for this book is available
from the British Library

Typeset by Yorkshire Web, Barnsley, South Yorkshire
in Bembo 10 point

Printed by
Redwood Press Limited
Melksham, Wiltshire

CONTENTS

To the memory of

John Eyton-Jones
Alan Curtis
Gordie Batt, DSC
Nick Taylor

and for my two boys
Kristian and Ashton

Glossary

A&AEE	Aircraft and Armament Experimental Establishment at Boscombe Down
AAR	Air-to-Air Refuelling
AAWC	Anti-Air Warfare Control Ship: the ship with the responsibility for controlling the Group's air defence assets. No air movements should be made without the AAWC's explicit knowledge and authority
ACM	Air Combat Manoeuvring: fighter combat, dog-fighting
ACT	Air Combat Training
Aden cannon	30-mm air-to-air and air-to-surface gun with high-explosive or armour-piercing ammunition. The Sea Harrier carries two cannon mounted in pods on either side of the fuselage belly
AEO	Air Engineer Officer
AEW	Airborne Early Warning
AI	Air Intercept: 'Do some AI' means 'Do some Air Intercept training'
AIM	Air Intercept Missile, as in Sidewinder AIM-9L
Air Staff	Representing the RAF in the Ministry of Defence
Air taxi, to	To move the aircraft from point A to point B when in the hover
Angle of attack	An aerodynamic term which defines the angle at which the chord line of the wing is presented relative to the airstream
AWI	Air Warfare Instructor
Axis, attack/threat	The geographical bearing along which an attack or threat is expected
BAe	British Aerospace: manufacturer of Sea Harrier
Blue Fox	The mono-pulse radar fitted to the Sea Harrier to support its Air Intercept, Surface Reconnaissance and Surface Attack Weapon System needs. It represents the heart of the aircraft weapon system. An exceptionally reliable, user-friendly system specially designed for single-seat fast jet operations. Information from the radar can be fed directly to the HUD in conjunction with information from the Navhars and other black boxes
Blue on blue	Engaging — and injuring or damaging — friendly forces by mistake
Bogey	Enemy air contact
Booties	Royal Marines
Brass Hat	Officers reaching or exceeding the rank of Commander, Lieutenant-Colonel, Wing Commander, have gold braid on the peaks of their caps
Buccaneer	Conventional carrier-borne fighter-bomber
'Burner'	Slang for jet engine reheat, i.e. burning extra fuel in the engine exhaust, thus greatly increasing thrust
Cab	Aircraft
Canberra	A British built, twin-jet bomber/reconnaissance aircraft that once held the world altitude record. Not to be confused with the name of the passenger liner that carried our troops to the Falklands
CAP	Combat Air Patrol. Aircraft can conduct a roving CAP or, as in the defence of the Task Group, can be told to patrol a particular part of the sky in order to detect, deter, intercept and destroy attacking aircraft
CCA	Carrier Controlled Approach: as opposed to a visual approach conducted by the pilot. Employed at night and in bad weather, with ship's radar information being used to guide the pilot down a specific glide slope to the deck
Conventional flight	A term developed for the VSTOL world to indicate normal as opposed to hovering flight (with, in the Harrier types, thrust nozzles pointing aft, as with all other aircraft)
'D'	Direction officer based in a ship to provide Air Intercept control and assistance to the pilot
DA	Direct Action, as in a bomb fuse. The fuse is triggered on contact unless there is a time delay set to achieve penetration of the target
Dagger	See Mirage Mks III and V
Departure	...from controlled flight. When the aircraft is pushed beyond its aerodynamic limits and takes charge of the pilot

Down the throat	Coming directly towards from a head-on position
Downwind	An aviation term denoting the position in the landing circuit that is opposite to the point of touchdown (abeam the ship and heading in the opposite direction)
Duskers	Landings conducted on a carrier deck at dusk and in the gathering gloom of dark. A pre-requisite in the Fleet Air Arm for pilots before their first night land-on
Exocet	An active radar-homing, sea-skimming, anti-ship missile with a stand-off, over-the-horizon launch capability. Range about 100 kilometres, speed 550 knots. The air-launched variant was carried by the Argentine Super Etendard. The ship-launched version is fitted in many fleets throughout the world
FAA	Fleet Air Arm
Fast jet	Pseudonym for a military fighter or fighter/ground-attack (FGA) aircraft
Fish head	Aviation slang for a Seaman Officer
Flag Officer	An Admiral appointed by Their Lordships (of the Navy) as the operational commander and administrative authority of a fleet or group of ships at sea, or of a shore-based command, e.g. FONAC. Often abbreviated to 'the Flag', which, in practice, is an expression including the Staff of the Admiral
Flyco	The aviation 'bridge' usually jutting out over the flight-deck from the island, from where aircraft movements on deck and in the local skies are controlled
FONAC	Flag Officer Naval Air Command — responsible for all shore-based operations of the Fleet Air Arm
Fox One, Two, Three	A pilot's call of 'Fox One away' means 'I have released a head-on missile'. 'Fox Two' means a stern missile shot, and 'Fox Three' means a guns kill
Front-line	Operational as opposed to training or support
Full braking stop	A detent in the Harrier's nozzle quadrant which allows the pilot to place the nozzles forward of the vertical and so provide a braking force on the jet either in flight or on the ground
Gannet	Conventional propellor-driven carrier-borne Airborne Early Warning aircraft
G	The force of gravity. Referred to in unit form to indicate how much centrifugal force is being experienced by the aircraft and pilot during manoeuvre
G suit	A special inflatable garment which fits tightly around the pilot's stomach and legs. When the pilot is pulling G in a tight manoeuvre, the vertical forces in his body tend to prevent a normal supply of blood to the brain. If nothing is done, the pilot then blacks out. The G suit inflates when the aircraft is under G, squeezing the abdomen and legs and preventing blood pooling in that area, thus sustaining an adequate supply to the brain
Goofers	Deck space on a carrier's island from where 'goofers' can 'goof' at interesting events on deck and in the air
Goon suit	A rubberised neck-to-toe, water-resistant garment worn by naval aviators when operating in cool/cold climes over a cold sea — an essential safety aid in the Falklands
Harrier GR Mk 3	The RAF Ground-Attack and Reconnaissance Harrier. Abbreviated to GR3
Hotline gunsight	The air-to-air gunsight provided to the Sea Harrier HUD by the Smiths Industries Electronics Unit. The computerised display shows the pilot where his cannon shells will go at any moment of firing. It is a state-of-the-art, effective aiming system that can be either manually or radar controlled
Hover stop	The detent in the Harrier's nozzle control quadrant that marks the position of the nozzle control lever when the nozzles are set for hovering. The pilot does not need to look at the quadrant when selecting the hover stop
HUD	Head-Up Display. A see-through display directly in front of the pilot upon which flight and weaponry information is projected. This allows the pilot to keep his eyes on the real world outside and, at the same time, to monitor his flight conditions without looking down inside the cockpit, and is a great aid to flight safety and to good weapon delivery
IFTU	Intensive Flying Trials Unit: a squadron specially commissioned to evaluate and test a new aircraft and its weapon systems on entry to service. The IFTU's task also includes developing operational tactics and converting pilots to the new aircraft type
Instrument flying	When a pilot uses his flight instruments (artificial horizon, altimeter, air-speed indicator, angle of attack indicator, etc.) as his principle reference for controlling his aircraft in flight
Island (a ship's)	The vertical superstructure on the right-hand side of an aircraft-carrier's deck, housing the ship's funnels, radar aerials, the bridge, and Flyco
Jet-borne flight	Term used to describe VSTOL aircraft when they are in the hover (or close to the hover) and all their weight is being supported by the thrust from the vertical nozzles (as opposed to by the wing)

'Judy'	Fighter pilot intercept jargon. A surface-based Direction Officer may be calling ranges and bearings of the target to the pilot. When the pilot sees the target on his own radar and is happy to take control of the intercept, he calls 'Judy'
Laydown	A type of bombing attack: passing over a target at low level and releasing the bomb at very short range (very accurately). Retard bombs are used for laydown bombing; they have parachute-type airbrakes to slow the flight of the bomb down relative to the aircraft. This allows the aircraft to be well ahead of the bomb when the latter hits the target
Lepus flare	A 6-million-candlepower flare, dropped or tossed from fast jets to illuminate targets for reconnaissance or night-attack purposes
Life preserver	A waistcoat worn by the pilot with an inflatable stole to keep him afloat plus other aids to survival and rescue (light, whistle, heliograph, radio etc.)
Mach	Measurement of speed in units of the speed of sound: e.g. Mach 1 = 660 knots; Mach 0.85 = about 550 knots
Mark I eyeball	Exaggerative aviation slang for the eyes or eyesight
Milliradian	An angular measurement used to set the depression that a pilot needs for a weapon attack. Defined as the angle subtended by one metre at a range of 1000 metres
Mirage Mks III and V	French-built, delta-wing, supersonic (Mach 2), single-seat jets. The III is a fighter fitted with a simple air-to-air radar, air-to-air missiles and guns. The V, known as the Dagger, is a fighter/ground-attack variant carrying guns and air-to-surface ordnance
MOD (PE)	Ministry of Defence (Procurement Executive)
'Mother'	Pilots' jargon for their aircraft-carrier
NAS	Naval Air Squadron — as in 801, 820, 800, etc. The '8' depicts a front-line squadron; a '7' depicts a second-line or training squadron, e.g. 700A — the Intensive Flying Trials Squadron. The abbreviation is also used before a place name to indicate a Naval Air Station, as in NAS Yeovilton
Navhars	Sea Harrier Navigation Heading Attitude Reference System: a computer-based system of first-generation Inertial Navigation System accuracy which receives its attitude reference from a sophisticated oscillogyro platform. It gives the pilot navigation and attitude information, gives him cues to follow, and can be easily updated by the pilot using radar or visual information. Unlike a back-seater, it doesn't talk back!
Navhars destinations	There are several memory banks in the Navhars which can be programmed with different destinations to suit a pilot's navigation needs
'Nuking'	As in description of USS *Nimitz*, which is nuclear powered
Picket	A destroyer or frigate placed up-threat of the main body of ships to provide early warning of attack and to contribute to defence in depth with its weapon systems. Beyond air defence pickets would be stationed air defence aircraft, i.e. Sea Harriers on CAP
Pickle button	The weapon release button. To pickle is to press the button
Pole-handler	Pilot, also referred to as 'jet-jockey'
Port	Left
Position destination marker	A marker on the radar screen that shows the pilot where his avionics system thinks a particular pre-programmed destination is situate
Pucara	Argentine-built twin-turbo-prop, twin-seat, heavily armoured, ground-attack aircraft armed with rockets, guns and bombs
Puffer jet	Jet exhaust nozzles in the nose, tail and wing tips of the Harrier which allow the pilot to control attitude when in jet-borne flight, e.g. the hover
QFI	Qualified Flying Instructor: trained to teach academic flying to student pilots and to monitor non-operational standards and practices in front- and second-line squadrons
Radar acquisiton cross	The symbol in the HUD that shows the pilot the point in space that the locked radar is pointing at, e.g. an aircraft, a ship, a school of killer whales, etc.
Radar pick-up	A radar contact
Round-down	The aft end (back) of an aircraft-carrier's flight-deck. It is rounded down to prevent aircraft on a too low approach catching the edge of the deck with the tail-hook
Royal Air Force	Referred to in the text by well known pseudonyms: crabs, the Light Blue (after the colour of their uniform)
Rotary wing	Helicopter
RP	Rocket Projectile. Sea Harrier carries pods of thirty-six 2-inch RP for use as an area weapon against thin-skinned targets
RT	Radio Transmission: or, simply, the radio
SAVO	Staff Aviation Officer: a member of an Admiral's Staff specially appointed to advise the Admiral on all operational and training aviation matters

SARBE	Search And Rescue Beacon: a two-way emergency radio transmitter/receiver carried in the pilot's life preserver
Sea Harrier SHAR	Fighter, reconnaissance, strike aircraft. Single-seat, subsonic VSTOL aircraft with all-weather operational capability. The Mark I aircraft as described in this book is armed with Sidewinder air-to-air missiles; 30-mm Aden cannon for air-to-air; bombs; rockets; Lepus flares and, now but not during the war, the Sea Eagle air-to-surface stand-off missile for surface and ground attack. It is nuclear-capable. Its avionic systems are amongst the most modern available and include the highly successful Blue Fox mono-pulse radar. The Mark II aircraft now entering service is fitted with a more sophisticated look-down radar and the Advanced Medium Range Air-to-Air Missile (AMRAAM) as well as other weapon systems. Nicknames used for the Sea Harrier throughout the book include SHAR, Sea Jet and Jump Jet
Senior Observer	'Observer' is the Naval equivalent of the RAF's 'Navigator'
Senior Pilot	Otherwise known as the SP, Splot or Senior P; second-in-command in a Sea Harrier squadron
Senior Service	The Royal Navy
Shrike missile	An American missile, based on the Sparrow, which homes on to a radar emitter
Sidewinder cross	The symbol in the HUD that tells the pilot where the missile seeker-head is looking
Sighting angle	The depression of the pilot's aiming mark. It differs for every weapon type, every dive angle, every release speed, and has to be calculated by the AWI
Silent Service	The Royal Navy
Six o'clock, the	The area directly astern of (behind) the aircraft. Twelve o'clock is ahead, three o'clock is right 90°, etc.
Ski-jump	The upward curve at the end of the UK carriers' deck runways which gives the aircraft an upward velocity at launch, allowing it to leave the deck at less than flying speed. Before upward momentum is lost, the aircraft accelerates under its own power to partially wing-borne, partially jet-borne flight. Known as the 'runway in the sky', it is probably the easiest way of getting a fast jet airborne
Sky Hawk	Also referred to as the A-4. American-built fighter/ground-attack aircraft, single-seat, subsonic, no radar, armed with bombs, rockets and guns
Starboard	Right
Super Etendard	French-built, transsonic, single-seat, maritime fighter/surface-attack aircraft fitted with simple air-to-surface radar. Armed with Exocet air-to-surface missile, guns and bombs
Task Group	A group of warships, in this case a Carrier Battle Group, subordinate to the command of the Task Force Commander (Admiral Sir John Fieldhouse) and working in parallel with, but without any executive authority over, other 'groups' such as the Land Forces (Major-General Jeremy Moore) and the Amphibious Group (Commodore Mike Clapp)
Topside	On deck
Tracer ammunition	Bullets or shells which are given a special coating that lights up the round in flight. This allows the firer to correct his aim, and it also frightens the pants off the target
Trade	A target or targets that the fighter will attempt to intercept
Transition/ing	A VSTOL term indicating the period of flight between wing-borne and jet-borne flight, e.g. transitioning to the hover (from jet-borne flight)
Translating	Moving the jet sideways in the hover
'Type 64 warship'	Jocular term for a combination of two ships, Types 42 and 22, whose defensive weapon systems (Sea Dart and Sea Wolf) complement each other
Update fix, radar	To check that the aircraft navigation system is aligned with the real world, the pilot can update his sytem by locking his radar onto a known geographical point feature, the co-ordinates of which have already been programmed into the Navhars. If there is a misalignment, the real world fix can be fed into the system to update it
Up-threat	Between the threat and the defended unit(s)
Vector	A voice command from surface controllers telling the pilot to turn onto a specific heading
VSTOL	Vertical and Short Take-Off and Landing
VT	Variable Time, as in a bomb fuse. This misnamed fuse has a proximity sensor which can be set for the bomb to explode at different heights above the ground or sea
Weapons-tight	A weapons-readiness state in which no one is allowed to fire at anybody who is not firing at him
Wing-borne flight	A term describing VSTOL aircraft in conventional (normal) flight, with the thrust nozzles facing aft (as opposed to vertically down for the hover). The aircraft's weight is totally supported by lift from the wing
'Wings'	Nickname for Commander (Air), the officer responsible to the Captain for all aspects of aviation on board — the Air Boss
Your tail is clear	There is no one behind you or threatening you from the rear

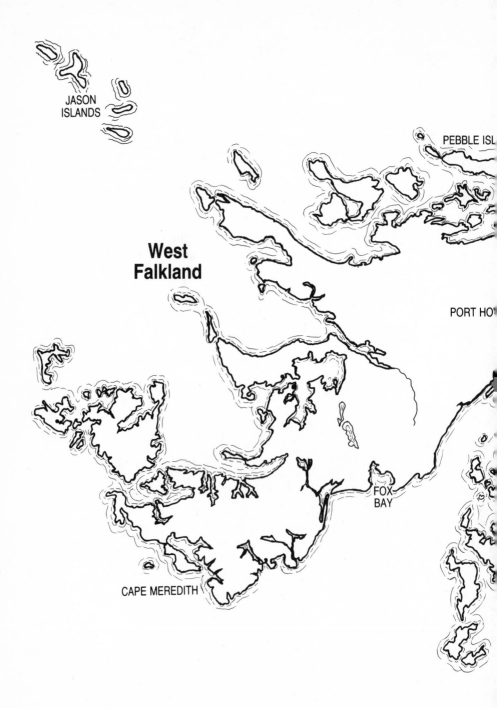

JASON
ISLANDS

**West
Falkland**

PEBBLE ISL

PORT HO

FOX
BAY

CAPE MEREDITH

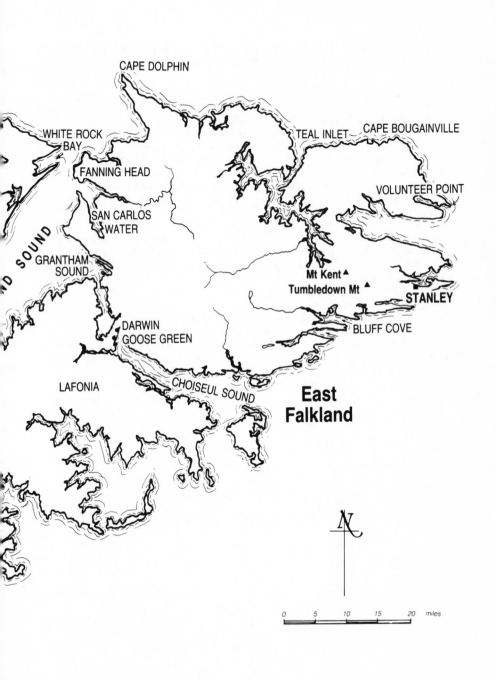

CAPE DOLPHIN

WHITE ROCK
BAY

TEAL INLET   CAPE BOUGAINVILLE

FANNING HEAD

VOLUNTEER POINT

SAN CARLOS
WATER

ND SOUND

GRANTHAM
SOUND

Mt Kent ▲
Tumbledown Mt ▲

STANLEY

DARWIN
GOOSE GREEN

BLUFF COVE

LAFONIA   CHOISEUL SOUND

East
Falkland

N

0   5   10   15   20   miles

Acknowledgements

To the designers, engineers and craftsmen who produced the Sea Harrier and its weapon systems; especially John Fozard of British Aerospace, Greg Stewart of Ferranti, and Andy Cameron of Smiths Industries. The reliability and performance of their products were key factors in the success of the campaign.

To Rolls Royce who provided the power plant for Sea Harrier in the form of the Pegasus jet engine with its astonishing reliability and performance.

To the RAF Wittering Harrier Conversion Unit, who ensured that we in the Navy knew how to operate safely in the VSTOL regime.

To the engineers and maintainers of 700A, 899 and 801 Naval Air Squadrons, whose extraordinary and consistent performance prepared the aircraft so well for war and sustained remarkable availability and serviceability during the fighting.

To the Captain and crew of HMS *Invincible* – there could be no better team with whom to go to war.

To Ralph Wykes-Snead and 820 Squadron for looking after us all in 801, and for rescuing Ian Mortimer.

To Dusty Milner, my Boss, whose energy, and enthusiasm for the Sea Harrier and its operational capability pushed me and my pilots to the limit and beyond.

To my wife, Semiha; to Major-General Julian Thompson, CB, OBE and Jane Thompson; to Pat and Judy Barnard; to Simida and Tom Carswell; and to George and Liz Laville, for all their help, encouragement and support.

And finally, to Toby Buchan, Barbara Bramall and Leo Cooper, whose charm, professionalism and enthusiasm have made the timely publishing of this book not only a reality but a pleasure as well.

Preface

...Very quickly, the Mirage was in Paul's sights. The Sidewinder growled its acquisition, he pickled on the firing button and called 'Fox Two away!'

The missile thundered off the rails like an express train and left a brilliant white smoke trail as it curved up towards the heavens, chasing after the Mirage which was now making for the stars, very nose-high. Paul was mesmerised as the angry missile closed with its target. As the Sidewinder made intercept, the Argentine jet exploded in a vivid ball of yellow flames. It broke its back and then disintegrated before its remains twisted their way down to the cloud and sea below.

'Splash one Mirage!' called the excited SHAR pilot. Then the incredible moment was over and he looked around hurriedly for his leader and the other Mirage. 'Where are you, Steve?.'...

It is probably true to say that in the eye of the average beholder, a modern fighter aircraft is nothing more than a noisy beast that can be seen at public air shows. To most laymen a fighter makes a lot of noise, goes fast and turns tight corners to please the crowd. It is also expensive, it fires expensive weapons, and occasionally it crashes.

To the educated military observer it is a sophisticated weapons platform that is there to provide an important contribution to the defence of the country.

But what of the 'driver'; the pilot?

'What is it like to be a fighter pilot in the modern world?'

'What does it take to be a good fighter pilot?'

'What is it like to be a fighter pilot at war?'

Certain Army 'wallahs' are inclined to be astonished when they find out that fighter pilots do indeed drive their own machines. 'I say, old chap! That's a bit awf! I don't know what I'd do without a driver in my tank!'

Thanks to such revered aerobatics teams as the Red Arrows, the Blue Angels and others, it would not be surprising if the majority of the public viewed a fighter pilot as one of those lucky guys who go around in vivid-coloured flying suits having fun as celebrities and doing everything in formation (or nearly everything).

Occasionally, a glimpse of the true fighter world breaks through the razzmatazz, even at an air show. One of the blue-eyed boys makes a mistake that costs him his life; perhaps the lives of others too. The message comes through that it is a dangerous business, and so it is. Formula 1 Grand Prix racing is equally as dangerous and is, perhaps, a reasonable parallel to the art of being a fighter pilot. You have to be at the top of your trade, think fast, react fast and put your machine in the right place at the right time to achieve the desired result. In a Grand Prix that means passing the chequered flag first, and your attempts to do so are constrained by the rules of safety, the car you are driving, the type of track you are on, and your ability to out-perform the opposition.

Your desired result as a fighter pilot may be stated simply as being able to place your fighter aircraft in a position in the sky that allows you to bring your weapons to bear on the opposition without allowing the opposition the same facility. But unlike a Grand Prix driver, you are not constrained by the physical width of the racing track. There is no tarmac road to limit your movements; just a limitless expanse of sky. The laws of physics and aerodynamics, and the hard deck below, are your race track. And these constrain you to work within the limitations of your aircraft and within the rules of flight safety, ensuring survival. You must apply these simple disciplines at all times to your air combat ability and your tactical expertise in order to out-perform the opposition.

Understanding a fighter pilot is almost as simple as that: provided that you have some idea as to what the game of air combat is all about. And provided that you understand that in war and peace there are other constraints on the pilot, such as working in close co-ordination with other fighter pilots and the rest of the defence effort. Most other personnel within the 'defence effort' understand what guns, missiles and bombs are. But in a frustratingly naive way, many believe that because fighter pilots have guns, missiles and bombs to use then, QED, they themselves understand fighter aircraft and the fighter pilot's art. This misconception can and often does cause the fighter pilot great frustration — and it can also place him in considerable danger.

Being a fighter pilot and being able to fly an aircraft are quite definitely not one and the same thing. That would be like comparing Nigel Mansell or Alain Prost with a learner driver who was competent at starting, stopping and driving along a road. And just as Nigel Mansell might make rather a frightening bus driver, so a fighter pilot who couldn't change his style would not necessarily be the best commercial pilot to have flying you around the world on your holidays. Nor would the best commercial pilot have any chance of acquitting himself well as a fighter pilot, at least not without the right aptitude and an extra three or four years' training.

All that being said, the story of the air war in the Falklands can only be properly understood if you have some genuine feeling for what it takes to be a fighter pilot and some understanding of the intricacies of the modern air combat scene. This book tries to give you that feeling and understanding (a simple guide to the basics of air combat is provided in Appendix II). It looks into the mind and feelings of a fighter pilot who was fortunate enough to be in the right place at the right time, and was strong enough a character to influence events on the surface as well as in the air.

The book combines a view of air combat with the feelings and experiences of its author prior to and during the war. It doesn't pull any punches. And it attempts to answer those questions:

'What is it like to be a fighter pilot in the modern world?'

'What does it take to be a good fighter pilot?'

'What is it like to be a fighter pilot at war?'

Sharkey Ward
Marmaris, Turkey, 1992

Prologue

When you arrive at Dartmouth Royal Naval College as a raw officer cadet, you are told by a pompous, somewhat subhuman apparition in uniform with an over-used tongue in his cheek that, 'The ideal Naval Awficer Cadet only has 'alf a brain! The other 'alf gets filled in by us! Ho, ho, ho!' Standing there amidst ranks of equally bewildered and apprehensive young men (all dressed as though they were auditioning for a gentleman's tailor's advert) I didn't really have a clue what the Petty Officer Gunnery Instructor was trying to say.

Looking back on my time in the Senior Service, I sometimes wonder whether the purveyor of such wisdom was correct. After a few years of toeing the line and getting to know how the system worked, the longer I served the more difficult I found it to conform to the 'accepted' way of getting on. That could be because I had less than half a brain at the start and the Service didn't manage to fill the vacuum entirely; or, biased as I am, I believe the real reason I became, in some people's eyes, a 'bit of a maverick' was that I already had a full brain cavity. My ability and desire to question the order of things, and to try to remain my own man, proved to be unusual and was not the best way to climb the promotion ladder, particularly in the Silent Service. But even with the balance that comes with advancing years and the benefit of hindsight, there are few things that I would change if I had to run the same course again. I might indeed be less tolerant of fools than in Round One. But that might well have denied me the opportunity of a lifetime, and I would much prefer to retain the satisfaction of looking back at a war well fought than at a second Court Martial well lost. (My first and only Court Martial resulted from a pleasant couple of hours' beating-up the beaches of Cornwall, Devon and Somerset.)

The 'war' I refer to is the South Atlantic affray in 1982, when Britain sent a major Task Force 7,000 miles to the Falklands to recover the islands from General Galtieri's force of occupation. It was a brave and an honest decision by Britain's first woman Prime Minister, and it was taken in the face of general opposition from world opinion.

Looking back over the years, it almost appears as if the United Nations lacked integrity in its attitude to the British initiative. There was little support for our sabre rattling. After all, the Falklands was only a small outpost of the long-dead British Empire, and was inhabited by little more than a few million sheep and 1,800 mainly Cornish expatriates. The fact that these hardy people who originated from Britain wished to remain firmly under the Union Jack and pay allegiance to the Queen was not considered very relevant in UN Headquarters, nor was the fact that Galtieri's sins at the helm of a police state were about to come home to roost, and that he wished to divert the minds of the Argentinian people away from home troubles. Invading the Falklands — or 'the Malvinas', as Buenos Aires would have them called — gave the Argentinian people a *cause célébre*, and the majority were soon happily immersed in a nationalistic crusade to liberate the islands, quickly forgetting Galtieri's track record at home.

Come 1990 and Saddam Hussein's invasion of Kuwait, the United Nations suddenly came alive. How terrible that this important Emirate should be annexed by Big Brother Iraq! Old chap, we really cannot allow this to happen in the modern world! World opinion spoke with one voice against the invader, although not because of any altruistic feeling of sympathy from members of the UN; it was because of commercial and economic necessity. If Saddam took Kuwait and was allowed to get away with it, then Saudi Arabia would be next. And what would happen to everyone's economic future with a madman controlling the most important oil fields in the world? But what a pity that even such an august and revered body as the UN should be seen to adapt its principles in less than a decade to suit its own ends. Wrong had been done in 1982 but all the boys at the club had turned a blind eye; all, that is, except for three nations.

New Zealand showed no malice about being kicked in the fork when Britain joined the Common Market. Instead, her erstwhile Prime Minister offered physical military aid in the form of a fully manned frigate ready for war. It was the only such offer from any of our Commonwealth brothers.

The United States had to play politics in her approach to 'her oldest ally's problem' but, under the discreet and capable helmsmanship of Casper Weinberger, provided the UK with strong moral backing and considerable under-the-table support. Sadly, it was on the same sort of terms as the assistance rendered in the two world wars: 'We'll help you, but you have to pay!' Suddenly the price of US weaponry doubled. But what can you do when you are out on a limb and you need a friend's help? All you can do is pay up and shut up.

The third UN club member to show great interest was the then-Great Russian Bear. Here was a member of NATO sticking its neck out on a seemingly impossible task. Would Britain get smacked, as the majority of the world thought? Or would it come up smelling of victory and roses?

2

There was no doubt that, for the Moscow audience, watching the UK Task Force's progress was going to be better than viewing any imported soap opera.

With the Prime Minister's announcement on 2 April 1982 that we would fight to regain the Falklands, patriotism and jingoism returned to the British countryside, and a great debate began on television as to who was going to win and what the odds were against success. The pundits kept on coming back to one very valid point: what is the Task Force going to do for air defence? The surface and sub-surface threat was pretty well catered for, but what could a handful of Sea Harriers do against up to 200 Argentinian military aircraft? There were Mirage IIIs and Vs (faster than the jump jet, and they could pull more 'G' as well), Navy Sky Hawk A-4s, Etendards armed with Exocet, Pucaras, and many more. It was a valid question and it was up to me as the senior figure in the Sea Harrier world to help answer it with actions — and successful ones, at that.

In order to give the reader a better feel for 'what it was like during the war', and before attempting to recall the excitement of the action, it is worth reviewing certain events and episodes in my own Royal Navy Fleet Air Arm experience, as an aid to understanding the attitude of mind of the Navy fighter pilots as they set off south for war.

It is also important to understand that, although being a true fighter pilot is a vocation and demands 100 per cent dedication and application, each pilot is an individual with his own special view on events, on life and on death. Each has his fears and aspirations, his family and his responsibilities, and all the boys heading south had been spawned (or at least grew up) in years of peace and stability. For some, going to war was a shock; for others it was a dream come true. The latter was the case as far as I was concerned.

Now to the story I want to tell. I tell it as I saw it. If my perception does not accord with other commentaries on the war, then readers will have to judge the validity of my opinions in the light of their own experience and the experience of other authors. What I am about to relate are the facts as I saw them. My story gives away no state secrets about Sea Harrier or other weapon platforms, but it does present the truth in a way that has not been published to date.

Part I

THE LEAD UP TO SAILING
SOUTH WITH THE
CARRIER TASK GROUP

1

It was 1982 and the new year had dawned, the stormy sea and sky were painted warship grey by day, and the outside air temperature was low enough to freeze the proverbials off a monkey. I and my Sea Harrier squadron were embarked in HMS *Invincible* off the coast of Norway and, in spite of the chillingly unfriendly weather, NATO Exercise 'Alloy Express' was going well.

Since mid-1981, when the squadron was commissioned, 801 Squadron had already operated with the American Fleet in the Atlantic and had also visited the US Navy in Norfolk, Virginia. Our new aircraft had proved itself to be a reliable and effective fleet defence all-weather fighter by day and night, but was now being asked to operate in conditions that prevented even the mighty USS *Nimitz* from conducting flying operations. Whether 'nuking' her bulk through the ocean at more than 40 knots or, as she was now, pitching like a bitch as she battled with the elements, she was a magnificent sight. And, as the American admirals would say, come hell or high water, if she needed to launch her 100-plus air group in earnest then she would. Getting the jets back on board would not be so easy but her devastating offensive punch would have been delivered against the Soviets on cue, and that is what mattered to NATO.

Exercises such as 'Alloy Express' were realistic enough, but when the weather deteriorated beyond reason in peacetime there was little sense even for *Nimitz* to risk losing half an air group by operating beyond the limits of prudence. The smaller, graceful *Invincible* seemed almost like a destroyer escort beside the mammoth US carrier, but rode the sea better and had a fighter on board that could be pushed harder when it came to bad weather.

It had been easy enough launching the Sea Harrier (SHAR) from the deck when the British carrier was hiding in the calm of the Norwegian fjords, where no other fixed-wing jet could think of taking off or landing. Indeed, it had been a lot of fun playing with the 'enemy' Fast Patrol Boats that attempted to attack *Invincible* with torpedoes. As soon as the tiny boats had run in for their attack and were sighted rounding the immense buttresses that formed the sides of the narrow waterway, it had meant a rapid scramble for the 'alert' SHAR pilot to get airborne from the 'ski-jump', haul-arse the little jet round towards the FPB targets, simulate arming the Aden cannon and then beat seven bells of hell out of the appreciative Norwegian sailors (passing only feet over their heads at 500 knots plus): a quick professional kill within minutes of the threat being observed and well before the FPBs came into torpedo range.

Out in the North Norwegian Sea it was a very different game. The threat was 'round the clock' from regiments of Soviet bombers carrying air-to-surface missiles, and the calm of the fjords was replaced by continuous gale-force winds, a heavy sea and, on occasion, solid cloud from 200 feet to more than 30,000 feet.

On first going to sea in July 1981, the 801 Squadron remit was to prove the Sea Harrier and its full radar and weapon system under operational conditions, and there was no one on earth keener to do this than myself, the Squadron Commanding Officer. (Proving the aircraft under operational conditions meant carrying out a full investigation into its capabilities. Was it the right aircraft for the job? How good was it at that job?) The SHAR was my personal protegé, my baby, and had been since the jet entered service in 1979. I had a great team working for me and together we had already shown the military world that the little jump jet could always equal and often surpass the capability of other more recognised fighters, particularly in fighter combat and also when conventional naval aircraft found the weather conditions too tough to handle. 'Alloy Express' afforded the opportunity to test the aircraft and its pilots in the most atrocious conditions.

Certain limits had been placed on the operation of the SHAR aircraft by the Test Pilot Establishment at Boscombe Down: limits in ship movement (pitch, roll and heave), and in weather. These very conservative constraints had long been forgotten as the squadron's enthusiasm to prove a point had prevailed. My own attitude to the task had also become infectious to a degree where the flying boss on board the ship, Dusty Milner, was still pressing the squadron to fly at night when the conditions were well 'over the top'; or in squadron pilots' eyes, near-suicidal.

'Come on now, Sharkey! You've flown in conditions as bad as this before. What's the problem? Is 801 losing its bottle?'

It was not really the best way of persuading me to accede. The one thing that my pilots didn't lack was bottle. Who else in peacetime would fly a single-engined jet 300 nautical miles or more away from a carrier in bad weather over a freezing sea, with little hope of a timely rescue if you went down?

'The problem, Sir,' heavy emphasis on the 'Sir' bit even though Dusty and I were on first-name terms when off duty, 'is as follows: the deck is pitching 7° and our theoretical Boscombe Down limit is 2°; the ship is rolling like a pig; she is heaving up and down about 30 feet; the cloud base is reported to be 200 feet but looks worse to me; tops are reported to be in excess of 38,000 feet with no gaps; and last but not least we are talking of night flying! We have never operated before with such a combination of out-of-limit factors, and I don't wish to push our luck without good reason.' It was the last statement that represented the real reason for not wishing to fly. There would be no 'enemy' aircraft launching from shore to attack the fleet that night (the land-based RAF team who were playing at being 'orange forces' or Russians would never dream of taking off in such weather just to play with the Navy) – so why bash your head against a brick wall if you don't need to? Night flying was fine when there was something to do. But sitting in a cramped cockpit on your tod, looking at a set of flight instruments and a blank radar screen for an hour and a half in thick clag with no one to play with, seemed pointless.

At thirty-eight, I had already begun to cogitate on the certain fact that my operational flying career in the Royal Navy Fleet Air Arm was soon to come to an end. Listed for promotion to Commander in July, the writing was on the wall – Commanders don't fly aeroplanes, they fly desks. I knew that I should stop resisting the wishes of my seniors if one day I wanted to wear Admiral's rank, but common sense and logic had always tended to rule my judgement, not personal ambition. I could hardly be described as the norm for a dedicated career officer, and was certainly not ready at the ring of my masters' bell to become transformed into a permanent bureaucratic Whitehall Warrior and 'yes man'.

I had already tasted the joys of being a staff officer in the Ministry of Defence when serving as the SHAR desk officer and there I had found that if you wanted rapid promotion, it generally meant toeing the line and agreeing with superiors. Sadly, superior in rank does not necessarily always mean superior in operational experience, logic or common sense, but to get on in the service you had to play the game. I despised 'yes men' and would prefer to stand up and be counted rather than conform for conformity's sake. And over the previous three years as 'Mr Sea Harrier', I had had to buck the system many times and struggle like hell to change entrenched views and get the Sea Harrier operational.

This had been largely due to the fact that the majority of my naval masters appeared ready to abandon the fight to keep the Fixed Wing (Fast Jet) Fleet Air Arm going. In the constant inter-Service battle for resources, the RAF had demonstrated a tenacious appetite for 'knocking' the Fleet Air Arm, and it appeared that the incessant sniping by the junior service was bearing fruit. *Invincible* was about to be flogged to the Australians after only two years in service, and the RAF were to 'assume a greater responsibility for defending the Fleet at sea'!

How many times would the corridors of power in Whitehall ring to the arrogant and nonsensical phrase created by the Light Blue (RAF) to serve their own interests: 'The indivisibility of air power'? It was ludicrous that some Air Marshal who may never have served on a front-line squadron in his life should be able to dictate the operational needs of the Navy and say, 'We are the RAF and therefore everything we say about flying and air warfare is gospel!' And even more ludicrous was the fact that senior Civil Servants would blindly accept the logic of such a crass statement. If air warfare experience was to be a meter in judging capability, then how was it that the only aircraft that the RAF had shot down since the 1940's were their own — by accident? So much for quoting experience.

And yet, whilst the aircraft-carriers of the realm were at sea during the fifties and sixties, sacrificing many lives in the course of duty — and at the same time providing the nation with realistic naval air defences — the Air Force was becoming more of an Old Boys' Club than a fighting service. They had learned that if you tell a big enough lie with a straight face, then the people in charge of the purse-strings will believe what you say. Proof of this pudding had come in the late sixties, when the decision to discontinue the Navy's aircraft-carriers had been made.

Why was this decision taken? Because the Air Force claimed that they could defend the Fleet at sea and Britain's interests anywhere on the high seas between Greenland and New Zealand. To prove their point and support their arguments, they appeared to have manufactured a new map of the world to use in their briefings on the carrier debate: they had to have a new one, because the old one had Australia in the wrong position for their purposes. They were trying to show that their fighter and bomber aircraft could support the Fleet anywhere in the Indian Ocean and, when they drew the extended aircraft ranges on the old map from Australia, there was still a big hole left in the centre of that ocean that they could not reach. The easy answer was to move the Australian sub-continent to the left (by several hundred miles). Aircraft operating from Aussie could now cover all the Indian Ocean, albeit only on paper. And the Civil Servants and Government were satisfied: no more carriers.

Nobody stopped to think and to ask the RAF how far they had been able to demonstrate their claims of world coverage. Even the Navy didn't ask the question — after all, if you are called the Silent Service and you are proud of it, why ruin your reputation?

As Dusty — or 'Wings', as all Commanders (Air) are habitually known — continued to insist on 801 Squadron flying in spite of the conditions, I gave in ungracefully and agreed that I and only I would fly. It was definitely too dicey for some of the more junior pilots, and although Ian Mortimer could easily handle it, one jet airborne on a shitty night was less risky than two.

The subdued deck lighting was less welcoming than usual as I went on deck, found my aircraft in the wet murk and then strained against goon suit, G suit and life-preserver to get my right leg high enough to reach the bottom rung of the Sea Harrier cockpit access ladder. (The goon suit was made of heavy rubberised fabric, was waterproof to a degree, and had tight rubber seals at the neck and wrists to prevent water ingress. The G suit was fitted inside the goon suit around the stomach and legs and was inflated when the aircraft was under G to pressurise the lower body and prevent all the blood draining from the pilot's brain — without it, a pilot would black out more easily under high G and would get more tired in combat. The life-preserver fitted around the torso, and included an inflatable stole, oxygen regulator, emergency radio and other goodies. When fully dressed in all the gear, a pilot's movements were rather restricted.)

Above me the night sky over the North Norwegian Sea was as black as the ace of spades. The sea surface was barely visible in the rain and was in turmoil, there was no visual horizon (making recovery on board more trying), and the aircraft creaked up and down on its oleos as the ship twisted and buffeted its way through the gale.

As usual, the plane captain (a squadron junior rating who was directly responsible for the condition of the jet) had prepared the cockpit well. But you stayed alive longer in single-seat jets if you always put safety first, so before strapping in I used my personal torch to check that the rocket-powered ejection seat was 'safe' and all the right switches were in the right places. The light from the torch was dim so as not to wreck my night vision (when you go from a brightly lit room into a dark space, it takes some time for your eyes to get used to the dark). Whilst attending to the routine, if vital, checks my thoughts wandered back to the story behind the first ever night sortie by Sea Harrier from the deck of an operational Royal Navy carrier; from the same deck — HMS *Invincible*.

2

Gaining approval for the front-line squadrons to fly the Sea Harrier from the deck at night proved to be no easy task. Both as the Sea Harrier desk officer in the Ministry of Defence and as Commanding Officer of the Trials Unit, 700A Squadron, I had to cope with many entrenched attitudes about the role and the importance (or otherwise) of the new aircraft to the modern fleet.

Since the 'Carrier Decision' in the late sixties, many senior naval officers who did not want to be seen to buck the system were cautious in the extreme about stating a need for any fixed-wing organic air power at sea (that is, the Navy owning its own air-defence, attack and reconnaissance aircraft). Some saw the introduction of the new jump jet as a sly reversal of the 'Carrier Decision' and did not wish to draw any political attention to the aircraft or its capabilities. At the same time, the Air Staff were more than keen to limit the recognition given to the Sea Harrier's potential. They saw the aircraft as an obstacle to their plans to rid the services of the Fleet Air Arm altogether.

Because of the general opposition to and lack of enthusiasm for the SHAR, it was a long hard fight to persuade the 'system' that the aircraft was more than just a means of shooting down shadowing enemy aircraft by day, and that it was an essential all-weather component of the defence of the Fleet. (Following the military's legendary dedication to exactitude, a Navy 'All-Weather Fighter' may be literally translated to mean 'All-Weather, Day and Night, Fighter, Interceptor, Ground-Attack and Reconnaissance Aircraft'.)

But test pilots at A&AEE Boscombe Down and well-researched aviation medicine opinion at RAE Farnborough had pre-conceived views about the SHAR flying from the deck at sea by night. 'It would not be possible for the average front-line pilot to cope with the difficult flying task. Therefore it should not be permitted.' This rather cloistered view from medics and scientists had been backed up by some extraordinary events during the aircraft's Boscombe Down trials, when the test pilot world carried out their first embarked night-handling checks of the Harrier aircraft on board HMS *Hermes* in early 1979.

As 'Mr Sea Harrier' from the Ministry of Defence, I was privileged to be allowed to witness the performance of these trials; and, as the Navy's official representative on board, I had objected strongly to the trials team about the level of night deck experience that they planned to use. 'Night deck experience' refers to the experience of a pilot or pilots operating fixed-wing aircraft from the deck of an aircraft carrier at night. Night flying from a deck at sea represents the most demanding aspect of all domestic military flying operations and should not be approached lightly or without adequate practice: too many aviators have died learning that lesson. But who was I to criticise the magical capabilities of test pilots, and in particular their lack of professional preparation for the task that lay ahead? Their skills would carry them through! Would they not? My objections were overruled.

One of the civilian trials pilots from British Aerospace, Hatfield, represented a less-than-ideal combination of night experience and hands-on time in the Harrier. He had carried out about four night sorties from land during the previous four years and had never operated from a deck before in his life. And he had a further limitation that did not become obvious until he was airborne.

I sat in *Hermes* on the end of a radio link and listened to events in the air unfold. It was a clear night with a good natural horizon and, on the approach to his first deck landing, the Hatfield Ace demonstrated that he was one of the few pilots who could not assimilate information from instruments that were lit with red light. (In simple terms, this means that specific pilots find it difficult or impossible to read and digest information from instruments lit in this colour. The instruments in the test aircraft were illuminated precisely thus.) As a result, the TP whiz-kid panicked and froze on the controls during the approach to land-on. There he was in a multi-million pound aircraft, the loss of which would cause huge delays to the date at which the SHAR could enter service, and he was incapable of controlling the aircraft at the most dangerous part of the flight profile, the approach to landing.

Just by chance, the aircraft that he was flying was a two-seater Harrier and the 'passenger' in the back seat was none other than Commander Richard Burn, AFC, Royal Navy, the Harrier Project Officer from the Ministry of Defence Procurement Executive (MOD [PE]). Although no longer in a flying appointment, Dick was 'along for the ride' and, as a Navy pilot with considerable experience and significant talent (even for a test pilot!), he was able to take control of the aircraft. When all had seemed lost, he saved the jet from a watery grave.

Well done, Dick! But the official Procurement Executive and Boscombe Down view of the incident appeared to be one of, 'I told you so, the aircraft is too much of a handful'.

There was more to come.

A second test pilot from BAe Hatfield, this time with a Navy background, got airborne in a single-seat jet on the same trials. Again he was assessing the level of difficulty associated with handling the aircraft on the approach to the deck by night. He had little Harrier experience and even less night deck experience. Getting airborne was no problem but on the approach to land-on, his God-like attributes as a test pilot were brought into play. The approach was awful. He sank like a stone below the prescribed glide path, over-corrected, continued in towards the ship like a yo-yo on a string, nearly crashed into the 'round-down' (the stern) and finally settled ungracefully on deck in an untidy heap. During his approach he had been given accurate and helpful advice over the radio from the Naval Deck Landing expert in Flyco, but had ignored all that was said. During the debrief after the trip he stated, 'Look, I'm a test pilot and I don't have to listen to the likes of you or obey your calls on the approach!' (Exactly the opposite of what one should expect from a professional naval pilot... perhaps he was a member of the breed who consider that any landing you can walk away from is a good one!)

He also claimed that the aircraft was too difficult for squadron pilots to handle ('I found it hard so they will find it impossible'), and this word from 'God' was believed by the boffins, the scientists and civil servants on board.

What could have been the final nail in the coffin for approving the SHAR as a night-operable aircraft for deck operations came when a third test pilot again almost lost a jet on the approach. He had left the Royal Navy recently, having been one of its best fighter pilots, and he was also a dedicated and balanced test pilot.

During the approach to the deck (at about 180 mph), his aircraft nose started to pitch strongly up and down. This is particularly dangerous in a Harrier and caused great concern on deck (too high an angle of attack, or nose-up attitude, on the approach can lead to the aircraft taking charge of the pilot and turning itself upside-down − a fatal condition). As he approached close in to the ship, the nose movement subsided and he carried out a stable and normal deck landing. However, a great debate arose afterwards as he was debriefed by the boffins because he swore that throughout the approach he had held the control column still and central and 'had certainly not induced the nose movement through his own cockpit control.'

'Ah-aah!' sighed the boffins and the detractors, 'This aircraft really is not safe for night deck operations without major modification!'

Minutes later, after hearing the result of the debrief, I was examining the electronic readout gathered from instruments inside the aircraft during the approach. This quite clearly showed that the nose pitching had definitely been demanded (caused) by the pilot's handling of the control column. He was actually moving the joy-stick forward and aft without realising it.

This type of lack of recognition by a pilot of what his hands are doing on the approach is quite common, and one does not and should not blame him for misinterpreting such events in his cockpit. Many pilots are susceptible to such human aberrations but on an approach to a ship, as opposed to a large runway, precision flying is a necessity and aberrations like this need to be corrected.

Unfortunately for the Sea Harrier's immediate future, the boffins had already made their minds up about the safety of the aircraft (after all, was it not they themselves who had confidently predicted the difficulty in aircraft handling before the trials took place?). The electronic readout evidence was pushed hastily aside and, as luck would have it, the Director Harrier (the newly appointed Procurement Executive Boss of the whole trial set-up) was still green at the gills from almost continuous sea-sickness. 'He could not be disturbed by irrelevances from non-test pilots', and subsequently he refused to clear the aircraft for night flying from the deck.

I did not blame him for his decision. The man had listened to all his scientific advisers and pilots (whose total collective experience of night flying in the Harrier was negligible) and he had to base his judgement on such 'approved advice'. He was just badly served; but once his decision was made, nothing could change it.

So eventually we had embarked in HMS *Invincible* for Operational Trials without the necessary paper authority for night flying. And if things stayed that way, there could be no all-weather fighter capability.

It was therefore a very good thing for the future of the aircraft in service that *Invincible* was first commanded by Captain Mike Livesay, and that he was closely advised on all air matters by the Commander Air, a flamboyant, extrovert and disciplined officer called Neil Rankin (also a brilliant pilot and Air Warfare Instructor). Both Livesay and Rankin were destined for high rank and achievement in the Service, and although they followed the 'rule book' with diligence, they were able to apply extensive aircraft-carrier and flying expertise to the important task of working-up their new ship and its air group.

Having already conducted the land-based operational trials for SHAR, I and my squadron pilots were more experienced at Harrier night flying than anyone else in the world. I also had several years of F-4K Phantom night deck landing experience under my belt, and my right-hand man in the operational trials, Flight Lieutenant Ian Mortimer, had years of productive land Harrier experience behind him. The pair of us knew that there would be no black art about night flying the SHAR from the deck.

On the contrary, we could see no reason for not getting airborne straight away and proving it.

A special combination of circumstances enabled us to achieve this goal. Livesay and Rankin were reasonable men who listened to logic and had more than enough front-line aviation experience to make reliable judgements. I pestered them for days on end to let me fly the SHAR from the ship at night. Then, during the Flag Officer's inspection of the ship, an old acquaintance with considerable conventional night deck experience in Sea Vixens and Phantoms arrived on board as the Staff Aviation Officer (SAVO). In his presence I spoke to the Captain and Wings: 'If you let me launch tonight, I shall take full responsibility for anything that may go wrong. The night is going to be clear and I shall have a good visual horizon with the lights of Chesil Beach and Portland Bill only a few miles away. If I have any problems I shall divert ashore – but that's not likely.'

Wings was clearly delighted to be able to say yes; 'OK, Sharkey, be it on your own head! But before you get airborne, SAVO will want a word with you.'

I could hardly believe my ears, and never ever knew whether Wings and the Captain were authorising the flight off their own bat, or whether they had consulted some higher beings.

Just before I walked out on deck for the all-important and much-cherished sortie, SAVO (Commander Hunneyball – or 'Nectar-Nuts' as he was often affectionately known) collared me and said: 'Take this brown envelope and open it in the air before you recover to the ship. It is an emergency drill and I want you to play it for real.'

Such brown envelopes were two-a-penny during inspections, and usually signalled gloom, despondency and inconvenience as the Staff looked on laughing hysterically at the recipient's ineptitude or lack of knowledge. But on this occasion adrenalin was already pumping through my veins and I received the offending envelope almost gratefully.

As always, the take-off or launch from the ship's ski-jump was a non-event. By day or night it is the easiest and safest way of getting any aircraft airborne, and I and my team had practised it by night from the land-based ski-jump at Yeovilton many times. The pilot taxis the aircraft onto the deck's short runway, ensures he is precisely aligned with the centre-line with its double row of lights, applies full power (giving him a kick in the back better than any sports car), keeps the accelerating jet straight with rudder and gets pressed down hard into his seat as the aircraft hits the ramp (ski-jump). The aircraft can then only go one way, and that is up. The pilot then uses his aircraft exhaust nozzles to provide both lift and acceleration. Before the ski-jump-induced upward momentum is lost, the jet attains full flying speed and flies away with nozzles aft (as with a conventional jet). Leaving the ski-jump on launch feels very much like taking a hump-back bridge at excessive speed in a car.

Following that first night launch, the setting was startling but familiar. I had overflown the same area by night on many occasions but it was impossible not to revel in the perfection of it all; alone with a million stars, a black sky and sea, and a coastline extending from Portland Bill to the west that looked like the Blackpool Illuminations. Offshore, *Invincible* was also lit up like Oxford Street at Christmas.

The Sea Harrier was functioning perfectly. The Blue Fox radar screen and the Navigation Computer together kept me fully informed at all times as to how far I was away from the ship or from other possible destination airfields.

After about half an hour of interception work against shore-based aircraft, I returned to the vicinity of the ship, took off my kid leather flying gloves and, with the help of light from my torch, opened the brown envelope: 'before recovering to the ship you are to declare a complete fuel tank pressurisation failure and to recover on board as dictated by that emergency'.

The failure in question, if it was for real, would leave me with no more than three or four minutes' flying time before I ran out of gas. However, thanks to the tuition and perseverance of Bertie Penfold, the Headquarters QFI (Qualified Flying Instructor) on loan from the RAF Harrier world, I and all my pilots had learned the emergency drills backwards. So I knew exactly what had to be done and how the ship should respond.

I flew in to a position about 15 miles from the ship, stationed the aircraft on her beam (to one side of her) and transmitted: 'For exercise; Mayday, Mayday, Mayday. This is Gold Leader with complete fuel tank pressurisation failure. I am 15 miles on your port beam at 10,000 feet for immediate recovery. I only have three minutes' flying time before the engine stops.'

'Roger, Gold Leader. Vector 160 for CCA.' The reply came promptly from the Direction Officer, Tony Walker, but a CCA was a time-consuming procedure and meant that I was to proceed to the south on a heading of 160° and prepare for a Carrier Controlled Approach, in which the ship's radar team guides the aircraft down a prescribed flight-path/glide-path to the landing point. It would take too long.

'Negative. I don't have enough fuel for a Carrier Controlled Approach. I shall have to make a visual approach and landing. Please pass me ranges to go to Mother.' ('Mother' being the ship.) I could of course check ranges to the ship on my own aircraft radar and did so, but any additional information at night was always useful.

From there it was plain sailing. Conditions were perfect and the emergency dictated what had to be done. SAVO had been sensible in his choice of emergency drill. If a pilot could handle this type of recovery on board on his first night deck landing in the aircraft type, then the Sea Harrier had got to be OK for night deck work.

I descended on a southerly heading towards a point well astern of the ship at 400 knots-plus with the engine throttled right back. Reducing the rate of descent at 2 miles to go to touch-down, I turned hard onto the extended centre line astern of the carrier and selected the nozzles down to vertical. This acts like a very efficient air brake and slowed me down fast. As the airspeed decayed rapidly I lowered the undercarriage and flaps and began feeding on power to compensate for the loss in wing lift. At half a mile to go, speed was well under control — about 150 knots. I switched the radar to standby (thus preserving the marital status of the men on deck — strong radar waves being notoriously bad for one's ability to procreate) and came to the hover at nearly full throttle just to the left of the ship and opposite the after-deck, which had been cleared of all aircraft, equipment and personnel. There was no air turbulence to distract me or cause discomfort or difficulty in aircraft handling and, checking my nose was into wind at all times, I banked a little to the right and glided horizontally and sideways over the deck edge until I was sitting at about 30 feet above deck level. A little bank to the left to arrest the sideways movement; check no fore-and-aft movement relative to the ship and that the aircraft was directly above the centre line of the runway.

Not surprisingly, my breathing was heavy as I concentrated on maintaining a steady hover. Below me the deck was brightly lit but the perspective was quite different from in daylight. Even with the lights of Chesil Beach in the distance giving a decent horizon I felt almost detached from reality. It seemed like someone else's left hand on the throttle as I eased it back to give an adjustment of power to get the jet going down positively. Back on with the power to maintain a stable rather than an accelerating descent, then a firm thud as the wheels touched and I slammed the throttle shut. I checked my watch. Just less than three minutes; perfect!

Sweating, excited and very pleased, I was instructed, 'Gold Leader. Well done! Shut down where you are'.

'Roger.' Now for a well-earned pint of beer and a celebration.

It had been a good celebration, with champagne from Wings and the Captain. And it was a far cry from my mundane sortie in the North Norwegian Sea in Exercise 'Alloy Express', with nothing but instrument flying to look forward to.

I put the past behind me as I started the Sea Jet, positioned for take-off on the wet, windswept runway and launched from the deck in high dudgeon. I returned an hour and a half later to carry out the land-on in atrocious conditions. There was no horizon at all. The rain on the windscreen caused a distracting deformation of the ship's usually welcoming lights, and I could feel the heavy buffeting from the gale force winds. *Invincible* was rolling, weaving, pitching and heaving and, as she was my only source of visual reference, this made the land-on task more onerous. At least it was a bit of a challenge and added spice to what had otherwise been a totally boring flight! Swearing under my breath at Wings and the world, I stabilised the aircraft over the deck amidships as best I could. The superstructure of the ship's island was only a matter of feet to the right and, as the ship rolled heavily to port, the huge wall of grey metal seemed to approach ominously close to the wing-tip. Maintaining a steady hover was more like flying in formation on an unwilling leader, so eventually I took pot luck, selected a firm rate of descent and waited for the heavier than usual touchdown as the deck came up to meet me. A jarring thud and I was there.

There must be more to life than this, I thought. Little did I know then that trouble was brewing in the Falkland Islands and it would soon bring me what I had always wanted: the chance to see some real action.

3

The first clue that something unusual and exciting was afoot came when the squadron had returned from *Invincible* to the Royal Naval Air Station at Yeovilton in Somerset. It was mid-March 1982, and Easter leave was due to commence at the beginning of April. Spring was in the air and the prospect of a well-earned break was uppermost in everyone's mind.

The ship-to-shore disembarkation of squadron aircraft had gone without a hitch and, before landing at Yeovilton, I led my six Sea Harriers in close formation on a tour of the local area around the airfield to let the families know that 801 had returned. Hazelgrove Prep School near Sparkford was to me the most important part of the unofficial flypast. That was where Kristian, my eldest boy, was boarding and I had promised by letter to 'pay him a visit' before landing. The Headmaster later told me that the youngster had glowed with pride and embarrassment as the peaceful spring morning in class was shattered by the sudden roar of six Pegasus engines at low level overhead. He knew that Dad was back!

In the not-too-distant past it had also been common practice — almost a prerequisite — for front-line squadrons to 'wake up' the airfield before landing when disembarking from sea, but the new station commander was distinctly lacking in a sense of humour when it came to dealing with noisy jet jockeys. He had a helicopter background (a 'farmer' as opposed to a 'cowboy') and so rather than risk a very unpleasant interview, I led the jets down quietly and without fuss. Not like the old days at all; sometimes it seemed that there was no fun left!

Once ensconced in the squadron buildings ashore, we began preparing for leave. The flying rate was low and the bar bills in the Wardroom grew logarithmically larger by the day.

Then, out of the blue, all squadron commanders received a secret communication. It warned us that our squadrons should be kept 'ready for any eventuality' and that personnel going on Easter leave overseas should be ready for the possibility of a rapid recall to duty. Initially, I had no idea of exactly what was about to take place, but a bit of thought coupled with some media emphasis soon brought the South Atlantic into focus.

Although they were termed very much in cloak-and-dagger fashion, the orders were a clear enough indicator that we might be off to war and so I decided to take an initiative on two counts.

First, it had become clear during the previous two years of intensive flying trials and aircraft assessment that the Sea Harrier's white belly might have looked good in photographs, but it had already proved something of a disadvantage in fighter combat. Our practice combat engagements were usually initiated with one set of fighters intercepting a target pair from beyond visual range, with opposing fighters closing towards each other either under ground control or by using information from their own radar systems. Pilots engaging in combat with the SHAR would often first see the flash of its white belly in the sun before having picked up the Sea Jet itself with the Mark I eyeball, and this gave them an earlier opportunity to manoeuvre than they would otherwise have had. This obvious giveaway needed to be rectified if there was serious business ahead.

The second thought in my mind concerned the aircraft's weapons. The fit for combat consisted of twin Aden 30-mm cannon and twin Sidewinder AIM-9G missiles. This mark of Sidewinder had served the Navy Phantom force well in *Ark Royal* but, from my recent experience in the MOD Sea Harrier desk, I knew that the latest version of missile, the AIM-9L, was already on order for the Sea Harrier community from the United States. This missile variant was more agile, had a better seeker head than the AIM-9G, and was also capable of engaging targets at lower altitude (very close to the ground). It could also see and hit a target from a head-on position. Clearly it was a must if there was some real air-to-air combat in the offing.

Two weeks before the official announcement came that a Task Force would be formed to sail south for Operation 'Corporate', I picked up the phone and called the Fixed Wing (Jet) desk officer of the Flag Officer, Carriers and Amphibious Ships (FOCAS) at Portsmouth. Tim Gedge had recently left the Sea Harrier world to work for the Admiral and it was he who received the call.

'Hello, Sharkey! What can I do for you?'

'A couple of things, actually, Tim! Can you please get on to the MOD and ask them to provide us with warpaint to hide the white belly of the SHAR? And also please ask them to expedite the order of AIM-9L missiles from the States. I think you know why I'm asking: it's very urgent and it will pay great dividends if we can get this organised quickly. OK?'

'Fine, Sharkey. We'll get on to that straight away.' And he put the phone down.

During the next two weeks, the squadron Air Engineer Officers, Dick Goodenough, Colin Thornhill and their team of nearly one hundred squadron maintenance engineers, ensured that all six 801 aircraft were in pristine condition. Morale was high because the lads had won all the Naval Air Arm honours for flight safety and operational efficiency. They were very proud of their squadron and their machines. The latter gleamed like new dinky toys on the hard-standing every morning, waiting to be used. They flew every day in spite of the run-down in flying effort prior to leave and were 100 per cent serviceable for 95 per cent of the time. There was no such thing as a 'hangar queen' in the squadron (that is to say, an aircraft used for spare parts to keep the others going).

Just prior to leave commencing, I cleared the lower deck of all ratings and addressed them. I couldn't tell them exactly what was afoot, but I was obliged to explain that their well-earned leave might be curtailed and I wanted 100 per cent effort from everyone to get back quickly should certain circumstances arise. The squadron personnel gathered round me in the hangar and listened carefully to what I had to say. My black labrador pup, Jet, sat by my side, drawing almost as much attention as I did at such gatherings.

I realised that the chances were that every manjack of them knew more about what was on the cards than I did; but they didn't let on and I was pleased to see that all the team, having worked like Trojans for the previous nine months, were in high spirits and ready for anything.

I was very lucky to have such a first-rate team of engineers and I knew that I could rely on them to come up trumps in any time of crisis. They too knew that if they were in trouble, I would put my neck on the line to help them out. It was a very healthy 'tit for tat' relationship.

I remembered very clearly the day when one of the Senior Chief Petty Officers had requested to see me to explain that he had been accused of shoplifting and was going to be prosecuted.

The desperately disheartened Chief explained that he had been in one of Yeovil's main supermarkets for the weekly shopping with his daughter, had filled his trolley with what he needed, and then had walked out of the store towards the car park having totally forgotten to pay. He felt a hand on his shoulder, 'Excuse me, Sir, I don't believe you have paid for those goods'. He thought that he had and felt in his top pocket for the grocery money. It was still there.

He apologised and said he had a lot on his mind, but to no avail. He was to be taken to court.

I knew that John did indeed have a lot on his mind. His wife was crippled and he had to do everything for her, including lifting her in and out of the bath. He had two young children to look after, was the local village Scout Master and was a strong supporter and member of his local church. On top of all that he had his very demanding squadron duties as the Line Chief.

'What you need, John, is a good lawyer and some moral support. My lawyers in Wincanton are excellent, so I shall have a word with them on your behalf.'

'Thanks, Sir, but I don't have a hell of a lot of cash to pay lawyers.'

'Don't worry about that! We'll sort this out together. There is no doubt in my mind that you intended to pay but forgot.'

My lawyer and friend, Fenton Rutter, was indeed the man for the job. Tall, distinguished and a pillar of local society, he was fascinated by the case and went to work immediately, researching the exit and pay facilities at the scene of the incident, and at other supermarkets. He engaged the services of the best barrister in the south-west of England and was well-prepared for the day in court. He was very fond of the Navy and would not hear of charging the Chief for his services.

The magistrates listened carefully to the defence case, which was brilliantly presented by the caring Fenton and his barrister. My job was easy; I appeared in uniform and gave the Court my testament as to the good character of the Chief Petty Officer.

John was acquitted.

Easter leave commenced on Thursday 1 April, and it was a time for one and all to go home, enjoy family life, play with the kids and forget the strains and stresses that come with operational flying at sea in the front line. I had two fine boys, Ashton, who was still not yet old enough for prep school, and Kristian, who was in his second term as a boarder. Kris had finished school a few days earlier and was up in the Midlands staying with his grandparents prior to my leave commencing. That is where I headed on the Thursday afternoon in my ageing, light blue Volvo estate car.

That night — at 4 o'clock on the morning of Friday 2 April — we were recalled for duty! I was awoken by my very concerned mother-in-law.

'It's the Captain of Yeovilton on the phone, Nigel. He wants to speak to you urgently.'

Several thoughts flashed through my mind; the prime one being that we could be off to war. 'Bloody hell!' I thought, 'Is it really happening?'

The content of the message passed to me on the phone was well worth the interruption of my sleep, though: 'Sharkey, from the Command, you are to mobilise your squadron for sea immediately.' That was all.

The phone message was quite clearly an order. The warning of two weeks past that we might be off to do serious business in the South Atlantic was coming alive and I welcomed the news. The Government had decided to call Galtieri's bluff.

It took less than half an hour for me to initiate the squadron call-out plan by telephone, to get my eldest son Kristian out of bed, and to set off for the Fosse Way and Somerset in the Volvo. 151 miles later (which included 30 minutes of very hairy driving in thick fog) and at 6.45 in the morning, I delivered Kristian into the care of his mother and little brother, Ashton, had a quick breakfast, and then drove to the Royal Naval Air Station at Yeovilton.

The squadron buildings were already alive and buzzing with activity.

The Chief Regulating Petty Officer was on top of the call-out plan and Dick Goodenough, the Air Engineer Officer, was well ahead of the game in preparing the jets for sea.

The buzz around the squadron was that we were to embark in HMS *Invincible* that afternoon and set off south for the Falklands. Aircraft and pilots from the Headquarters Training Squadron (899) were being seconded to my squadron (801) and to 800. 801 were to receive two extra aircraft, bringing the squadron strength up to eight. HMS *Hermes*, being a larger deck and therefore having more space, was to sail with twelve Sea Harriers.

The knowledge that my pilots were well up to speed and that my six squadron aircraft were in excellent order gave me considerable peace of mind, and the only real idiocy of the day seemed to be the panic to get on board ('You are to embark immediately' was the theme of the Air Station's advice). My own motto in such circumstances was 'slowly, slowly, makee monkey'. I had never been one to 'jump' just for the sake of being seen to conform; especially when important things such as the welfare of my men were at stake. So before contacting the ship, which had been the squadron home for the previous nine months, I checked on the status of pertinent things such as when the Carrier Group was likely to sail, when would the main armament arrive on board, and so on.

It was patently obvious that the Task Group could not sail before Sunday at the earliest (*Hermes*, the Flagship, being empty of all stores and covered in scaffolding for her planned refit), and so I recommended to *Invincible* that we should embark no earlier than Saturday afternoon and, preferably, on Sunday. The Captain, one J. J. Black, MBE, agreed the proposal and so whilst 800 Squadron scrambled on board *Hermes* as soon as her deck was clear, 801 settled down to the serious business of preparing a programme of weapons trials for the aircraft. The majority of the SHAR's inventory of weapons were still awaiting trials by the Boscombe Down organisation.

The bureaucracy of the modern Services, and the Civil Service in particular, was such that although a modern warplane may 'enter service' on a particular date, it was unlikely that it could be fully utilised in its operational role for at least three years. This arguable waste of resources was directly attributable to the empire-building that had taken place within the Procurement Executive of the Civil Service which, to cut a long story short, meant that before a front-line, all-weather fighter pilot could use any equipment or weaponry in his aircraft, a special clearance had to be given by the test pilot world at A & AEE Boscombe Down.

I had no particular quarrel with the principle of test pilots being used to explore the operational envelope of an aircraft or to check the physical safety aspects of flying with new weapons or equipment; but when the tail wags the dog to the detriment of the service's ability to react to a crisis, then I believed that something was seriously wrong.

The Procurement Executive of the Ministry of Defence was set up to serve the interests of the individual services, not to hinder them; but it never seemed to work out like that. I often reflected on this and other associated 'evils' when en route to the South Atlantic. And there was no doubt in my mind that one of the first priorities on sailing would have to be a comprehensive weapons trials programme. That was something all the pilots would look forward to.

A quick call to Tim Gedge at FOCAS resulted in the news that the AIM-9L missiles were being expedited and I could expect to receive them before the squadron reached the South Atlantic. The warpaint was also on its way to the fleet. That all sounded pretty satisfactory, but things didn't turn out quite so well.

The ship carrying the Admiral in command of the Task Group, HMS *Hermes*, enjoyed the privilege of receiving and redirecting all air stores destined for other ships in the force. There were only two carriers, *Invincible* and *Hermes*, and so it did not seem too difficult a task for the Flag (as the Admiral's team was collectively called) to ensure that aircraft stores got to both ships in an orderly fashion. Sadly, and even in a prospective war scenario, one-upmanship appeared to come to the fore for the first of many times, and the warpaint never arrived in *Invincible*. It did, of course, arrive in *Hermes*. This was mildly frustrating, but there was to be rather more frustration later over the allocation of the AIM-9L missiles that I had ordered.

Dick Goodenough, our Air Engineer, was not at all put out by the inability of *Hermes* to redirect warpaint; 'Don't worry, Boss. I wouldn't allow that messy stuff to touch my aircraft. You'll have the aircraft repainted properly before we get near the action.' How right he was. The squadron ratings worked night and day to strip down the 'old' aircraft paint scheme and replace it with a dark charcoal grey. Everything had always got to be up to scratch with Dick, and with the lads as well. They were proud of their work and proud of their squadron; nothing but the best was good enough for their pilots. It was a great team to go to war with (or, with whom to go to war, as Churchill would undoubtedly have said).

The squadron eventually embarked on the Sunday morning in Portsmouth Harbour. We had embarked in harbour several times before (a capability unique to the Harrier breed with its vertical landing capability) but this occasion was very special and serious. Coming to the hover over the still harbour waters, I thought of the noise being inflicted on the locals. I also remembered with some amusement our harbour embarkation in Norfolk, Virginia. Ships moored close to *Invincible* had not been warned of the noise and there was a German frigate lying alongside the quay at the carrier's stern. The wind direction was from *Invincible's* bow and so the SHARs approached the deck from astern and passed very close to the

German warship. One of that ship's officers had just settled down on the loo for his morning 'constitutional' when he thought his world was coming to an end. The roar of the Pegasus jet engine at full throttle deafened him, frightened him off his seat, and gave real meaning to the saying that 'if you are likely to be very frightened, then you should wear brown trousers!'

On that Sunday, 4 April 1982, the locals of Portsmouth needed no warning of noise and mayhem. It was a naval port and the inhabitants knew full well what was happening. Landing on the deck, I could almost feel the tremendous support that all those good people were giving to the mobilisation of the Task Force. Later, I found out that although more than half the Naval Harbour workforce had been made redundant as of 4 o'clock on the Friday afternoon, they all turned up to work voluntarily over the weekend to get the ships stored and ready for sea.

After climbing out of my jet, I reported to Wings and the Captain on the bridge, and watched the remainder of the aircraft land on. My request to brief the Captain, Wings and the Operations Officer, Rod O'Connor, that evening was granted and I made my way down to the squadron crewroom to address my team.

4

On my way down to the crewroom from the bridge, my thoughts turned to the additional four pilots who had been seconded to the squadron for the operation ahead. From my point of view as the Squadron Boss, the most important newcomer was a really old friend who had been a close colleague since the early days of our flying training, Robin Kent.

Robin had joined the Navy on the lower deck, as a sailor rather than an officer, and had been selected for officer training at Dartmouth in very quick time. I met him first at RAF Linton-on-Ouse, near York, where all fixed-wing Navy Air candidates did their basic flying training. My first impression of him was of a remarkably good-looking and dedicated sub-lieutenant. He was a keen pursuer of the ladies and his finely chiselled bone structure soon won him the nickname 'porcelain features'.

He now hailed from the Buccaneer world, had survived an horrendous high-speed, low-level ejection which broke his back, and had enjoyed many high-spirited escapades during his seventeen years of flying. One in particular came to my mind.

I most vividly remembered the time that we had crashed a car together during our tactical flying training at RNAS Brawdy, near St Davids in South Wales. It was a Sunday and the Training Squadron Boss, Fred de la Billière, and his wife Sue had thrown a party for all the squadron aircrew, including the students. Drinks at lunchtime extended all afternoon and as it was getting dark Robin had suddenly remembered that we both had an invitation for tea (and to watch Tom and Jerry cartoons) at a friend's house in Haverfordwest, some 10 miles distant. Neither Robin nor I could walk without assistance thanks to Fred's more than liberal hospitality, and so amid much merriment we were carried to my Lotus Cortina and set off erratically down the winding coast road at an ever-increasing speed. That would not have been too bad in itself but we decided to share the driving; with me on the pedals and Robin on the wheel.

Shortly after passing a flat-hatted grockle (local) with wife and kid bouncing along in their little Austin A35, the lights went out! This was probably a result of the Lotus hitting the near-side banking, which then threw the car across the road and head-on into another vertical mud and stone bank at about 85 mph. At this moment, we both lost our lights as well and I woke up lying on the road gazing in awe at my pride and joy, which was sitting inverted on the tarmac in a very crumpled condition. Both front wheels had been pushed back under the driving seat and the only car panel that was in one piece was the boot lid.

The sad condition of the car occupied my befuddled brain for a minute or so before I remembered Robin. I had been through the windscreen, but where was my dear old pal? I remember staggering around the remains of the car through the stench of leaking petrol and eventually espied my co-driver lying unconscious inside the cockpit on the inverted roof. He looked remarkably peaceful and unmarked, but the first threads of full sobriety and fear struck me as I wondered whether he had actually gone to join the Big Fighter Pilot in the sky. I crawled into the wreck in a panic, switched off the ignition and after a couple of rough shakes awoke my partner from his beauty sleep. If we had been using unleaded petrol Robin would have been dead − burnt to a cinder.

'Hi, Sharks! Gosh you look terrible!'

This wounded me not a little when I realised that my face was indeed a mess and Robin's extraordinary good looks remained unimpaired. And as I was pulling him out of the car through the side window, streams of blood from my face dripped all over the new suede waistcoat that I had lent to Robin for the party. It just wasn't my day. But at least we were alive and in one piece.

In what appeared to be no time at all a car pulled up next to us in the dark. It was an officer from Brawdy.

'I think you two need a lift to the Sick Bay, don't you? You'd better get in!'

'But I'm bleeding like a stuck pig! It will ruin your back seat.'

'Never mind that! Get in quickly before the police arrive.'

At the Sick Bay, I realised the extent of the damage. My scalp had been torn apart at the eyebrows and pushed an inch or so up over my forehead. There was blood everywhere as the young Surgeon Lieutenant placed me on the operating table and started to stitch. I felt no pain but immediately fell in love with the nurse who held my hand throughout the sewing lesson. My overtures of boozed-up passion did not get a result from the young lady, though, and soon it was Robin's turn on the table.

He had only received a cloth-like tear in the back of his scalp, but whether because he wasn't quite so drunk or for other reasons his stitching hurt like hell. It was some consolation for me as I sat listening to his muffled screams with delight.

The police arrived before the Doc had finished stitching Robin, and I was instructed by the medical staff to hold my breath throughout the short interview and to feign total shock. This I did and the police rapidly gave up trying to solicit a statement from me. Soon we were both on our way to the Haverfordwest hospital for overnight observation. When we returned to the Air Station the next day after a suitably unproductive interview with the police, it was evident that trouble was brewing; our accident had not gone unnoticed. Self-inflicted injury during flying training is deemed a sin by Their Lordships because it wastes the taxpayers' money and slows down the flow of aircrew to the front line. Even broken limbs sustained whilst 'jock-strapping' (playing rugby for the Air Station, for instance) are severely frowned on, and incapacitation from alcohol-induced car prangs is considered over the top. A very officious and sober-faced Fred de la Billière began his formal bollocking. He asked how we had managed to get so drunk and act so irresponsibly during flying training. Didn't we know the rules? What the hell was going on?

'Actually, Sir,' replied Robin, 'we were invited to a drinks session which turned into a party. I'm afraid we got legless!'

'That's just not good enough! You're supposed to be big boys now, not fucking Girl Guides. You've got to learn to control your drink or there's no place for you in the Fleet Air Arm. I'm now seriously considering your position on this flying course.' It was a real threat, but underneath both offenders hoped that Fred was just enjoying frightening them. After pausing for breath, he continued, 'By the way, whose party was that?' He glowered in impressive style.

'Yours, actually, Sir!'

It was time for more bullshit as Fred realised his part in the incident. After much posturing, swearing and threatening he waved his great hairy arm as a sign of dismissal. That was the end of the interview and no more was said.

'Good days,' I thought as I negotiated the final ladder down to the crewroom deck. Robin was to be my Senior Pilot (SP) during Operation 'Corporate'. Doug Hamilton, who had served the squadron so well as the SP since its formation, had been found to be allergic to the ship's air-conditioning system and had to be left ashore for treatment. Naturally, Doug was shattered when he realised that he was to be left behind.

Robin had taken his place as my second-in-command at very short notice. Although sad not to have Doug along, I was more than confident that Robin would fit equally well into the squadron. He was a strong character with a lot of self-discipline and a lot of go. Just the ticket for going to war.

'Attention in the crewroom!' the new Senior Pilot barked as I entered and took my customary position on the raised dais with my back to the blackboard.

'Thank you, Senior Pilot. Do sit down, gentlemen. Welcome aboard and a special welcome to our reinforcements from 899 [the Headquarters Squadron]. John, Paul, Mike and of course you, Robin; you are now 801 Squadron pilots and a full part of the *Invincible* team. I am delighted to have you with us.'

I then addressed the team as a whole.

'The squadron has three important tasks ahead: prepare for war; carry out all the weapons trials that are still outstanding; bring the newcomers up to full speed.

'The first task is well within our compass. I believe we are at least 95 per cent proficient in all the Sea Harrier operational roles and we already have a good night-qualified team. Thanks to Dick and all the lads, the aircraft are in A1 condition. We can expect a delivery of AIM-9L missiles before the action starts and the engineers have already begun to give the jets their war colours. But, and it is a big "but", I have had no indication at all from the Flag that any detailed planning has been done for the air war and that must therefore be our priority over the next few days. We have received zero intelligence from anywhere concerning the threat but you will all have heard from the know-alls on television that we are completely outnumbered and don't stand a chance.

'Horse-shit! We have already shown that we can beat the best fighters in the world in combat and so ten to one odds are not too much of a problem as I see it.' I could tell from the faces that not all present were fully convinced.

'What we do have is three Air Warfare Instructors (AWIs) within the squadron and that should stand us all in good stead. John Eyton-Jones is the most experienced; then there is Morts and myself; in addition, Alan Curtis has important first-hand knowledge of the A-4 Skyhawk and the Mirage III from his antipodean days with the Kiwis and Aussies. On completion of this briefing, we four shall get together in my cabin to sort out our ideas and a lot of planning tasks. Then tonight we shall brief the Captain and Ops Team on a way ahead.

'That brings me to the second task; Weapons Trials. As you all know, Boscombe Down has only cleared a few of our weapons for use up till now and it is up to us to test the remainder of the aircraft/weapon capabilities. We have no paper mandate for this but as we are off to war we have no choice but to crack on with it. Morts has already worked out what is needed and he will get together with Splot [Senior Pilot] today to plan the trials flying programme.

'The third task is to get the newcomers up to speed. You all have excellent experience behind you and so that shouldn't be a difficult task. However, I do want you to learn the way 801 does things and I want you all on the night team as soon as possible. So at the first opportunity, Rob, you can get duskers programmed.' Duskers means literally what it sounds like – flying non-night deck qualified pilots to the deck at dusk before letting them loose at night.

Without a full night-flying capability, any front-line pilot or aircraft could not be considered up to scratch. I had already been astonished at how well a few of the established squadron pilots had taken to the task of flying the Sea Jet to the deck. Morts and I together had carried out the majority of the early night work from the deck. Each of us had about seventy-five sorties under our belts and other 801 pilots were progressing. Alan Curtis was up to twenty-five and my two young 'protégés', Steve Thomas and Charlie Cantan, were about to start. Not bad for their first embarked squadron tour! Pressing for full night-flying status for Sea Harrier had been a hard battle for my trials squadron and now that the fleet faced action it was clear that our stubborn perseverance was going to pay dividends. In the other squadron in *Hermes*, none of the 800 Squadron pilots had more than one or two duskers sorties under their belts. Duskers is a gentle introduction to the challenge of the dark, but is in no way the real McCoy.

'Finally, gentlemen, we have the press on board; six journalists varying in pedigree from *The Times* to the *Star*. Treat them with respect, look after them in the bar, but there is to be only one official mouthpiece for 801 Squadron and that is me. Understood? Then if any crap flies we all know where it should land, don't we?

'That's all I have for now. This is a new game for us all and I want 100 per cent effort as usual. Any questions?' Short pause. 'Thanks Robin! Drop into my cabin when you've finished please and we can talk with the AWI team together.'

To date the 801 Squadron regime had been a happy one, and at this critical time I did not want the existing balance of endeavour and achievement to be disturbed. How would the new boys make their presence felt? Some were very senior aviators but none had operated from a deck at sea since the *Ark Royal* days. They would, I thought, need a lot of flying to get rid of the cobwebs that come from flying from ashore and to get them up to an operational standard, but that was no real problem. There was plenty of flying time before the ship reached the South Atlantic. Even so, deep down inside I was intensely proud and jealous of the performance of the squadron over the past year and did not really want to dilute the level of expertise that we had achieved by day and night.

I was also fully aware that my own style of command and leadership differed greatly from the norm in the Fleet Air Arm: I disliked supervision for supervision's sake and work for work's sake. If one of my subordinates knew what he had to do and did it, then the Boss was happy! I had a very efficient team and because of that there had never been any rumblings of discontent or disruptive factions formed. Nor did I want any now.

After showering and changing, and as I sat in my cabin waiting for Robin to arrive, I looked back on the early days of the Sea Harrier in service.

I had been very lucky to be appointed as the boss of the Sea Harrier Intensive Flying Trials Unit, 700A Squadron. It had been one of my tasks to write the terms of reference for the squadron when at my desk in the Ministry of Defence, London, and when I arrived at Yeovilton Air Station in mid-1979 to take up my post, I had been more than a little surprised at the level of self-help that was necessary to get the squadron moving. Initially, my staff consisted of a Senior Pilot, a Special Duties List Aviation officer as Staff Officer, a Squadron Engineer, myself and my dog. Tony Ogilvy was the Senior Pilot and he, like Robin, hailed from the Buccaneer world, where he had qualified as an Air Warfare Instructor and was indeed a first-class pilot.

'Tony, you don't really know me yet even though we served together in *Ark Royal*. I expect you are going to find me a little unusual as a Commanding Officer. I'm not going to be looking over your shoulder and I don't expect you to come to me with day-to-day problems if you think you can solve them yourself. I am sure you'll make mistakes, but I'm also sure that they will be honest ones: and when you do I am not going to hold it against you in any way. We have a whole new free world here and it is up to us to make the Sea Harrier work. If we have to work all the hours that God gives us, fine. But that is not my intention. I plan to leave the office every day between five o'clock and five-thirty and once you have got organised, I expect you to be able to do the same — and I expect your pilots to do likewise. Understood?'

Tony had looked bemused and confused at the same time. He obviously wasn't sure that he liked this style of leadership and would probably have preferred a bog-standard Commanding Officer ('You are here to work hard and run a tight ship!' and all that rubbish). It actually took him about three months to realise that his new boss was not a lunatic, was genuinely happy with him and his work, and preferred a fun squadron to the staid and often oppressive atmosphere that prevailed in other high-visibility units.

I had used a similar speech of welcome and direction to all my officers and men as they joined. And from day one I had left my office no later than 5.30 (unless I was night flying) and allowed each Head of Department to conduct their work to their own satisfaction. Without exception, other Commanding Officers at the Air Station would sit in their offices until at least 7 in the evening and possibly as late as 9 or 10. And while they were there they would expect most of their officers to be there as well, whether there was work to do or not. Why they stayed so late, I couldn't really fathom; either they were totally inefficient at their paperwork or they wanted to stay around just in case some senior officer called (the things people do to get bonus marks!).

For the first year of the squadron's existence, either the Captain of Yeovilton or Wings would call me on the phone every day between 5.30 and 6 and never once did they find me available. This could have been a very bad thing for me if my new squadron was not functioning properly and the trials task was not being achieved. However, this was not the case. Each officer and man knew his responsibilities and what he had to do, and was pleased to be able to get on with it without the Boss interfering and perpetually looking over his shoulder. Morale rapidly blossomed and even though our new unit had to face many teething problems these were overcome by the lads without any undue fuss.

Amazingly, on squadron formation all that had been provided for my new team was a hangar and some dirty, empty offices. There was no furniture, no carpets, no filing cabinets, no safe, no lights, no telephones: just an empty space that needed to be filled. The Staff Officer, Charlie Stirling, went to work with a vengeance immediately; scrounging, begging and borrowing from other units and from the Air Station offices. It wasn't long before even I had a desk to sit at and a chair to sit on.

The arrival of the first aircraft from British Aerospace was a day to remember. But infinitely more exciting and challenging was the invitation I received a few days later, when Commander Neil Rankin (later the Wings of *Invincible*) telephoned.

'Sharkey, how do you feel about landing your Sea Harrier at the television studios in the centre of Birmingham for the *Pebble Mill at One* programme?'

Thinking very rapidly, and fully aware that I had flown the new aircraft less than half a dozen times, I replied ostentatiously, 'No problem, Sir! When do you want it to happen and why are the RAF not doing it?'

'About ten days' time is the answer to your first question. And as for the Crabs [friendly name for the Light Blue], they have turned it down but haven't said why. I reckon they think it's a bit risky and if there is a problem, heads will roll. You know the Light Blue.'

While Wings was talking, I was analysing what needed to be done. 'What we have to do immediately, Sir, is reconnoitre the proposed landing site — whether car park or whatever — talk to the local police and fire brigade and then publicise the event properly to warn the Brummies about the noise. I shall need to visit the vertical landing-pads at Wittering to brush up on my precision vertical work and also seek the advice of BAe's Chief Test Pilot, John Farley.' (There were no pads at Yeovilton; only marks on the standby runway which meant that it wasn't so serious if you made a mistake during a precision landing.)

'OK. But hold your horses until I've spoken to the Admiral to get his clearance. Then if it's cleared, you'd better get your slippers on and come and see me to give me a full brief on the pros and cons.' As I listened, I could visualise my boss in his office in the Control Tower. One of his favourite expressions was 'get your slippers on', and this usually meant that you had incurred his displeasure. Small in height but totally dynamic in every way, he would continuously hitch up his trousers when concentrating on giving a lecture or a bollocking. Rather similar to another old favourite and friend of mine who had been my Commander Air, Derek Monsell. His penchant was for scratching his arse when he bollocked you or when a difficult decision had to be made in a rush!

As predicted by Rankin, the Admiral gave the go ahead and a few days later the fun event occurred. A metal landing-pad was laid on the grass outside Pebble Mill studios by a bunch of obliging Royal Engineers; the Squadron QFI, Bertie Penfold, posted himself on top of the studios with a radio; the Admiral and his guests attended a champagne lunch; the local zoo was evacuated or the animals sedated; the police stopped the traffic; and I took off from Yeovilton 15 minutes before the planned land-on time. I found Birmingham by heading up the M5 motorway and contacted the studios by radio. I had been briefed to follow a specific route over the city in order to remain as far as possible over the unpopulated green park spaces and the like, and this I did, turning right from the motorway to the north of the studios. I was then heading east and as I descended in the turn towards the tall white structure of Pebble Mill I was obliged to tighten and tighten the turn until, as I was approaching the zoo, I had a lot of bank on the aircraft and my speed was excessive. I had a habit of talking to myself in the cockpit when things got busy.

'Shit! I'm too fast! Full braking stop!' This meant pointing the four jet nozzles under the belly of the aircraft as far forwards as they will go; thereby applying a decelerative force of up to two times the force of gravity (2G), dependent on the aircraft's speed.

Approaching the planned hover point above the landing-pad, I heard the QFI call, 'You are too fast. You'll have to take it round.'

'No I won't!' I said to myself. 'Not live on television!' And I didn't. As I came to the hover precisely over the pad (through good luck rather than good flying), I disengaged the braking stop, ensured I was absolutely aligned with the two sets of white markers that had been set up on the ground to guide me to the correct touchdown point, and commenced the vertical landing down between the trees. As my wheels hit terra firma I slammed the throttle shut and heard the QFI call. 'You are right at the back of the pad; move forward before shutting down.'

'Roger!' I replied, and inwardly thought 'Who was the idiot who placed those markers. Doesn't he know that the pilot's eyes are at the front of the jet, not in the sodding middle!' A couple of yards further back and my rear puffer jet would have dug a 9-foot hole in the ground and probably wrecked the aircraft. (There are puffer jets at nose, tail, and each wing-tip, to control the attitude of the aircraft when it is in hovering flight. Their operation is activated by movements of the pilot's control column or joy-stick. When in use they emit very high-velocity, high-temperature air taken from the engine and it is this exhaust air that can dig big holes in soft ground in very quick time.)

I taxied forward a few yards, applied the brakes and shut down. My landing had been recorded for the *At One* programme and I was to take off live at the end of it. There were a couple of hours for interviews before that and in these I was asked to put across my views about the Sea Harrier. Although I had learned much about the aircraft as the MOD Project Officer I had still only had six flights in the Sea Jet, and thirty hours on RAF Harriers at Wittering. This had been enough to convince me that the aeroplane breed was quite remarkable and, to me, the most remarkable aspect of the jet was its extraordinary manoeuvrability in fighter combat.

From an operational angle, the SHAR was being officially provided to shadow and, if necessary in time of conflict, shoot down Soviet maritime reconnaissance aircraft such as the Bear; hopefully before the latter had been able to guide waves of Badger, Blinder and Backfire bombers in to attack the fleet at sea. The Bear would sit off from the NATO naval units observing its targets on radar from very long range. There was no surface-to-air missile system afloat that could 'take out' such an aircraft shadowing the fleet, and so the only answer to the problem in war would be to despatch carrier-based fighters to deny the shadower the ability to gather information and, at best, to shoot it down. The effort required to keep shadowers at bay was magnified by the certainty that any conflict would usually be preceded by an indeterminable period of tension, during which it was essential continuously to deny the enemy targeting information about the fleet. This meant keeping fighters on task and available to the command at sea for twenty-four hours a day.

In order to win approval within the corridors of power in Whitehall for the *Invincible* class of carrier and the SHAR, the Naval Staff was forced by the RAF and the Whitehall mandarins to agree not to call *Invincible* a 'carrier' but to refer to the new ship as a 'Through-Deck Cruiser'; they had also had to agree that the *raison d'être* of the SHAR was purely and simply to be able to counter the shadower threat. It had therefore been instilled in the minds of many senior staff officers in MOD, and certainly in the minds of the RAF and the Civil Service, that when the SHAR went to sea it would have one and only one principal task — "hack the shad".

The previous generation of fixed-wing naval aircraft in UK carriers had consisted of Phantoms for air defence, Buccaneers for air-to-surface strike and attack, and the Gannet for Airborne Early Warning (necessary to detect the approach of a low-level air threat). After the demise of HMS *Ark Royal*, the last of the old carriers, the Navy had been committed to doing its duty at sea in defence of the realm without any organic fixed-wing air capability. Theoretically this was to have been provided by the RAF both in peacetime exercise and in any form of conflict or war. I would not have been unhappy if, indeed, the RAF had been able to provide the promised support for the fleet at sea and I would have been relatively content to operate the SHAR purely in its intended role against the shadower. But I knew only too well the difficulties that arise when one is trying to provide air defence and other services for a fleet at sea when that fleet may be 700 nautical miles or more away from the UK base. These difficulties included the simple matter of time of response, distance to on-task position, and the ability to react effectively to a threat that suddenly looms over the horizon. Unless fixed-wing air defence fighters were in place over the fleet on Combat Air Patrol (CAP) at the time of need — that is, when under attack — then there would be no outer ring of defence for that fleet and attacking forces with stand-off weapons would have a free hand and a relatively easy task in attaining their aim, the destruction of the fleet.

To have one's air defence forces sitting ashore 700 miles or more away (two hours' flying plus scramble time and the need for air-to-air refuelling tanker availability) was not only illogical to me and to all my Fleet Air Arm colleagues, it was also irresponsible and verging on lunacy. Simple mathematics showed that with all the publicly declared resources of the RAF fighter and tanker forces combined, it would not be possible to maintain Combat Air Patrol defence of a fleet at distance from shore in a satisfactory manner for any length of time at all; and certainly not for days and days and days of tension. If indeed, and it was a very big 'if', the RAF were willing to sacrifice the defence of the UK mainland and concentrate on defending the fleet at sea (and it was their agreed responsibility to defend that fleet) it was possible that a certain level of CAP air defence could be provided for limited periods — but not without major gaps in that defence. And who in command ashore would sacrifice defence of the mainland for defence of the fleet at sea?

In a situation of war with the Warsaw Pact, the RAF resources were already stretched beyond reasonable limits (if analysed logically and dispassionately in the cold light of day). They were committed to supporting the Northern Flank, the Southern Flank, defending the UK base from attack over the North Sea and from the north, patrolling the Greenland-Iceland gap, and supporting land forces on the European Central Front. All of these tasks needed air-refuelling tanker support for their fighter and attack aircraft and should a war with the Warsaw Pact have materialised, I knew that the fleet at sea would get a very poor service indeed. There were neither enough tankers nor an adequate number of fighters for the task.

It was therefore with some relish that I had taken up my post as the boss of the Sea Harrier world, and I knew that I and my team had to do everything humanly possible to transform the blinkered plans for the SHAR into a realistic multi-role war-fighting capability.

As I took off vertically from the Pebble Mill landing-pad and bade farewell to my hosts on the radio, I had no illusions at all about the task ahead. I knew that when the aircraft did go to sea the command would need to have a full fighter, attack and reconnaissance capability. My team had to come up with the best possible answer that could be found from the new jet.

The First Sea Lord had wished me well in my task and commented, 'The eyes of the Navy and the world are watching you. Don't let us down. Good luck!' It was a challenge that I took to heart.

Sitting in my cabin on the threshold of a possible war and waiting for my Senior Pilot, my thoughts drifted back over some of the key points in my flying career that now assumed importance in relation to things to come.

5

I and all my pilots were lucky, I reflected, to have been exposed to the wealth of operational experience that had been gathered by the aircrew of Britain's post-war carriers. There had been eight of the capital ships after the war but only three left when I first embarked in *Ark Royal*. And it had been more than obvious to me then that I was surrounded by professionals who had learnt their trade the hard way; from practical experience and from listening to the advice of their older and bolder predecessors. The Naval Flying Training system reflected the no-nonsense attitude of the seasoned front-line aircrew and there was little forgiveness for professional failings. Even less forgiving was the attitude of the staff of the Air Warfare Instructor School, the legendary 764 Squadron. All the war-fighting skills and essential disciplines of air leadership that had been learned over the years had been distilled out of the front line and used to create 'The' fighter pilot's course. Many above-average aviators had been delighted to be selected for this specialist training, only to be psychologically destroyed by failing to make the grade when on course. It was the most respected qualification in the Fleet Air Arm, made *Top Gun* look like a holiday, and, particularly to the young and green pilots joining their first front-line squadron, the AWI was more akin to God than the Squadron Boss.

You didn't learn to fight in the air from books and manuals. You learned from the AWI. And when you didn't get things right you got your arse kicked from breakfast-time to God knows when. This led to fierce professional competition in the air and a very healthy and aggressive atmosphere on the deck. Experience was passed on from one mini-God to the next, ensuring that the youngsters at sea reaped the benefit of the knowledge of the generations of fighter pilots before them.

The gap in time between the demise of *Ark Royal* and the introduction of the Sea Harrier to service was sufficiently brief to provide the new VSTOL world with some experience of the important skills and lessons of the past. Several ageing aviators bridged the short gap in time, and one of these was myself.

What particular benefits had living in the old world given me that I could now apply to Operation 'Corporate'?

Five years flying Phantoms from the deck of *Ark Royal* by day and night, firing all types of ordnance and missiles; Air Warfare Instructor qualification — terrific training for the task ahead; Instrument Rating Instructor; and, last but not least, three years moulding the SHAR's operational envelope to my liking: soon I would know if I had got that bit right — not that I had any doubts about it. I could be quite an arrogant bastard on professional matters, and certainly had the courage of my convictions.

Compared to most Fleet Air Arm colleagues of similar age, I had relatively few flying hours under my belt. I had qualified as an AWI when well below the stipulated minimum number of hours normally needed to be selected for that course. I had become Senior Pilot of the Phantom squadron when still a Lieutenant and with senior officers serving under me. Of course I had worked hard at it in the air but my shortage of flying hours had best been compensated for by rubbing shoulders with and learning the tricks of the trade from a top-class team of pilots and observers. Thanks to them I had been forced to use those hours in the Phantom to good effect and had learned some very important lessons that should now stand me in good stead.

When I had joined the Phantom world in 1969, direct from operational flying training, I had been surprised and a little disappointed to find that one's ability in fighting the aircraft in its operational role was often judged less than objectively. On occasion, seniority in the Fleet Air Arm counted for more than ability and, when it came to fighter combat, the results in the air were not always reflected in the debrief on the ground after the flight. 'Winning' a fight to some meant being able to use seniority and shout loud enough in the crewroom rather than performing well in the air. As a result, and depending whom you were flying with, less benefit was gained from some of the front-line training and operations than would otherwise have been the case.

At least that is how I then viewed my baptism into the fighter pilot's world at sea and, when I became the Senior Pilot of *Ark Royal's* 892 Squadron, I and the Senior Observer, Doug Macdonald, attempted to bring some extra realism and order to the manner in which air combat training was conducted. Doug was a fiery, despotic, tyrant of an AWI with a heart of gold. He took his relatively inexperienced Senior Pilot in hand and showed him the meaning of true aggression in the air and in the crewroom. As a back-seater, it was most unusual to have achieved the status of AWI, and this was a valid pointer to the true quality of the man. Nothing but the best would do, particularly in weapon delivery or combat. And it was in combat that I learned the most from the wily Scot.

We used to quarrel all the time in the air over domestic flying practices, but when it came to a dog-fight I would button my lip and attempt to follow the directions and tips of the older campaigner. He and several others like Dick Moody had enjoyed exchange service with the United States Navy and, from the home of the F-4 Phantom, had learned most of the tricks that you needed to know.

Doug was particularly adept at the rolling scissors manoeuvre (see 'A Layman's Guide to Combat' at the end of this book) and eventually got me not only to understand it but to perfect it. Taylor Scott, the accredited 892 Squadron AWI, also taught me much in combat − initially by shooting hell out of me every time we fought. And as time progressed, the know-how was transferred from the experienced to the not so experienced ... until I ended up at the top of the ladder.

Apart from aspiring to beat the old and bold in all forms of weaponry and combat, there had been various other triggers which led to my search for more personal objectivity in operational training. The first was directly connected with the power plant of the Phantom F-4K (twin Rolls-Royce Spey reheated engines delivering a total thrust in excess of 20 tons), on the back of which I had 'bored holes in the sky' for a considerable time.

The Phantom was a high-speed, swept-wing, twin-seat all-weather fighter and whenever engaged in aerial combat most of the earlier pilots would take great delight in 'horning' it round the sky on full 'burner' (reheat) in order to maintain fighting energy and achieve a position of advantage over the opposition fighters. Such was the Phantom's excess of power over and above that of other fighters of similar vintage that the aircrew came to rely on power in a fight and, at low level, would burn approximately 1800 pounds of fuel per minute when flat out (throttle in the left hand corner and blood dripping from the corner of the mandatory snarling mouth!). This of course had two effects, the first of which was frightening the hell out of the sheep and the grockles (tourists enjoying the sun) on Dartmoor, in the Highlands of Scotland or wherever the opportunity arose. The second, more important effect was that the aircraft ran out of fuel quickly and had to return to base or make an uncontrolled landing, colloquially known as a crash.

That second effect may not be much of a problem in peacetime on land, but, in serious action, the man who runs out of fuel first loses the fight without the opposition firing a single shot. This was successfully proven by the Israeli fighter pilots on several occasions when toying with Syrian fighter opposition during the several Middle East confrontations.

At sea, in carriers such as *Ark Royal*, the duration of one's flight was strictly regulated by the launch and recovery cycle on the flight deck. That was because flying programmes lasted all day (and sometimes all night) and the deck could not be used for landing-on at the same time as aircraft were being launched from the steam catapults amidships and up forward at the bow. The deck runway was angled away from the main aircraft park forward of the island, to allow aircraft attempting to land but who failed to hook on to the arrester wires with their tail hook to apply full power and take off once more. This obvious conflict of deck-space interest meant that a very strict discipline of fuel control in the air had to be maintained, because an unnecessary recovery to the deck at the wrong time would result in the next launch cycle being cancelled and the embarrassed pilot getting his balls torn off by Wings & Co. for screwing up the whole flying programme.

The rule of the day, therefore, when I was a nugget (junior pilot), was that air combat training should continue up to the point where protagonists had sufficient fuel to endure at economic speed in the air and still make their scheduled hook-on time on the deck. Pilots burning their way around the sky in reheat in a developed dog-fight would call 'Rabbit!' or 'Chicken!' when they reached the appropriate fuel state. This was not a way of ordering lunch, merely a code-word telling all concerned that they had some form of limitation — in this case fuel shortage. It meant that the fight had to be knocked off immediately — and was a convenient way for certain seasoned but less able pole-handlers to avoid being 'shot down'.

I saw this practice as an illogical way to prepare for war and so, when I became Senior Pilot, I began to advocate combat with limited use of burner or no use of it at all. This was reinforced in my mind by a second trigger which was the result of several combats with the non-reheated Buccaneer and the slow yet manoeuvrable Gannet aircraft. I found it somewhat invidious that the fleet's air defence fighter should be unable to cope in combat against a fighter-bomber like the Buccaneer purely because one's fuel state dictated that reheat could not be used. I had spent many sorties manoeuvring hard against both types of aircraft in simulated combat without reheat, sometimes successfully and sometimes not.

The third trigger was the return to the squadron of one of the Fleet Air Arm's more charismatic characters whose nickname was 'Hooligan'. He had left the Phantom world three years earlier to become an Empire Test Pilot, and having qualified was returned to the front line. Before leaving the squadron for his ETP course he had been well-known for never being able to fly his jet peacefully in a straight line; he always had to have G on the aeroplane and was an exciting pilot to fly with. On his return and once he was fully 'back in the saddle' at sea, he was written into the flying programme for one-against-one combat with Splot (myself).

As I got airborne from the waist catapult, I was very confident that I was going to win the combat training session, but I was in for a big surprise. During his Test Pilot course Hooligan had learned how to fly the Phantom to its limits in a safe fashion. In combat between two relatively evenly matched opponents, it is more often the case than not that the fight degenerates into a stalemate with both aircraft manoeuvring at the pre-briefed safety height, out of energy and unable to achieve any advantage

41

over the other. When the fight got low and slow against the Hooligan, I found I was less than evenly matched because the prodigal son could handle his jet better in the slow regime of the fight.

Having completed the sortie and landed back on board, I made a simple but key decision in my mind which was later to materialise into one of the hallmarks of the three squadrons that I was to command in the Sea Harrier world. Instead of bullshitting and arguing the toss about the finer points of the combat session (thereby reducing the impact of being comprehensively beaten), I decided to compliment Hooligan and to try to learn how to fly the F-4 his way.

'Hooligan, that was amazing! I was more than impressed and I want you to teach me everything you know about fighting the F-4 at slow speed. I want us to go through each combat now, step by step, and I want you to explain where and how you managed to gain the advantage – in other words, where was I going wrong?'

The Hooligan was only too willing to comply and he led the debrief in a very systematic and organised manner. He pointed out several areas where I was not getting the best out of the jet. Other pilots and observers in the crewroom thought it was a considerable joke that the Splot had been beaten in combat, but this didn't concern me (for a change). My main interest now was to be able to fly the F-4 to its limits as the Hooligan had been able to do.

Several fights later, I had learned fast, was able to hold my own against the Hooligan at slow speed, and had regained my position as the man to beat. I then wiped the smiles off the faces of the other pilots by addressing them all at a squadron briefing.

'You will all have noted, I am sure, that when the Hooligan returned from Boscombe Down he was able to beat shit out of me in combat at slow speed. Gentlemen, that is no longer the case! But what is more important is that I have learned a lot from that experience and can now cope with the Phantom in combat at very slow speed, with or without burner and at low level. I know much more than I used to about the aircraft's handling in that dangerous regime, its limits and characteristics – all thanks to the Hooligan. Now, gentlemen, I want you to learn the same tricks of the trade. What I am about to ask you to do is undoubtedly risky and dangerous if approached in the wrong manner or the wrong frame of mind.

'Talking about frame of mind, I refer of course to your macho images in the crewroom and to certain individuals' inability to admit that they were well-beaten in the air. That, gentlemen, has to change forthwith. In order to fly well low and slow, you have to be on the limits and you are going to learn nothing if you kid yourselves interminably in the air or on the ground.

'We are about to embark on a programme of low and slow combat. From today onwards, whenever you return to the ship as a pair, the Number

Two is to bounce his leader [attack his leader] without warning and engage in fully developed combat. Normal return height to the ship will be 2000 feet and that is to be your base height. You will not use reheat other than to regain full control of the jet! I realise that the height I have chosen is well below the normal safety height for developed combat but I don't believe you will get full advantage from this training programme unless there is no room for error — or cheating! That is why I emphasise the flight safety angle.

'What I definitely want to see is a marked improvement in squadron low-speed, low-altitude combat. In order to assist you in this programme, the Hooligan will give a squadron phase brief on the F-4's handling characteristics in this environment. Bend your ears back. Listen carefully. Because, gentlemen, if we have to fight for real one day, it will be no good saying to me, "Sorry Splot, but I ran out of fuel and I couldn't continue the fight". Should that situation arise, you will probably get your feet wet before returning on board — if you return at all.'

After a couple of months, the programme transformed the 892 Squadron pilots into a team that did not have to rely on burner to win a fight. Morale was high, but the most important benefit from the phase as far as I was concerned was that my pilots had learned how to acknowledge being beaten without bullshit and go on from there to learn from their shortcomings. It was this approach to training that I carried with me to the Sea Harrier world.

6

During my three-month conversion to the VSTOL Harrier at RAF Wittering, I had been astonished at the versatility of the unique aircraft type. There were many ways of landing the jet, varying from vertical, through various forms of short or slow landing, to the conventional landing in which one made an approach at approximately 170 knots, that is to say a similar speed to the old F-104 Starfighter. Conventional landings were practised only to take account of a nozzle failure in which the nozzles could freeze in the fully aft position (for wing-borne flight). The majority of shore-based landings would be slow ones with about 60° of nozzle, and all deck landings would be vertical.

I had been privileged to watch the first ever carrier deck landing by an RAF Harrier on board HMS *Ark Royal* in the early seventies. The pilot and squadron boss elected to carry out a slow landing rather than a vertical one and half of the carrier's air group were up on top of the island (housing the bridge) to watch the event. This sunny deck space was known as 'goofers', as it was where all and sundry would come to watch flying operations. To the seasoned deck operators assembled, the Crab Harrier was obviously too fast as it touched down about a third of the way up the angled deck from the stern. The pilot realised this too and used full braking stop as well as his wheel brakes to slow down – but he had not allowed for the slippery surface of the well-worn deck paint. His main undercarriage wheels locked and he skidded towards the end of the angled deck, out of control. A huge cheer went up from goofers; nobody wanted an accident but it was always exciting to see one!

The cheer had turned to a sigh of disappointment as the Harrier turned sideways on to the deck, somehow avoided slipping over the side into the briny, and came to rest amidships just forward of the angle.

Years later, and under the direction of the cream of the RAF, I found that landing the aircraft in its various different modes required a lot of thought, concentration and care. Putting a Phantom or Hunter down on a runway could be done virtually blindfolded, but for any form of landing in the Harrier full concentration was needed. There were also strict limitations to be observed in the VSTOL aircraft whenever transitioning from wing-borne flight to jet-borne flight, that is, to the hover. Going outside those limits could mean a very rapid departure of the aircraft from controlled flight with the jet turning upside down involuntarily. You had to be extremely lucky to survive such a loss of control during an approach to land. Whilst training at Wittering, I had witnessed such a departure.

A very seasoned Crab pilot was practising mini-circuits over the airfield. He commenced this evolution by establishing the aircraft in a steady hover and then, by lowering the nose of the jet or cracking the nozzles a little aft from the vertical, he induced forward airspeed. He then 'flew' or 'air taxied' the jet round the sky very slowly in a racetrack pattern through 360° to the point where he first started from; or in this case he attempted to do so but did not succeed. He must have allowed the aircraft nose to yaw away from the relative air stream and this induced a Harrier phenomenon known as Yaw Induced Intake Momentum Drag. (This is where the airstream being sucked into the engine intakes situated at either side of the nose becomes unbalanced and the imbalance forces the aircraft nose viciously to the right or left. This accentuated yawing moment increases the lift on one wing and reduces lift on the other; causing the jet to roll rapidly with the yaw. As it rolls its thrust vector is no longer vertical and so the aircraft begins to drop out of the sky. It is an uncontrollable situation.) Suddenly and very rapidly the aircraft banked over starboard about 120°. It then swung back over to port just as quickly and dropped like a stone out of the sky onto the grass. (Harriers can and often do land on grass fields, but not this way.)

The jet still had a lot of forward momentum on it as it hit the ground and it ploughed its way across the main runway before coming to rest in a bedraggled heap, its back broken. The crash alarms rang and the rescue crews were swiftly on scene, axing away the remains of the cockpit canopy and lifting out the injured pilot. I went to visit him in the RAF Hospital at Ely where he had been rushed by air ambulance, and although he looked more like a suntanned god than a crash victim, he was a little the worse for wear, and had an interesting tale to tell.

'I'll tell you what, Sharkey, I can hardly believe I'm still in one piece. When the aircraft departed I thought, Christ, this is it! It seemed to take an eternity for the jet to hit terra firma and I had plenty of time to decide my fate. I knew that if I banged out and timed it wrong, the rocket seat would nail me into the deck. And if I stayed with it, the chances were that I was going to burn. I guess I decided the latter course and I really believed my time had come. The aircraft was impossible to control and all I remember was hitting the deck because the impact fucked my back! The next thing I recall was an eerie silence. I didn't really know where I was but I had an idea that I must be in Heaven because I could hear this strong male voice saying, "Are you alright, mate?" I thought it was one of the angels! It took me some time to realise I was still alive and that the voice belonged to one of the rescue boys from the crash wagon.'

The VSTOL landing repertoire was challenging, but it was in the air combat environment that the little jet really inspired me. Like every fighter it had good points and bad points, and the trick to being successful in combat was to keep away from the bad and to stick with the good.

Being a physically small jet, the Harrier was difficult to pick up visually at long range in the air. Its Pegasus jet engine exhaust was smoke-free, ensuring that no tell-tale trail could guide an opponent's eyes to the aircraft's position in the sky. It had very fast acceleration up to in excess of 400 knots but peaked at less than supersonic speed when in level flight. When at full power and at low level (the worst situation for high fuel consumption) it used very little gas; less than 200 pounds of fuel per minute (compared with the F-4's 1800 pounds). This latter attribute meant that it could outlast any other known fighter in fully developed combat — a truly excellent characteristic. Its principle disadvantage (other than being limited to subsonic air speed) was a relatively poor turning circle in conventional wing-borne flight. That is to say, whereas an F-5E Freedom Fighter from the States could pull an instant 7G at 320 knots, the Harrier would be limited to much less G at the same speed, so, in a straight turning fight, the F-5E would win every time. To win in the Harrier, you had to avoid the normal practice of just pulling like a rigger and developing piles, and use your other assets instead.

There were two further unique characteristics in the Harrier's combat inventory. The first was its ability to decelerate incredibly rapidly through the use of 'full braking stop'. The four exhaust nozzles of the jet are controlled with a simple lever in the cockpit. The lever is set in a quadrant that has variable 'stops' on it that can be pre-selected for different types of take-off. With the lever forward, the nozzles face aft and this is the normal position for wing-borne flight. Pulling the lever as far back as it will go moves the nozzles down and forwards until they are in the vertical, for hovering flight. By pulling the lever further back through a restrictive detent, the nozzles can be moved forward of the vertical into the full braking stop position. With moderate to high engine power and at a speed of about 400 knots, placing the nozzle lever in the full braking stop detent makes the pilot feel as though he has run into a brick wall. A deceleration of 2 or more G occurs and nothing else in the sky can match that.

Advantage from the aircraft's acceleration and deceleration capability can be obtained by the pilot in combat by using one or the other to place the jet in the precise speed regime that suits him but, critically, does not suit the opposition.

The second characteristic that is unique to the Harrier and ultra-beneficial in combat, is its handling at slow speed, where it is without question the best fighter in the world. The excellent slow-speed handling has nothing to do with the operation of the nozzles. With engine power reduced almost to idle and with nozzles aft (normal flight), the Harrier's wing should stall and the nose of the jet should drop at about 160 knots. However, at the sort of power setting one would expect to use in a dog-fight, say 85 per cent plus, and provided the jet's nose is above the horizon, speed can be bled off (by pulling through the stall buffet or simply climbing steeply) until the aircraft has entered a speed margin of somewhere between 70 knots and 120 knots. In this regime, the pilot has the control column hard back in his belly (on the back stop) and he keeps it there, still retaining full lateral flying control of the jet. This appears totally contrary to the normal laws of aerodynamics and I later addressed this phenomenon to British Aerospace for explanation. They could not give one; nor did they know that the jet could be flown quite so slowly in full control.

To me, there was a simple and logical explanation of this useful characteristic. With the aircraft's nose pulled through the normal stall position and at a very high angle of attack (up to 50° above the horizon in level flight), the high-speed jet efflux from the four nozzles under the belly of the jet was hitting the airstream and being bent up towards the all-moving tailplane. This either impinged directly on the tailplane or, more likely, induced an air-flow over the tailplane that was strong enough to give the pilot continued nose-up pitch authority over the aircraft.

In the RAF Harrier, this phenomenon remained even when the nozzles were cracked down about 20°, thereby allowing further positive attitude control from the wing-tip, nose and tail puffer ducts (which only operated when the nozzles were down). I found that the geometry of the Sea Harrier differed somewhat from the RAF Harrier GR Mk 3 because cracking the nozzles down in the Sea Jet at very low speed generally caused an immediate loss of controlled flight – the exhaust-induced airflow over the tailplane being removed to below the tailplane. However, it did not seem to matter much because with the nozzles aft the SHAR could still be made to obey the pilot's wishes. The normal lateral attitude controls, the ailerons, still worked effectively, albeit reluctantly, and it usually needed repeated demands of full aileron and full rudder to induce the jet to respond satisfactorily to demands to turn right or left. Swearing and screaming at the aircraft also seemed to help when it was being stubborn! It was intriguing that to get the SHAR to turn adequately when at very low speed, one had to apply what in any other aircraft would be pro-spin controls. And one had to be really vicious with the controls in certain weapon configurations to get the jet to behave as you wanted.

The key to flying the SHAR successfully in combat, therefore, was to know the regime in which you wanted to fight and to suck the opposition into fighting in that regime. Naturally, you chose the regime that the opposition could not handle. You also had to know your aircraft, be fully competent at handling it in all regimes, concentrate 100 per cent and learn from any mistakes. Dependent on pilot aptitude, application and aggression in the air, it could take considerable training time to become proficient. But there was one final handling characteristic that proved to be a boon in training and more than useful for getting out of trouble when in a dog-fight. That was the aircraft's departure characteristics and, particularly, the ease with which one could regain controlled flight with a certain predictable height loss following a departure.

'Departure from controlled flight' simply means that the pilot loses any form of positive control over the aeroplane (the aircraft assumes a mind of its own) and it is usually represented in swept-wing jets by an often violent entry into a spin, from which recovery can not always be assured. It is therefore a 'no-no' in the swept-wing world and often prevents pilots from operating their jets to near the limit, thereby restricting their war-fighting capability.

A departure in the SHAR can be a most enervating and electrifying experience. It is best induced by putting the nozzles down when in normal flight and applying full rudder, elevator and aileron controls at the same time. A bucking bronco from a rodeo is a tame affair by comparison with the unusual manoeuvres that follow. Fortunately, being strapped into the jet helps the pilot and allows him to sit back and enjoy the ride. The aircraft yaws, pitches and rolls extremely violently and all at the same time. It tumbles 'arse over tit' and gyrates laterally in a most extraordinary way. (I had once demonstrated a departure for the benefit of the Commander-in-Chief, Fleet who was being flown in an accompanying jet. I put on a very good show and literally tumbled violently — out of the sky. The C-in-C had been a fair passenger until that point, but the visual impression created by the impromptu 'aerobatics' very nearly induced an involuntary technicolor yawn from the Admiral.)

Recovery from a SHAR departure could not be easier. Place the nozzles aft and centralise the cockpit controls; or better still, take hands and feet off the controls and let the aircraft sort itself out. As if by magic, the jet stops gyrating, assumes a nose-low attitude and, as forward airspeed increases, it can be rapidly recovered from the shallow dive. Height loss from the commencement of recovery is very predictable.

When the Harrier flight envelope was being demonstrated to me at Wittering, I had been extremely cautious about slow flight in the aeroplane because of my swept-wing background. I admitted this to the staff pilot and asked him to demonstrate the departure and recovery characteristics. He was delighted to do so and for about ten minutes the aircraft was put through its paces, often with zero airspeed on the clock. After being initially horrified, I revelled in this new game and immediately began to realise the advantages that could accrue from the forgiving aspects of the jet when close to or beyond normal flight limits.

I was already planning in my mind the training of convertees to the SHAR; they would all have to become fully proficient at aircraft handling throughout the flight envelope, and the best place to monitor their progress and capability would be in the fighter combat arena.

For the first months of service at Yeovilton, the SHAR was still not fitted with its full Head-Up Display facility or its air-to-air radar, both of which were still undergoing manufacturer's trials and fine tuning. The new trials squadron (the IFTU) could not therefore commence trials or training in the primary role of air intercept, so it was an ideal opportunity for all pilots converting to the Harrier to explore fully the jet's flight envelope. I therefore dictated that the majority of early flying would indeed be combat because I knew that when confidence in full aircraft handling had been achieved and the pilots had learned to operate it to its limits safely, they would find little trouble with the academic flying tasks associated with other aircraft roles such as ground attack and air intercept.

The programme went predictably, with the ex-fighter jocks finding combat a little easier than those from the Buccaneer world. Within my team I found a newcomer to the Navy who was very much a kindred spirit in his approach to flying. Ian Mortimer hailed from the Crab Harrier world and was expert in the VSTOL, low-level ground-attack and reconnaissance roles. He admitted to having very little fighter combat training and was very keen to get up to speed. He was aggressive, intelligent, loyal and full of initiative, and soon became a very close friend. With the friendship there grew a friendly rivalry in the air, each pilot respecting the other's talents. 'Morts', as I liked to refer to him, could handle the jet as well as anybody and his only deficiency in combat initially was knowing the right tactics to use at the right time. But he learned very fast and soon outstripped all the squadron cowboys, carving himself the reputation of being a man to beat in a dog-fight.

Although I always managed to retain the edge over him in 1-v-1 combat, he was much better than me at teaching other pilots (particularly those from the flying training pipeline) where they were going wrong. I would lead a student combat sortie and inevitably return to land having won all aspects of the fight. I would then attempt to explain where the other pilot had been found wanting or had made mistakes. Morts would lead a similar sortie and purposely make mistakes to demonstrate their importance to the trainee. We actually complemented each other well and as time progressed, Morts became my unofficial right-hand man.

The first opportunity for combat against a dissimilar type of aeroplane came when the squadron managed to organise a combat phase against the USAF Aggressor Squadron at RAF Alconbury. By then the IFTU pilots had already established a capability ladder and the top three, myself, Morts and a legendary character called Dave Braithwaite, flew our shiny new jets to the Aggressor base to do battle. There we were warmly welcomed by the Aggressors and three days of intensive fighter combat training began.

USAF Aggressor Squadrons consist of specially selected USAF fighter pilots and were formed specifically to give the best possible fighter combat training to USAF squadrons throughout the world, and to NATO squadrons in Europe. They are highly regarded for their professionalism and expertise. They allow no bullshit in their post-flight debriefs and their simple aim is to improve the fighting capability of the squadrons that they work with.

On the first day, the two teams briefed each other about their own aircraft characteristics (the Aggressors flew the F-5E) and then got airborne for 1–v–1 fighter combat. The F-5E is even smaller than the SHAR, turns much better and can accelerate to supersonic speed extremely quickly in a nose-low situation. Its armament is the same as that of the SHAR, Sidewinder missiles and guns.

The results of the first three 1–v–1 combat sessions were: I had four kills and none against; Morts had three kills and one against; Dave scored two against two. The Aggressor pilots were astonished. Later that day, one of their staff pilots approached Mortimer.

'Jesus Christ, Morts! Who are you guys? What's going on? Have you been sent here to evaluate us?'

Morts assured him that that was not the case. The Aggressors were intrigued that a fresh-from-formation squadron team could do so well against them, and so we agreed to fly some special combat evaluation sorties with them to give them a better chance of understanding the SHAR.

'What I suggest we do,' I briefed, 'is set up each combat with your F-5s in a position of clear advantage over us. That is to say you can take up the "perch" at about 2000 feet above us, about 800 yards on the beam and 2000 yards back. We shall commence each combat when you turn in on us. We'll be watching you and when you turn in we'll counter [turn] hard in towards you. At that point you will be able to track us and attempt to get an acquisition with your missiles. As you come into missile range, we shall deny you a shot by hiding our jet exhaust from your missile. In the SHAR that is relatively easy to do: we just drop about 30° of nozzle. This will pitch our nose up instantaneously about 20°, diffuse the hot gases of our exhausts and hide the exhaust from you by placing our wing between your missile and the source of heat. You will still be able to track us with your nose and by this time you should have a lot of overtake, that is, you will be closing in rapidly towards guns range. Before you get to guns range we will commence a high-G braking stop barrel roll which you won't be able to follow. This will allow us to roll over you and decelerate to a position behind you where you will be in our gunsights. That's the aim of the game, gentlemen; let's go and see if it works, and see whether you can come up with an answer to our moves.'

The combats went as planned with about the same ratio of kills as on the first sortie. Missile shots were denied to the F-5s and as my own opponent closed in towards guns range I pulled the joy-stick fully back in my midriff and used a combination of aileron and then full rudder to corkscrew the jet into the vertical. Breathing hard from the excitement, I relaxed the flight controls and swung the nozzles down and forward into the full braking stop position. Suddenly the F-5 was no longer pointing at me but was being sucked and pulled down below me. Nozzles aft again and full rudder, aileron and elevator to pass through the inverted and then roll down behind the F-5. The fight was over. Either with missile or gun, the Freedom Fighter was finished.

On day two of the detachment I flew against the Aggressor Boss and was beaten in one of the four combats that took place. The fight had progressed until both jets were near to base height, and slow. It was almost stalemate and in that situation I should have walked it. But one of the F-5's specialities is being moderately capable in the slow-speed regime, and although it can't fly as slow as the SHAR it can manoeuvre more freely at a slightly higher speed. Our two jets were crossing over each other in our attempts to point at the other aircraft and shoot (a manoeuvre known as horizontal scissors) when I momentarily let my jet's nose drop below the horizon. I had briefed my team that on no account must they let this happen against the F-5 or that fight would be lost.

I was furious with myself as I had wanted to return to Yeovilton with a clean sheet. Nevertheless, it was a highly successful first look at dissimilar combat, with the team kill ratios against one of the best outfits around being 12:1, 9:3 and 6:6, making an aggregate kill rate of 27 to 10 in the SHAR's favour. All the lads on the IFTU were delighted and I submitted a short paper to the MOD to report the detail of the Aggressor visit. It was an honest report, and it complimented the Aggressors on their professionalism and integrity. But it pulled no punches on the score-line, or the capabilities of the Sea Jet.

As a matter of internal MOD courtesy, a copy of the report was passed to the appropriate RAF Harrier desk and from there it was passed on up the line to the hierarchy. It was apparent that the courtesy was neither welcomed nor honoured at higher level because within days of the initial report being submitted, an Air Vice-Marshal stormed into the Aggressor Squadron Commander's office at Alconbury, threw a copy of my report down on the table, and asked, 'Have you seen this, Colonel?'

Obviously, the Crabs didn't relish the idea of the SHAR being a successful fighter and were presumably trying to question the validity of the report. This rather underhand intrusion caused unnecessary embarrassment all round and was a most unwelcome gesture. The Boss of the Aggressors was rather upset by the incident, but his staff did get in touch with me by phone to say that the report was a good one, and valid.

A few days later, the telephone on my desk at Yeovilton rang.

'Good morning, Sir. This is the F-15 Eagle Squadron at Bitburg in Germany. Could I speak with Commander Sharkey, please?'

'Certainly! Speaking!'

'Sir, I hear you had a good experience against the Aggressor Squadron at Alconbury, recently. Is that correct?'

'Yes, that's right.'

'Well, Sir, if you're happy with the idea we'd be delighted to come across to Somerset to do some combat with you. We'd bring over four F-15s to see how you get on against our jet. We hear you did pretty good against the Aggressors.'

'That would be splendid!' I replied. 'We would love to see you here at Yeovilton and to fly with you. Just let us know when you expect to arrive and we'll be at your pleasure for the duration.'

Word had got around fast and the elite of the USAF in Europe couldn't resist the chance to see how good the SHAR was − and whether Alconbury was just a flash in the pan. True to their word, the Bitburg boys arrived at Yeovilton with four of their magnificent fighters for a day's Air Combat Manoeuvring.

It was agreed that the aircraft should operate in pairs against each other, which brought fighter tactics really into play (as opposed to just matching aircraft for aircraft, pilot for pilot, in a 1-v-1 fight). The visitors were fully equipped with their radar and were simulating Sparrow AIM-7E missiles, Sidewinders and guns. The SHARS were without radar but were fitted with their radar warning receivers and were simulating Sidewinders and guns. The two combat sessions were set up over North Devon and the Bristol Channel, with the dissimilar pairs running in towards each other from a distance of about 40 nautical miles. My team were given radar direction from ground radar by a brilliant Direction Officer of many years' experience named Harry O'Grady.

Having spent years flying the Phantom and using the Sparrow missile, which has an excellent head-on firing capability, I knew how to deny the F-15 a valid Sparrow shot from head-on and had briefed my pilots accordingly. The tactic worked well. There were no head-on claims from the F-15s as they ran in and, as the two aircraft types entered the same airspace, fully developed combat began.

Initially, the F-15s had the advantage. Their radars pinpointed the SHARs and directed their pilots' eyes on to the smaller jets. The SHARs flew at about 12,000 feet, which was where we wanted to meet the opposition, and so the F-15s came in from very high level (30,000 feet plus), rolling over and looping down towards the stern of our Sea Jet formation. This was when the SHAR was most vulnerable. It was essential that visual contact was made. Morts came to the rescue.

'High in the 6 o'clock, Boss! Break port and up! They are about 3 miles and closing fast!'

The aircraft shuddered in the hard turn with the nose rising to meet the threat. 'Tally-ho! On both! I'm flying through the right-hand man and reversing on him. Your tail is clear.'

The nose of the Sea Jet passed through the vertical, with my head strained round as far as it would go to keep tabs on the F-15 which, feeling threatened, had engaged burners and had also pulled vertically upwards and over the top (about 5000 feet above me). As the 15 came down the other side of the vertical manoeuvre he found me still pointing at him all the way. Trying the same move twice was not a good idea, but that's what he did. I predicted the move, sliced my nose early through the vertical and found myself sitting astern the two white-hot plumes at the back of the US fighter. 'Fox Two away!' I called, simulating the release of the Sidewinder missile. Morts fared just as well.

The detailed post-flight debriefs showed a 7 to 1 valid kill claim by the SHARs. The Alconbury experience had been no flash in the pan. The Sea Harrier had really arrived on the fighter combat scene.

Although I placed maximum emphasis on combat in those early months of the IFTU, the more mundane but no less important tasks of proving the aircraft and all its black boxes (computers, and so on) continued on track. The Smiths Industries Head-Up Display System and the Ferranti Attitude Reference Platform and Navigation computer arrived, were fitted and produced excellent results from day one. Hundreds of data-gathering flights were conducted, records collated and the information passed on to British Aerospace and Boscombe Down.

A very comprehensive IFTU report was written by aircrew and engineers and submitted to the MOD every six weeks, and an equally close liaison was maintained with the Admiral's staff, the Ministry and the aircraft manufacturers on all aspects of the aircraft operations and progress. The Aeromedical Team at Farnborough monitored all reports closely to see how the pilots were coping with the cockpit workload, and the Navy Flight Safety Centre at Yeovilton gave excellent moral support to the squadron as they waited for the first 'nasty'. When the Harrier AV-8A had gone into service with the United States Marine Corps there had been a plethora of serious accidents, and it was not unrealistic to suppose that the IFTU would have its own fair share of incidents during the early days of the SHAR in service.

No nasties or crunches occurred, and there were three reasons for the accident-free track record. The fundamental reason was that the RAF had learned from their own mistakes and had passed on all their flight safety knowledge to the IFTU aircrew during the Harrier conversion flying at Wittering. The second reason was that the RAF had lent the Navy an experienced Harrier Qualified Flying Instructor, Bertie Penfold, who provided an absolutely outstanding service, monitoring and directing domestic flying standards and practices. The third reason was that I backed the QFI to the hilt and came down like a ton of bricks on anyone who showed signs of taking liberties with the aircraft when in the landing and take-off arena.

During the three years of service up to the outbreak of the Falklands conflict, my three squadrons, 700A, 899 Headquarters Squadron, and 801, maintained an accident-free record. It was the best flight safety record of any military jet aircraft entering service in history. But 801's sister squadron, 800 NAS, spoiled the record soon after their formation. Their Senior Pilot, Mike Blisset, lost control of his jet when flying past *Invincible* and hit the ski-jump. Blisset ejected and the aircraft was lost.

He had been taking film for a television programme with a camera strapped under the belly of the aeroplane. The initial aim had been to have a second aircraft flying in close formation, astern and below Blisset's jet, with the TV camera facing aft and filming the second aircraft overflying the deck. 800 couldn't produce a second aircraft for the flight and so I offered one from my squadron, 899. Had the offer been accepted, which it was not, the second aircraft would have had no chance of surviving the flypast of the ship.

To me it was all a dreadful waste. It was my strongly held opinion that the accident could have been avoided.

Differing standards of airmanship obviously prevailed in the two squadrons.

A knock on the cabin door interrupted my mental review of past events. It was Robin, the Senior Pilot, and there could be no more time for day-dreaming; at least not until after the Captain had been briefed, and the bar was open.

7

'Come in, Robin, and sit down. What's the score?'

'Thanks Boss! After you left the crewroom we had a bit of a chat about things in general. The boys are in good spirits, but some have let me know in private that they have a few misgivings about the size of the task facing us. To be frank, so do I; we seem to be up against considerable odds and we shouldn't kid ourselves that it's going to be easy, but that's by the way. One thing is for sure, and that is they are all pretty excited at the thought of some action. The best thing for all of us will be to get to sea and get on with the job.'

One thing about Robin was that he didn't bother to dress up a point. It was essential that the new Senior Pilot was going to be completely open with me about anything to do with the flying task or the pilots' morale. Splot continued.

'As we discussed ashore yesterday, Boss, I briefed the guys on us all pairing up into permanent fighter combat pairs and training together until the action starts. The idea has gone down pretty well so I should have a proposed team list for your approval by tomorrow night. As we only have eleven pilots, someone is going to have to be the "loose deuce", but that's unavoidable.' He paused. 'There is one teeny weeny snag, though. Our new arrival on the squadron, Soapy Watson, nearly flipped his lid when I mentioned that he would be pairing up with you. As far as he is concerned, that is a definite "no-no".'

I was quite taken by surprise by this revelation. I liked the custom from World War II of the CO flying with the junior squadron 'joe' on his wing, and I agreed with it, and that's why I had suggested that Soapy should fly on my wing. My first choice as a pairing would have been Mortimer, without question − but I also knew that that would not have been right or fair.

'What did Soapy actually say, Robin?' I didn't know Watson all that well yet but the man's reputation had come before him. He was reported to be affable, devastatingly witty and amusing, and was not afraid to call a spade a spade.

'Well, Boss, and I quote, "I'm not going to have anyone being my fucking nursemaid, Splot. I want to take my chances like the rest and without any special favours. Tell that to the Boss and tell him to shove it in his pipe!" You see what I mean, Sharkey. He feels pretty strongly about it.'

'You're not joking, are you?' The funny side of it was getting through. 'Speak to him again and try to persuade him to see reason. If he still feels the same by the time we get to sea, I'll have a word with him myself.'

We then got down to the serious business of preparing a brief for the Captain with the AWIs. Soon all five of us were gathered in the small cabin, the AWIs sitting where they could on the bunk seat, the desk and the deck. I felt very lucky to be supported by the officers who sat facing me. Their expertise and experience were a priceless asset to the squadron and ship.

'OK, AWI,' I began, addressing Mortimer, 'What's your plan?'

'There are several tasks in front of us, Boss. The first one is to fine tune the organisation of the outstanding weapons trials. Second, we need to look at the threat, quantify it, and use all available intelligence to carry out a threat-reduction exercise. Third, we should try to predict all possible enemy offensive tactics. Fourth, we have to plan the best possible use of our available assets for countering the projected air threat. Last but not least, we need to examine options for an air-strike on Port Stanley airfield.

'I would like,' he continued just as I was about to butt in, 'to suggest an allocation of tasks as follows. I and the Senior Pilot should plan the weapon trials and get them out of the way as soon as possible. Alan Curtis should get to work on the threat: he's the best man for that having flown A-4s and Mirages himself, and he should be able to glean a lot from the ship's intelligence files and incoming signals. John Eyton-Jones will examine the specific scenarios of possible enemy offence and, Boss, I think you are the best-qualified to plan the use of our resources. We can look at an air-strike on Stanley airfield after we have finished the other tasks.'

I was impressed. They hadn't missed anything as far as I could see.

'Fine, gentlemen. We shall all attend the Captain's briefing this evening and propose your way ahead. Then we'll try to go for a formal briefing recommending specifics 72 hours later. I shall act as the link man on all this, so when you are ready, all inputs to me.'

They departed, and a few minutes later I was off on my rounds of the various squadron departments in the ship. First stop was the hangar to see how the lads were progressing with the aircraft. They had an immense amount of work to do preparing for the weapons trials, giving each 'cab' (aircraft) in turn its new colour scheme and, at the same time, continuing routine maintenance. Smiths Industries had forwarded the new computer tapes for Head-Up Display (HUD) weapons release guidance and these were being run on the bench rigs, checked and then loaded into each aircraft system. Radars were being checked for tuning and the armourers were busy in their task of preparing to load Sidewinders, guns, 1000-pound bombs, 2-inch rockets and Lepus flares.

Next stop, the squadron staff office; then a quick hello to the ship's Commander (second-in-command) and to the Air Operations Officer, Rod O'Connor (an ex-Phantom observer and an old friend); and finally a return to 3U cabin flat to call on the Commanding Officer of 820 Sea King Anti-Submarine Squadron, Ralph Wykes-Snead.

There was none of the latent outdated rivalry between rotor-heads and jet-jockeys that had existed in *Ark Royal* and its predecessors. Instead, when I first met him Ralph put his offer of friendship and co-operation quite bluntly.

'Sharkey, I hope you and I are going to see eye-to-eye. We've just had 800 Squadron on board for a few months and they couldn't get it into their heads that my officers number about fifty and theirs less than ten. So Wardroom hooliganism between squadrons was a bit onesided! They wouldn't get the message and were always confronting my guys. And it always ended up the same way — with all of them on the deck! From what I've heard about you, you and I should hit it off well, so how about some harmony rather than aggro?'

From that first meeting mutual respect and friendship grew rapidly and the two of us were able to put on a united air group front to one and all. This was extremely useful when negotiating conditions for aircrew such as beer after hours and a hot meal for aircrew who came down late from night flying. The two of us were pleased to be going south for action together. Following the lead of their two COs, the aircrew of both squadrons were inseparable when off duty and this made for a very happy ship's Wardroom.

After greeting each other with genuine pleasure, we settled down for a chat about the way ahead. Ralph had embarked on the Friday before when the balloon had gone up and one thing was worrying him.

'You may know that the Captain plans a Command Briefing session twice a day, Sharkey, at 0800 and 1800. All Heads of Departments [HODs] are invited to attend but Wings sees himself as our HOD and he has said to me that Squadron COs are not required! What do you feel about that?'

I didn't like that at all and I had every intention of representing the Sea Harrier point of view personally to the Command on a regular basis. If we were going to war, then I didn't want middlemen misinterpreting what I had to say. 'Let's go and see him now, shall we?'

Dusty Milner was a good hand in every way. He was loyal in both directions, to seniors and subordinates alike, and had a genuine interest in the welfare of all personnel under his control. I had a keen respect for the man with whom I had already served in the MOD for two years. It was Dusty who as my immediate boss had apprised me of some dreadful news back in 1978. He had invited me for a drink in the little wine bar close to the Embankment Underground and had raised the subject with some delicacy.

'Sharkey, I've watched you operate here in MOD now for a few months and I'm very pleased with what I've seen. But I have a hunch that you don't realise that your name is more than controversial with the Naval Secretary and the promotion team?'

'Go on, Dusty, I haven't a clue what you are talking about.' It sounded ominous to say the least. The Naval Secretary's Department was headed by a Rear-Admiral and it received, collated and appraised all officers' confidential reports. It was also responsible for deciding which job and career pattern was suitable for individual officers. Like most people in life, I was keen to succeed in my career and the phrase 'more than controversial' didn't sound too good.

'No, I didn't think that you did. From what I can gather the last Director [of our Department, Naval Air Warfare] put a confidential report in about you that was the worst report that the Naval Secretary's Department have ever had on a General List officer. In fact it was so bad that they wouldn't accept it as it didn't match any of your past reports. They sent it back to the Director via the Vice-Chief of Naval Staff for it to be rewritten. It then bounced backwards and forwards for about three months with neither side giving way, until finally the Naval Secretary had to accept it as it stood. As you know only too well, you are right in the middle of the promotion zone for Commander and you don't stand a chance in hell of promotion if we don't do something about this. I've spoken to the new Director, Lyn Middleton, who knows you pretty well and he has agreed that an injustice has been done. So we are both going to push you extra hard for promotion. Have you any idea what caused the problem?'

I was astonished at the news and more than a little depressed. No one had apprised me of the contents of the report; on the contrary, when I had attempted to solicit information concerning its contents, I had been lightly informed 'Oh, you're doing fine, Sharkey. A bit noisy at times but generally fine.'

Now that Dusty had been good enough to put me in the picture it didn't take me long to guess why I had been marked down so badly. I explained that I had had a pretty volcanic altercation with one of my superiors over my absence from the office one day when my au pair girl had fractured her skull. I had taken her to the hospital early on a Monday morning, was three hours late for work and had then made the mistake of standing on my dignity when I was subsequently 'carpeted'. I was no 'slacker' and wouldn't tolerate being called one.

'I don't accept your bollocking, Sir!' had been my last words before storming out of the room.

My behaviour had been tactless in the extreme. But, that was no justification for my peers misleading me about the contents of my report. I had had the guts to stand up for my own opinions so why couldn't they be equally forthright and honest? It was very good of Dusty to put the record straight.

'Thanks, Dusty, for telling me the bad tidings. I think I'll cross those bastards off my Xmas Card list!'

Dusty and Lynley E. Middleton did much more than just tell me about what had gone on behind the scenes. They worked hard to repair the damage done and because of them my name had at last appeared on the promotion list in December 1981. I would put on my Brass Hat at the end of June.

Although loyal and grateful to Dusty, I didn't ever let my personal feelings interfere with operational need. I was quite prepared to have a row with my boss on the issue at hand — attendance of Squadron COs at Command Briefings. I knew that Dusty might be difficult to persuade, but in spite of a certain level of obstinacy about the issue, he eventually agreed to put the matter to the Captain.

That was good enough for us and we soon received the nod from the Command that Squadron COs were welcome to attend Command Briefings.

Everything seemed to be going adequately smoothly, and the 801 briefing that evening was no exception. Captain J.J. Black listened intently to our 801 team and said he would look forward to the detailed briefing in a couple of days' time.

The morrow was the day that the Task Group sailed from Portsmouth. I retired to bed after the bar closed following a very convivial evening with the two squadrons. There was only one subject of conversation in the bar: the action that lay ahead. And it was very obvious to me even at that stage that most people on board had one major worry — the Argentinians' numerical superiority in the air. Everyone wanted to know how we expected to cope with the odds against us because their lives depended on our success. I went to sleep dreaming of Mirages and thanking God that it was Thatcher at the helm of the nation and not Foot. This was a chance not to be missed.

Part II

THE PASSAGE SOUTH
TO ASCENSION
– PREPARING FOR WAR

8

Monday 5 April 1982 was a perfect spring day. The hazy sunshine warmed the green-and-grey decks of the Task Group ships as they prepared for sea, and was kind to the many well-wishers who came early to claim the best vantage points at the narrow entrance to Portsmouth Harbour to wave farewell to the boys in blue.

On this very special day, the build-up to leaving harbour was an even more emotional period than usual for all on board. No one knew what would happen to them or to their ship in the months to come. But each man had his own job to do and I kept my mind from wandering back to Somerset and my family by working in my cabin on plans for the fight to come, as did the other AWIs. Robin sorted out the afternoon flying programme (we were to start flying as soon as the ship had cleared the approaches to the harbour) and the AEO organised the presentation of aircraft on deck. A lone Sea Harrier stood on the ski-jump near the bow of the ship and the Sea King helicopters of 820 Squadron were ranged neatly along the flat flight-deck.

As the ship slipped from alongside, I remained below. I knew there would be many a lump in the throats of the hardened sailors on deck and I preferred to be alone with my thoughts. But if I had been on deck or on the bridge I would have observed a tremendous send-off. The record of Rod Stewart's 'Sailing' was played from ashore amidst all the Union Jacks, handkerchiefs and frantically waving families. It was most moving and none could have wished for a better farewell. Morale in the fleet was at a peak, even though news had just come through of Lord Carrington's resignation. This was regretted by all, as was Mrs Thatcher's decision not to accept the resignation of Mr John Nott, the Minister of Defence.

The news media were still full of the diplomatic initiatives being made to resolve the crisis peacefully, but we somehow knew that Galtieri would lose too much face by withdrawing without a fight. And in my heart of hearts, I wanted a fight. Peacetime flying had been fun; more than that, it had been terrific. But it wasn't the real McCoy and only the real thing was going to show us all if our training and tactics were good enough. Like many others I was tired of peacetime constraints and bureaucratic interference in operational matters. For us, the defence of British territory was no longer a make-believe game controlled by the Whitehall mandarins. Instead it was time for professionals to take over and use what little equipment we had — following years of defence cuts — to do the job.

I knew, like all the others on board, that I would feel some trepidation before going into combat for the first time against shooting opposition. In fact, I would probably be frightened fartless! But the past two years' achievements by my squadrons against the best that the West had to offer gave me just cause for considerable confidence. And although I can not explain why, not for one minute of time during the coming weeks did I accept the possibility that I might be shot down by Argentine fighters. I believed in my heart that my team could pull it off; in spite of the odds and given a fair chance. Maybe I was kidding myself and not looking at the opposition rationally, but there is no point going into a fight if you think you might lose. So it was time to start believing in all the hype that goes along with the fighter pilot label:

'Yea, though I walk through the valley of death I shall fear no evil,

For I am the meanest motherfucker in the valley!'

And so it was down to business. I shut out all the soft thoughts of home. I would give myself the luxury of thinking of the family once a day only, before sleeping.

To date, no live retard 1000-pound bomb deliveries had been made from the SHAR and this was to be the first of the weapons trials that Morts had planned. 'Retard' or 'laydown' bombing entails flying very fast and low over a target and releasing the bombs very close to it. It is best employed against targets with a reasonable height. If one used this type of delivery with a standard non-retarded bomb, the bomb would reach the target at the same time that the aircraft passed overhead and both target and delivery aircraft would go up in smoke. (It's happened.) To overcome this problem, the bomb is fitted with an effective airbrake, like a parachute, which opens as soon as the bomb leaves the aircraft so that it rapidly decelerates and hits the target long after (several seconds) the aircraft has cleared the point of impact.

There is a very convenient live weapons range to the east of the Isle of Wight and the AWI had booked it for use with live ordnance for two hours after sailing. The Senior Pilot (Robin) had programmed E-J (Eyton-Jones) and Morts for the bombing and had given me an Air Combat Manoeuvring (ACM) sortie against Brian Haig. As soon as the deck had been cleared of the leaving harbour routine, the Sea Harriers were ranged, armed and launched.

Meanwhile, back on Portsdown Hill overlooking Portsmouth, the staff of Flag Officer Flotilla III were witnessing the departure of the remnants of the Task Group from the lawn outside the Wardroom. Gin-and-tonics in hand, they all wished they were embarked with the Force. There was a haze over the harbour in the noonday sun which limited visibility somewhat, but nevertheless made for a very picturesque setting. Galtieri seemed a very long way away. Then suddenly, the peace was shattered and the G&Ts rattled by the sound of a huge explosion from seawards. Disaster! Had a ship blown up? Damn the haze, we can't see a thing.

Phones rang and signals whisked their way through the ether. Eventually the source of the explosion was identified. It was Morts delivering the first live 1000-pound bomb on the range at sea. And the weather conditions were such as to carry the noise a very long way.

I was pleased with the results of the first bombing trial even though E-J and Morts could have done it blindfolded. But my own priority for day flying after completion of, or without detriment to, the weapons trials was, without question, Air Combat Training. The other priority was to crack on with getting as many aircrew as possible fully night-qualified: not just for landing on deck but also for air-to-air and air-to-surface weaponry at night.

I enjoyed my flight against Haig, who was progressing adequately although lacking in confidence. Naturally, it was hard for him flying against the Boss but you can only win in the air if you believe you can. And that belief comes only from being aggressive, confident and knowing the aircraft backwards. Brian had not yet had long enough in the SHAR to feel fully at home in the air combat environment, but he was making good progress.

After flying and back down on the deck, it was pretty clear that the planned night flying could not take place. Fog was forecast both in the Channel and at all possible diversion airfields such as Yeovilton and Portland.

But at least the fog gave me a good opportunity to get up to date on how all the operational planning was going.

The bad news came from Alan Curtis. The only intelligence available to the 801 planners was from personal knowledge and from that eternal non-classified publication, *Jane's All the World's Fighting Aircraft*. Alan was a little disappointed in the efficiency of the on-board intelligence system or, more correctly, the lack of it. It was, however, no surprise to me that the over-classified documents in the ship's safes revealed the square root of FA! I well remembered an incident at the weekly intelligence briefing in the MOD in 1978.

In a conference room full of desk officers from all MOD Directorates, I had listened to the intelligence community slapping themselves on the back about what they knew. But there was no talk of giving the highly classified information to the front line (the pilots at sea or the troops in the tanks).

During question time at the end of the briefing, I stood up and stuck my neck out (as usual).

'Can you tell me, Sir, how you intend ensuring that all this valuable information is going to be disseminated to the front line at a time of need? It is my experience at sea that all the important nitty-gritty never gets to the boys at the coal-face, and this situation needs to be rectified.'

Suggesting that things may not be as well-organised as they should be was, sure to get an indignant response. One of the senior officers at the briefing took great pleasure in following the party line.

'Ah, Sharkey! It had to be you! We have a very good organisation for updating the front line with all the intelligence that it needs to know and you should have hoisted that in by now. When the need arises the appropriate intelligence will be available.'

'Need to know' and 'appropriate' were the key words in the answer. In other words, the system led by armchair Admirals would decide who needed to know what and it was not a matter for discussion. Over-classification of data meant that it would go into a safe in Whitehall and never be seen again.

Returning to the present problem on board *Invincible*, I said, 'Well, there is only one thing for it, Alan, and that is to make do with what we've got. Several of us have fought against the A-4 and you have flown it. Some of us have fought with the French Etendard squadrons and we are already experts on the air-launched Exocet. We know the quality and performance of the air-to-air missiles that might face us and so the only real shortage of intelligence that we suffer from is performance data on the Mirage III and V. Even there, you have had to ride in an Aussie Mirage III and we may be able to get some more information out of the system. But even if we can't, we know some performance data from *Jane's* and we'll have to base our analysis on that. So the best thing for us now is for you to list all the relevant strengths and weaknesses of the different opposition types and then we'll all get together and add our bits of extra knowledge. From that position we can do the threat-reduction exercise.'

Lieutenant Alan Curtis had a very analytical mind and had flown a useful selection of front-line aircraft. V-bombers with the RAF, A-4s with the Royal New Zealand Air Force, and now Sea Harriers with the Royal Navy. Although a QFI rather than an AWI by qualification and at heart, he was a brilliant planner and a self-taught weapons expert, which is why I was happy to treat him as an AWI within the squadron planning team. He went off to do his work.

The lack of readily available intelligence had not surprised me. But it did mean that the MOD intelligence team had so far done bugger-all about getting information to the coalface during the two and a half weeks that the squadron had been on alert. I would have been very much more concerned if I had had a crystal ball and seen how much of the intelligence was to be passed directly to *Invincible* during the whole confrontation. I was soon to receive the only three signals that gave us any intelligence at all, and these proved either inaccurate or inadequate.

At the Command Briefing that evening, I briefed the Captain and Wings on the results of the laydown bombing trial. 'E-J and Morts did well, Sir, and the results appeared satisfactory. But we would only use this form of attack against an undefended or lightly defended target. There is no point in risking the loss of our limited air defence assets on low-value targets, but if we have to use it, we know it works fine. Tomorrow, we may need the splash target streamed for rocketing trials, and as from tomorrow I plan to arm all aircraft with live Sidewinder AIM-9G missiles. This will be of benefit in two ways: first, the missiles can be checked out fully in the air; and second, the pilots need to get used to the feel of the aircraft when it is fully armed.'

'Oh,' drawled JJ, looking hard at me with some amusement and a lot of devil in his eye, 'A lot of fundungus under the wing makes a difference does it, CO 801?' J.J. Black was a Gunnery officer by background and had seen real action before, in Borneo. He was about the only man on board to have that experience and was already quite philosophical about the risks that we would be facing. Tall, dark-haired and distinguished-looking, he was a born leader. He never talked down to even the most junior seaman, and was as laid-back as you could get when putting his subordinates at ease. He also had a sense of fun and humour that rivalled even Soapy Watson's. It was soon to become clear to all participants at the Command Briefing that it was not only a venue for briefing the Skipper but also a useful medium through which JJ could relax his senior troops and give them confidence.

It was also apparent from that first Command Briefing that the two squadrons were looked upon with a new respect by the other non-flying Heads of Department. It was as if they all realised for the first time that the noisy aircraft and aircrew were just about all that stood between them and disaster. The Captain had always respected the capabilities of his aviators, as had Wings, but the ship as a whole had often given the impression that they preferred the Air Group being ashore. It was now an entirely different situation. Instead of having to fight for decent conditions on board, suddenly the airmen, and the Sea Harrier team in particular, were blue-eyed boys.

Air defence of the ship had suddenly become a serious question of survival. Throughout the fleet, the atmosphere was the same. Even the Admiral, Sandy Woodward, who was a submariner by trade, had to adapt to the new situation. I had understood that he was not an advocate of air power at sea, and he had said as much in the MOD during official presentations: 'The days of needing fixed-wing carriers at sea are over'. Now, following the ill-informed remarks of various senior self-styled experts òn television, the country believed that the Task Force was bereft of air power. They had not properly recognised the existence of the Sea Harrier, and every man-jack in the fleet wondered whether the pitifully small number of fighters that we had embarked would be enough to do the job.

After the briefing, Ralph and I made our way aft in our flying suits for a much-needed shower. Evening rig in the Wardroom bar and the dining room continued to be Red Sea rig — open-necked, short-sleeved white shirt with stiff epaulettes; cummerbund; navy slacks and black shoes. By the time we arrived the Air group was already hard at it in the bar, 'spoofing' for who would buy the wine with dinner. That evening was my first opportunity to meet some of the journalists who had embarked. I was particularly taken with two of them, John Witherow of *The Times* and A.J. McIlroy of the *Telegraph*. Witherow was tall and laid-back, McIlroy short and aggressive. Although I didn't dine with them I promised them a seminar in the next few days to brief them on the Sea Harrier perspective.

820 Squadron were always ready to entertain, and after dinner they gave the Wardroom a rendition of their new song which— surprise, surprise — went to the tune of 'Argentina':

> You don't frighten me Argentina,
> The truth is we will defeat you;
> We'll sink your carrier with our Sea Harrier
> And with our Sea Kings subs'll be sinking.

> On your bike Argentina,
> The front line are getting airborne;
> You've gone too far now, we've left the bar now
> And soon the Falklands will be in our hands.

> Four and a half thousand booties
> Will take back Port Stanley!
> You might try to hold out but we will throw you out
> To Buenos Aires, you bloody fairies!

It was very well received and set the tone of the evening. I chatted with my noisy team of jet-jockeys and was kept up to date on the progress of the newcomers by Robin Kent.

Robin had flown an Air Combat Manoeuvring (ACM) sortie against one of the 801 regulars.

'How did it go, Rob?'

'Bloody hard work, Boss. There are so many things to sort out before you get airborne that are different from ashore, especially aligning the Navigation Platform. I found myself working flat out throughout the sortie just to keep up, and so did E-J.'

It was good to hear Rob's openness. 801 had thrived on honest self-criticism to date and it was a relief to know that the Senior P was already in the groove. He was not a straight yes-man, though.

'There are a couple of things I want to discuss, if you don't mind, Boss.' He dragged me off to a moderately quiet corner. 'That list you gave me nominating officers who can authorise a flight from the deck? I don't agree with it. Paul Barton shouldn't be on it yet. He may be an authoriser ashore but he needs to find his way around at sea before having that responsiblity here. Am I right?'

I grinned, 'Dead right, Batman! I'm getting too over-enthusiastic about all this and you are going to have to hold me in check. You amend the list and get it up to the Air Staff Office for Wings's approval. What else is on your mind?'

'You're looking at him over there in the far corner of the bar. Soapy! What a bloody character! He's already a blood-brother to the 820 crowd.' Soapy was obviously enjoying himself relating stories to the group gathered round him and didn't fit at all with the image of a new boy on board. 'Mind you, he used to be a Sea King pilot, didn't he? So he probably knows most of the guys already. Anyway, it is his first flight from the deck tomorrow and I understand from Morts that you have ordered live missiles on all flights. Is that what you want for Soapy as well?' Robin was being tactful. He obviously didn't like the idea.

'Yep! He's old enough and wise enough and says he doesn't need a nurse-maid. I'm sure he's right when it comes to straightforward flying – with or without missiles. Have you talked with him again about pairing up with me?'

'No, but I will tomorrow.'

'OK. Maybe we can have a chat together tomorrow night. I'm off to hit the sack now, Robin. 'Night.'

It had been a good first day to get the ball rolling, and I slept like a log.

At the morning briefing I found that my plans for a squadron work-up were not going to progress unhindered. Wings broke the bad news to me: 'I'm afraid 801 is going to have to change its flying programme for today, Sharkey. The Flag wants some air strikes on the carriers to exercise ships' defences and we've been told to provide them.'

'Sir, that is just not on!' I retorted angrily. 'I have new pilots on board who have to be brought up to speed in combat as quickly as possible. That is not going to happen if we are not allowed to get on with training and stick to planned programmes.' I looked hopefully at the Captain for support.

'Don't look at me for help, Sharkey. We've been given an order and we have to comply. It's a pity, but it can't be helped.'

I didn't give in that easily.

'But we can't have them fucking around with our flying programme at every drop of the hat!'

Wings interrupted with a mixture of sadistic and masochistic glee. 'I'm afraid it's worse than that. They have told you exactly how far out from the Carrier Group you have to proceed and from what direction you are to run in for your attack. How does 80 miles sound?' It was a ridiculously short range and if the defences were also to know of the heading from which we were to mount the attack there would be little benefit gained by anyone.

'That isn't going to exercise anyone at all, is it?' I was more than a little frustrated. 'Please will you talk to the Staff Aviation Officer [SAVO] about it, Sir?'

'No. But if it happens again, then I shall.'

Robin Kent and the AWI, Ian Mortimer, were equally annoyed when they heard the news. What it meant was sacrificing a day's good ACM training in order to provide a series of predictable and entirely unrealistic attacks on the fleet. The attack aircraft should, at least, have been given a free hand to attack as they pleased, so that the defending ship's radar operators would have to work for their living.

At the pre-flight briefing, it transpired that on one sortie 801 would attack the fleet and 800 (the *Hermes* squadron) would defend it; the next sortie would be the other way round. Rather put out by it all, I decided to add an extra ingredient to the 801 attacks.

'We shall of course obey orders and strike *Hermes* in accordance with the Flag's instructions, but I want the attack aircraft to get in to the target unscathed and without being intercepted. That will give those no-hopers something to think about, and we can still get some value out of the exercise in air combat training. So the plan is this. Your pair, Morts, will carry out medium-level Air Intercept [AI] training at 100 miles in a position 60° off the briefed attack bearing. When the time comes to run in and attack, you will set off at medium level, say 15,000 feet, direct for the Flagship, *Hermes*. They will think that you are the attacking pair even though you are off the briefed heading. My section will depart the ship in the opposite direction to the attack axis and conduct low-level AI training well out of sight of the fleet. By the time that you are running in for your dummy attack we shall have transited to the briefed attack heading at very low level and will run in on the deck to complete the real attack. Make sure you entice any 800 Combat Air Patrol [CAP] aircraft towards you when you feint in towards the ships. And make sure you shoot them down, too!'

It was a simple plan, and it worked like clockwork. The *Hermes* defence radars monitored the approach of Morts's section and despatched the CAP aircraft from 800 Squadron to intercept them. The *Invincible* controllers were monitoring the whole situation and warned Morts of approaching 'trade'.

'Gold Leader, you have two bogeys [hostile aircraft] at 40 miles down the throat [head-on].'

'Roger. Descending.'

'Bogeys now 040/25 [on a bearing of 040° at 25 nautical miles].'

I was listening in to it all as I began my low-level run in from 80 miles on the pre-briefed heading. After a short pause I heard, 'Judy!' from Morts. That must have been a 20-mile-plus radar pick-up and I knew I would hear no more of the fight until Morts's pair called their kills on the 800 opposition. My own Number Two was in good battle formation on my port side (800 yards on the beam) and I checked regularly to see that his tail was clear of any threat, that is, that there were no bogeys creeping up on him from astern. We were cruising in at 550 knots and at a height of 50 feet on the radio altimeter. After eight minutes we were visual with *Hermes* at 16 miles and had not been detected. I jinked a fraction to port to put the grey bulk of the Flagship on the nose, and prepared to simulate a laydown bombing attack. As we passed over the target and pulled up, we called 'Bombs away!'; my Number Two slotted into neat formation and we made the short transit to *Invincible* to join the circuit for landing-on.

Morts's pair soon joined us on deck having achieved two theoretical missile kills on the 800 CAP aircraft. It was a good start to the flying day and subsequent sorties were equally successful from the *Invincible*/801 point of view.

I spent the remainder of the day working on the Argentinian threat, watching Soapy's maiden deck landing and preparing my mind for night flying. During the afternoon my phone rang: 'The Captain would like to see you on the bridge when convenient.' 'Roger.' That was typical of JJ. He was thoughtful enough to intimate that there was no rush or panic. About fifteen minutes later I entered the bridge.

'Hullo, CO 801. How's it going?' He meant in the air, of course.

'Pretty well, Sir. We haven't failed to hit *Hermes* yet, and we have intercepted the 800 attacks on all occasions.'

'Good!' A short pause as the Captain gazed out of the bridge windows. 'Did you want me for something?' His unconcerned absent-mindedness was all an act − and a good one.

'You asked to see me, Sir. Said there was no hurry.'

'Ah, yes! Sharkey, I have had two quite amazing signals which have confused the hell out of me. Have a look at them, will you?' He handed the two sheets of pale blue print over. One was from Yeovilton and one was from the MOD. Both addressed the same subject, that is the pilot's sighting angle for 2-inch rocket delivery in a 10° dive. One gave the angle as 22 mils (milliradians); the other gave 94 mils.

'A great lot of fucking use they are, wouldn't you say?' The Captain's eyes were moist with amusement. As a Gunnery officer he was an experienced weaponeer and realised that if you were just 2 mils out in your sighting picture (aiming point) for the release of rockets then you could miss the target by over 50 yards, dependent on the angle of dive. The disparity of 72 mils between the two sighting pictures offered from ashore was a joke.

'No, they're not too helpful. The right picture is somewhere in the middle, and my AWIs are each working it out right now. Let's see what they come up with.'

'OK. Let me know what the right answer is later, will you?'

'Aye, aye, Sir.'

Passing the crewroom on the way back to my cabin, I told the Duty Boy to get the AWIs down to see me as soon as they were free. I was not in a sparkling mood. My flying programme had been snookered by the Flag, and now I had received unsolicited help from ashore which was totally conflicting. We had managed nearly three years of operational trials without such help and it was the AWI's job, not the Staff's, to calculate weapon-release data.

I related the facts to Morts, who could hardly believe his ears. 'Well, Boss, E-J and I have independently come up with figures of 51 and 52 mils. That's good enough for me and so the squadron will use 51 on the trials. The Air Force do, however, use two different sighting angles for the SNEB 2.75-inch rocket. Single-shot delivery is 2 mils less than ripple-firing.'

'Why is that, Morts?'

'During a ripple-firing there is much more gas exhaust from the rockets and this tends to flow over the tailplane and affect the pitch attitude of the jet. The nose dips quite discernibly.'

'OK. Thanks for that titbit. Do you think that we need to go for two sighting pictures or shall we suck it and see?'

'Let's just give it a go at 51 mils, Boss. You, E-J and I will do the trial firings and we can film the results and work it out from there.'

'Right, Morts, I'm happy with that. Well done!'

By the time the evening Command Briefing came, it was clear that night flying was going to be written off again. The Met Officer, Bob Young, had given a gloomy picture of more fog and Wings cut the programme on the strength of that. Wednesday's day forecast was no better and it was decided to forgo flying on the morrow and allow the Task Group to make full speed towards sunnier climes. That was very convenient as far as our presentation to the Command was concerned, and would also give some much-needed time for squadron phase briefs on weaponry and intelligence. It would allow the engineers time to get on with repainting the jets, too.

That night I enjoyed dinner in the company of the 'three musketeers' — Bob Clark, Surgeon Commander, Neil Harkness, Dental Surgeon Commander, and Bob Young, Met Office Commander. The three were inseparable when off duty, and had become close friends to me during the previous nine months. I felt somewhat akin to d'Artagnan in their company and cherished their friendship. They were always ready for a good laugh, and their present mood was no less frivolous than usual, but they also registered their doubts about the threat of Argentinian air attack. I briefed them on what to expect as best I could.

'You have all heard the nonsense spoken in the media about our "lack of air assets". To some of the pundits ashore we, the Sea Harrier world, do not exist. I want you to disregard all that crap and look at the facts. In the North Atlantic last year we demonstrated to the USA and NATO that with only five Sea Harriers on board we could defend a 180° sector of the fleet from Soviet and Exercise aggression. We had at least one jet airborne on CAP for five days and nights with no breaks, and at the end of the exercise we put all five cabs up just to show NATO what a reliable jet we have available. Remember that that was with only six pilots! At the end we were all shattered, but we did the job. We now have eight aircraft embarked and eleven pilots. *Hermes* has twelve aircraft and about eighteen pilots. My team are already planning how we should run the air defence of the fleet down south and provided that we get co-operation from the Flag, I can see no problems — other than fatigue, that is.'

'Yes, I can see that, Sharkey,' replied the somewhat cynical Neil, 'but what about the odds we will be facing down there? People are talking about 200 aircraft against us; and that is ten to one in anyone's book.' The twinkle in the eyes had temporarily disappeared, replaced by serious concern.

'I haven't really got an answer to that. At least not an answer that you are going to swallow hook, line and sinker. My boys are worried by the same problem. And although it sounds stupid, I for one am not that concerned. Let me explain why. First, the Argentines haven't fought a war for 150 years. They may have relatively modern hardware — missiles, jets, etc. — but I believe that the last bit of up-to-date training they received was from Adolf Galland, the great German fighter ace from World War Two. He stayed with them for nine years and, if my information is correct, they have had bugger-all new blood since then. That should mean we are well ahead of the game in tactics.

'Second, we are talking of defending a fleet at sea at perhaps 400 miles from the enemy air force's bases. Their carrier and its Sky Hawks are a different kettle of fish, but we can cope with them. They, the Argentine Crabs, will undoubtedly be like our Crabs — flying missions more than 100 miles offshore may not make them wet their knickers, but it won't make them feel good either. They will have the advantage of being able to mount attacks on the fleet at a time of their choosing, but we should be able to anticipate most of the strikes and have the right number of CAP aircraft airborne to meet each attack. That will give us the correct balance of defence in depth.

'Finally, we have a track record to show that we are red-hot at fighter combat. And that isn't bullshit! We have consistently beaten the best that the USAF or the RAF can throw at us. Our record against the RAF Phantom in combat must be of the order of twenty-five to one. It's the same against the F-14 Tomcat. And against air superiority fighters like the F-15 it is at least three to one. And we can prove what I say. Our hardest sessions have been on fully instrumented Air Combat Manoeuvring Ranges against the F-15 and the Aggressors with their F-5Es. There is no lying about results on those ranges and, as an example, let me give you my best personal tally. Flying as a single Sea Harrier against two F-15s and two F-5Es, I claimed and was awarded seven kills with no claims against me.

'So, yes, I am concerned about fatigue and the number of pilots available, and I would like more aircraft. But at the end of the day and all things being said, I can't wait to shoot shit out of them! We can and we will do the job.'

Although not fully convinced as to the end result of the coming air war, the three musketeers retired happy in the knowledge that there was no shortage of confidence in 801. I believed all that I had said, and was now in just the right mood to have a chat with the rebellious Soapy Watson. I collared Robin Kent, who was chatting with Brian Haig, and left the bar for the privacy of Rob's cabin. We had a few cans of beer available and Brian went off to collect Soapy.

Soapy was in a very happy and cheerful state. 'Hullo, Boss! What's all this about then?' he chuckled as he parked himself on the cabin floor and cracked a can of beer.

'You know bloody well, Soapy! And I want to hear what you have to say direct about flying as my wing man.'

'Well, it's like this, Boss. I'm new in the squadron but I'm not the average green student straight from flying training. I'm much older than the average and I've flown helos [helicopters] for several years in the front line. So I'm no chicken and I think I've got my head screwed on. Now Splot tells me that I am to be paired up with you like some "nugget" pilot who doesn't know what he's doing. Well, I don't want to be nursed like a baby and, no offence, but that means I don't want to be seen to be your Number Two. It's nothing personal against you. I just don't want to hang on your apron strings.'

I hadn't given up. 'Who do you suppose is going to get at least as much flying as anyone else in this war, Soapy? You can bet your bottom dollar that it will be me. Don't you find that attractive?'

'Yes, I do. But I still don't want to be your Number Two!'

'You know that if you maintain this attitude then you will have your way, Soapy. I don't like it at all, but that is by the by. There is no way I'm going into a fight without a willing team. You know of course that with eleven pilots, someone is not going to be paired up and so will get less of the action? The way you are talking, that someone is going to have to be you.'

'Doesn't worry me, Boss. I really am sorry, but my mind is made up.'

In peacetime, I would have had none of this nonsense and Soapy would have received a serious bollocking for what was without doubt a stupid and ill-considered attitude. But there were more important things for me to worry about. I had given the new boy a fair chance to be my Number Two, and the lad had blown it!

Soapy left the cabin as happy as a sandboy, but Robin and Brian were clearly embarrassed by what they had witnessed and the Splot was in the mood to hang Soapy from the yard-arm. 'Leave it, Rob! I can't make him want to fly with me, nor can I have a Number Two with the wrong attitude. That would be dangerous. I'll take either Steve Thomas or Charlie Cantan. They are both great youngsters and I'll leave it to you to decide who it should be. Although I'm sure this is a one-off, you had better watch Soapy carefully to see how he progresses. And it goes without saying that he has to be the loose deuce. I'll see you in the morning on the planning side. 'Night, both of you.'

Although a little frustrated, I slept well as usual, and was up with the lark.

9

Wednesday 7 April saw the Carrier Group steaming south-west through the often-treacherous Bay of Biscay towards Finisterre. Frequently in turmoil when whipped to a frenzy by Atlantic storms, for once the waters of the bay stood grey and relatively calm under the overcast sky. Although fog was threatened it was not evident, and *Invincible* cruised silently out of sight of land. The Task Group was spread out over several hundred square miles of ocean linked only by the unseen but all-seeing radar and radio waves. We knew that the passage south would take about three weeks, but there was much to pack into this limited time. It was a chance to prepare thoroughly for war and the precise position of the Group was not uppermost in the minds of squadron personnel. Instead, the aircrew were intent on learning more about the different weapons now available to them and absorbing all the important details of new weapon-delivery profiles. For the majority of 801 aircrew the day was spent in the crewroom listening to phase briefs by QFIs and AWIs. A 'phase brief' would normally be given whenever new or different operational or domestic flying routines were to be used. In the old days, all the associated data had to be remembered (with the assistance of notes taken on the pilot's knee-board) but now, with modern technology providing computerised head-up displays for the pilot to watch while flying, the emphasis had changed from a straight memory game to a need to understand the computer software. There was still a hell of a lot to take in and while the younger pilots were being brought up to speed in the crewroom, I and my team of planners devoted most of the day to preparing the presentation for the Captain.

The air threat known to be awaiting the Task Force was a varied one, but the first point we wished to emphasise was that whoever had better control of the airspace above and around the Falklands would probably win the day. This may appear to be stating the obvious, but the successful conduct of war is based on obvious hard facts and on a thorough analysis of those facts. And it was my job as JJ's Sea Harrier expert to brief him fully on all appropriate points, however obvious or simple they might appear. It was not possible for us to talk in terms of comprehensive air superiority or airspace denial for several reasons.

The Sea Harrier was only armed with a short, within visual-range air-to-air weapons fit (Sidewinder and guns), and its radar was limited in two ways: it could not search for and acquire small targets when looking down over land or over a rough sea; and against small fighter targets such as the Mirage, its optimum detection range would be no more than about 15 miles — if you were lucky. In the expected confrontation with enemy fighters the Sea Jet would therefore have to rely on ship-based radar for the early detection of small, medium- and high-level targets. For low-level targets over land and below the detection lobes of ships' radar (below the horizon), the Combat Air Patrol aircraft would have to rely on the Mark I eyeball. The lack of an Airborne Early Warning (AEW) aircraft such as the Gannet was a severe operational disadvantage for the Carrier Group and could only be partially compensated for by maintaining a strong CAP presence at low level. (What use now the RAF promises of air defence coverage world-wide!) Without being able to detect the movement of all enemy aircraft in the area of interest it was not possible to ensure full air superiority or airspace denial.

However, by stationing well-armed air defence frigates and destroyers (pickets) up-threat and placing the CAP aircraft beyond the pickets at medium to low level, there was a good chance of detecting both inbound fighters and enemy air-to-surface fighter-bomber raids. Chances of reliable detections would be best if the Carrier Group remained at long range from the Argentine bases, thereby forcing the enemy fighters and attack aircraft to make high-level transits towards the force.

In spite of the various aircraft shortcomings and expected gaps in the Group's air defence cover, my Planning Team agreed that a level of airspace superiority could nevertheless be achieved by the SHAR if, on day one of any action, the SHAR could be given an early opportunity to shoot down Argentine fighters. We would therefore suggest to the Command that a maximum possible number of CAP aircraft should be employed on day one over the area of immediate interest, Port Stanley, to ensure engagement with enemy fighters. Once combat superiority had been established (and we were confident we could achieve this), the presence of CAP aircraft would act as a real deterrent to any air raids by enemy fighter and ground-attack aircraft; and such deterrence was half the battle in establishing air superiority. Should there be large formations of jets attacking the fleet, these would of course be more easily detectable on the Sea Harrier radar than a single enemy jet, and if such raids materialised the Sea Jet would undoubtedly be able to demonstrate its autonomous intercept capability.

Point One to the Command was, therefore, to mount a maximum CAP presence in the Port Stanley skies at the outbreak of hostilities and to force early combat with the Mirage fighters. The Sea Jet's track record in a dog-fight was such as to support the probability of a high success rate against the opposition.

Intelligence gleaned from *Jane's* indicated that the Argentine Air Force had already taken delivery of five Super Etendard aircraft armed with Exocet air-to-surface missiles. This aircraft weapon system represented the most serious threat to Task Force ships and it was the Team's view that the limited Exocet resources would undoubtedly be targeted against the two carriers. If either carrier was disabled or sunk, then all hope of mounting a realistic air defence would be gone and the Task Force might just as well go home.

What then could the Super Etendard achieve?

It was capable of air-to-air refuelling (AAR) from one of two Argentine Air Force Hercules aircraft fitted for the role. This could extend its maximum effective range quite considerably. But AAR tankers were vulnerable and easy targets for fighters (as had been demonstrated on many occasions in NATO exercises), and as it was most unlikely that they would be sacrificed lightly, then their range of operation from the Argentine mainland was probably going to be limited by their command. 801 AWIs guessed that the tankers would venture no further afield than the coast of West Falkland. Bearing this in mind, as well as the known maximum transit range of the Etendard, it was fairly easy to calculate how far out from their bases the Etendards would risk mounting an attack on the Carrier Group. Having to face CAP aircraft and radar pickets, they would be forced to run in for any attack for a very long distance at low level. This reduced their options further, and the result of all calculation and deliberation was that there probably would not be any Exocet-armed Etendard attacks at ranges greater than 425 nautical miles from their Argentine air bases.

Point Two to the Command, therefore, was that the prime air threat was the Exocet-armed Super Etendard, but that if the Task Group remained outside 425 nautical miles from the Etendard-capable bases, then the carriers would probably be safe.

The Team went on to address the air-to-surface capabilities of the Mirage V 'Dagger', the Canberra, and the A-4 Sky Hawk. Point Three to the Command was that calculation showed that the 'safe range' established for the Etendard was equally applicable to these types of aircraft. A singleton Dagger might be able to menace the Task Group at longer range, but it would not present the same Exocet threat and as a result could be dealt with more easily by the CAP and the ships' weapon systems.

This 'threat-reduction exercise' was conducted on all threat aircraft types. The maximum aerodynamic range of an aircraft would be modified downwards by the limits that the defences could place on its operation. 801 was, of course, working on all the options without any knowledge of what the Flag actually intended to do with the Task Group. The Weapon

HMS *Invincible* sets sail from Portsmouth with the Carrier Battle Group, bound for the Falklands, 5 April 1982. Four 801 Naval Air Squadron Sea Harriers are on deck, with two 820 Squadron Sea King helicopters in the background. The jets still have the white-painted undersides of their peacetime livery. Photograph taken from Flyco.

HMS *Hermes*, 1980, before her 'Jimmy Durante' ski-jump was fitted. Two Sea Harriers from the Intensive Flying Trials Unit, 700 Squadron, about to land on. One jump jet already on deck.

HMS *Invincible*. Two SHARs of 801 Squadron on deck, one about to touch down aft and a fourth in transition to the hover (top right). Note the disturbance on the sea surface from the Pegasus jet engine exhaust. These two photographs clearly show the differences between the older, larger carrier above and her more up-to-date sister.

Invincible at sea in a Force 9 gale, with a Sea Harrier from 899 Headquarters Squadron just about to land on. The surface wind speed is 60 knots—about 70 mph and well out of limits. Typical of some of the bad weather in the Falklands and Exercise 'Alloy Express'.

Hermes refuelling from the Royal Fleet Auxiliary *Tidepool* on the voyage south, with *Invincible* in the background. Clearly visible is the take-off ramp or 'ski-jump' on *Hermes*, which was added in 1981. Streaks of rust can also be seen, which gave her a curiously raffish and experienced air.

'Crossing the Line' ceremony on board *Invincible* on the way south—Sharkey Ward about to be heaved backwards into the ducking-pool, after various other indignities to his person.

Lieutenant-Commander N. D. (Sharkey) Ward—one of the less official representations of him.

Effort Planning Team therefore had to look at the possibility of a shorter-range confrontation with the enemy, that is, well within what we had calculated as the 'safe range'.

At long range (400 miles plus) it was adjudged that the Argentines did not have adequate tanker resources to support an attack involving large numbers of aircraft, but at shorter ranges this type of attack was a distinct probability. And in such circumstances it was likely that the mixed formation of attack aircraft would enjoy fighter escort from Mirage IIIs and would contain an Etendard/Exocet element. The Exocet represented the most dangerous single factor, but large numbers of more simply armed attack aircraft could also be used to saturate defences and they would have to be stopped.

There was some disagreement within the Planning Team concerning the optimum way to deal with this threat scenario and so, having listened to all views, I dictated the air defence moves that would be put forward to the Command. E-J had proposed the likely formation of attack aircraft and fighters and had suggested that the Exocet-armed aircraft would undoubtedly come in below the main formation of attack aircraft or on a separate axis to the larger group. This was agreed and the tactics to be employed by the defensive CAP aircraft were based on that assumption.

The key to disrupting or dissuading a large number of aircraft from attacking was to get in amongst them with a small number of easily controlled fighters. One pair let loose against ten or fifteen bogeys could easily keep track of each other, whereas the opposition would have great difficulty in sorting out friend from foe. I had experienced this on several occasions in the past during exercises.

On the first detection of a major incoming air raid, the nearest CAP pair would be vectored down the throat of the threat. The Leader would attempt a head-on kill on at least one target in the larger formation of aircraft and the Number Two would 'hook' round the side of the formation and go for stern missile shots. The pair would not hang around but would fly straight through the enemy formation and make a clean getaway, joining up as soon as they were clear of the fight to give each other mutual support. Without doubt, with two or three of their number having been shot down, mass confusion would be created in the attackers' minds and their resolve to continue would be weakened.

Whilst the first CAP pair were being vectored down the throat of the threat, adjoining CAP pairs would make best speed towards the threat axis at right angles to it. They would then sweep up the threat axis at low level, searching for the Etendards as their prime target. If detected, the Etendards would be fully engaged in combat, which would probably force them to jettison their Exocet missiles in order to survive. If no detection was achieved on the Etendards, the remains of the larger attack formation would be engaged in hit-and-run fashion. In the meantime, aircraft being held at alert on deck would be launched and vectored up the threat axis. It would be for the Command to judge whether a second threat axis existed, that is, whether the Etendards were coming in from a different direction. Whatever was decided, CAP aircraft would be available for trade and individual ships could take early and appropriate Exocet counter-measures.

Point Three, therefore, was to propose to the Command the ideal tactics for countering a multi-aircraft raid.

The final air threat element to be considered was the possibility of an air strike being launched against the Task Group by the Argentine aircraft-carrier, the *Veinticinco de Mayo* ('25th of May'). This would consist of a limited number of A-4 Sky Hawks attacking the Group with bombs, rockets and guns and could take place at any range from shore. The defences of the Group were well up to coping with this threat, and my team considered that it was only a realistic threat if it was supported by a co-ordinated attack from other forces, either air or sea. A plan of action for 'taking out' the carrier was proposed.

Having examined the threat in some detail and proposed counters to each of its elements, it was not a difficult task to decide on how available Sea Harrier assets should be used to counter the differing threat possibilities.

The Team's best judgement had indicated that there was really only a day-fighter capability against the Force. The Mirage III was the principal fighter and did not have good enough radar or avionics systems to allow its pilots to intercept and shoot down other fighters in dense cloud or at night. (The SHAR was well up to this task and had already demonstrated its efficiency many times in NATO exercises.) The same daytime-only limitation was also applicable to all the attack aircraft except for the Etendard. However, for the Etendard to do its job at night it needed third-party help to find and acquire its target. This was available only from the outdated Neptune maritime surveillance aircraft still in service with the Argentine forces. And for the Neptune to do its task of spotting the Carrier Group, locating the prime targets (the carriers) and passing the information to the attack aircraft, it too was open to detection by Task Group radars. That meant that there would be adequate warning time for alert CAPs to get airborne to deter any Etendard attack whenever the Neptune came up on ships' radar at night.

Educated judgement therefore decided not unreasonably that the air threat at night was going to be minimal. Point Four for the Command strongly advocated that the main Sea Harrier flying effort should be concentrated on daylight hours as far as defence was concerned. An alert aircraft posture should be maintained overnight but not at too much cost, in terms of fatigue, to the aircrew.

Point Five suggested that, by day, three pairs of CAP aircraft should be kept airborne at any one time to cover the westerly hemisphere of the Carrier Group. The CAPs should be drawn in rotation from both carriers making full pro rata use of all twenty Sea Jets, and an alert CAP section or pair should be on deck ready to go at all times in each ship. By night, the level of alert held should begin with a total of two aircraft, but this should be modified by experience as the action progressed.

'Well done, fellers! I think we've got the basis here for a good presentation as well as a useful brief for the Flag to chew on. I hope and trust that 800 Squadron will have been doing the same type of threat-reduction exercise. I shall be seeing them and the *Hermes* command in the next couple of days and will put our thoughts to them. No doubt JJ will brief the Admiral separately.

'The presentation this evening will be at 1900 after the Command Briefing and will be in our crewroom. Although I shall introduce it, you, Morts, will be the main presenter and you can introduce E-J and Alan to do their bit as you think appropriate. I'll give a brief summary at the end, hand over a written brief to the Captain, and ask for questions.'

As expected, the Captain, Wings and the Air Ops organisation attended the presentation. It turned into a very useful and professional discussion and my team's proposals were all accepted. Wings was a little cynical about our use of the phrases 'air superiority' and 'airspace denial', and was also keen to get the squadron view on how we planned to attack Port Stanley airfield.

'We haven't had time to refine our ideas on that yet, Sir, but what I can tell you is this: daylight or dawn raids against heavily defended targets are, in my view, for the birds and for John Wayne. We must achieve surprise when we attack and every man and his military dog down there will be expecting a "surprise" dawn raid! The most professional and the safest way to hit them will be in the small hours of the night. It has to be a very well-co-ordinated attack and time spent over the target must be minimal, say no more than thirty seconds from first to last aircraft. We already have four pilots fully qualified and capable of doing the job and by the time we get down there I expect to have at least eight — to match the number of aircraft. Whether we stick at eight or ask 800 to provide another four can be decided when we know how far they have got with their night flying. As you know, they have been to sea for over a year and have still only managed a couple of duskers flights. If we may, we shall brief you on the detail of a planned night attack against the airfield later when we have got our act fully together. Anything you would like to add, Morts?'

'Not on the airfield attack, Boss, but I think it would be useful to brief the Captain on a few fringe subjects that you might be discussing tomorrow with *Hermes*. The main ones are Cluster Bomb Units [CBUs], Helicopter

Tactical Direction of Air Strikes [TACDIs], Close Air Support [CAS] routines and our interest in the water-purification plant.'

The Captain was keen to listen.

'OK Morts, you kick off with CBUs and CAS and I'll cover the rest.'

CBU stood for Cluster Bomb Units; small bomblets clustered together in a streamlined dispenser pod under the wing of the aircraft. They were designed for dropping against thin-skinned targets such as aircraft, personnel and lightly armoured or unarmoured vehicles. On release from their pod at high speed and low level, the lethal individual bomblets would spread over a large area and give the ground forces a real headache.

'Right, Sir!' Morts began, addressing the Captain. 'The Boss tells me that *Hermes* have embarked CBUs and although we don't want to get too embroiled in the secondary task of ground attack, I believe we should have some of them available for our use. For example, if we carry out a night strike on the airfield they will come in most useful. Can we ensure that we do get some on board?'

The Captain nodded.

'The next thing, Sir, is Close Air Support. It's quite possible that we may have to give Close Air Support to our ground forces and this demands specialist flying techniques to ensure that the pilot delivers his weapons exactly where the ground force commander wishes. We have in our possession all the officially approved Crab routines for the air support of ground forces, and I am fully familiar with those routines, having had two front-line tours in Germany. They are, however, very complicated and it takes quite a lot of special training to get to grips with them. I'm afraid we just haven't got enough time or the right facilities to do the training on the way south. The Boss argues, rightly I think, that we ought to ditch the official Crab routines and revert to the more simple practices that the Fleet Air Arm has always used. Of course, before, the pilot was carrying round a back-seater to cope with navigation which has to be spot-on with CAS – especially when attacking positions close to our own troops. But our navigation computer is well up to the task of providing the right navigation cues to the pilot and, given the simple Navy routine of one identification point close to the target plus a range and bearing to the target from that IP, I am sure the boys can cope. They certainly won't cope with the Crab routine that is being advocated by the Flag.' We had already had word from the Admiral's Staff that RAF CAS routines were to be adopted.

The Captain looked at Wings, who gave a nod of approval. 'Now what else do you want to change, Sharkey?' JJ was absorbed by all that he had heard, but he didn't want change just for the sake of it.

'Not a lot really, Sir. You will remember how smoothly our over-the-horizon targeting and attack work went in "Alloy Express". We struck those frigates at 220 miles with simulated weapons and they didn't know we were coming until we flew over the deck. That was done without any coded ranges and bearings and without any unnecessary use of the RT [radio]. Well, the Flag now wants the SHAR community to work to the Lynx helicopter tactical direction rules. That means a lot of useless chatter on the radio, interpreting codes in the cockpit while flying at low level and high speed and in general is an unprofessional pain in the neck! I wish to retain the routines that were worked out by my squadron under my official hat as the Chief Tactical Instructor, Sea Harrier. Both 800 and the Staff should already be fully acquainted with the approved Sea Harrier procedure for over-the-horizon targeting, but in case they are not I have taken the liberty of laying it all out on paper again along with the new CAS routines. Perhaps you would like to pass them over to the Staff and 800 in *Hermes* tomorrow?'

'All right, CO 801, so be it. Now what's this about water?'

'Well, we've been studying the maps of the Port Stanley area and we've noticed a water-purification plant at the end of the Sound away from the town. It seems an ideal priority target to me. There are supposed to be a lot of Argentine troops in Stanley and if we can knock out the water supply it will give them real problems. It won't help the residents either, of course, but, with local knowledge, they should be able to manage all right.'

The Captain didn't object. 'Have a word with the Flag's staff about it tomorrow, will you? And thank you, gentlemen, for an excellent brief. I like the way you are thinking and it all seems pretty logical to me.'

JJ was obviously content with the planning effort and suggested to Dusty that the written briefing and all proposals should eventually be forwarded to the Flag for consideration.

It had been a very useful non-flying day. The next major item on the agenda of preparation was to get the weapons trials out of the way.

10

Thursday 8 April signalled the start of the 801 Weapons Trials programme, which was to last three days. It was also the day for the planning meeting between *Invincible* and *Hermes* to discuss the way ahead.

It was fresh but not so cold on deck as the Captain, Wings, Rod O'Connor and the two Squadron COs, Ralph and myself, boarded the Sea King helicopter in our berets and ear defenders for the short hop across the water to HMS *Hermes*. The weather had cleared of all risk of fog, the sun had broken through the layer of cloud, and it looked a perfect day for flying. As we approached *Hermes* we were reminded that there had not been time to repaint her hull in Portsmouth and so the old lady looked a bit of a sight with large streaks of rust down the side. But she was definitely functional, as witnessed by her deck full of aircraft and air stores, and that was the main thing for this operation.

Lyn Middleton, the Flag Captain, met us on deck personally and escorted us off the flight-deck and down to his sea cabin in the stern of the ship. He looked extremely fit and I was delighted to be able to chat to my old boss again.

As we entered the Flag Captain's cabin, we were more than a little surprised to see that it had already been prepared for war. No mirrors or pictures on the bulkheads (wall), no tablecloths or napkins with the coffee, and the furniture, tables, chairs and cabinets had all been lashed into place with rope. Privately I thought it all a bit unnecessary as we were still steaming off the coast of Portugal. I thanked my lucky stars that I was from the *Invincible* squadron; there would be plenty of time to prepare the ship for action when we got closer to the war zone.

My private little prayer was reiterated during the subsequent polite conversation in the cabin before the official 'Way Ahead' or 'Conference of War' meeting started. The *Hermes* Sea King Squadron CO was present. He was a giant of a man with a huge and rather shaggy, spade-like beard in the old Navy style, when if you grew a beard you were supposed to leave it untrimmed (making you look more like a Viking than a naval officer). I was also the proud owner of a beard; but a smart, short, well-trimmed affair. In a well-timed moment of gross tactlessness, this very large 'food-mixer' pilot addressed me in a loud voice.

'When are you going to shave off your beard, Sharks? We've got to do ours tomorrow.' It felt like being back at school — and prep school at that.

'Yes, Sharkey,' butted in Lyn in his mild, South-African-tinged accent, 'when are you taking that mess off your face? You know what Ships' War Orders say, don't you?' He grinned.

In peacetime, War Orders were always kept locked in a safe, but they did indeed indicate that a beard could be a hazard in action and should be removed. 'Oh yes, Sir. That I do! But having looked at the threat I'm not aware of any chemical or biological problem, and I'll take my own chances with fire in the cockpit.' The chemical bit referred to the need for a tight-fitting gas-mask, which was not possible with a beard.

Lyn looked across at J.J. Black. 'Don't look at me, Lyn. Sharkey is old enough and bold enough to decide these things for himself.' Good old JJ!

The small group left the Captain's day cabin after coffee and we made our way to the Wardroom Annexe for the serious discussions on the way ahead. We all sat at a long, highly polished table with Middleton at the centre, JJ on his left, and myself to the left of him. After the pleasantries and when we got down to the nitty-gritty of the meeting, it was more than apparent that 800 Squadron and the *Hermes* Air Ops team 'hadn't had time' to address themselves to the operational problems that lay ahead. Andy Auld, the 800 CO, admitted as much, and so the Sea Harrier discussion was very much one-way traffic. I outlined the content of the presentation that my team had given to the Captain. There was no disagreement around the table concerning the threat or the proposals as to how to counter it. Much to my surprise, the 801 plans for Close Air Support and TACDI were also agreed readily. *Hermes*'s Captain also promised CBUs for *Invincible* but didn't say when they would be forthcoming. I continued my spiel on the way ahead:

'I am sure it is well understood, Sir, that my squadron has had its full radar system fit for some time and that we have already carried out the associated operational trials. Because of that and because you, Andy, have only had your radars for a short period, may I recommend that should there have to be a split in resources, with one team concentrating on ground attack and one on air defence, then 801 and *Invincible* will lead on the air defence.' I knew that Lyn, as an expert ex-Buccaneer ground-attack CO, would not quarrel with the suggestion. Nor did he. It was accepted in principle. Later, and in private, JJ asked me why I had bothered to raise the subject. I replied that it was just a hunch that Lyn's background would lead to an over-emphasis being placed on ground/surface attack, and I wanted no part of that.

Turning to the next possibly contentious issue, I then gave a brief outline of my Planning Team's ideas for attacking Port Stanley airfield at night. This drew a very different reaction from the *Hermes* group. Night surface or ground attack in a single-seat fighter! There was open astonishment that it was even suggested. Lyn Middleton led the onslaught against my proposal.

'Gentlemen, night ground attack in a two-seat aircraft is probably the most dangerous and difficult flying task in the world. And I should know as I've done enough of it in a Buccaneer. It can't possibly be done in a single-seat aircraft. What do you think, Dave?' He knew that Dave, his Air Ops man and an ex-Buccaneer back-seater, would have the same view.

'Its a ridiculous idea, Sir. Can't be done!'

As usual, an entirely predictable response from the old brigade, I thought, as I returned to the attack. 'I realise that you have a lot of experience in this area, Sir, but that was in the Buccaneer which did not enjoy the advantages of modern avionics. I've done a lot of ground attack by night in the F-4 Phantom as well, and I recognize what hard work that was with old systems. But it is different in the Sea Jet and we have a lot of good night experience under our belts now in my squadron. The avionics system is a great aid to safety, and I am now stating from an experienced viewpoint that co-ordinated night ground attacks in Sea Harrier are not only possible but they can be done safely and effectively. And a night attack on Port Stanley airfield should be seriously considered.'

The Flag Captain was still not convinced, but neither did he turn down the idea out of hand. He turned to JJ, 'What do you think about it, Jeremy?'

Quick as a flash, but in a very relaxed manner, JJ supported his CO. 'Gentlemen, you and I know that Sharkey Ward is as mad as a fucking hatter!' Short pause and a sigh of approval went round the table. Then the punch-line: 'But if he says he can do something, believe me he can. So you'd better believe it too.'

I was delighted at such praise, and after some further discussion it was agreed that 801 would demonstrate a co-ordinated night attack on the *Hermes* splash target within a week.

It had been an excellent morning with all the right results. We thanked our hosts and were escorted to the flight-deck for departure. Before we left, I had the opportunity to discuss the water-purification plant at Stanley as a possible target with the Staff SAVO, Chris Hunneyball.

'Mmmmm...' he pronounced, sucking on his pipe strongly. 'I don't like that idea. It may be in contravention of the Geneva Convention. Better forget that one, eh, Sharkey?' So we did.

Back in *Invincible*, I changed rapidly into my flying kit and headed for the crewroom. The first 2-inch rocketing sortie was about to take place and I didn't want to miss it. Morts, as the AWI, was leading it and was taking E-J as his Number Two. I wished them good luck: 'Make sure you get rid of the splash target!'

The 'splash target' looked something like a sledge. It was about 6 foot square, made of timber, and was towed behind the ship at the end of a 600-foot wire. It had various cross-members between its side-boards which ensured that it stayed on the surface and that it threw up a plume of spray as it was towed through the water. The plume of spray was easily visible from the air and made it ideal as a weaponry target. Generations of pilots had delivered their practice weapons against the splash and their fall of shot was accurately measured in angular terms from the towing carrier and from a helicopter or frigate stationed aft of the beam and at 90° to the target. Firing aircraft were controlled from Flyco, whose job it was to ensure that the safety arcs beyond the target were clear of third parties and that no dangerous flying took place (such as late releases, low pull-ups, and so on). The line of attack was from 45° on the port bow of the carrier, and this made it easy to monitor the actual angle of dive. In this way it was possible to gather maximum data on each weapon delivery, data which was backed up by film taken through the pilot's aiming picture in the Head-Up Display. Interpretation of data and film after the flight by the AWI ensured a useful debrief on each delivery. When the splash target was shot away, the shipwright or 'chippie' on board would furnish a new one.

Before going up to Flyco to witness this first trial, I despatched one of the Acting Sub-Lieutenants to the Air Crew Refreshment Bar (ACRB) to get me a much-needed beefburger and coffee. Two youngsters on hold from flying training had been seconded to the squadron for Operation 'Corporate' and were very usefully employed as Squadron Duty Officers. This relieved the pressure on the aircrew and also made the Senior Pilot's programming task a lot easier. They were to prove to be worth their weight in gold once the action had started.

Flyco was the preserve of Wings and his Deputy, colloquially known as 'Little "F"'. They controlled the movement of aircraft on deck and in the local area around the ship.

As the two SHARs launched in quick succession from the ski-jump into the blue yonder and rapidly joined up in battle formation, Flyco became more and more crowded. 'Get these bloody goofers out of here would you, "Little F"!' growled Wings, and the hangers-on were despatched to other vantage points on the island superstructure to watch the fun. The embarked journalists were there in force — I hoped that the two AWIs were going to put on a good show for the media. I had little doubt that they would.

'Black Leader, in dry.' Morts's voice crackled over the RT.

'Black Leader, you are clear in dry. Wind over the splash is 15 knots at 7 o'clock.' "Little F" approved the dry pass.

'Two, in dry.'

'Clear in dry.'

In the air, the two pilots would be working hard to get the briefed release conditions exactly right. After a couple of dry passes, Morts was obviously happy with the release sight-picture that he was getting and called 'Black Leader, in live.'

'You are clear live, Black Leader. Wind 15 knots at 7 o'clock.'

The small jet had crossed the bow at 2000 feet and suddenly banked hard to port. Approaching the line of attack, the jet over-banked in the hard turn, dropped its nose through 10°, and rapidly rolled wings-level. It arrowed down the shallow dive until almost level with Flyco, then there was a puff of smoke from under the port wing. The needle-shaped rocket accelerated towards the splash and as it impacted the water the crack of sound from its supersonic flight penetrated Flyco. Already the SHAR was arcing upwards away from the sea surface and, as it started an early turn downwind I knew that Morts would have his head craned round over his left shoulder to see for himself where the rocket had landed.

'10 yards at 6.30, Black Leader.'

The two SHARs peppered the splash with single shots for seven dives, and then the AWI called, 'Black Leader, in live, ripple'. This meant he was to empty his pod by ripple-firing all remaining rockets, with only micro-seconds separating each rocket.

'Clear live ripple.' The same for Black Two.

This was where the best chance of shooting off the splash target would come. In turn the jets raced down the dive to release point. A trail of dirty brown smoke appeared under the wing and flashes of rockets firing could be seen. The impacts surrounded the splash target. But it survived.

'Delta Hotel, Black Leader. Delta Hotel, Black Two. From the Command, good shooting!' 'Delta Hotel' meant 'direct hit'.

It had been a first-class professional effort, and the journalists were agog with excitement, as were all the other goofers. None of the rockets had been further than 20 yards over or short of the splash, and all had been in line with it. If the boys had been aiming at the vertical side of a ship, the dispersion around the actual point of aim would have been a few feet — even for the furthest rocket. Now to get the film developed and analyse the firing.

All the pilots were in the crewroom for the debrief and to see the Head-Up Display film. Each of the single rocket firings was painstakingly analysed. If it hadn't hit the target then there was a reason for it, and the reason could always be established from the data gathered. I was particularly keen to see the film of the ripple-firing to note whether the aircraft did indeed nod as the rocket exhaust hit the tailplane. And it did. But it didn't seem to affect the fall of shot (accuracy of the rockets) markedly. Maybe that was because the nod only affected the later rockets. I would fire a full pod tomorrow to establish the answer once and for all.

One thing that was for certain was that the AWI's sighting-picture calculations of 51 mils had been right on the button.

Having congratulated the two AWIs, I returned to my cabin to get an hour's sleep. I was night flying that evening and wanted to be fully fresh for it.

By the time I launched from the deck, the two carriers had separated. *Hermes* had disappeared from view and above the choppy sea there was about 4/8ths cloud cover (cloud cover is always given in eighths) and a good horizon. The deck had virtually no movement on it from the sea, so it was a perfect night to get back in the groove. I was airborne on my own and practising CAP routines for the benefit of the ship's controllers when I realised that *Hermes* must have taken the bit between their teeth at last; they had an aircraft airborne only 20 miles away.

The Direction Officer passed a range and bearing for the 800 cab and that was enough for me to set up my own intercept. As I turned towards the direction of my quarry I asked for the radio frequency that 800 were operating on and tuned in. I recognised the voice of the pilot immediately, Ted Ball, a fine young Crab officer on loan from the RAF. My Blue Fox radar picked up the target straight away at about 18 miles. I locked on to it immediately to ascertain its height and then worked out its heading. Within minutes I was sitting behind the unsuspecting aircraft at missile range. My live Sidewinder growled angrily as it detected the target's exhaust.

I broke off to return to my CAP station and, once there, repeated the exercise. This time it wasn't so easy because the *Hermes* controllers had seen me at last and had warned the pilot. It took a little longer to close to a firing position on the evading aircraft, but I managed it without too much fuss and called 'Fox Two away' on the *Hermes* frequency. ('Fox Two away' indicates the firing of a missile from astern.) What I couldn't understand at the time was why no real effort was being made by Ted to turn the tables and intercept me. I was later to find the reason, and it was all to do with the standard of radars and radar expertise in the other squadron.

The landing back on board went smoothly and there was still time to change and make the bar before it closed. Things were going well on all fronts and I felt I deserved a couple of pints of beer before hitting the sack. Whilst I was chatting to Witherow of *The Times*, Robin, the Senior Pilot, approached. He looked a little concerned about something. 'Excuse me, John, do you mind if I grab the Boss for a minute? There is a little problem I need to discuss in private.'

We moved to a relatively quiet corner of the Wardroom amidst the tables of ship's officers playing their umpteenth game of bridge. 'What's the problem, Robin?'

'It's a tricky one really, Boss. And a bit annoying, too. You know we chatted about ensuring that no cliques should be established within the squadron? One faction against another and all that?

'Well, Boss, one of the pilots is letting off his mouth about how things are done in the squadron.'

'Tell me more.'

'He's giving the impression that he knows how to run things and do things better than you, and if we don't watch it there will soon be a split in loyalties.'

I was pleased to get the early warning from my chum. That's what Senior Pilots were all about. The good of the squadron must come first always and anyone threatening trouble had to be dealt with. 'How are you going to sort it out, Sharks? Do you want me to have a word with him?'

'No thanks, Robin. I'll deal with this one myself. Just get all the aircrew and engineers in the crewroom tomorrow morning five minutes before my rocketing sortie brief. I don't want any other hangers-on in there. And put our friend on the programme as my Number Two. Thanks for keeping me in the picture; now let's get back to the bar and have a nightcap.'

Later, in my cabin, I thought about the problem. The officer in question was a very experienced pilot and was used to stating his opinions freely — that was his trade. He probably did disagree with the way some things were done in the squadron, and I was sure that he meant no harm in letting off his mouth to the other aircrew. Of course there would be an element of competition in what he was saying and feeling — that is natural for a fighter pilot — and he probably wished he was in charge of the show instead of me.

'Tomorrow,' I yawned to myself, 'I'll have to put him straight. 'Night, boys!' I always said goodnight to my two lads before sleeping.

11

9 April dawned blustery and overcast, but pleasantly warm. Most of the 1000-plus ship's company on board rarely saw the real light of day unless there was a special reason for going topside during their limited time off watch. The cause of this almost perpetual incarceration was that *Invincible* had been designed to cater for modern warfare at sea. Nuclear fall-out, chemical and biological contamination were all risks that had had to be taken into account by the designers, and this had led to the ship's exterior having very clean lines with a minimum of windows and scuttles. The cleaner the lines and the less cluttered the external surfaces, the easier it would be to wash off nuclear dust, chemical agents, and other potentially lethal contaminants.

And being an aircraft-carrier operating during a period of tension, the flight-deck was no place for a casual 'walk-about' whenever it took one's fancy. It was inevitably busy with flying operations and the Sea King helicopters of 820 Squadron flying twenty-four hours a day, and because of this it was out of bounds to most personnel for most of the time. Add to this restriction the rigorous watch routines that the lads had to work and one could easily understand that sleep was at more of a premium than getting a glimpse of the sea and the sky in the precious off-watch hours. There were a few open deck spaces for 'Jack' to get some fresh air if he wanted to — the forecastle deck, the lifeboat stations and the quarterdeck, although the latter was generally reserved for officers.

After an early breakfast and before the 0800 Command Briefing, I took a stroll on the quarterdeck to gather my thoughts. The day ahead was an exciting and important one from the trials point of view. It was busy for me, too. I was on the programme for rocketing, tossing a live 1000-pound VT-fused bomb, and then night rocketing and Lepus against the ship's splash target. The new boys would also be starting their duskers programme and I had to be in Flyco for that if possible. Things were getting hectic and the ship was coming alive. Each flight included 45 minutes' briefing time plus any preparation work by the leader, and about 30 minutes' debrief time — longer if there was Head-Up Display film to analyse. In effect the whole day was taken up, a pattern that was to be the same for the rest of the deployment. So five minutes' solitude and fresh air on the quarterdeck did me no end of good. I thought about the dissent and felt I could have done without the hassle. But it was not a major problem and I knew exactly how I was going to deal with it. I crossed my fingers and hoped that my plan of action would have the right end result.

By the time I arrived in the crewroom, the Duty Officer had already gathered the specific wind information that I needed to calculate the sight-picture for the release of rockets, and the briefing diagrams had been drawn on the board by the AWI. The rocketing part of the sortie would in any case be briefed by Morts. As the AWI in charge of the trials, it was his privilege to be able to make sure that all trials pilots knew exactly how he wanted things done. The Boss was no exception.

'Squadron! Sit to attention! All present and correct, Sir.' The Senior Pilot had gathered together all squadron officers and I could see from their faces that they were mystified as to the reason for this special gathering.

'Thanks, Robin. Please sit at ease.' I looked slowly and deliberately at the attentive faces in front of me.

'Gentlemen, I've called you here because we, 801, have hit an unusual problem. It has been brought to my attention that there is a certain level of dissent in the ranks, and so I am going to remind you all of who we are and what this business is all about. I shouldn't have to say it but there is only one Sea Harrier squadron in this ship and there is only one Sea Harrier boss. Those of you who have served with me for some time realise that I am always open to discussion and, if appropriate, criticism on a one-to-one basis. You have never been bollocked or shoved sideways by me just because you don't agree with me. I have welcomed, and will continue to do so, your views and ideas on any matter, especially operational subjects. In that way we can air disagreements in a sensible manner and, to date, this approach has ensured that we are going in the right direction. We are streets ahead of 800 in every department and that is the way it is going to continue. Nothing but the best will do.

'When we embarked, less than a week ago, I welcomed several of you as newcomers to the squadron. So far, you have all been given a fair crack of the whip by me but I hear that one of you has been complaining about squadron practices behind my back – instead of coming to see me with your views.' I allowed no pause for any response. 'That disappoints me… And it must cease forthwith! If you want to get the better of me for some reason there is only one place to do that; in the air — and, if you manage to do that, I'll be surprised but pleased!

'I am now going to put the man in question through his paces in the air so that he can demonstrate his talents and expertise in the right way. You are all welcome at the debrief.

'As far as any further hidden dissent is concerned, my message to anyone so inclined is "grow up and act like a man". We are preparing for war and we don't need to waste any more time on problems like this. That will be all!'

The crewroom cleared like magic and the ship's Ops Team entered to give their part of the coming sortie brief. Morts then ran through the rocketing data. Each aircraft was fitted with two 36-rocket launchers; eighteen RP in the port launcher and thirty-six in the starboard. We would fire seven single rockets and then ripple-out the balance of rockets on the last dive. The AWI briefed everything in detail. Then it was my turn.

'Right! Before the rocketing, you and I will burn off some fuel by doing low-level, fully developed fighter combat. There will be no base height and each combat will commence from a head-on pass at 2000 feet. Claims for kills will only count if they are registered on the HUD film and fulfil the established kill criteria [in range and tracking steadily]. When I'm ready to do so we shall knock it off and join the rocketing circuit. Any questions?'

There were none, and I could see that he was raring to go.

'Let's go!'

There was almost zero RT between us in the air. I led us a few miles away from the ship and called, 'Outwards split for combat. Go!' The two jets countered away from each other through 45°. Whilst still within visual range and when the other jet was just a dot against the white clouds above the far horizon, I called, 'Inwards turn for combat. Go!'

The two jets turned hard inbound and closed each other quickly. I kept my speed back to about 400 knots and was already pulling back hard on the stick as the two jets passed each other head-on, canopy to canopy. I kept my nose just above the horizon and maintained back stick through the heavy buffet, never taking my eyes off the other aircraft. Relaxing the G, I pointed below the jet, which was still in the turn, and by the time we were passing for the second time I had pulled my nose up through the vertical, the airspeed reducing through 150 knots and the aircraft then corkscrewing round to point the other jet, which still had a fair bit of speed on it. He couldn't get his nose round towards me before we passed again. This time my nose was again high but I was slow enough to slice the nose in yaw through the sky with the hot-line gun-sight passing through my target for a snap shot. Seconds later I was firmly locked on to my target, tracking and filming him as he bucked and weaved ahead of me in my 12 o'clock. 'Fox Three! Knock it off!' ('Fox Three' denotes a guns kill.)

It had taken about a minute to achieve the first kill with guns. We set up again for the next combat, and the next, and the next. All with the same result, which was what I had anticipated. I had been flying the Sea Jet for a lot longer than most and there was little that I didn't know about its handling or the correct tactics to use with it in combat. When I thought that my opponent had got the message satisfactorily, I called off the combat and the two jets entered the rocketing circuit.

Goofers was packed for the event, and with adrenalin running very high in both cockpits we gave the splash our best. I had three Delta Hotels (direct hits) out of seven. But the other pilots rockets were equally good. Then it was time for the ripple-firing. I was cleared in live by Flyco and entered the dive at about 12°. Camera on; safety flap on the release button up; steady tracking upwind of the splash, which grew larger by the millisecond; and at about 1250 yards I opened fire. It seemed like an eternity of time as the rockets twirled their way towards the splash, brown burnt cordite filling the air between me and the target. The nose visibly nodded down before the last rocket had gone and I pulled hard up and away from the ship's wake. As soon as the jet was going up I rolled onto my back to look at the fall of shot and at the same time put my armament switches to 'safe'.

'Delta Hotel, Gold Leader! We need a new splash target. Good shooting!' The splash target had been shot away and my number two was left with nothing to fire at. He brought his rockets back on board.

We recovered to the deck in the weak morning sunshine, grabbed a coffee and entered the crewroom. It didn't take long for the HUD film to arrive and the AWI went through the combat film first. My opponent didn't have any film of my jet, but his aircraft filled the frames of film from my own camera and five gun kills were awarded. The rocketing results were just the icing on the cake. I didn't rub it in. There was no point. He had got the message and took it well. There was no more trouble behind the scenes — on the contrary, everyone put their best into preparing the squadron for the successes to come.

The next item on the day's agenda was tossing a live 1000-pound bomb with VT fuse a distance of about 3 miles to its target. In the old days this would have been achieved manually by pulling up at a specific range from the target, as measured on the aircraft's radar, and releasing the bomb at a particular, carefully calculated, moment in the pull-up. Speed would have to be spot-on, as would the rate of pull-up for release of the weapon. With modern technology all that had changed; or most of it had. The software in the HUD would give the pilot cues to follow and would release the bomb automatically when it 'knew' that the bomb should hit its designated target. Of course, the pilot had to designate the target correctly in the first place.

It was agreed with the ship's Staff that the 'target' point of impact should be 1000 yards on the port beam of the ship and level with the bow. The Sea Harrier would set up its attack from ahead of the ship and would be monitored by ship's radars to ensure that no mistakes were made. The last thing *Invincible* needed was a live 1000-pounder landing on the flight-deck!

On completion of the bombing run, I would carry out a similar attack profile and toss a Lepus flare at the ship.

'VT' stood for 'Variable Time', meaning that the bomb could be programmed to detonate at a specific height above the water or above its target. The fuse itself was a sensitive proximity sensor (so sensitive that in the past several aircraft have been blown up by their own weapons going off underneath them). What the ship expected to see, therefore, was the bomb detach from the jet during pull-up and then explode abeam the ship and at a pre-set height of 50 feet above the water. Visual techniques would be used to measure the rough accuracy of the delivery.

Again it was a popular event. Live bombs weren't dropped alongside every day and after I had got airborne the flight-deck was opened up once more to goofers. I had planned to do a dummy run and then a live run.

In the cockpit, I set my radio altimeter warning at 50 feet and then concentrated on programming the other equipment. (Whenever I allowed the jet to go below 50 feet a red light would illuminate and the radar picture would flash.) I was going to use one of the 'destinations' in the navigation computer as the ship and insert an offset of 1000 yards, or 0.5 nautical miles, against that destination in the appropriate direction. That would then be my target. The ship was heading 180° at 15 knots and I programmed the chosen destination with this course and speed (the bomb aim-point would then travel in the same direction as the ship and at the same speed); the offset being 090°. In order to synchronise the weapon-aiming system with the real world I would lock-up the ship on radar during my run-in and 'fix' the radar range and bearing information into the chosen destination.

I ran out after launch to about 15 miles south of the ship and then turned to port for the first run-in. I locked the radar onto *Invincible* and fixed the offset position into the weapon system. The ship confirmed that my heading appeared to be correct and at 500 knots I watched the range decrease. At just before 3½ miles to go the cues in the HUD demanded a 4-G pull-up, which I followed. All seemed to be working correctly. The ship was happy with the dry run and so I turned out for the live run and again descended to 50 feet.

Having set up the correct profile on the run-in and checked with the ship that all was well, I called, 'Clear live?'

'You are clear live' came the immediate reply.

This time as I pulled up on the HUD cues I had the armament switches all live and the pickle button safety flap open. I pressed the bomb-release button and held it down. At about 40° above the horizon the HUD cues told me to relax the G gradually. Suddenly, I heard the 'crump' of the explosive ejection unit in the pylon and felt the whole aircraft lift slightly as the bomb departed on its way.

Calling 'Bombs away!' and pulling clear to starboard, I reversed the turn to try to watch the flight of the bomb, but failed to see it. I continued in at an angle away from target position and after about 25 seconds watched the bomb explode. It looked about right for position, and even at that distance was an impressive sight. A bright orange flash was followed by a puff of smoke the size of a small cloud, and I could see the blast shock-waves running outwards over the sea surface. Shrapnel from the blast turned the sea into a maelstrom underneath the burst and there was little doubt as to what it would have done to a ship's superstructure and radar aerials.

Next on the agenda was the Lepus flare. This was to be tossed ahead of the aircraft in a similar fashion to the bomb release, but I had been warned by Smith's Industries that the programming was not yet correct and so the flare would not go as far as the weapons system software indicated. In the event this proved to be the case, and although the Lepus functioned properly as a flare it burst well short of the ship. And so for Lepus delivery down south there was no alternative but to revert to old and established practices of manual release from the aircraft. I had delivered many a Lepus in the F-4 and knew the manual delivery backwards. It was as easy as riding a bike.

Back on board after the sortie, there was no time to stop and think. Charlie Cantan, Steve Thomas, Brian Haig and the Senior Pilot, Robin, were all preparing for their duskers rides. They would launch about an hour before darkness fell, carry out 45 minutes' Air Intercept (AI) training and combat, and then fly to the 'wait', ready to be marshalled down to the deck by the ship's talk-down team of approach controllers. For obvious reasons, night flying from and to the deck had always appeared a bit of a challenge, and in normal circumstances would not have been countenanced by the Command without there being a reliable diversion airfield close at hand. That was just not possible on the way south. Only one of the littoral states on either side of the Atlantic would have anything to do with supporting the UK Task Force, so the duskers team had the extra pressure on them of having to land-on, come what may. There was nowhere else for them to go.

Robin had of course carried out many a night deck landing in the Buccaneer, but the other three pilots were understandably nervous, even though this was just a dusk land-on with a good horizon. Alan Curtis gave them a very detailed brief on what to look for reference the ship's night-approach lights, which had been fitted at considerable expense and were found useful by some pilots. I personally had never even noticed their existence on any of my night deck landings and instead used the perspective of the ship as a whole to give me the right cues. I and Morts also provided the benefit of our experience to the duskers team, and it was to be Morts who would be up in Flyco talking them down for their land-ons. I would be getting airborne for the final trial of the day; rocketing on the splash target under the illumination of a Lepus flare that I was to toss myself.

All the duskers pilots acquitted themselves very well and each flew perfect land-ons. As full darkness fell, my lone Sea Harrier launched from the ski-jump and the goofers again started to gather on the island superstructure.

There could be no such thing as a dummy run for night Lepus work. It had to be a first-run attack and there would be no prizes for messing it up. When the ship was all prepared, the relative wind-speed over the splash target was passed to me in the air and I was cleared in live for the attack. I planned that the final heading for the release of rockets would be on the beam and that meant I had to make my initial attack heading 45° on the port bow of the ship.

'5 miles.' An information call. I was at 100 feet and 450 knots and was measuring the distance to go on my own radar. As the phosphorescence of the sea's white horses flashed by underneath the jet, the ship was still a tiny cluster of lights in the blackness ahead. I double-checked that I had selected the correct pylon for releasing the Lepus and that the RP selector was set on rapid ripple. There would be a lot to do shortly when I pulled up to release the flare and I didn't want to have any finger trouble with the switches. I changed scales on the radar and as the green blip on the screen that was *Invincible* hit the 1.7 miles to go range I pulled 4 G.

'Pulling up!'

As the nose of the SHAR raced through 43° nose-high, I pickled on the bomb button and felt the Lepus go. Immediate over-bank to starboard until almost inverted and pull like a rigger to prevent ballooning too high. Wings level and a positive check for level flight at about 2000 feet. (If you didn't pause to do this you could end up hitting the sea in no time at all.) A short pause, then off with the Lepus pylon and on with the rocket pylon selector (making sure that the release-button guard was safe and down before I did so). I was now on a heading parallel to the ship. A further short pause and then into a hard turn to port through 90°, letting the nose drop through about 10° during the last 30°. Wings level in the dive, and I had just begun to wonder if the Lepus was going to work when my dark world was lit up with 6 million candlepower.

The flare hung smoking on its parachute just beyond the splash. Perfect! It was like daylight and I only needed a small adjustment in heading and I was on the splash with my HUD sight, in a dive of about 9°. The flare continued to gyrate seawards leaving a corkscrew-like trail of white smoke. 430 knots was a bit slow, so on with the power as I prepared to fire. Low and slow, so adjust the release-sight picture. Fine! Up with the safety flap and — pickle! The rockets left the pod in rapid succession, each one trailing flame and burnt cordite behind it. With all my concentration on the aiming-point I felt as if I was travelling at high speed in a brightly lit, smoke-ridden tunnel. Releasing the firing button, I pulled hard. At night, the splash looked closer than I remembered. Check all switches safe and head for the recovery pattern. I was covered in sweat and breathing hard.

'Sharkey, Delta Hotel. From the Captain, well done!'

As I came down the slope towards the hover I felt the usual symptoms of a night deck landing coming on — an irresistible desire for a pint of beer.

Morts and Robin met me in the crewroom. 'That was great, Boss. Looks far more interesting by night and better than any fireworks display.' Morts was to have the pleasure of carrying out the identical sortie on the following night. Together we all went aft, showered, changed and told old flying stories in the bar until closing time. The ship's officers had enjoyed the 'display' too. The smell of hot cordite around the ship seemed to have put morale one step higher.

12

Preparations for war seemed to be going pretty well. The Senior Pilot ensured that all the aircrew enjoyed at least one RP sortie to give them a feel for delivering the new weapon. All were already fully at home with the finer aspects of weapons range safety, and it was agreed that each pilot would need to practise with no more than eighteen rockets. The firings went well and it was a boost to the confidence of the Command and the ship's company to witness all rockets fired landing on or near the splash target. Everyone on board wanted to witness weapons being released effectively — the better the weaponeering, the better our defences would be.

At the morning Command Briefing on the 10th, I outlined the coming day's events for the Captain. 'Highlights today, Sir, are the Sidewinder AIM-9G firing against a Lepus flare target — Alan Curtis will fire the missile and E-J will toss or drop the flare; a live 1000-pound HEMC Direct Action bomb will be tossed by Morts against a free-floating dan-buoy target; we shall do one release of high-angle 1000-pound dive-bombing; and, tonight, the AWI will conduct a 2-inch RP attack on the splash under a Lepus flare. The rest of us will be doing academic rocketing, Air Combat and Air Intercept training. And to round off a pretty busy day, the duskers pilots from yesterday's programme will do their first night sorties.'

'Hmmmm! I enjoyed the fireworks last night. Sounds like an interesting day. What on earth does HEMC stand for?'

'High-Explosive Medium Capacity,' responded Wings, 'and before you ask, Sir, Medium Capacity indicates the balance between the weight of explosive and the weight of metal or shrapnel in the bomb. The higher the capacity, the more blast effect you get, but at the expense of losing some volume of shrapnel.'

Wings was being pretty chirpy, I thought to myself. Let's hope he stays that way. A happy Wings means a happy Air Group.

All the HODs had their say, but it was something that the Ops Officer brought to the Captain's attention that sparked off a little speculative discussion. 'Hermes [that is, Lyn Middleton] has signalled to the Flag to request permission to close Gibraltar. He wants to provide a diversion for the first flight from the deck of one of his SHAR pilots!' The rules which surrounded, and often threatened to suffocate, front-line flying demanded the availability of a diversion for any pilot's first deck landing and, even in the excitement of mobilisation, or with this new aircraft type which was easy to deck-land, Lyn was not going to be caught out. I knew that my old boss was a stickler for the rules but all at the briefing agreed that there must be more to it than met the eye. After all, the Flag had told the Task Group that details of its progress south were to be kept secret — no one other than C-in-C Fleet should know exactly how far the fleet of warships and support vessels had proceeded. Permission to close Gibraltar and give away our position to the world was refused, and the young *Hermes* pilot had to fly without a diversion. But Lyn's back was covered. At least he'd tried to follow the rule book.

I was never to find out for certain whether there was any friction between Middleton and Woodward. Lyn was a professional naval aviator through and through; Woodward was a submariner who didn't appear to have much time for aviators or aviation. And now this guy was running a show which depended very heavily on organic air power for its success.

But it was a very busy day ahead for me and I concentrated on the immediate demands on my time. I was only scheduled to fly once; AI and Air Combat against Paul Barton, who had been one of my officers during my time as Boss of the Headquarters Squadron. Paul was a good pilot, pretty fair at combat, and so the flight would not take much time to brief. That would allow me more time up in Flyco talking to Wings and watching the progress of the weapons trials.

Dusty was a very experienced fighter squadron CO from the Sea Vixen world. "Little F ", Brian Prendergast, had equivalent experience in the helicopter world, and the two were an ideal pair for running the *Invincible* Air Group. It was usual practice for one of the more senior squadron pilots to be in Flyco whenever squadron flying from the deck was taking place (launch and land-on) and, today, I was to be there for nearly all flying serials.

Most of the ship's company had never witnessed a Sidewinder shoot, and so the Captain specially approved a deck walk-about for those who wanted to see the event. E-J dropped the Lepus flare on the beam of the ship at just less than a mile from us, and Alan ran in from the stern for the first ever SHAR missile release. Even by day, the flare could easily be seen from several miles away. Alan called 'Visual the flare!' and continued in towards his target using the ship's radar echo to tell him exactly how far it was to go before he was in range. At low level, the missile's maximum and minimum ranges are not that far apart, leaving only a few seconds' firing time for the attacking pilot.

'I have acquisition!' Alan called over the radio. That meant his Sidewinder had seen the flare and had locked on to it.

Checking visually that the sea ahead of the ship was clear of shipping and receiving a nod from the Captain, Wings gave the green light.

'You are clear to fire when in range.'

'Roger. Clear to fire.'

All eyes were on the Sea Jet, which initially had been just a small black dot traversing the horizon but which was now growing larger by the second as it ran in towards the ship. It was at about 1000 feet and some 2½ miles from the deck when the dot transformed itself into a Sea Jet.

'Missile away!' came the call. After a very short pause a plume of white smoke ran out astern the SHAR from under the port wing. Micro-seconds later the missile was on its way, accelerating rapidly to a position well ahead of the aircraft. Initially it tracked smoothly towards and slightly below the flare in the sky, but when its control fins were unlocked the sensitive guidance of the missile head took over and the path to the flare became a gentle, corkscrewing weave. In a matter of seconds it had closed to impact point and hit the flare fair and square. Its spent body then continued its flight until it impacted the sea ahead of the ship. The trial was over.

The aircraft system and the missile had functioned correctly, and that was enough for 801 and *Invincible*.

All of the trials that day went according to plan, except for the 1000-pound bomb toss trial. The dan-buoy target was launched satisfactorily from the quarterdeck but the wind had risen to about Force 5 and was blowing against the radar reflector. This pushed the buoy over on its side, hiding the reflector from the aircraft's Blue Fox radar, which meant that Mortimer could not hold a radar lock on the target. Not being a man to let small things beat him, he called me up on the radio in Flyco.

'Boss, I'm having trouble seeing the buoy on radar and so I intend to revise my routine and do a reversionary attack and fire against that position. OK?'

'Affirmative. You are clear to go ahead.'

'What's the meaning of all that mumbo-jumbo, CO 801?' JJ was keen to know all about the change in plan.

'As the AWI can't hold the dan-buoy on radar in this weather, Sir, he is now going to overfly the buoy and fix its position accurately into his navigation kit. He will then run outbound from the buoy for about 15 miles before turning back in and locking his weapon system onto the navigation fix. Of course it won't be as accurate a delivery as with a continuous radar lock, but it should suffice for this trial's purpose.'

Morts did as he had proposed and the bomb impacted the sea and exploded about 200 feet downwind of the target.

The remainder of the day was generally rewarding and successful. In less than 48 hours the eight-aircraft squadron had flown nearly 50 sorties. The engineers had loaded about 400 rockets (each one in a pod having to be correctly sequenced), three 1000-pound bombs, and several Lepus flares. There had been no malfunctions at all and this was a real testament to the technical excellence of Dick Goodenough's armourers. No less impressive had been the performance of the navigation and weapon systems. Neither could have produced good results in the air without the guys in the workshops tuning things to perfection.

By and large, I had the same team that had been with me in the IFTU and Headquarters Squadrons. All the sailors had volunteered for 801 Squadron when it had been formed and recommissioned and this made me a very happy man. It made others jealous, too. And that evening in the bar, after witnessing the new night-flying team of Charlie Cantan, Steve Thomas and Brian Haig land-on without any problems and seeing Morts score an impressive Delta Hotel against the splash target on his first night rocketing sortie, I heard from the young squadron pilots and from the 'borrowed' Headquarters Squadron experts a few interesting truths about the past.

When they, the youngsters from Flying Training and the older pilots from Harrier Conversion, had first arrived at Yeovilton to join the Sea Harrier community, the place was full of talk about the IFTU and 801. The trials results on shore and at sea were excellent – but were they too good? After all, they had been presented by the Trials Squadron itself... When 800 formed and did not manage to achieve similar results, the honesty of myself and my team started to be questioned by many — though no one had mentioned such doubts to 801!

'You see, Boss,' Mike Broadwater, the well-respected Command QFI explained, 'to the outsider, and we were all outsiders initially, there was such a difference between your opinion of the kit in the aircraft and that of Tim Gedge's crowd in 800 that we didn't know who to believe. I am sure that went for the Staff as well.' Mike had just completed his first duskers land-on and was in high spirits. He was a very good talker.

'For example, the Navhars kit has never been properly trusted by 800 aircrew because, when they first used it, it wasn't giving them the right results. And you were saying in the IFTU and in 801 that it was a nigh-on perfect system – your results from trials were excellent and well up to the equipment's specification. Of course your pilots were saying the same thing. But if you were on the Staff, how would you decide who was right between two squadrons whose opinions are miles apart?' The answer to that seemed perfectly simple to me.

'Phil's quite right, Boss,' interrupted the ebullient — and slightly inebriated — Charlie Cantan (and who wouldn't have had a jar or two after his first night deck landing?). 'We all thought you were a bullshitter to begin with! And all thanks to those arseholes in 800! Buy you a drink, Boss? Same again?' And off he went to the bar.

What the boys were saying all fitted in surprisingly neatly with various events past, and would fit with several that were to come. I mulled it all over in my mind. It certainly would account for some of the very funny attitudes I had come across when training 800 personnel. Well, maybe the progress report that I had sent to *Hermes* through JJ that very evening would make them sit up and take notice. It read as follows:

801 NAVAL AIR SQUADRON WORK-UP PROGRESS REPORT
1. Principle effort devoted to primary role of Air Intercept and Air Combat Manoeuvring. Newly joined squadron pilots adapting well to the Front-Line learning-curve.
2. Full evaluation of the following weapon roles/modes already completed.

   a. 3 x live 1000-pound HEMC retard bombs delivered. Good filmed results. Sight setting 135 milliradians depression for 200ft 450 knots release.

   b. 1 x live 1000-pound HEMC VT fused bomb with 952 fuse delivered in LOFT mode of new HUDCAS software tape 3A. Further live 1000-pound HEMC Direct Action bomb also delivered using HUDCAS 3A LOFT mode. Both successful, filmed deliveries with good accuracy from over 3 miles.

   c. 1 x live 1000-pound HEMC Direct Action bomb delivered in high angle 30° dive. Successful delivery.

   d. 1 x Lepus flare tossed using HUDCAS software guidance. Software programme incompatible with this attack i.e. range of pull-up demand too great. Flare deployed normally. All Lepus deliveries require manual toss.

   e. 400 x 2-inch RP practice rounds fired against splash target by day and by night. Attack profile 10 to 15° dive with a slight setting depression of 51 milliradians. Rockets fired in all combinations of ripple and single shot. Extremely good results all on film with one splash target destroyed. All aircrew fired a minimum of at least 18 rockets each.

   f. 2 x night Lepus and RP trials carried out on ship's splash target. Lepus manually tossed from 1.75 nautical miles and rockets delivered by Lepus drop aircraft. Profile and results as in 'e' above. Delta Hotel achieved on both sorties.

   g. 1 x proof firing of Sidewinder AIM-9G carried out alongside ship against Lepus flare. Highly successful.
3. Night flying proceeding with three fully qualified and experienced crews. Seven more pilots in various stages of night qualification.
CO 801 NAS   10 April 1982

There was no immediate acknowledgement of the report, but two days later, on Monday 12 April, the squadron had a very welcome visitor from *Hermes* in the shape of a small but wily Irishman called Desmond Hughes. He and I had flown together in the Phantom as a crew and later he had served in the IFTU, teaching all the pilots the art of radar handling. He had also been in charge of the Navhars trials. He was a brilliant Observer and worth his weight in gold to any squadron. 800 NAS were lucky to have him seconded to them for the duration of the coming action.

Ostensibly he had come on a liaison visit to exchange views and information. But he was obviously somewhat downhearted and needed a break from the Flagship.

Desmond was a perfectionist when it came to operational skills and was more than a little disappointed to relate that the effort he had put into training certain pilots to use the Navhars and radar had borne little fruit. Apparently some had no trust in either piece of equipment; hence the poor air intercept ranges claimed by the 800 aircrew.

The situation was exacerbated by the fact that the *Hermes* Command were pushing the squadron to concentrate on surface attack and visual reconnaissance training. It was, of course, the prerogative of the Command to decide which of the threats facing us all was the greatest, and it was the surface threat that appeared to have grasped the attention of our sister carrier. As a result, air intercept training was not given much priority and there was nothing that the 800 Squadron command could do about it. The emphasis being placed by *Hermes* on the surface threat did not accord with either Desmond's views or our own in *Invincible*.

I left Desmond with Splot and went off to fly. It sounded really difficult for the squadron in *Hermes* but they, the 800 command team, were all coming over on the next day for a get-together on the way ahead — I would be able to chat to Neil Thomas and Andy Auld then.

My flight was a mixture of AI, combat and a special trial against the ship. It was the latter that interested me most. The object of the trial was twofold: first to become acquainted with the noise made by the ship's Sea Dart missile system when it locks on to the aircraft (the 'noise' being transmitted to the pilot's headphones by the aircraft Radar Warning Receiver kit [RWR]); second, to see if it was possible to evade lock or break lock by manoeuvre. The reason for this was that the Argentine Navy had two Type 42 destroyers armed with Sea Dart as supplied by the UK. If we had to attack those ships we needed to know what we were up against.

When Sea Dart's acquisition radar locks on to your aircraft, there is no doubt at all in your mind that something evil is pointing at you. That part of the trial took very little time. The second part was a more lengthy process and, to say the least, was not frightfully successful. In theory, a particular manoeuvre by a fast target could temporarily break the Sea Dart lock, but, try as I did, I failed to do so. If I had to attack a Type 42, I would have to use different tactics. And my AWIs had already been working on that for the afternoon's presentation to the Captain.

Two plans were submitted to the Command that afternoon: a night attack on the Port Stanley airfield, and a daylight attack on the Argentine carrier and her escorts. The airfield was the simpler affair.

There would either be an eight- or a twelve-aircraft attack; four pairs from *Invincible* and two from *Hermes*, if they could provide. The aim of the attack would be to signal to the enemy that they were vulnerable and to destroy any aircraft on the airfield at the time of the attack. Bonus points would come from destroying radar aerials and personnel. The safest way of achieving the aim would be to toss VT-fused bombs all over the runway and hard-standing area. But that would not ensure the destruction of aircraft, nor would it allow a real-time inspection of damage caused. As the attack should really achieve the element of surprise (being planned, as it was for the early, dark hours of the morning), it was unlikely that defensive systems would be very effective, and so my 801 team recommended Lepus illumination of the target followed by low and fast rocketing, gunnery and laydown bombing — all from different directions.

'How are you going to manage to co-ordinate up to twelve aircraft and get them all through the target in about 30 seconds?' Dusty had asked the right question, as usual.

'The lead pair will toss their Lepus from the north so that their final run-in to the pull-up is shielded by the ridge to the north of the target. That will be their task completed. The other three or five sections, as the case may be, will time their weapon deliveries accordingly; the first being in a shallow rocketing dive within 2 or 3 seconds of the Lepus flares illuminating the target. The rockets will be fired in fast ripple at the hard-standing area close to the control tower and at the tower itself. The remaining sections will attack from different directions with laydown bombs, each pair being targeted on a different part of the airfield to ensure deconfliction from bomb shrapnel. All aircraft will fire their cannon on an opportunity basis.'

'Subject to your approval, Sir,' I addressed the Captain, 'we intend to demonstrate a limited version of this attack tomorrow night on *Hermes*'s splash target.'

The plan was discussed at some length before the AWI went on to present our first thoughts on taking out the Argentinian Type 42 destroyers during any attack on the enemy carrier group. This led to more discussion, with Wings and the Captain raising a couple of valuable points.

At the conclusion of the presentation JJ was clearly content. 'That seems to be shaping up fine, gentlemen. If *Hermes* don't want to play tomorrow night we shall use our splash for the demonstration attack. Thank you very much.'

By the time I retired to my cabin, I was pretty shattered. I was looking forward to chatting with Andy Auld and Neil Thomas in order to get a fuller perspective on the problems that seemed to be facing our sister Sea Harrier squadron. My whole mind and being was focused on preparing my team for action, and I just couldn't imagine anyone else in the Carrier Group having a different approach. But I was lucky; I was in *Invincible* and the Staff were in *Hermes*.

13

Invincible and the armada of warships and supporting vessels were now steaming southwards through tropical climes. The island of Ascension would be reached by the weekend and it was expected that the progress of the Carrier Group would be halted there for at least twenty-four hours. On deck it was warm and pleasant, and the weather pointed to the likelihood of some good night flying conditions, with a calm sea and, with luck a reasonable horizon to give heart to the night deck qualifiers. All the squadron were well practised at night flying from the shore; it was just landing on deck at sea that gave most pilots a few butterflies to begin with.

At night, a pilot has to use his flight instruments to tell him what is happening to his aircraft. He can and often does use external sources of light to give him some of the same information that he gets from his instruments. For example, on a bright moonlit night with no cloud, the earth's horizon is clearly visible and the pilot can use this as a major altitude reference. But even on clear nights, it is easy to confuse bright stars in the sky with far-distant lights on the ground. This can be very dangerous if you are not monitoring your flight instruments − you think you are flying straight and level but you are not, and the next thing you know you have hit the deck or the oggin! And when flying in cloud at night or below complete overcast with no moon, there are no external references at all for the pilot to use, especially when at sea. Everything he does must be done by reference to his instruments.

Couple these facts with the demands of military operational flying (having to throw the aircraft around a lot) and it is easy to understand that a pilot can rapidly become disorientated. That is to say, his mind can be confused by what his natural senses are telling him and what his instruments are telling him. Often, the two can be diametrically opposite, so that he may feel that he is in a level turn to the left when in actual fact he is in a steep spiral dive to the right.

With two aviators in the aircraft, as in a Phantom or Buccaneer, both aircrew monitor what the aircraft is doing at all times. The back-seat man is as much responsible for safety as the pilot. In a single-seat jet like the Sea Harrier there is no second string and so when it comes to the more difficult or dangerous night-flying tasks (deck landing, for instance, or night weaponry against surface targets) the pilot has to have all his wits about him and work hard at staying alive. A short lapse in concentration means curtains.

The art of night deck landing in a conventional fast jet such as a Phantom is very demanding, and if you get it slightly wrong you can easily be off to join the Big Fighter Pilot in the sky. Because of this, as well as other inherent dangers of flying at sea (such as having nowhere else to go) a considerable mystique has grown up about night deck operations. So one's first night deck landing can be a traumatic experience, even if everything goes well. And doing your first night landing off the coast of North Africa, where there is the highest concentration of sharks in the world, doesn't help. Either you make it back on board safely or you feed the big fishes. The latter are usually faster to a ditched pilot than the rescue helicopter.

But all that is life in a blue suit with wings on your arm, and the young pilots, especially, usually cope very well. My junior officers were no exception and, with any luck, by the coming weekend ten of the eleven 801 pilots would have a minimum of at least two night deck landings under their belts, giving a squadron total of about 200.

On Tuesday 13 April, flying continued apace for all the squadron except for myself. My whole day was taken up with hosting the *Hermes* visitors and conferring on the way ahead, as well as the usual Command Briefings, Flyco watches, etc. In advance of the main Conference of War, due to be held in the afternoon round a table with the *Hermes* staff, I was able to get together with Desmond Hughes, Neil Thomas and Andy Auld.

Andy was unquestionably a dour, reserved Scot at the best of times, and had shown himself in the Phantom world to be a good pilot. We chatted as a foursome in the Wardroom. *Invincible* had not prepared the ship for action yet — that would come when we left Ascension — and so I was able to lounge with my guests in armchair comfort, coffee being served by the well-turned-out Wardroom stewards. This all took Andy by surprise. He looked drawn, tired and dispirited, but was still game enough to have a go at his host ship.

'I see you guys haven't got the bit between your teeth yet, Sharkey. This is more like a five-star hotel than a ship going to war!'

'Glad you're comfortable, old chap. I understand you are almost on a full war footing in *Hermes* already. That must make training a little fractious at times.' I had been tempted to say 'getting up to speed' instead of 'training', but didn't want the discussion to degenerate into a slanging match. Neil Thomas, a real gentleman in every sense of the word, quickly butted in.

'Actually, Sharkey, you have hit it right on the button. We have a lot of work to do to get up to speed but we're not being allowed to get on with it. Lyn Middleton is very concerned about the surface threat, and so we are spending more time training for that than for air intercept. And the Flag's staff on board are not much help to us. "Nectar Nuts" is the Staff Aviation Officer [SAVO] and he certainly knows what he's talking about, but he is in a minority and his views tend to be overruled by fish-heads [seamen officers] with no knowledge of air tactics at all. So we are piggy in the middle.'

I looked at the CO 800. 'Yes, Neil's right I'm afraid. And your report on the progress of weapons trials hasn't helped either. Middleton wants us to carry out a similar programme ourselves now instead of getting on with other much-needed training.' At least that would be a step in the right direction, I thought.

It was then that the conversation got down to specifics of how we were going to meet the threat. I raised the subject of using the 'Polish heart' tactic to intercept and destroy incoming raids — one aircraft going for a head-on missile shot and the other of the pair going round the back. It would be important to know what the other squadron was trying to do if both teams got embroiled in the same fight. Andy had very different views.

'How can you possibly use that tactic with the radar contact ranges available from the Blue Fox? I've heard all about the contact ranges claimed by 801 and, to be frank, I don't believe them.'

'Are you calling me and my team liars, Andy?' It was a pretty toned-down reply, but I felt I had to give up trying to be nice to the man. 'Our normal radar pick-up of another Sea Harrier on Blue Fox is 23 miles head-on and never less than 21. If it is less than that, I get the engineers to look at the radar tuning. That range is plenty for any hook manoeuvre and we've done enough of them in this squadron, and against all sorts of opposition too. I think you can accept that we talk from proven experience.'

'Nonsense!' came the reply. 'We have worked with the radar for nearly a year and our best pick-up is no more than 11 miles – and often less.'

I remembered the time at Yeovilton when 800 had received their radars from Ferranti. My team had been carrying out the operational trials in 899 Squadron and when I heard that 800 were only getting poor results I had offered the services of my radar artificers to give a hand with tuning the radars. The reply to the offer was negative. 'We don't need your help, Sharkey. We can sort out our own problems.'

Seeing an argument developing, Desmond tactfully broke in to the debate. 'Actually, Sir' — he always addressed me this way in company — 'we have signalled to the UK for some help on this from the manufacturers and expect their expert to arrive on board at Ascension. That should help sort this all out.' It would save a lot of effort if 800 swallowed its pride and accepted our help, I thought to myself.

'Thanks, Desmond.' I was trying to keep cool. 'Why don't we forget air-to-air radar for a minute and address the possible ways of attacking Port Stanley airfield instead? The subject will come up officially round the table this afternoon and we really should try to present a united front on the matter. I think you will remember, Andy, that at our last meeting I proposed a surprise attack in the middle of the night. And although Lyn didn't think it much of a goer we said we would put on a demonstration this week. Well, we've been working hard at it and are ready to do our thing tomorrow night. How do you feel about it?'

Andy had very different views. 'Look Sharkey, come down from your dream world to reality. I have adequate night experience from the deck in this jet now and I agree with the Captain that your idea is a total non-starter. The aircraft isn't up to it. Especially for a co-ordinated attack.' Auld was not AWI qualified and this was more than apparent from his remarks. But, giving him the benefit of some doubt, I responded quietly, 'How much night deck work have you actually got under your belt in the Sea Harrier, Andy?' Perhaps my information had been wrong and some aircrew in 800 may have achieved a few more hours than I had suspected. The man had just said that he had adequate night experience to make a judgement. If so, then I would have to take his views more into account, even though they did not accord with the views of any of my own pilots.

'Two night deck landings including one duskers.' I was amazed. But he was serious. 'And how many night deck landings do you have, Sharkey?'

'Actually, Andy,' I replied almost sweetly, 'about seventy-five. So has my AWI. And I really don't believe there is much point in progressing this conversation further. We are talking from experience and in future you would be well advised to listen.'

Our 'polite' get-together was adjourned.

At the afternoon meeting I commented that by the end of the week I would have ten out of eleven fully night-deck-qualified pilots and restated my offer to demonstrate a co-ordinated night attack on the *Hermes* splash. I was backed up by JJ. Somewhat reluctantly, Lyn Middleton agreed, and so the event was set for the following night.

It was to be just a three-aircraft attack. Alan Curtis would toss the Lepus flare to illuminate the target and then he would strafe the splash with 30-mm Aden cannon. I, as leader of the sortie, would tip in to the dive after Alan but from the opposite bow of the ship and fire out two half-pods of 2-inch RP in rapid ripple. Morts would then fly through the target from a third direction at high speed and low level and deliver practice retard bombs. The flight brief was comprehensive and was attended by Wings and the ship's Ops Team. Before concluding, I addressed Wings: 'Sir, if there is any problem with *Hermes* we would like to attack the *Invincible*'s splash as our alternative target.'

'That will be fine. Have a good trip.'

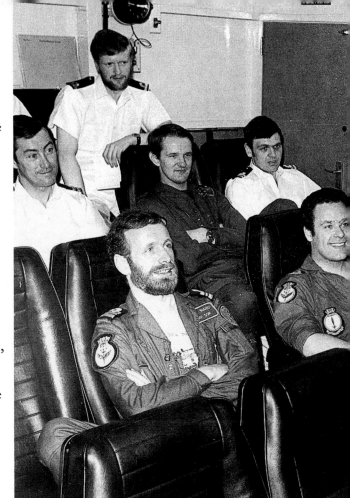

Sharkey and fellow officers in 801 Squadron's crewroom aboard *Invincible* during a briefing.
Charlie Cantan to his left, Steve Thomas behind Charlie and Alan Curtis behind the Boss.

The CO 801 with some of his officers on the flight-deck of *Invincible* at the end of Falklands War.
Back row: Dougie Hamilton, Steve Thomas, Dick Goodenough, Paul Barton, CO, Soapy Watson, Colin Thornhill, Ian Mortimer, Robin Kent. Kneeling: Charlie Cantan, Dave Braithwaite, Alisdair Craig, Squadron 'D', Brian Haig.
A number of pilots are wearing the home-made shoulder-holsters.

An 801 Squadron Sea Harrier returns to 'Mother' from CAP; the empty
pylon shows that the port AIM-9L Sidewinder missile has been fired.
The aircraft in the foreground is manned in readiness, and the SHARs'
white undersides have long since been painted over.

001 off on CAP to protect the Task Force—the 801 Sea Harrier clears
the ski-jump, probably the swiftest and most effective way of getting
a fast jet airborne.

The Argentine pilots christened the Sea Harriers '*La Muerte Negra*'—'The Black Death'. 801 pilots would tune their radios to the enemy frequencies and chant 'La Muerte Negra ees-a coming!'

The 801 Squadron engineers and maintainers worked tirelessly throughout the campaign, often in vile conditions, to make sure that the Sea Harriers were always ready and in perfect flying order. Here an 801 SHAR is armed with an AIM-9L Sidewinder missile.

Bad weather, a slippery deck and a strong sea could make working conditions on deck uncomfortable and difficult, if not downright hazardous.

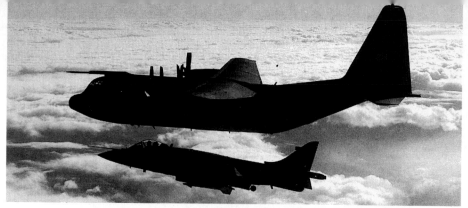

Sea Harrier escorting a C-130 Hercules transport. Sharkey's third and last kill of the war was an Argentine Hercules—these aircraft, which brought in much-needed supplies, matériel and reinforcements to the enemy garrison throughout the campaign, were a persistent thorn in the British command's flesh and, when operating by night in the latter stages of the war, were almost impossible to find and shoot down.

Lieutenant-Commander Ward in full flying kit during the war. Insensitive tasking from *Hermes* led to 801 Squadron being pushed beyond prudent limits, despite having fewer pilots and aircraft than 800 Squadron in the Flagship. The lines of strain and tiredness show in the CO's face, but the eyes tell a different story.

On deck, it was sultry and close. The night was dark with no moon and there was about 4/8ths light cumulus cloud cover. So we had some light from the stars, though not enough to give us a natural horizon. The whole flight would be conducted on cockpit instruments. We manned aircraft, started engines and taxied onto the centre-line. Post-launch, we carried out the standard procedures that followed every take-off, including checking our radars.

The RT crackled. 'Sorry, Boss. I've got a problem... ' It was Alan. His radar wouldn't come on line. And without his radar he couldn't measure the pull-up range from the target for tossing the Lepus. 'Shall we abort the sortie?'

'Negative!' There was no way that I was not going to hammer *Hermes*'s splash after all the talk. 'Continue east at 2000 feet and I will join you in trail.' My mind had switched back to an exciting experience from Phantom days when Desmond Hughes had been my back-seater.

The *Ark Royal* had been in a major exercise in the Atlantic for some time and all the aircraft were suffering from the intensity of flying. Most unusually, all the Buccaneers were 'down' (unserviceable), as were all but one of the Phantoms, when a signal arrived from the Flag tasking the ship to attack a group of three frigates at a range of some 150 nautical miles. It would normally have been a Buccaneer task but there was no choice but to give it to the versatile Phantom. The serviceable F-4 was rapidly loaded with Lepus and rockets and we launched from the waist catapult into a wet, murky night with low cloud and no horizon. Post-launch, Desmond spoke on the intercom. 'Bad news, Sharks! The confounded radar is down so we are stuck. If we could find the target visually we could still attack the splash, but there's no way we can do that in this weather without help.'

There was a short pause before he went on. The little Irish wizard always came up with an answer. 'Isn't there a Gannet airborne tonight? Why don't we see if they can direct us?'

And that's the way it was. The Gannet Observer guided us as far as he could towards the targets. We stayed at low level in the clag and as we approached the vicinity of the three frigates some gaps in the oppressive low cloud appeared. Before sighting our prey Desmond raised another pertinent issue. 'The Gannet can't give accurate enough ranges for a tossed Lepus delivery, so we are going to have to do an over-the-shoulder shot; then come down and do the business with the rockets.' Neither I nor Desmond had practised this manoeuvre, but we knew that it was well-used by our predecessors. We therefore planned to overfly the target fast, plug in the afterburners and pull up through the vertical, releasing the Lepus when about 20° past the vertical. The Lepus would go very high and then, if we had got it right, would drop and illuminate directly above the target.

We did get it right, and after releasing the flare had plenty of time to reposition for an accurate dive against the splash target that one of the frigates had streamed. It was a lot of fun and was capped by the frigates sending a 'well done' signal to *Ark Royal* — Delta Hotel was recorded.

Sitting strapped into my Sea Jet and airborne behind Alan's aircraft, I mused that if the Gannet could do the job then so could I. The discrimination on my radar was much better than the Gannet's and therefore plenty good enough to guide Alan in to the correct pull-up point for the Lepus toss. So I briefed Morts over the air that the attack was still on as briefed and then got down to concentrating on flying my jet and directing Alan exactly where to go. The formation descended to low level and ran in for the target. Morts split from our pair to set up his own line of attack.

Not only did I have to place Alan's jet just right for pull-up, I had to get the whole thing timed exactly right so that co-ordination over the splash with Mortimer was correct. Otherwise there could be a nasty. It was hard work but by the time we were inbound to the target at 15 miles, the Navhars indicated the correct time to go and no problems remained. Speed 450 knots. Armament switches selected; just the safety flap to lift when in the dive. Check sight depression. How far to go to call Alan to pull up? My mind was working overtime.

'*Hermes*, this is Omega Leader inbound at 15 miles as briefed for a first-run co-ordinated attack on your splash. Over.'

No reply! I called again at 12 miles. This time there was a reply.

'Omega Leader, this is *Hermes*. Sorry, but reference your last we do not have a splash streamed. I say again, there is no splash target. You are not cleared to attack. Over.'

After all the talk and the effort on the ground and in the air, *Hermes* was letting us down. It seemed that someone on board didn't want to be proved wrong and so the ship had refused to stream the target for the demonstration. I was furious but tried not to let it show.

'Roger, *Hermes*. Now switching to *Invincible* frequency and conducting my attack on Mother's splash. Goodnight. OUT.' I didn't wait for a reply. 'Omega division, stud four, go!' We switched to *Invincible*, checked in and explained the problem. We were cleared in live for our attack, which went as planned and without any further hitches.

The squadron gained excellent training value from the mission and *Invincible*'s command were pleased to have been able to witness a good co-ordinated night attack. But there was no sound from *Hermes*. I wondered whether there had been an unfortunate problem that had prevented *Hermes* streaming her splash target.

At the morning Command Briefing next day, JJ let everyone know that the incident had been most regrettable but that *Invincible* should get on with its work-up regardless of such pettiness. And with great flair and judgement he changed the tone of the briefing by questioning the MEO (Marine Engineer Officer) about the troubleshooting that was going on with the ship's main propulsion gearing. The MEO had commented that the interior of the gearing could be and was being examined without taking off the covers by using a glass-fibre 'Intrascope'.

'What exactly is that, MEO?' enquired an innocent-looking Captain.

And after the explanation he immediately came back with, 'Aahh! You mean an arsehole scope. Now I understand.'

Although he joked about it, he knew that the MEO's problem was very serious. Changing the reverse coupling in the main gearbox of the ship was a 'dockyard job'. 3½ tons of metal had to be lifted out and replaced. 'Well, we can't go back to Portsmouth to have it fitted, that's for sure. So you, Dan, had better assist the MEO in ordering a new part and having it flown to Ascension. Then you'd better think of some way of getting it on board'

'Aye, aye, Sir!' responded Commander Shorland-Ball, the ship's Supply Officer. Like Neil Thomas, he was, in my book, a gentleman through and through. And he was undoubtedly on top of his job because the 'spare part', all 3½ tons of it, was later delivered to *Invincible* off Ascension Island by Chinook helicopter. Then, with enormous industry, initiative and efficiency, the MEO and his stokers fitted the part at sea. It was, by any standards, a terrific job well done.

Before the briefing closed, Wings reminded the Captain of the main event of the day, the 'Crossing the Line' ceremony on the flight-deck. Legend had it that whenever a ship crossed the Equator carrying sailors who had never 'crossed the line' before, King Neptune would visit the ship and carry out an initiation ceremony on all the 'virgin' sailors. It was a hilarious and festive occasion and, whether you had been across the line or not before, if you were a squadron commander or indeed the son of the Monarch, you were automatically initiated.

His Royal Highness Prince Andrew was embarked as a helicopter pilot in Ralph's squadron, 820. When at sea or with his squadron ashore he was treated very much on merit as a pilot and junior officer. And there was no doubt that he was an excellent pilot and a very promising officer. To make life easy for everyone, he was content to be referred to as 'H' by fellow officers on board, and became very popular not only within 820 but also in 801. Charlie Cantan (known often in social circles as Champagne Charlie) had become a good friend to the Prince, and he in turn became a good friend to 801 by keeping abreast of all that happened in the Sea Jet squadron.

In the tropical sunshine off West Africa, King Neptune had a field day. The average age of the whole ship's company (including the Old Man) was twenty, and because of the resulting amount of business that King Neptune had to get through a special stage was rigged on deck by the island with a canvas swimming (or ducking) pool below it. Initiates were sat on a chair, plastered with foul-tasting shaving soap that certainly didn't come from the barber's shop, shaved with a huge razor and then tipped backwards into the pool, where further strong hands ensured a good ducking. Any objection to the King's ministrations resulted in another mouthful of the vile soap — there were few objectors. JJ, Wings, 'H' and the Squadron COs participated half-willingly, and everyone on board benefited from the fun and relaxation. For most of the crew it was the last afternoon off duty for months — until well after hostilities had ceased.

14

AS we neared Ascension Island, the Air Group had to adapt to the heat and humidity of the Tropics. But life within the hull of the ship carried on as usual, with the air-conditioning system doing its best to take the edge off the equatorial sun. In the heart of the ship was the Operations Room, and it was here that the majority of war-fighting decisions would be made by the Command.

There were essentially three elements of naval warfare which had to be controlled and directed from the Ops Room: Above the Surface (Air), On the Surface, and Under the Surface (Anti-Submarine). The three were very much interbred and interdependent, thanks to the variety of modern weapon systems available to the fleet and the sophistication of the modern threat. It was therefore no easy task to collect and collate information from all the ship's sensors (including aircraft sensors and information from other platforms) and present them to the Command in readily digestible fashion. All friendly units in each element had to be continuously plotted and information from the separate levels of defence recorded, so that *in extremis* the Command could judge priority and take the appropriate action.

Defence in depth had become the war-fighting philosophy of the day. Against the air threat, the outer layer of defence could be air-to-air and surface-to-air systems provided by a third party and deployed at some point between the source of the threat and the fleet at sea. In the South Atlantic there was no such layer available and the Task Group had to rely on its organic defensive weapon platforms.

The outer layer of air and surface defence was the Sea Harrier on Combat Air Patrol. Whenever the threat assessment made air attack highly possible or probable, then CAP aircraft would be stationed up-threat to deter and/or engage the attackers. (Should a surface attack be predicted then the SHAR would be despatched over the horizon to search for the enemy units.) Air-defence radar pickets (warships fitted with suitable sensors and weapon systems) would also be stationed up-threat but inside the CAP stations, to provide information to the CAP and to the Carrier Group itself. These pickets would be armed with a variety of surface-to-air weapons and represented a second layer of defence. The next layer of defence was the medium- or long-range surface-to-air ship-borne missile system. Sea Dart fulfilled this role for the Group. Attackers or their air-to-surface missiles that managed to penetrate through these outer layers of defence would then face the next designer weapon – the Short-Range or Point Defence Missile Systems such as Sea Wolf. And, as a last-ditch defence (on the hard-kill side), high-rate-of-fire, radar-directed guns such as Phalanx fitted the bill. Soft-kill options such as jamming and chaff were also an important integral part of the air-defence-in-depth scenario.

If one analyses the probabilities of engagement and kill of each of the different layers of defence, and calculates the overall probabilities of engagement and kill of the cumulative system, it is fairly easy to demonstrate mathematically and in practice that money spent on defence in depth is far better than spending the same amount of money on a single 'all-singing, all-dancing' weapon system. The latter can never be perfect or 100 per cent efficient and if it has weaknesses, which it surely will, the threat will be certain to capitalise on those deficiencies and circumvent the system. The separate layers of defence in depth each act as a deterrent to an enemy, and each are capable of causing attrition to attacking forces.

It is the Commander Task Group's job to ensure that where possible he does not place his force in a position which denies that force the full benefit of its defence-in-depth systems, whether by geographical location or by misuse of a particular asset or layer.

The under-surface threat has to be approached in the same manner as the air threat, utilising third-party resources, long-range organic sensors such as Towed-Array Sonar, Anti-Submarine Warfare (ASW) frigates on a screen between the threat and the group, anti-submarine helicopters on the screen and at other appropriate locations round the group, and last but not least sonars fitted to the ships in the main body. Each of the anti-submarine platforms must be capable not only of locating the threat submarine but also of prosecuting it with appropriate weapons. And with the submarine threat being ever-present and very difficult to detect, the various levels of defence have to be working at 100 per cent efficiency for twenty-four hours a day when in a threat zone.

There were, of course, to be no third parties of any description providing defence for the Task Force in the South Atlantic; no Nimrods, no air-defence fighter barriers, and no shore-based Airborne Early Warning (AEW) aircraft. The decision to 'do away with' aircraft-carriers as taken in the late sixties was now coming home to roost and added immeasurably to the sense of vulnerability felt by the average sailor embarked in the Carrier Group. We would all have felt much more secure with a couple of modern, conventional attack carriers at our disposal.

The *Invincible* Ops Team had to cope with all aspects of the threat all the time and had to be ready to give the Captain a clear picture of the status quo at any time by day or night. But they were well up to the task and, thanks to pressure put on the Flag by J.J. Black, it had been agreed that *Invincible* would have the job of Anti-Air Warfare Control (AAWC) ship in the action that lay ahead.

This gave me considerable satisfaction, for it meant that provided we were indeed allowed to get on with that job, a robust air defence in depth of the Carrier Group could be maintained and the limited SHAR assets could be used to best effect.

Although the 801 Squadron threat-reduction exercise had already indicated that air defence by night would be less of a problem than by day, it was essential that the Air Group should be fully prepared to cope with any eventuality, and that was why 801 persisted with its intensive night-flying work-up. The days before arrival at Ascension reflected this, with a heavy night-flying sortie rate. And those pilots who were night deck qualifying in the SHAR for the first time had an additional problem to contend with (apart from the sharks that followed each ship looking for waste).

This problem arose because of the increased outside air temperature. The higher the ambient air temperature, the less efficient a jet engine becomes. This is because the thrust derived from a jet engine is generated by taking cold air, heating it up to expand it, and then accelerating it rearwards out of the jet exhaust. This reaction from expansion and acceleration is thrust. If you start the process with hot air rather than cold air, then the thrust achieved is reduced. The ingenious Pegasus engine designers anticipated this problem by providing the aircraft with a water-injection system. The pilot has a switch to control a flow of water which, when required, is sprayed onto the face of the jet engine turbine. The turbine sits in the hottest part of the engine and its rotating blades take energy from the superheated hot gas exhaust to drive the engine compressor — it is the compressor that draws in the cold air through the air intakes. At a critical exhaust gas temperature, the turbine blades will melt and this governs how much fuel can be burned in the engine to expand and accelerate the air passing through it. Too much fuel burned would raise the temperature of the exhaust gases to above the melting-point of the turbine. The application of water to the turbine cools it and allows more fuel to be burned, which in turn gives more thrust − for as long as the water lasts.

In the hover, the Sea Harrier sits on four columns of thrust from its four nozzles. When operating in high temperatures such as those we were experiencing in the Tropics, the thrust available is less and so the aircraft can not maintain the hover at the same weight as in cold temperatures. So something has to be sacrificed to reduce weight, and that something is fuel. The alternative is to use water for the duration of the landing sequence, thus allowing the engine to burn more fuel and thereby increasing available thrust and allowing more fuel to be carried. More fuel means more safety for the pilot. He has more fuel-burning time to sort out his approach and landing and, in cold weather, he has plenty of fuel for more than one approach and vertical landing. But in very hot weather, a point is reached at which you have to enter the hover with a very low fuel state and you have to use water as well in order to be able to maintain the hover. Then there is no margin for error, which is not really the best time to be sent up to do your first night deck landing.

I was already wound up for action, though, and wouldn't let anything get in the way of the planned work-up programme. Mike Broadwater, Paul Barton and E-J were seasoned aviators, and so I therefore decided that they should carry out their first recovery to the deck at night as planned in the work-up programme and in spite of the hot conditions. I was in Flyco with Wings as they started engines. It was a calm, almost breathless night with no moon — they were in for a real black one.

'Flyco, this is 004.' Aircraft side-numbers were used for communications on deck; 004 was Broadwater's aircraft. As the Command QFI, he knew his aircraft systems backwards and was a stickler for common sense and flight safety.

I took the Flyco radio. 'Go ahead 004. What's the problem?'

'I only have one igniter working.' Pre-start checks included listening to the engine igniters. There were two of them and although one would do the job of starting the engine, it was normal practice to abort the sortie if both were not fully serviceable and available. If your engine igniters failed in the air it was no problem — unless your engine 'went out' for some reason and you had to do an emergency re-light.

Without reference to Wings, I instructed 004 to start up on one igniter. I then turned to Wings: 'If it starts OK on the deck it would also start OK in the air. I want to send him anyway.' As soon as I had said it, I wondered whether I was being a bit too get-up-and-go. Wings didn't reply.

A minute or so later came the call, '004 on deck'. That meant he was started up and all systems were ready to go. There was a short pause.

'Flyco, 004. What are your intentions?' Mike Broadwater was not at all happy. Not unreasonably, he did not want anything or anyone compromising his personal safety, however small the risk might be.

'You are to get airborne.' My instruction was uncompromising. I had worked out the risks in my mind and decided that they were negligible. The work-up must proceed.

'Roger!'

At this stage in the proceedings, Broadwater still had the option of deciding not to go, even if it meant him having to invent some other problem. That wheeze had been pulled off by pilots for generations — but he stuck with it.

The three SHARs thundered down the deck in quick succession and disappeared into the night for their Intercept training. It was a short sortie with the main emphasis on the approach and landing. After the launch Wings was silent for a few moments. He was obviously working out how best to rebuke and caution his Sea Harrier Squadron Boss. I could sense that he appreciated my wish to get on with the job but there was also a case for sensible restraint. After all, it was Mike's first night deck landing and he only had one shot at it with water in the hot conditions. In other words, the pressure was on him already without having additional worries about his engine.

Eventually, Dusty just remarked, 'We are not at war yet, are we, CO 801?'

'No, Sir.' I hoisted in the message. But in the depths of my maverick soul I heard a little voice saying 'No, but we bloody soon shall be!'

The three experienced aircrew completed their sortie and returned to the deck in text-book style. There were no hiccups and, from where we watched in Flyco, no sign that this was a first for them; it was as if they were old hands at the game (which in one sense they were). I talked them down on the Flyco radio out of the black night. 'That's a good approach height, Mike. Hold it level. Your speed looks fine. You're a fraction high in the hover. Bring it down before you come over the deck. That's perfect.' The jet glided smoothly over the edge of the deck, banked slightly to arrest the sideways movement, paused above the centre-line, and then made a well-controlled descent to touchdown. The throttle was slammed shut and the aircraft settled firmly on its undercarriage like a mother hen settling on her eggs. We could almost sense the relief in the cockpit as Mike taxied clear of the runway to make way for the next jet.

'Well done, 004!'

Morts, the AWI, had also witnessed the land-on, and when all three were down he volunteered to debrief the sortie. 'I'll see you in the bar later, Boss.' It was a tactful move.

On my way to the Wardroom, I poked my head into the crewroom. 'Well done, you three! I couldn't see any problems there. I'll go and set up the beer!'

E-J and Paul Barton joined me in the bar, but there was no sign of Mike Broadwater. The two jet-jockeys were pleased with their performance but both admitted it had been very hard work. Mike had still not appeared by the time the bar closed and I didn't find out why until the next morning. Robin Kent chatted to me at breakfast.

'Mike didn't seem at all happy when he got down last night, Boss. He said nothing in the debrief and hasn't said anything to anyone since then.'

'Oh, I expect he will come and see me if he has anything special on his mind.'

After breakfast there was a knock on the cabin door.

'Come in!' A calm, if slightly ruffled, Broadwater entered. 'Hullo, Mike. Grab a seat. How did it go last night?'

He ignored my question, sat down and came back with a question that caught me totally by surprise. 'When you examined my log-book after I joined the ship, did you read it, Boss?'

'Not in detail, Mike, no. I saw that you have four and a half thousand hours' jet time — more than twice the amount I have under my belt — and I decided, rightly I think, that a detailed examination was unwarranted for the Command QFI.'

'Well, if you had read it as you were supposed to you would have noted my night deck experience.' Broadwater seemed more than a little put out.

'Agreed. So how many night deck landings did you have in *Ark Royal* and other carriers? Educate me.'

'None! I have never been night-deck-qualified before.' I was astounded.

'You're pulling my leg, aren't you?'

'No. And so I don't think it was very sensible of you to launch me with only one igniter on my first night deck sortie, do you?' He was definitely upset, and needed consolation.

'I'm sorry, Mike. I missed a trick there, didn't I?... and I apologise.' But I couldn't resist adding, 'Nevertheless, you made an excellent landing, and now that's out of the way let's get on with the job, shall we?' With all those Fleet Air Arm hours under his belt, I couldn't help wondering how it was that Mike had never joined the night team before. I wasn't too disturbed by his obvious discomfort and annoyance − his 'christening' had been well overdue.

I expected my pilots to be able to take the rough with the smooth — to work hard, play hard, and get it right. Because once you were up in the single-seat Sea Jet with a problem facing you there were only two people who could sort it out; yourself, and the Big Fighter Pilot in the sky. Playing hard might get you into a tight corner but, with confidence, the same qualities that had pushed you too far could also be usefully employed to get you out.

It wasn't only the newcomers to night deck operations who had to overcome problems in the dark. A night sortie of my own earlier in the week had underlined that.

After a very rewarding and enjoyable low-level intercept training flight I had approached the ship from the marshal, carried out a precision approach under carrier control, and had started my transition to the hover from forward flight. It was a lovely night but black as the ace of spades, with no horizon. Although I had plenty of fuel to allow for a second approach, my weight on this first approach was marginal. In that heat there might not be enough engine power to support the aircraft in the hover, and so I double checked that the water was selected 'on'. As I approached a point level with the stern of the ship I was a little fast, so I selected nozzles to braking stop to slow my aircraft down more quickly. My throttle lever was by this time hard up in the left-hand corner (I was at full power), but the jet still would not maintain its height. I was rapidly sinking towards the briny. I immediately decided to take it round again. I nozzled away carefully and sank to flight-deck level before the jet worked up enough forward speed and wing lift to arrest the rate of descent.

I was quite happy and unperturbed as I climbed ahead of the ship before turning downwind for a second approach. We had often relaunched after a night landing just to get more practice, so taking it round was no problem.

My fuel was fine, but not really enough to take it round a further time. I turned in towards the glide slope from downwind and was in good voice contact with the Air Direction Officer, Tony Walker. On my first approach I had switched off my radar when close to the ship and was now relying on ranges to go to the deck being given by my controller. My Number Two that night was Alan Curtis, and I could see his aircraft coming down the slope behind a third aircraft. I suggested feeding in behind Alan.

As can very easily happen, a slight misunderstanding then occurred. In the ship, Tony assumed, with good reason, that I had elected to feed myself in visually for approach and touchdown. In the air, I was of the same mind but was expecting some ranges-to-go to be passed to me (judging the distance to a deck by night is not easy when the deck lights are the only reference you have − my first night sortie off Portland had been under very different conditions with a good horizon and I then had my radar working). Tony must have presumed that my radar was still on line and so he switched frequency to talk to the next aircraft coming down the slope. This left me on the same frequency as Alan, who was now approaching the hover ahead of me. Robin Kent was in Flyco talking Alan down, so I couldn't get a word in edgeways.

Not having a clue how far it was to the ship, I did realise that I was high on the prescribed glide slope, adjusted for that, and felt a little uneasy. Suddenly I realized that I could see the spray being kicked up from the sea's surface by Alan's jet, and I then knew I was too close and too fast. I was still doing 130 knots with 60° of nozzle and, as Alan's aircraft suddenly loomed large before me I had to take evasive and corrective action. I jinked left to miss Alan's jet and slammed the nozzles to the full braking stop position. My fuel state was about 700 pounds — not enough to go round again if there were any more fuck-ups!

I cruised on past the ship decelerating as I went and ended up in the hover very wide and very high and with no visual references at all. It was a black night with no horizon, the ship was back over my right shoulder and the velocity vector symbol in my Head-Up Display had disappeared from

121

view. I was completely in limbo, not knowing whether I was going up or down, fighting harder than ever before to control the aircraft and expecting to crash at any moment. For what seemed about 30 seconds I was in serious trouble and on the point of ejecting from the aircraft. But then the ship cottoned on to the fact that something was wrong and took action.

Brian Prendergast acted before speaking. He switched on the flight-deck floodlighting, then called 'You're high!' At last I could see the ship and gain some perspective. Robin Kent then transmitted: 'You are very high.' In the aircraft, I immediately felt more comfortable. I kept my eyes on the floodlit deck by craning my head around to the right and throttled back to bring the jet down to a realistic hover height. Now I had to get back to the deck from my position ahead of the ship, and used a little braking stop nozzle to start me moving backwards. Nothing seemed to happen. I was making no progress and fuel was running low. I selected full braking stop and, as I started to move backwards alongside the ship, I suddenly got heavy rudder tramping. The rudder pedals were trying to thrash left and right against my feet. That meant I was doing about 40 knots backwards! It was a most unnerving experience and I couldn't really understand what was going on. Soon, however, I was in a position to return the nozzles to the hover stop, stabilize alongside and carry out a normal deck landing. I then found out that there was a wind over the deck of more than 10 knots from the stern. No one had passed this critical information to me, which is why I had found it so difficult reversing to the correct hover position.

After a safe touchdown and whilst still in the cockpit, unstrapping, I was cursing Wings and the world in general. I was definitely going to have someone's guts for garters, blah, blah, blah! But by the time I had cooled off walking down the flight-deck my sense of humour had returned. I said nothing to Wings beyond pleasantries, and told Tony that none of it was his fault. Then I went down to the bar, where the ever-present and understanding Senior Pilot listened to my story over a couple of pints.

Part III

THE CONFRONTATION

15

Invincible remained off Ascension Island for only six hours; time enough to load the new reverse coupling for the ship's main gearbox. It appeared that all the political initiatives to sort out the Falklands crisis back home were failing. The Flag had left Ascension in *Hermes* with the balance of the Task Group shortly after we had arrived on the 18th, and had told *Invincible* to catch up as soon as she was ready and able to do so.

On board, the main event for all personnel was the receipt of mail and an opportunity to despatch letters home. One and all wrote to their loved ones and told them not to worry — 'It will all work out fine and when the job is done we'll be home.' It was the last time mail would be offloaded or received for the foreseeable future. My letters were no different to the rest. I missed my family as much as anyone, but for most of the time my job was keeping me and my mind fully occupied. There was no time for daydreaming. It couldn't be the same for my wife and two boys. They must be wondering if they would ever see their old man again.

When we had left the UK on a wave of national support, the prophets of doom had already started to discuss the fate of the Sea Harrier boys. And I had been reminded of this by the third and last intelligence signal that the ship was to receive.

Flag Officer Naval Air Command had signalled to report the results of some practice air combat sorties flown between Sea Harriers and Mirage IIIs, the fighters that we were about to face. At the close of the Command Briefing one evening, J.J. Black passed the signal to me with a look of genuine concern in his eyes. The report described how three unnamed Sea Jet pilots had fared in 1-v-1 combat against the French-made fighter. It would have been depressing reading to anyone but myself — the three had hardly held their own against the supersonic fighter, and were certainly not trying to claim that they had come out on top.

'Don't worry about what this says, Sir. I know exactly who these three SHAR boys were from the remarks made by them in the report and from how they acquitted themselves in combat. They are not what you would wish to call "aces of the base" in fighter combat and they certainly don't measure up to our own team. Their tactics as described by the signal were inadvisable, but predictable for the individual pilots involved. None has flown against the F-15, F-5E, F-16, as we have, and those fighters will all knock spots off a Mirage III — and you will remember that we have easily held our own against those top jets. So, in my view, the report isn't worth the paper it's written on.'

JJ looked half relieved, but not totally convinced.

'Are you blowing smoke up my arse again, Sharkey?' I had pulled the wool over the Captain's eyes once before, or so JJ had thought. Was it happening again? He wanted the truth, and no messing.

'Mostly certainly not, Sir! Our ability to cope with the Mirage III must be judged on our proven performance in the air against similar jets on instrumented ranges, and on two other factors: our confidence in combat — knowing that we can and will win; and our own personal levels of expertise, or "time in the saddle". Regular air combat training is particularly important in the Sea Harrier so that you learn to use the aircraft aggressively and to fly it smoothly at one and the same time. We have had stacks of practice — much more than the boys back home — and we know that we can do the job.'

Wings intervened in the discussion. 'I think you can accept Sharkey's opinion of this signal, Sir. He knows all the pilots pretty well, especially in combat. And I would rather believe his expert view than anyone else's.'

JJ relaxed more and the signal was forgotten. I later went through it with my pilots to extract any useful tips on Mirage III performance, then ditched it. It was fortunate that I didn't know FONAC's personal assessment of the combat risks facing Sea Harrier or his estimate of the likely casualties that would result from the operation. If I had I would have hit the roof. Back in England, the Admiral (who was no aviator and probably could not therefore judge the issue) remarked to his Personal Assistant that he feared that only 25 per cent of the Sea Jet boys might return. The Personal Assistant then passed this message on to the senior squadron wife, my Alison, with the helpful comment, 'Keep it to yourself. I just thought you would like to know'! Alison took it bravely on the chin and, as time went on, got used to the idea that her husband would not be coming home.

But I knew nothing of this sitting in *Invincible*, and once my letters home were posted at Ascension, I put my mind back on the single track of war and kept it there.

Although the real enemy was still 3500 miles away to the south, I was beginning to realize that I was going to have to fight others within the Carrier Group, as well keep things going in the right direction with my squadron. Events of the past week had indicated that there could be major differences of opinion between ships as well as petty rivalry, and that now seemed to be confirmed. *Hermes* had received the AIM-9L Sidewinder missiles when off Ascension, as well as some chaff and flare dispensers for the Sea Jet. The ALE 40 dispensers allowed pilots to decoy radars and missiles aimed at them. Naturally, I wanted a fair share of both the missiles and dispensers for my pilots (especially, I thought, as it was me who had galvanised Tim Gedge into action over the early supply of the AIM-9L in the first instance!). *Hermes* was not altogether helpful, however.

It took the Captain of *Invincible* three very frustrating days of signals and requests to get a result from the Flagship. Eventually, the 9L arrived on board, but no ALE 40s arrived until the last day of the war — even then there were only two, and both had been crushed in transit and were unusable.

As *Invincible* set sail at high speed to catch up with the Task Group everyone now felt that action was really on the cards, and as a result there was a tangible rise in tension within the Task Force. This accounted for one or two odd attitudes coming to the surface; nor was it possible to ignore *Hermes* and the Flag for long.'

The *Invincible*-planned flying programme for the morrow, Monday 19 April, had been passed to the Flag as usual and indicated a morning of non-flying for 801 followed by full afternoon and night programmes. Splot had scheduled some much-needed tactical briefings for the forenoon, but during the night the Flag changed the programme without so much as a by your leave. So I awoke to find that all had changed and an Air Defence Exercise (ADEX) had been ordered for the morning. The change might have affected the pilots' training programme, but what was infinitely worse to me was that my engineers had to interrupt their planned maintenance and hurriedly prepare the jets for getting airborne. Dick Goodenough always briefed me every morning before breakfast on squadron aircraft status and never complained when a change of plan was thrown at him. He always came up trumps. But I hated my boys being buggered around and didn't hold back from telling Wings and the Captain so at the morning briefing. JJ promised to have a word with the Flag, and did so. But he admitted that he wasn't sure that it would have any effect.

The first serial in the surprise ADEX was for a division of four *Hermes* aircraft to launch from the deck and depart the group until well out of sight over the radar horizon. They would then run in to attack the carriers, while 801 would provide airborne CAP aircraft to defend the same. It didn't turn out quite like that, however. *Hermes* was only about 15 miles away from *Invincible* and when her aircraft launched they turned in directly for the sister carrier to conduct their attack. It struck me as a valueless departure from the briefed exercise, did not allow time for any of the ships' Ops Teams to get properly involved, and in all senses represented a total waste of effort. Nevertheless, 801 played the game, scrambled from the deck and managed to claim kills on three of the four attackers before they reached their target (which is some achievement against an attack launched at 15 miles). In Flyco and on the bridge it was definitely a question of 'What the fuck are you doing, *Hermes*?' and, later, 'Well done, 801!'

JJ, Wings and I were all seething with anger and frustration at the stupidity of it all. No advantage had been gained. Exercising the ships' defence-in-depth had been the aim of the ADEX, but that aim had been utterly ignored. A very curt signal went from *Invincible* to *Hermes* and all on board hoped that the second and third serials would prove better training value. They did.

I was flying with my new Number Two, Steve Thomas, on the second serial and we established a CAP station at about 60 miles. The other CAP was taken by Robin Kent and Brian Haig. The first sign of the ingressing attack aircraft was the ship's radar detection of a singleton jet at medium level. Robin's pair were directed to intercept. Meanwhile, I was searching below me with my Blue Fox radar and picked up a pair of targets inbound at fairly low level — so much for 800's assessment of the radar. I and Steve descended towards them. They were almost head-on to us and there was plenty of time to build in some lateral separation for the turn in to the kill.

'Right 20, 10,000 below,' called Steve. He was just letting the leader know that he also had contact. 'Looks like they are in close battle, Boss.' He was referring to their formation, and it appeared that he was right. They were probably about 800 yards apart.

'I'll go for the left-hand target; you take the outside man.'

The two attack aircraft were weaving gently through towering white and grey cumulus and were easy to spot against the light background. 'Tally ho! Your tail is clear.'

'Likewise,' came Steve's reply. He didn't waste words in the air and I liked that. As I barrelled down onto the stern quarter of the right-hand man I placed the Sidewinder cross of my HUD on the target's exhaust and immediately got the tell-tale growl letting me know that the missile could 'see' the target and had acquired it. I could have acquired earlier if I had left my radar locked on, but that could have warned the opposition of our presence. As I closed to within release range I watched Steve out of the corner of my eye swooping down like the avenging angel onto the tail of the left-hand man. We called 'Fox Two away!' (claiming a missile kill) almost simultaneously, and were closing to guns range before the 800 pair saw us. As they started to manoeuvre, I called Steve to 'Knock it off!' and we returned to our CAP station.

In the third and final serial of the ADEX, 801 provided the attack aircraft and launched two pairs. *Hermes*, having screwed up the *Invincible* day by insisting on the ADEX in the first place, only launched one pair of aircraft to act as CAP. Then, hearing from their controller in *Hermes* that the two 801 sections were attacking the ships from different directions, they threw away the game completely by splitting their CAP section and sending a single aircraft to intercept each attacking pair. (What they should have done was leave one attacking pair to ships' missile systems and engage the other with both CAP aircraft.) The result was entirely predictable. I watched the combat on the Ops Room radars and listened to the commentary. Each *Hermes* aircraft was 'shot down' in very quick time, without menacing the *Invincible* aircraft.

In spite of differences of opinion with *Hermes* on Sea Harrier capabilities which seemed to be multiplying as the fuse of the crisis got shorter, spirits were definitely high in *Invincible*. We all felt ready for the job that had to be done.

The planned night attack on Stanley airfield looked as though it was to be an all-801 affair, with a follow-up attack from *Hermes* by day; 800 had admitted that they couldn't provide crews for the night mission. It was definitely going to be a challenging event in anyone's book, but I was masochistically looking forward to it. If the choice was between day and night I would far rather take the night option, and had discussed this at length with Wings, JJ and my pilots. The latter all backed up my choice and were keen to get on with the job. I had also spent a considerable time discussing the cost-effectiveness of various types of attack that the SHAR might be involved in.

There were only twenty jets available, and that starting-point was less than adequate. Every jet lost would be a severe blow to the Air Group's ability to provide a robust air defence for the Task Force. It was, therefore, my very strongly expressed view that it would be counter-productive to risk losing aircraft in direct attacks against low-value, heavily defended targets. And because of fatigue amongst the aircrew, which was already beginning to build up, the loss of a pilot would be even more critical to the defence effort than the loss of a jet.

Why then was I keen on mounting the proposed attack on Stanley airfield at all?

Calculation showed that although the runway was short, it was just capable of operating the A-4 Sky Hawk and, at a pinch, Mirages. The A-4s certainly were fitted with deck-hooks and could use many different types of arrester gear for landing. Should there be any fighters or fighter/ground-attack aircraft based at Stanley, it was important to destroy them and equally important to deter the enemy from thinking of operating such aircraft from the airstrip. Otherwise they would represent a continuous short-range threat to the Carrier Group and to the embarked land forces. It was therefore a risk worth taking, especially with surprise being a highly probable element of the attack.

In parallel with all the briefings, deliberations and discussions, the flying programme continued to address tactical problems and ideas. On the night of the 19th, I flew with my new Number Two, Steve, on the self-imposed task of examining the feasibility of conducting hook intercepts in the dark. The 'hook' or 'Polish heart' was the tactic used by day to engage a threat with one aircraft from head-on and the other from the beam or stern. To do the same thing by night could lead to collision, and so it had to be looked at carefully. Another 801 jet was used as the target for the mission and I had briefed the game-plan with great care.

'Right, Steve, we shall do the first run with anti-collision lights on in all aircraft. The "D" will set up a head-on split of 30 miles and we shall run in with you in extended battle-two formation − when we go without lights you will have to keep formation on me using your radar, and I want you to be able to illuminate me as well as the target.' It meant that Steve would be behind me by about half a mile and about 30° to one side. 'Your job will be twofold; to hang on to me and to search for the target.' Steve was a dab hand at the radar and, when operating from the shore, had used it many times by night to follow his leader round the sky.

'Whoever gets the contact first will automatically become the "shooter" or head-on aircraft. On the call of "Judy", the other man will take an immediate split and pile on the coals. Take the split in the direction that you best judge will give the optimum lateral separation for coming round the back of the target. The shooter will pass ranges-to-go to the target and, very important, call the height at which he will pass through the target position. The hook man will then remain clear of that briefed height. Equally important, the hook man must call "splitting right" or "left" because after the shooter goes through the target he must turn away from the hook man and, when steady, call his final heading. It will then be the hook man's responsibility to engage the target and then fly through, establishing radar contact with the shooter. We'll then join up and do it all again. When I'm happy, we'll give it a go with lights out − but only if it all goes like clockwork.'

It did work well and proved to be no more difficult a task than the normal type of air intercept that the squadron had been practising by night. At the debrief, I asked, 'Any problems at all, Steve?'

'No, Boss. It was all pretty straightforward and it gets us into and out of the fight without giving the opposition a chance to come back at us. I like it!'

'Good. And well done. I liked it too.'

The squadron were to be briefed on the new tactical procedure and all the night crews would familiarise themselves with it in the air before the end of the week.

When I retired to my cabin, I sat at my desk and considered myself very lucky to have ended up with a Number Two like Steve Thomas. He knew the aircraft backwards, was excellent at handling the radar and the Navhars, was good in combat, and took to new procedures and challenges easily and without fuss. Although new at night flying from the deck he seemed fully at home in the dark, and already we had finalised between us the 'silent' procedure for launching from the deck and proceeding on task without use of the radio.

As you accelerate off the ski-jump at night, it gives the same sort of impression as running from a brightly lit room into a coal cellar. Whilst still on the deck, you have a full visual perspective of where you are relative to the ship, the sea and the sky — even though the forward part of the deck is only lit dimly with runway centre-line lights. Suddenly you are in a different world, where all you can see is your cockpit Head-Up Display and your dimly lit head-down instruments. First actions are to get to wingborne flight and 'clean up the aircraft' — putting nozzles aft, raising flap and undercarriage — and then you have to get the radar on line and prepare your weapons for use. At the same time you have to control the jet to the pre-briefed speeds and conditions, say 400 knots and 1000 feet. Whilst all this is taking place, your night vision should have adapted and you might be able to pick up a visual horizon, phosphorescence on the sea surface (if it is rough and if you are low enough), and very black areas in the sky denoting clouds. If there is eight-eighths cloud cover in rain with no moon then you can see nothing at all outside the cockpit.

My routine for getting joined up with my Number Two, post-launch, was simple. 'Whoever is launched from the deck first' (it might be either jet, dependent on aircraft location on deck) 'will turn onto the briefed heading, hit 400 knots at the briefed height, and wait for the other man to fly past. The second to launch will also stabilize at 400 knots on the same heading, establish radar contact on the aircraft ahead, and then check out his missiles on the lead aircraft jet efflux. Once you have established that you have a good tone on both missiles, increase speed to fly past the lead aircraft close enough to be seen. The lead jet will then go into trail and check out his own weapon system, then fly up alongside the other jet. From there we continue the sortie or mission as briefed.'

The whole evolution took very little time, didn't prevent us getting on with the job and, without the use of radio, enabled both aircraft to do a full check on their weapon systems. Steve and the other pilots took to it like ducks to water.

It was on the evening of the 19th that the Captain took me on one side at the conclusion of the Command Briefing. 'Sharkey, a little word of comfort. I just want to let you know that I've been in touch with C-in-C Fleet, the Admiral himself, concerning all the press comment that has been coming out of this ship from you and me. The word is that they are quite happy with it ashore and you can continue making comments. But when I give you the nod, which will probably be soon, then it's got to stop. OK?'

'Certainly, Sir, and thank you.' What other Captain would have taken the time to let me know that all was well? Not many.

Each day, JJ devoted about half an hour to briefing the press men on board. This was a significant sacrifice of his time — there were a thousand and one other matters that he had to address each day — but he believed it only good manners and common sense to permit the media men the courtesy of a daily interview. And they responded by respecting his confidences when asked to do so.

I had talked to the press men in the bar on most days since leaving Portsmouth and had given many quotes for publication. Essentially I wanted to get across to the British public, and indirectly to the Argentine pilots, that the squadron was in very high spirits and that so far as the enemy was concerned, there was trouble on the way. I had referred to the immense success of the Sea Harrier in combat, and how I and my team would use the enemy pilots like 'splash targets in the sky'. This may not have been a brilliant analogy, but since the press had witnessed the accuracy of weapon delivery against the splash target by day and night, it was a useful way of giving them confidence. Whenever things were relatively quiet on the press front, either John Witherow or A.J. McIlroy would approach me in the bar and ask for a quote. They were never let down.

Robin Kent did get rather upset one day when, although a bachelor, he was reported as being married with two kids. On seeing the ship's press release he blew his top and demanded a retraction. It was readily given.

The squadron ratings were happy to see the squadron name going out in print regularly; their families would draw comfort from it. Happy, that is, until the day that the *Sun* got together with the AWI and myself after a few beers. Tony Snow, the *Sun* reporter, had an idea that the great British public would like to get involved with the action, and suggested having names and messages written on the missiles and bombs that were being prepared for action. The first munition so inscribed and delivered against the enemy would result in a cash prize for the named party. Most of the aircrew considered it a good wheeze, but not so the lads. A deputation led by the Chief Regulator came to see me to say they were horrified by the idea. It was immediately shelved.

On the morning of the 20th, 801 arose to find that yet another surprise ADEX had been scheduled by the Flag. This time the master plan was for attacking aircraft to run in to attack the group from a distance of only 40 miles — it was becoming so ridiculous as to be funny. *Invincible* didn't know whether to laugh or cry. Later, and with hindsight, I could only conclude that neither *Hermes* nor the Flag had any trust at all in the Sea Harrier radar, and perhaps even considered Air Intercept exercises to be a waste of time. So why not run in from a point where the aircrew had no time to devote to radar search? Let them get on with a bit of combat, and blow the defence-in-depth theory....

Come 21 April, one reason for ensuring the proper use of the Blue Fox radar became apparent. The Task Force made its first contact with the enemy.

16

Whether there was a known threat and there were Sea Harriers airborne or not, the fleet's Ops Rooms did of course maintain a vigilant twenty-four hour watch on the skies around us, as well as on the sea for surface and submarine threats. Above the water, the main area of interest was towards the south-west and the Argentine mainland, and on the morning of 21 April a buzz of excitement swept through the fleet. The long-range detection radars in several ships, including *Invincible*, picked up a high-level contact approaching the Carrier Group up the threat axis. Internal ships' intercoms came alive: 'Captain, Ops Room at the rush! Possible enemy contact!'

Individual detections of the bogey were passed from each ship to the Flag in *Hermes*. The atmosphere in *Invincible*'s Ops Room was electric as the command viewed the small green echo that was closing the Group at nearly Mach 0.8. 'Looks about 40,000 feet, Sir! Subsonic but motoring!'

'Stand by to scramble 801.' The Captain gave the order which allowed Flyco to give an update to the aircraft that was already being manned on deck. '002, we have a bogey to the south-west at 150 miles-plus approaching the force. Start up and stand by for launch.' We were all prepared and ready to go.

It was at that point that all radars in the Group, except for those in *Hermes*, were ordered to cease transmitting.

What on earth was going on? We couldn't understand the logic of the order. Why shut down all warning radars except one? Was the Admiral hoping to hide the Task Group's position or constitution? On its present heading, the Argentine jet would see the Group visually in about twelve minutes. And why keep *Hermes*'s radars on line with everyone else's silent?

Eventually one of the *Hermes* jets was launched and the bogey was intercepted. It turned out to be an Argentine Air Force Boeing 707 reconnaissance aircraft. It turned away before overflying us.

Rules of engagement (ROE) were rapidly signalled from the UK on how to react to this intruder. Although it couldn't launch any weapons against the ships, it was important to the Argentines to know exactly where the Carrier Group was, and to this end the 707 was carrying out the classic shadowing role. The ROE did not give permission to fire at the intruder. Instead, Sea Harrier CAPs were to 'visibly escort the aircraft and dissuade it from overflying the force.'

From the moment of that first contact, two significant changes in Task Group routine occurred. At all times by day and night there was to be a Sea Harrier airborne or at alert on deck, ready to intercept intruders. A Missile Exclusion Zone (MEZ) was also declared around the group. All Sea Harrier domestic training missions had to be conducted outside this MEZ, and recovery to the ship had to be via pre-briefed 'safe lanes'. At last things were getting on to an operational footing.

In the dark early hours of 22 April, Brian Haig was sitting in his aircraft at alert on deck when the intruder was detected inbound again. 'Scramble the Sea Harrier!'

Although having been in the front line for only six months and having only just night qualified, Brian did an excellent job. Before the 707 had approached to a range of 60 miles from the force, the young fighter pilot was sitting on his tail at 3 miles and 5,000 feet below, ready to fire if so instructed. It had been a perfect intercept to an excellent high-level firing position. He then approached the bogey for a visual identification (which by night is no easy task) and reported confirmation that it was our old friend from the day before.

The 707 turned away, but returned a few hours later during daylight. This time an 800 aircraft was despatched to intercept. Their Sea Harrier pilot showed just how it should not be done. He attempted to turn in behind the target at missile-release range, and instead of achieving this ended up 'sucked' by 10 miles (that is 10 miles behind and with no hope of firing a weapon). He then 'chased' the intruder inbound for 140 miles, by which time the 707 had flown well over the centre of the force; only then did he achieve a firing position.

Later that same day *Invincible* received a signal from the Flag. The Admiral 'didn't think much of the intercept flown by 801'. JJ immediately passed the message on to me, though my simple reaction was the same as the Captain's: 'Fucking cheek!' What, we wondered, had been the content of any message to the *Hermes* Air Group after their disastrous intercept?

I didn't get a chance to try to intercept the 707 myself until the 23rd, by which time the enemy aircraft was getting quite canny and cautious. It obviously had a radar warning receiver fitted because as soon as it was illuminated by my Blue Fox radar it turned away without closing the Group to less than 150 nautical miles. I sat on my high-level CAP station awaiting the intruder's return, but to no avail. The sortie was not wasted, however. Of first importance was the fact that the CAP had dissuaded the intruder from getting close enough to the Carrier Group to gather useful information. This was a clear demonstration of the Sea Harrier being effective in its conceptual role. Of secondary importance, but equally intriguing to me, was this opportunity to look at how high the Sea Jet could be reasonably operated in its full war configuration of fuel tanks, missiles and guns. I took it well above 40,000 feet and held it there on a race-track patrol for half an hour or so. It performed much better than 'the book' suggested it might.

On landing back on board, I was more than keen to find out how the only 'ship's visitor' was getting on. At the request of the Flag, the Ferranti radar trials expert had joined *Hermes* at Ascension to try to help sort out the deficiencies in the 800 Squadron radars. Having done his work in the Flagship he had come across to fit a Ferranti modification to the *Invincible* SHAR radars. I met him in the 801 crewroom.

'Hullo, John! Long time no see, eh? How the devil are you?' We knew each other pretty well from the IFTU days. 'Come on down to my cabin and let's have a chat. I'll introduce you to the Captain later — he's looking forward to saying hullo.' It was a genuinely warm welcome, and I could see that the Ferranti engineer was quite taken aback by the atmosphere in the ship. He looked tired and a little hassled after his few days in *Hermes*. Soon we were sitting in my cabin surrounded by all the paraphernalia of a CO at sea. 'Excuse the mess, but I'm a bit untidy at times and have stacks of paperwork to catch up on.'

'Actually, Sharkey, I was thinking the opposite. It is pretty spartan in *Hermes* now with everything prepared for war. No seat cushions, mirrors, etcetera. And although I can see the rest of this ship is prepared in a similar way, your cabin looks pretty luxurious.'

'Well, that's just me. I hope you will keep it to yourself but the Chief Steward is a good friend of mine and I have told him that on no account is anything to be changed or touched in this cabin. I like my comforts and reckon that if I'm going into action I might as well be well rested when I do. Anyway, as soon as the threat level gets high, this is the last place I'll be found. Other things to do, you know. Now, how are things in *Hermes*?'

John began his story.

'The first thing is that when I arrived on board I found that the squadron radars were not well-thought-of by the aircrew. They have more sets than you do, by the way, but none of them seemed to be fully tuned. Andy Auld was complaining that the maximum contact range on Sea Harrier was about 10 or 11 miles. That is well short of what Ferranti expected. On the other side of things he reckons that 801 claim a normal pick-up of 23 miles? I find that a bit hard to believe.'

'OK, I'll cover that later. Do go on.'

'Well, I tuned all the radars and showed their artificers how to do it properly. Then after putting them right on that I went to work putting the wet-weather modification into the sets — which was the real reason for me coming down here to join the force.'

'I hope you're getting extra pay for it,' I laughed. 'The MOD have actually cut our overseas allowance while we are down here; to save money! Doesn't do a lot for fleet morale. You'll be all right if you stick with us in this ship, though. Are you going to stay?'

'No, my orders are to return to *Hermes* when I'm finished here. Now, what's the score in 801?' It was obvious from his face that he was hoping for better news about our radars.

'First and foremost, the Blue Fox is performing well up to specification. We are still getting the same results as we got in the early trials. 23 miles is our expected contact range on Sea Harrier head on. And on a jumbo jet it is over 60 miles, as you and your team should know from our reports.'

It was difficult for John to swallow the contact ranges that we claimed.

'I know that's what you have always stated, Sharkey, but our own Ferranti results only give a range on the SHAR of about 18 miles. 23 miles is a little hard to believe.'

'We can demonstrate that well enough, John, while you are here. You can talk to all the pilots on the subject and also witness actual results from the Ops Room displays. And that obviously means that we don't need to call on your tuning skills to provide help for our artificers. Now, to the wet-weather snag.'

As we had passed through the Tropics, the high humidity and rain had caused a fair bit of trouble with the radars in both ships. I explained the problems and said, 'Let me leave you in the tender charge of our lead radar technician, Chief White. He knows more about this than I do and he has something to show you. After you've been down to the workshop in the hangar we'll have another chat. But I'd like you to see what the Chief has to show you before we continue. OK?'

John was taken away by the ever-smartly dressed Chief Artificer and met me later in the bar. 'I need a drink!' was all he could say initially. The Chief had taken him to the hangar and, en route, the Ferranti man explained that he had a 'fix' for the radar humidity problems. When he entered the workshop, the squadron radar boffin simply pointed to the radar on the test rig and said, 'What do you think of that?'

The 801 maintainers had already solved the problem, had engineered the necessary 'fix' on site, and had fitted the modification to all squadron aircraft. John was totally taken aback. The cure was identical to the one proposed by Ferranti.

In the bar, I simply said, 'I told you we had a good team. Now go and talk to the pilots and check their views on radar contact ranges. Then I'll buy you another beer.'

By the time he left the ship there was no doubt in John's mind about radar contact ranges or anything else. To say that he had been impressed would have been a major understatement.

'Fixes' were by no means the sole prerogative of the engineers, though. Charlie Cantan had volunteered to provide one at the latest aircrew meeting ('shareholders', as it was called). The pilots all agreed that when they went into action they wished to carry a sidearm, and the 9-mm Browning automatic pistol was the obvious choice. But there were no suitable holsters on board – at least none that would fit under the all-weather 'goon' suit and leave the pilot unencumbered in the cockpit at the same time. 'What we need is a shoulder-holster, Boss. Leave that to me!' And within twenty-four hours Charlie presented me with the prototype. It was just perfect for the job, crafted out of heavy canvas, and made its wearer feel very much like James Bond. All the pilots were to be provided with a shoulder-holster within forty-eight hours and were issued with two magazines of ammunition.

Normal rules in the service required that the ammunition had to be signed out and signed in before and after every flight. It was not difficult to persuade Wings and the Captain that this was inappropriate for war, and it was agreed that one signature would suffice and the pilots could keep the ammunition on them for the duration. I explained my views on the need for a weapon to the squadron: 'As you know, I don't expect any of you will be shot down in combat, particularly if you keep your eyes open and cover each other's 6 o'clock. But there are many other reasons why you might end up in a parachute, and the last thing I want is for you to be hosted by the Argentine secret police having your balls squeezed between two bricks! Carrying a weapon should assist you in evading capture – and, if you end up in your rubber dinghy at sea, it might deter any killer whale that fancies using you as a quick snack. Might — but I can't promise.

'On a very serious note, if you do happen to fall into enemy hands, I hope the opposition will treat you in accordance with the Geneva Convention. As you all well know, all that you are required to divulge under that Convention is your name, rank and service number. But if things do go wrong and someone starts wanting to play with your private parts, then my instruction to you all is to tell them anything they want to know — and don't feel bad about it. Thanks to the media and aviation literature they will already know how many Sea Jets we have with us, how they are armed, and so on. They will also be fully briefed on all aspects of our ship's weaponry as most of their ship's officers have been trained in the UK. So you won't be giving anything away. Is that perfectly clear?'

There was no dissent. The boys were happy.

All on board were now convinced that going into action was merely a matter of time. Dick Goodenough's men had transformed the jets with their new paint scheme into evil-looking machines of war. They were painted dark charcoal grey and were much more difficult to pick up visually in the air than before, especially against a sea background. The engines had been uprated to wartime power, giving a noticeable difference in climb performance. And the battle for the provision of AIM-9L missiles was almost over; *Invincible* was soon to receive an adequate supply.

The Wardroom on board had been transformed from its five-star comfort into an action messing compartment. Self-service was the order of the day and the food became less exotic, though just as palatable as before. Shortages of various commodities were easy to forecast and ration – including the draught beer. Officers were limited to a maximum of two pints a day, but as most ship's officers drank very little, particularly when the action started, this left a satisfactory margin for thirsty (if not bloodthirsty) aviators.

Action stations were practised frequently at irregular intervals and all personnel became used to carrying their personal lifesaving waistcoats, gas-marks and white anti-flash gear, which consisted of gloves and a balaclava type of headgear. The flash from an explosion would melt exposed skin like candle wax, and so no one needed reminding to carry this important protection.

The closer to the Falklands, the higher the concern became about possible torpedo and Exocet attacks. Captain Black briefed the crew that anyone wishing to sleep above the waterline to escape the worst effects of torpedo impact and away from possible Exocet impact zones, could do so. The choice was up to the individual. In *Hermes*, there was no such choice. Even aircrew had to leave the sanctity of their cabins and doss down on camp beds above the water line. But JJ was a wise man. He knew that there was little point rushing from one part of a ship to another when under attack. It was an even chance that you would jump out of the frying pan into the fire. The Captain remained unruffled and philosophical about the risk of injury to himself throughout the action to come, and his laid-back example worked wonders with everyone on board.

I followed the Captain's lead on personal vulnerability and explained to my pilots the official advice for aircrew – sleep in your flying kit. I also explained that I, for one, could dress and get to the flight-deck in less than three minutes in emergency and that I would adopt my normal sleeping habits — comfortably esconced in sheets and blankets. They could do as they thought fit.

The reality of action was brought home strongly to all in the force on 23 April when two accidents signalled the first casualties of the operation. In South Georgia, an SAS team that had been lifted out of tropical climes and placed on the island to help reclaim it for Britain were suffering from exposure and had to be lifted out by a helicopter from HMS *Antrim*. Flying conditions were atrocious and two aircraft crashed in their rescue attempts.

A third helicopter succeeded where they had failed. Closer to home, a Sea King Mk IV aircraft was airborne from *Hermes* at night with just a pilot and aircrewman on board, and it either ditched or crashed into the sea.

Invincible's 820 Squadron immediately mounted a search-and-rescue (SAR) effort at the scene of the crash and recovered the body of the pilot, an old friend of mine from the *Ark Royal* days. Only the aircrewman's helmet was recovered and so, as the Task Group continued south on its ever more urgent mission, three ships were detached to continue the search for the missing sailor until shortly after daybreak. They found nothing more. While the 820 air search was proceeding, I sat in their crewroom with my sister squadron's Senior Observer. It appeared that there was great confusion as to where the downed helicopter had come from and it wasn't until nearly three hours after the incident that a *Hermes* helicopter joined the 820 SAR effort. This might, of course, have been because 820 were on the scene very swiftly and too many cooks could have spoiled the broth. But reactions to the incident only helped to concern the *Invincible* squadrons more about the way ahead, and so, to get myself up to speed, I requested permission to visit *Hermes* on the following day. Permission was granted and in shitty weather in the early forenoon Robin Kent and I climbed into a Sea King to make the short transit across the water to *Hermes*.

The aim of the visit was to get together with 800 to clear up any misunderstandings about the planned way ahead and, if the opportunity arose, to talk to the Staff about how the Sea Harrier should be operated to best effect. Our large helicopter emerged out of the howling gale and the spray from an angry sea to land on a ship that quite clearly did not expect us. Communications between the two carriers' Ops Staffs had obviously fallen over somewhere, and there was some consternation as we two 801 executives made our way across the deck and into the island.

Eventually we were escorted to the 800 crewroom where we were met by my three old friends, Desmond Hughes, Neil Thomas and Tony Ogilvy; none of them were original 800 Squadron officers, but they were the only three with whom I could communicate satisfactorily. Mike Blisset, the Senior Pilot, was also in evidence in the background and even ventured a rather grudging greeting: 'Hullo, what are you two doing here?' Briefly acknowledging him, I got on with my discussions about plans for the coming action. There was no disagreement with the three 'professionals' on the tactics to be used or on the harmonisation of effort.

Whilst chatting I noticed that the 800 Duty Officer was putting up details for the next 800 sortie. To show interest I excused myself for a minute and asked Blisset what was being planned. 'Actually, we don't plan our sorties any more. We get told what to do by the Staff. This sortie is for four aircraft to get airborne and fan out with 15° between each aircraft's track to do a visual search of the area to the north-east of the Carrier Group out to 80 miles. Then we are to join up and return to the deck.'

I was dumbfounded. 'Visual search! What do you mean?'

'I mean a radar-silent mission and using the Mark I eyeball to search for ship contacts.'

I really couldn't believe my ears. 'Whose fucking stupid idea is that? One Sea Harrier can sanitise more than that area of sea for surface targets with just one sweep of its radar. The sortie is a total waste of resources! You can't seriously let the Staff run your squadron for you. They obviously haven't got a clue what they are doing.'

'I'm sorry, but that's the way it is over here and there is nothing I, or you, can do about it.' Blisset seemed resigned to it. In spite of myself, I felt sorry for the 800 team – even though in my view it was their own fault that they hadn't shown the command what good results could be achieved with the Blue Fox radar.

'Visual search, my arse! You should tell the Staff to mind their own bloody business. Just give you a task and let you decide how to do it.'

At that moment, the SAVO burst into the crewroom. He looked quite concerned, and his opening shot showed why. 'Hullo, Sharkey. Have you come to see the Admiral?' The tone of his voice indicated the consternation behind the scenes. But on more than one occasion JJ had warned me about any confrontation with the Admiral. Instead I told SAVO, 'Not at all. Just popped across to see how things are going over here. And I can't say I like what I see! What is this nonsense about the Staff programming visual searches to the north-east? Haven't they heard of the Blue Fox?'

'I don't think I should comment on that because it's not your business.' Nectar Nuts was obviously being loyal to the system, so I dropped the subject.

We sat down with SAVO and went over the points that we had already raised with the three 'professionals'. I felt that he too was in full accord with our views on the way ahead, and for a time we started to feel that at last we were getting the right message through to the Staff. But our optimism over what had been agreed with him proved to be short-lived.

By the time Robin and I returned to *Invincible* we were both of the same mind. The Staff and *Hermes* together appeared to have an understanding of Harrier capabilities that did not match our own. It was essential, therefore, in my view that the job of directing SHAR air defence operations was left to *Invincible*. That was the main message we passed to Wings and JJ on our return.

'What I plan to do, Sir, is to put our refined thoughts about airspace denial and air defence on paper in a manner that would be suitable for the Flag to digest. When you have approved it, it can be sent to the Admiral with an accompanying request for confirmation that this ship will act as the Anti-Air Warfare Control ship.'

JJ was pleased with the papers that I later presented, sent them on to the Flag, and was later assured that the AAWC responsibilities would definitely lie with *Invincible*.

The weather played havoc with the flying programme over the next few days. Tropical sunshine had disappeared and been replaced with gales, rain, sleet and fog. Alert aircraft continued to hold their vigil on deck by day and night. And the 707 intruder continued to monitor the Group's progress southwards until 25 April. Each day it would approach to between 40 and 60 miles before departing under escort. But on the 25th the air groups received clearance to destroy the intruder if it persisted in its shadowing task. As if by magic, the aircraft didn't appear again. Somehow the Argentines had got the message that the shadower could take no more liberties.

Morale remained high in *Invincible*, and was given a terrific boost when Her Majesty's Ships *Antrim*, *Brilliant*, *Plymouth* and the Royal Fleet Auxiliary *Resource* engineered the recovery from Argentine hands of the island of South Georgia. The Royal Marines carried out a virtually unopposed landing and took the small enemy garrison into custody. There couldn't have been a better tonic for the Task Force as it made final preparations for action, especially when we heard that the Argentine submarine *Santa Fé* had also been attacked and captured.

My 801 team calculated that at the present rate of progress the ships would be within range of a possible extended strike mission by the Argentine Air Force on 29 April, and that was when it was proposed to go to full alert status, particularly by day. The Flag agreed and, according to the proposals that had already been accepted, the night alert state was to be balanced to reflect the perceived and then the observed threat. Alert on deck and airborne CAP duties were to be shared on a pro rata basis by the two Air Group SHAR squadrons. With *Invincible* having eight aircraft and eleven pilots and *Hermes* having twelve aircraft and about eighteen pilots, it seemed reasonable to expect that the alert and air tasking from the Flag would reflect the difference.

Unfortunately, things didn't work out that way. The first tasking signal from the Flag for the night of 29 April directed that *Invincible* would provide half the night alert. And the level of alert was to be two aircraft manned and ready to go on deck, with two further pilots fully kitted out in the crewroom ready to scramble. My first impression was that it was an overkill, but that it was understandable as a first offering. I and Robin Kent then did our arithmetic.

Steve Thomas returning from combat—both Sidewinder missiles have been fired and two Dagger kills registered.

A typical day on the flight-deck of *Invincible* during the 'shooting war'—looking forward, with the island at right. Flyco can be seen in the distance jutting out from the island.

An 801 Squadron Sea Harrier on *Invincible's* flight-deck armed and bombed-up. The aircraft carries three 1000-pound bombs, one on each wing pylon in place of missiles, and one slung centrally; either side of the central bomb are the pods containing the 30-mm Aden cannon, loaded either with high-explosive or armour-piercing ammunition; slung inboard of each wing-mounted bomb is a 100-gallon auxiliary fuel tank.

Sea Harrier firing an AIM-9L Sidewinder—Sharkey's second kill of the war, a Mirage V Dagger, was achieved with one of these missiles.

On 4 May, Sharkey ordered his AWI, Flight Lieutenant Ian Mortimer, to photograph the Type 42 destroyer HMS *Sheffield* ten minutes after she had been hit. The starboard view proved that the massive hole amidships was at 'Exocet height', that is, made by an air-launched Exocet missile and not, as the Command believed, by a torpedo. The Staff's poor understanding and tasking of the Sea Harrier, and unwillingness to trust in its capabilites and those of its pilots, almost certainly let the Argentine Super Etendards within Exocet range.

The Argentine trawler *Narwal*, one of the very few ships in history to have been captured from the air. Found within the Total Exclusion Zone, she was first shot-up by 800 Squadron Sea Harriers and then captured by the SBS troops dropped from 820 Squadron helicopters. Her crew proved to be bona fide seamen—if drunk—apart from an Argentine Naval Intelligence Officer, who was convinced that his British captors would shoot him.

SS *Atlantic Conveyor*, carrying vital stores for the British forces, on fire after being hit by at least one air-launched Exocet on 25 May. Luckily, the Sea Harriers and RAF GR 3 ground-attack Harriers she had been carrying had been flown off to the carriers, but all but one of the six double-rotor Chinook helicopters on board, badly needed to support the land forces in their advance towards Stanley, were destroyed.

HMS *Yarmouth* comes alongside to assist the blazing *Ardent* in Falkland Sound. Mercifully, loss of life was small, largely due to the courage and professionalism of the stricken warship's crew.

Seven hours of darkness — half the night — had to be covered. It was very cold on deck sitting at alert, almost 0° C, and so we couldn't risk having pilots in the cockpit for more than 1½ hours at a time. Even that was pushing it if they were to be scrambled at the end of their alert. If each pair of pilots did 1½ hours' crewroom alert, followed by the same period of deck alert, the squadron would have to use five pairs, that is, ten of its eleven pilots, to cover the tasked period. Had the Flag made any attempt to do the same calculations? And had they taken on board the need to conserve resources by night so that the Air Group would be ready and fit to take on the much higher threat by day? We guessed that the answer to the two questions was a firm negative.

We approached the Captain and Wings and explained the situation. 'I fully agree with your sentiments, Sharkey. Wings, would you have a chat with the Staff on the secure phone and try to get this resolved? I would have thought that one at alert on deck and one in the crewroom was quite adequate.'

'Aye, aye, Sir.' Wings made the call, but to no avail. The tasking signal was to be obeyed.

It was the same story on the following night and for some reason 801 was again landed with half the effort and was given the small hours of the night to look after. If it continued in this vein, the pilots were going to face a very long flying 'day' and would be buggered in no time. That would have an adverse effect on the efficiency of air defence which, as far as I was concerned, was simply not on.

'Not only is this pretty thoughtless tasking, Sir, it is unfair to this ship and my aircrew. We are being given slightly over half the night to cover with only two-thirds of *Hermes*'s SHAR assets. And we are getting the second half of the night too, which causes most fatigue. I don't know what the reason is, but it is very counter-productive. And it must be sorted out.'

JJ was as frustrated as Wings and myself over this latest signal. He spoke to the Flag personally, but again to no avail.

'May I suggest, Sir, that if the Admiral is immovable on this issue, then we should ignore his tasking signals and do our own thing? Otherwise we are going to start losing aircraft through fatigue rather than action.'

Wings was rather keen that the squadron should get on and do as we were told, but I would not accept that. After a short debate it was agreed that the squadron would only mount half the alert ordered by the Flag, but would have an additional pilot sleeping in the crewroom on a camp bed. Honour and common sense were satisfied for the moment, but as I retired to my cabin I dreaded to think what the Flag would dream up for the following night. That was when it was more than likely that the action would start, and when we would have the opportunity to attack Port Stanley airfield in the dark.

17

The last day of April 1982 dawned grey and blustery in the South Atlantic. The sea temperature off the Falklands was about 2° C and the air temperature not much higher. In the rising tension, the Carrier Group sailed back and forth to the north-east of the islands well out of sight of land. The only sign of life above the water was the gliding presence of an occasional albatross. This was home country to the big bird and we were intruders − though it didn't seem to care. But the UK did care about who visited the islands and a Total Exclusion Zone around the Falklands was declared by the British Government. The fight to recover them from the army of occupation was about to begin.

At the morning Command Briefing, the Captain gave his HODs the news that we had been waiting for.

'Gentlemen, tonight the action will commence. The master plan is as follows. Frigates from the force will strike the first blow at night with sustained naval gunfire bombardment against targets on Port Stanley airfield. This will be followed by a Vulcan attack on the runway. The aircraft will launch from Ascension with twenty-one 1000-pound bombs. 801 will provide fighter cover for its attack. At dawn, 800 Squadron from *Hermes* will conduct an eight-aircraft attack on the airfield and a four-aircraft attack on the airstrip at Goose Green. 801 will provide fighter cover for these attacks as well. On completion, the two Sea Harrier squadrons will confront any enemy air presence from CAP stations to the west of the Carrier Group.'

He paused to let the sequence of events as ordered by the Flag sink in.

'Sharkey, I'm afraid that puts paid to the night attack on Stanley airfield by your squadron. That's a pity, after all the preparation and hard work. But that's not all... Now, here's the really bad news! 800 Squadron aircraft and aircrew will be stood down tonight to prepare for their attack. All night alert duties will be carried out by 801.'

To everyone's surprise, I said nothing. I was too disappointed to speak, and was wondering what sort of idiot had proposed a Vulcan raid from Ascension.

'Oh, and the icing on the cake is that none of the Task Force is allowed to shoot at anything in the air for the period around the ETA [estimated time of arrival] of the Vulcan.'

It was priceless. First the gunfire from the 4.5-inch guns in the frigates would wake everybody up on Stanley airfield; then a lone Vulcan would attempt to cut the runway with some iron bombs after a 3500-mile flight; while the Vulcan was in the area, the Task Group ships would not be allowed to engage anyone firing at them; and then, at dawn, the cavalry would come over the hill and take the enemy by 'surprise'. It had to be special rules for the RAF, of course. Nobody else would have the gall to insist on a weapons-tight procedure in a war zone

What I couldn't fathom out was why send a Vulcan all that way to drop just twenty-one bombs. Four of my aircraft in a card formation could do exactly the same job and probably just as accurately − but I would have to wait and see the results before claiming that. Alan Curtis used to be a Vulcan pilot, so he would know the logistics behind getting the aircraft all the way down and all the way back. I would have to have a word with him after the briefing.

'Well, Sir, at least the Flag is giving us what we asked for in terms of air defence. We can't complain at that! And we should find out pretty quickly whether night CAP is going to be an important part of our flying task.'

Before the briefing was over, the Captain passed the new Rules of Engagement to his Sea Harrier CO. 'These came in as well. You'd better make sure all your team understand them − I'm buggered if I do!'

Ralph and I each went straight to our respective crewrooms to give our teams the news. Robin showed some disappointment about the sidelining of the night attack, and when he heard about the Vulcan he couldn't contain himself.

'You've got to be joking! You have just got to be *joking*! I don't believe it! Three-and-a-half thousand miles just to deliver twenty-one bombs. It's incredible! Trust the fucking Crabs to put their noses in somewhere!' Rob rarely swore (unlike his Boss), and when he did it meant he was really wound up. I had still to tell him about the special 'weapons-tight' rules surrounding the Vulcan sortie, and the fact that 801 had been given all the night alert to do.

'That really steals the cake!' He was almost speechless. 'Just because there is a Crab aircraft in the sky, we are not allowed to defend ourselves. How on earth did C-in-C Fleet agree to that?'

'I'm as surprised as you are, Rob. But not really surprised about the night alert − just disappointed.'

'You betcha! It doesn't take all night to put a few bombs and rockets on twelve aircraft. What is this? An 800 benefit?'

'Seems a bit like it, I must admit. However, I've got to go and digest these new Rules of Engagement now. Try and fix a time for shareholders today so that I can brief all the squadron. And you can plan to have me airborne on CAP when the Vulcan pays us all a visit, OK? And one last thing, let the AEO know that the night attack is off.'

I grabbed a quick coffee from the ACRB and went aft to my cabin clutching the ROE in one hand and a bacon-and-egg sandwich in the other. As I sat and studied the paragraphs of legalistic jargon I became completely lost. The ROE were obviously based on international laws and conventions but, equally obviously, they were totally unsuited to a fighter pilot sitting in the air in a single-seat jet with hostile aircraft all around. If you followed the printed word to the letter, you would have to be shot at before retaliating – and that was too late in the fighter game. I had already decided exactly how I was going to brief the squadron, and while I waited for the Senior Pilot to tell me when that would be, I got hold of Alan Curtis so that he could play with some figures on the Vulcan raid.

After he had been briefed, Alan gave the data that I wanted to know off the top of his head. 'For a round trip of about 7000 miles you would need about ten Victor tankers to support one Vulcan. The tankers would launch before the Vulcan and keep topping each other and the Vulcan up until only one was left.'

'How much fuel does a tanker hold at launch, Al?'

'About 100,000 pounds would be a safe bet. Could be more if they decided to take on an overload.'

'So to get twenty-one bombs to Port Stanley is going to take about one million, one hundred thousand pounds of fuel? Right?'

'Right!'

'Thanks a lot, Al. Here, take these new ROE and have them photocopied for the boys, will you? But don't hand them out before I've said my few words. You can let me have my copy back at shareholders.'

I enjoyed the next few minutes playing with my calculator. One point one million pounds of jet fuel equalled about 137,000 gallons. That was enough fuel to fly 260 Sea Harrier bombing missions over Port Stanley, allowing internal fuel only and a land-on allowance of 800 pounds. Which in turn meant just over 1300 bombs. Interesting stuff! Better put a few notes on paper for the Captain. Also better brief him on the new Sea Harrier high-level bombing technique worked out by Morts.

The AWI had been looking at the feasibility of using the radar and Navhars to give fairly accurate bomb releases from 10,000, 15,000, 20,000 feet. His work was to come in most useful in the weeks ahead and was certainly something that Wings and the Captain should be briefed on.

That day I sat at alert on deck and then flew a CAP mission before I had a chance to address the squadron.

'OK chaps. Bend your ears back. I have here the new Rules of

Engagement from the UK. I am going to read them out to you, and before you leave I want you all to get your personal copy from Al.' I read the mystifying paragraphs out loud. When I had finished I looked around and chose my man. 'Charlie. What do you make of that? Is it all clear to you?'

'Clear as mud, Boss. I didn't understand a word!'

There was a chorus of support for Charlie Cantan's sentiments, and he immediately looked less uneasy.

'All right. You can all digest the written words later, but in essence they are telling you not to shoot at anyone unless you are shot at first.' I was playing to them, and why not? For a second or two the crewroom was full of indignant and very foul language. 'Hold it down, will you! I am now going to give you my own rules of engagement. As far as you are concerned they take precedence over this or any other piece of paper. Understood?'

They all knew what was coming.

'When you are airborne defending this ship you will engage and shoot down anything that moves in the skies, provided that it isn't one of ours and it isn't a Red Cross airliner carrying nuns and school kids. It is as simple as that.'

Soapy Watson never missed a trick. 'Excuse me, Boss, but how do I know if the Red Cross airliner is carrying…?'

The Senior Pilot didn't allow him to finish. 'Wind your neck in, Soapy!'

The boys were happy, and ready to go to war. And it was obvious from their faces that they were pleased that I had covered their 6 o'clock on ROE. Hypothetical wargames in Whitehall were not quite the same as a one-on-one confrontation with a flag-waving Argentine in a fully armed fighter. We all wanted to go and beat hell out of the air opposition; what we didn't want or need were sheets of small print telling us to commit suicide by letting our opponents shoot first. I understood the need for British forces to be seen to obey international conventions of war, but that could just as easily be achieved by instructing the troops to 'apply common sense and decency' to the fight. The ROE had been written with a view to protecting reputations in Whitehall, and between the lines I could detect a bureaucratic understanding that we, as individuals, were little more than cannon fodder. Good chaps, yes, and as professional as they come − but dispensable if the cause justifies it…

Later, I was to hear a rumour that the Government had been prepared to sacrifice up to 10,000 men to win the day: that certainly put cutting our allowances into perspective.

What gave me confidence, as the outbreak of hostilities approached, was that the odds were stacked against us in the air and without us the Task Force couldn't do its job. In other words, we were *not* dispensable. And it was my job to make sure that the Flag and his Staff understood that and employed our resources wisely. I would have to stand up for my pilots in the coming weeks. There was nothing left to do now but wait for the night to pass — it would be a busy day for everyone tomorrow, and while the *Hermes* jet-jockeys slept in their sacks we sat on deck at alert, freezing our balls off!

Dick Goodenough walked with me as I went out on deck to man my alert aircraft in the early hours of the morning of 1 May. The foul weather had abated. There was little cloud over the fleet and the ship had stopped heaving around at last. My aircraft was parked down aft at the stern and, as I approached it, the dim light of my torch signalled to Steve Thomas that his time on alert was over. He could unstrap and go to get some well-earned rest.

'All the standard Navhars destinations are set, Boss. You'll need to raise the seat... Have a good trip, and don't shoot the Vulcan down!' Steve had a great sense of humour — his comment about raising the seat was just a friendly reminder that I was a short-arse compared to his six feet and a few inches. He quickly disappeared towards the island, swallowed up by the dark. 'See you later, Steve.'

Dick turned to me. 'Well, goodbye, Boss. And good luck.' Did he really mean that, or was it a slip of the tongue? He was just as concerned as all of us about how this first day was going to turn out.

'Thanks, Dick, see you in an hour or so.'

I walked round the jet checking that the two missiles and the cannon had been readied for flight and action. The plane captain went with me. 'Reckon you might get some action, Sir?' he whispered. 'We're all banking on you getting the first kill, you know.'

'I should be so lucky! I hope there is some trade around up there, but I doubt it. The fireworks won't be starting just yet.'

Having strapped in, I called Flyco on the deck intercom.

'003 on alert.'

'Roger.'

And the cold wait at alert began.

At least the stars were visible now. I could feel the steady vibration of the ship's engines through the undercarriage as I settled down to speculate on what the next few hours would bring. I also wondered how I would perform in action, and what form that action would take. Were the Argentine pilots as keen to fight as my boys were; and if not, how would they play the game? One thing was certain — the importance of coming out on top in the first few engagements. If that could be achieved then the psychological advantage would be won and that could pay huge dividends.

Right now, the Mirage pilots must be looking at all the pros and cons, just as the Sea Harrier boys were. The air war was definitely going to be fought in two phases: prior to the Task Force landing the troops; and after the troops had been landed. During phase one, the tactical advantage could well lie with the Task Force. Provided that the attack on the airfield was successful, it was extremely doubtful as to whether the Argentines would bother attempting to operate fast jets from Stanley. If the Vulcan could cut the runway, that would help. But it was an easy task to fill in a bomb crater, and so the main job in phase one must be to harass the airfield on a regular basis. That could easily be arranged. On each CAP mission the SHAR could drop a single bomb on the airfield from high level. A VT fuse would do the trick, with lots of shrapnel flying all over the place!

If they were denied the use of Stanley, the Argentine fighter boys would have to come a long way to help protect their ground forces. And the Carrier Group could remain closer to the islands, but still outside the Etendard/Exocet threat line.

Phase two would provide an entirely different tactical situation. Wherever the British troops were landed, the Sea Harriers would have to provide CAP protection for them. That would be a major effort, given our meagre resources, particularly if the beach-head was established any distance to the west of Stanley. I had already planned that the two squadrons should have six aircraft on CAP at low level at any one time, and that was going to take some doing. The Argentines, on the other hand, would then have the important advantage of being able to attack the beach-head when they felt like it.

'003, Flyco. You are clear to start.'

As soon as I was turning and burning, I put the radar to 'standby' to warm up and called 'On deck'.

'Roger. Ship's head is 340°; now, now, now! Your position is 55° 05' W and 51° 12' S.' The communication link between Flyco and aircraft on deck was via a wire, not radio.

The information passed was necessary for aligning the Navhars platform. My HUD had already showed me that the aircraft was pointing 2° to the left of the ship's centre-line, and so on the third 'now' I entered 338° into the system. Geographical co-ordinates were also entered, and I was ready for launch. I changed my dimmed navigation lights from steady to flashing to tell the deck personnel and Flyco that I was ready to taxi to the launch-point. Wheel chocks were removed, and with the engine still at idle I moved up the deck to abreast of the island.

Now my world was coming alive. My mind was clear of all the subjects that had given me a pain over the past few days and I concentrated on what I loved best. Nozzle stop set to 50°. Check engine with nozzles down. Looks fine. Nozzles aft. The whole aircraft nodded in tune to the movement of the nozzles. Set rpm at 55 per cent. Nav lights to steady. Check the flight-deck crew are to one side. Check the green light from Flyco. And even before the Flight Deck Officer had brought his 'Star Wars' green wand down to the deck I had hit the throttle to the left-hand corner and released the brakes.

The ski-jump loomed large ahead and then disappeared from view. I was pressed down in my seat for a second, and then I was free. I was airborne and automatically nozzled away into wingborne flight, cleaning up the aircraft as I did so. I left the radar on standby, switched off my nav lights, levelled momentarily at 800 feet and then, as I throttled back to maintain 420 knots, gently descended to a comfortable 200 feet above the waves and turned onto my opening heading towards the Falklands.

After clearing the area around the Carrier Group I smoothly applied power and climbed to 20,000 feet to await the arrival of the Vulcan. Dimming my cockpit lighting almost to extinction, I could see that the cloud cover over the islands was extensive. That was a pity, as I was hoping to be able to see the flash of shells and bombs exploding.

Twenty minutes or so later I heard the V-bomber boys check in. They were on a discreet frequency and so I welcomed them with 'Morning!' No reply came, so I didn't persist. My job was to be ready to intercept any aircraft threatening the Vulcan, and I was relying on radar pickets to come up on frequency should they detect any bogeys inbound. There were none.

For me, the flight was very much a non-event. I enjoyed being up under the stars but saw nothing of the action. After being airborne for 50 minutes I heard the coded call from the Vulcan indicating that my task was complete. The bombs had gone and now so had the bomber.

Recovering to the deck was going to be a little different from usual, the difference being that none of the ships would have any lights on at all – including *Invincible*. The carrier would only switch on the dimmest deck lighting when the Sea Jet was about 200 yards from touchdown. Then, as soon as the wheels touched the deck, it would be off with the lights and back to 'darken ship'.

I descended to low level and, using my Navhars, navigated through the briefed safety lane to where I expected *Invincible*'s aircraft marshalling area to be. Switching my radar to transmit, I found what I thought was *Invincible* amongst the many contacts on my neat green radar display and called the Approach Controller. '003 estimating 6 miles on the approach. 800 feet, gear down and locked, 2200 pounds.' I had stacks of fuel.

'Roger, 003.' It was Tony Walker's familiar voice. 'I have you at 5½ miles. Ship's head 320°. Wind over the deck 18 knots.'

It was an eerie feeling. There was I preparing to land, carrying out all the normal checks, but there was only total blackness ahead as I started the descent. Not a light anywhere. But the Blue Fox confirmed that at least one ship was ahead where *Invincible* should be, as did Tony's calls. 'Half a mile.'

I hit the hover stop, concentrated on levelling at and maintaining 100 feet on the radio altimeter, and started to feed on power as the wings lost their lift. Still blackness ahead. Approaching 100 knots and a quarter of a mile. Height good; angle of attack pegged on 8°; wind-vane on the nose in line. I called 'Lights!' and was amazed at the size *Invincible* assumed as the subdued deck lighting suddenly shattered the darkness. That was much more comfortable. There were no calls from Flyco as I established the hover, translated sideways over the deck edge, and settled onto the deck.

Soon it would be dawn. With luck an exciting day lay ahead.

In the crewroom I found E-J and Paul Barton getting ready for the off. They were to launch in the dark and be on CAP to the north of Stanley when the 800 Squadron airfield attack took place. In spite of a long night's alert on deck, practically all the pilots were gathered together to monitor progress. 'H' was there as well; never a day would go by in the next few weeks without him taking a strong interest in 801 activities.

'Morning, Robin. Morning "H". Before you ask, there was nothing for me to do up there. The Vulcan came and went and that was all there was to it. Weather is good, though.'

As the next pair set out for the flight-deck, I called 'Go for it, E-J! Don't come home without one!' E-J just grinned. It was obvious that he couldn't wait to get airborne and I knew that, given the slightest chance, he would be in there fighting and knocking them down like ninepins.

The faces of the other pilots were a bit of a mixture. All were undoubtedly apprehensive. Some showed it, some didn't. It was one time that I couldn't get into their minds to read them. And there was little inclination to chat, although Charlie, Morts and 'H' were adding up the pros and cons of the *Hermes* air attack. The boys from the Flagship would be on their way to the target now — at least they had all had plenty of air-to-surface practice! I envied them their task, and was crossing my fingers for them.

About forty interminable minutes after dawn the good news came through. All *Hermes* aircraft were safely through the target and returning to the deck. A flood of relief swept through the crewroom and soon everyone seemed to be back to their usual selves. Most of the tension had disappeared. Robin and Brian Haig had already manned their jets and would be launched before E-J and Paul returned.

Out over the northern coast of East Falkland, part of E-J's wish had come true. The crewroom was hushed as he and Paul debriefed what had happened.

Their air defence controller in HMS *Glamorgan* had warned them of the approach of a pair of high-level bogeys from the west. The CAP had been vectored towards them for 'trade' and the enemy aircraft had turned away. It was obvious that the Argentines had good area-surveillance radar installed on the islands and that they were keeping the Mirages informed of every move made by the CAP. When the CAP returned to its station, the Mirages again approached, only to turn away again as soon as the CAP made a move to intercept. This shadow-boxing went on for some time until the Mirages made a more positive move, descended, and seemed to be committed to an engagement.

The CAP pair had piled on the coals and headed towards the opposition. Just before intercept was inevitable, the Mirages turned away and retreated over the land with the Sea Harriers in hot pursuit. Whether it was a pre-planned trap or not, as soon as the CAP pair were over the coast the grey dawn sky around them was suddenly lit up with a fireworks display. Or that's how Paul Barton described it. For a few milliseconds he enjoyed watching the trails of light all around him — then he realised that he was under fire from surface-to-air guns using tracer. There was no indecision between the two Sea Harrier pilots. Breaking hard away from the retreating Mirages, they returned to the calmer skies over the sea.

It was their first taste of action and, from the sound of the debrief, they had enjoyed it.

Robin Kent's pair returned from CAP in a slightly different frame of mind. The ship's Ops Team had been monitoring their CAP frequency throughout the mission and had heard what sounded like a proper dog-fight developing. There was talk of missiles flying between the aircraft, although no claims of any kills.

When they entered the crewroom it was pretty obvious that Brian Haig was still a little taken aback by it all. A pair of enemy aircraft, probably Mirages, had played the same game as had E-J's and Paul's opposition until eventually there seemed to be an opportunity to get in close to them. The Mirages were much higher than the CAP and were descending towards the intercept point at high speed. Although apparently no visual contact was made, the tiny Mirages blending in with the blue sky, Robin and Brian couldn't help but notice the small white, finned missile that smoked its way towards them and eventually passed between them. While they were concentrating on evading that, the Mirage pair turned and ran for home.

It was all good stuff. Each pair had been exposed to the enemy fighters, and had gained some experience and a lot of knowledge from their missions. The Mirages were obviously not too keen on mixing it, otherwise full combat would have developed. Their tactics appeared to be to enter any intercept from high level with a lot of energy or speed. When they were met head-on they would release ordnance, turn away and return to base. It was early days yet, but already these tactics were making me feel a little frustrated. I wanted to see a result.

My turn on CAP came soon enough and, after Soapy's strong early resistance to being 'nursed' by me, it was poetic justice that he was programmed as my wing-man for this trip. Steve Thomas was getting some rest after his night alert and was to fly later in the day.

Our CAP station was about 10 miles to the north-east of Volunteer Point and only 20 miles from Stanley. As we set up the patrol in battle formation at 12,000 feet, we could see little of the islands with only one or two rocky mountain peaks jutting through a layer of low cloud. The tops of the cloud were a brilliant white and there were some breaks in it, which would be useful if we needed to get down below in a hurry. The 'D' in *Glamorgan* was directing us from a few miles to seawards of Port Stanley. There wasn't a sign of any Mirages.

From our pre-flight briefing we had learned that a couple of Task Force frigates were prosecuting a possible submarine contact to the north of Cape Bougainville and were susceptible to attack from any aircraft at Stanley. The anti-submarine operation was only about 20 miles to the west of our CAP station and so we were in a good position to provide assistance if needed. *Glamorgan* suddenly called us up.

'I have two, no, three contacts, slow moving, departing Stanley and turning up the coast to the north. Could be light aircraft or Pucaras.' The Pucara was a very sturdy ground-attack machine with excellent firepower. Our battle pair countered round to the south and commenced descent. 'Ten miles south of you now' called the 'D' in *Glamorgan*.

Both of us pilots were locked on to our radar screens. To my absolute delight, Soapy came up on the air: 'I have them, Boss! Three contacts on radar well below at 6 miles. 20° right.'

'Roger. They are probably below the cloud. Let's get down there fast and have a look.' We increased our rate of descent and were passing through a gap in the cloud layer when both of us saw one of the bogeys to the right, in our 2 o'clock at about 1½ miles. It looked more like a T-34 than a Pucara and was just pulling up into the cloud. It obviously knew it had company.

'Tally ho! Right 2 o'clock. Just entering cloud.' My voice was strained with excitement as I pulled maximum G towards the enemy aircraft. I checked my gun safety flap was up and commenced firing as I raked the gunsight from below and upwards through the target. It was close-range stuff but with no chance of steady tracking, and I continued firing until both I and the Argentine became engulfed in the cloud. The whole thing had taken just a few seconds, and I knew I was dangerously close to colliding with the T-34. I wasn't wrong! The dark shape of the other aircraft emerged suddenly from the dense fog ahead, grew very large and flashed underneath me, again lost from view. That was too close for comfort, I thought. Which way? Up or down?

I broke through the cloud-tops into brilliant sunshine, looked round rapidly, and realised I was on my own; so I rolled on my back and pulled hard down through the 2000-foot-thick cloud layer. As I broke the base of the cloud, there they were again! Standing out as bold as brass against the browns and greens of the Falklands coast. I could see all three of them this time, and they were jettisoning their under-wing stores. But I was practically above them and as I manoeuvred hard round to the right and down towards them they again went for the cloud and disappeared.

'I've lost them in the cloud, Soapy. Where are you?'

'I'm now above the cloud, Boss. Nothing up here.'

'OK. Stay above and I'll remain below. Tally ho! Oh, shit! Just passed one head-on, Soapy. He's in and out of the cloud heading south over the land.'

In the end, the cloud defeated us. We knocked it off before getting too close to the Stanley defences and returned to the CAP station. I was exhilarated, but annoyed with myself. How had I missed the bloody thing? It had been a snap shot with no time even to try to get a tracking picture — but all the same it was one chance blown. Still, I thought, feeling a little more cheered, those sods didn't get anywhere near the frigates to the north so it wasn't all for nothing.

'Leader, I have possible trade for you.' It was *Glamorgan* again. Things were getting busy. 'Three contacts bearing 190° at about 40 miles. They are very high, estimating 38,000 feet, and fast. Heading straight towards you.'

'Roger!' I thought fast and remembered E-J's shadow-boxing. 'Steady on north, Soapy. We'll spoof them into attacking us. Call the ranges, "D", and we'll turn into them late.' I was going to let the Mirages think that they hadn't been detected and that they had a clear shot at my 6 o'clock.

The *Glamorgan* 'D' continued to read out the range of the bogeys astern of us. '30 miles. 28 miles. They are now supersonic. 23 miles. Coming down the hill. 18 miles. 15 miles.'

'Counter port, Soapy!' Our two SHARs turned hard to the left through 180°. Half way through the turn, my radar lost its stabilisation. Manoeuvring against the earlier threat had probably upset the reference platform. I steadied, nose high, and my eyes searched hard against the pale blue of the sky to try to pick up the enemy fighters.

'8 miles.'

'Tally ho!' This was it. I didn't have blood in my veins any more, just pure adrenalin. 'Three trails, 12 o'clock high. I'm going for the left-hand man. You take the right; then we'll sort out the middle one later.' The 'trails' were smoke trails coming directly towards us in a steep descent. Were the Mirages passing through a condensation layer? I couldn't work it out. My Sidewinder cross was already on my chosen target but I could get no acquisition tone. Then I started to make out the target — it wasn't an aircraft, it was white, with fins... Must be a head-on missile. 'They're missiles, Soapy! Keep your eyes peeled for the aircraft.'

My excitement subsided as the 'missiles' ran out of steam and plunged towards the sea below before reaching us. I craned my neck up and around to try to spot the enemy, but there was just empty blue sky. Not even Soapy was to be seen. I felt suddenly vulnerable on my own without the cross-cover from my Number Two.

'I've lost visual, Soapy. Better head for the clouds.'

'I'm already there, Boss.' Soapy was obviously no fool. I felt all the tension go and laughed — at least Soapy had had the sense to run for cover when he lost the picture. We joined up with the help of *Glamorgan* and returned to the deck.

It had been an exciting sortie. *Glamorgan* had tracked the three Mirages running for home as I attempted to shoot at their 'missiles'. Again they had been unwilling to get stuck in. I was very disappointed that the squadron had still not registered its first kill. It took about three days for me to stop blaming myself for missing the T-34. Later, when the war was over, I found out that all the 30-mm that I had fired was not in vain. One shell had exploded in the rear cockpit of the T-34, but it was empty at the time.

As 1 May slowly passed by a real sense of frustration set in. The enemy was avoiding a fight and we could do little about it. All that changed, however, when Steve Thomas and Paul Barton got airborne together in the afternoon.

18

During the final three hours of daylight on 1 May our Sea Harriers were able to demonstrate their superiority to the enemy in convincing style. Predictably, and to my absolute delight, it was the 801 team that made full use of the aircraft weapon system and showed once and for all that the Blue Fox radar was worth its weight in gold. At least in my book, and to any unbiased observer of the events, we had put paid to all the sarcastic remarks about the aircraft's avionic systems and showed that the tactics and training of the three years leading up to the Falklands crisis had been both correct and worthwhile. Soapy Watson had already ensured intercept on the T-34s encountered in the morning by gaining an excellent look-down radar contact on them at low level. Steve Thomas and Paul Barton were now to provide the air intercept *par excellence*. And then the two QFIs, Alan Curtis and Mike Broadwater, were to finish the day off with the icing on the cake.

Lieutenant Thomas and Flight Lieutenant Barton launched for CAP duties, checked out their weapon systems on each other, and took up their station under the control of *Glamorgan*. The weather hadn't changed and their air patrol was sandwiched between a startlingly blue sky above and a brilliant white carpet of cloud-tops below. It wasn't long into their mission before they were advised of trade approaching from the west at high level. *Glamorgan* had made contact on what appeared to be a pair of Mirage III fighters inbound towards them.

Initially the Mirages played the same tactics as in the morning, closing towards the CAP pair and then retreating when menaced. But the Argentine pilots must have become as bored as we were by these cat-and-mouse games, and must have been adding up the odds for and against them. They could well have been forgiven for believing that they had a considerable tactical advantage over the Task Group fighters. This was a logical assumption because they were higher and faster and, when used to good effect, this extra energy of position and speed could be made to pay dividends in a dog-fight. They also were looking down against a white, cloud-top background which made it much easier for them to see their targets when in visual range — the Sea Jets would stand out as distinct black dots against the cloud. The SHAR pilots would have much more difficulty seeing the Mirages against the blue background of the sky. Obviously all these factors combined to give the Argentine pilots confidence, because they suddenly stopped shadow-boxing and committed themselves to the fight.

'Looks as though they mean business this time.' *Glamorgan* had detected them coming down the hill fast towards the CAP. Steve and Paul increased power, entered a gentle climb towards the opposition and put all their concentration into gaining radar contact on the Mirages.

'25 miles,' from the 'D' in *Glamorgan*.

'20 miles.'

Steve concentrated hard on the small, square radar screen. Was he looking high enough? They must be there somewhere. Am I on the right range-scale?

His doubts disappeared when suddenly the two small, thin radar blips appeared. He had contact at 17 miles.

'I've got them, Paul. 10° high at 17 miles. 10° right. Judy!' He took control of the intercept from *Glamorgan*. This is what all the months of practice had been for, and now he was in a perfect position to execute the 'hook' manoeuvre. '15 miles. I'm going head-on. You take it round the back.'

Immediately, Paul took a split to the left, allowing him to build up some lateral separation from the two Mirages so that he could turn back in on them without flying through their formation. He let his nose drop a fraction to allow the jet to build up more speed, and steadied. And all the time his head was down in the cockpit as he waited for confirmation on his own radar of the target position. 'I have contact! Right 30. 11 miles.'

Everything was running like clockwork. The only question was whether the Mirages would turn away. Not this time — they were either going to mix it or fly through. Things began to happen fast. The closing rate between the two sets of fighters was more than 1 mile every 3 seconds. Steve had locked his radar-beam on to his prey and at about 4 miles he visually picked out the tiny dot that was the Mirage through his Head-Up Display, neatly framed by the four arms of the radar-acquisition cross.

'4 miles. Visual. Attempting Sidewinder lock.' The Sidewinder wouldn't lock. The Mirage boys must have throttled back, thus reducing the heat coming from their jet pipes to prevent the head-on shot. What about their own head-on missiles? They were radar-guided rather than heat-seekers, and if the Mirage pilot had locked on with radar Steve could be in trouble.

Just as he was about to fly through the pair of delta-winged jets, slightly low on them, two shapes detached from the Mirages and smoked past Steve's cockpit. Nearly brown pants time!

Then he was through the enemy pair and reversing hard to follow them.

157

He had his control-stick back in his stomach and his head craned over his right shoulder as he juddered round to the right. Meanwhile, Paul had gained visual contact and was turning in hard on the two Mirages from their right. They were not in a good formation; one was ahead of the other and so they couldn't give each other cross-cover. As he turned into them, the trailing man pulled his nose up through the horizon and started a fairly gentle turn to the right. He can't have seen Paul coming, otherwise he would have been manoeuvring like sin — he must have been concentrating on Steve's aircraft position. Very quickly, he was in Paul's sights. The Sidewinder growled its acquisition, he pickled on the firing button and called 'Fox Two away!'

The missile thundered off the rails like an express train and left a brilliant white smoke trail as it curved up towards the heavens, chasing after the Mirage which was now making for the stars, very nose-high. Paul was mesmerised as the angry missile closed with its target. As the Sidewinder made intercept, the Argentine jet exploded in a vivid ball of yellow flame. It broke its back as the missile exploded and then disintegrated, before its remains twisted their way down to the cloud and sea below.

'Splash one Mirage!' called the excited SHAR pilot. Then the incredible moment was over and he looked around hurriedly for his leader and the other Mirage. 'Where are you, Steve?'

Steve had turned hard back into the fight, saw Paul on the tail of one Mirage, and then detected the second bogey in a tight spiral descent towards the clouds. This was a well-known and over-used classical defensive manoeuvre. It was supposed to make tracking by a menacing fighter difficult, but it was a mistake.

'I'm going for leader. Below you.'

Steve rolled on his back and pulled hard and down almost to the vertical. He tracked the Mirage and, when his Sidewinder growled, released the missile. 'Fox Two away!'

The little white messenger of death sped earthwards and intercepted the Mirage just as it disappeared into the cloud-tops. Steve couldn't be sure that a kill had been achieved so he didn't call it.

There was huge excitement in *Invincible* and *Glamorgan*. Both Ops Rooms had been monitoring the combat radio calls and cheers went up as Paul's call came in, 'Splash one Mirage!'

It was quite definitely a hero's welcome when the two landed back on board. One confirmed kill and one possible — that was more like it. The 801 pilots could hardly contain themselves as they listened to the story from the pair. They wanted to know every move in detail.

There was good news coming in from *Hermes*, too. Ten minutes after the Mirage IIIs were downed, Bertie Penfold had shot down a Mirage V supporting the attack on HMS *Glamorgan* and HMS *Arrow* off Port Stanley.

The enemy fighter-bomber had pulled off its target straight in front of Bertie's jet. And Bertie's Sidewinder had done the rest.

No one in the Task Force knew it at the time, but it later came to light that Steve Thomas's missile had proximity-fused on its target, that is, exploded next to it. The Mirage was still flying but very badly damaged, and the pilot knew he couldn't possibly attempt to make it back to the mainland. But he was under the cloud layer, close to Port Stanley airfield and had control of his machine. So he elected to fly to the airfield and either land or eject there. While he was making up his mind what to do he made it to the airfield's overhead, and then decided to clear his wings of all unnecessary weight. He jettisoned the under-wing stores (missiles) to make his aircraft more easily controllable during the approach to landing. It was his second and last mistake. The troops on the ground believed that they were being attacked and opened fire, shooting the stricken Mirage out of the sky.

Having listened to the debrief on the combat, I left the crewroom in very high spirits to take up my alert on deck. All the squadron engineers were celebrating too as I strapped in, called to Flyco that I was at alert, and switched on my radio. I selected the CAP control frequency and listened in to what was going on in the air. Alan Curtis and Mike Broadwater were airborne.

Daylight was nearly over when the 'D' in *Invincible* called up the CAP pair. 'I have a spoke bearing 320° and a possible contact at 120 miles. Suggest you investigate.' ('Spoke' was jargon for intercepting an electronic emission such as radar or jamming on a particular heading.) Was there something there or not? The possible contact had disappeared. Was it an aircraft in descent? It could be an air raid on the way in to attack the force.

Alan took no chances. 'Roger. Closing the bearing and investigating.' He took his CAP pair onto a heading of 050° and intercepted the 320° bearing at about 40 miles from the ship. 'Now outbound on 320 in descent.'

There wasn't much to go on but it was definitely worth a look, he thought. The squadron had practised low-level air intercepts like this many times, and as the sea was relatively calm the Blue Fox radar should be able to see what was there, if anything.

The CAP levelled off at about 3000 feet in the gathering gloom of dusk. Cloud-tops were about a thousand feet below them as they progressed outwards from the force watching their radar screens intently. Alan soon found out that there was 'something', and that it was inbound towards the force.

'Two contacts bearing 315 at 24 miles. They are on the deck and appear to be in battle formation. Taking it round the back!' My heart leapt. Curtis had gained contact. Good for you, Alan! He was going to do a standard intercept and approach the bogeys from their stern quarter.

Mike Broadwater followed his leader as they jinked to the right, and then he too established contact. 'There are three of them, Alan.'

'Affirmative. I'll take the lead aircraft.' It was definitely getting a bit dark as the two Sea Jets penetrated the cloud and descended towards the sea. From what Alan could gather from his radar, it looked as though the enemy was no more than 200 or 300 feet above the water. He commenced his final turn in to the targets, keeping it a little tight so as not to get sucked. There they were! Three Canberras!

'Tally ho!' The enemy aircraft were in a loose battle formation and had not detected the approach of the Sea Harriers.

He acquired the lead aircraft with his first Sidewinder and fired from just behind the wing line. The missile curved away from his jet and down to its target. It impacted the Canberra at the wing root and disappeared into the fuselage. There was no big bang. No reaction. Was he dreaming? Alan fired his second missile. As he did so, the Canberra exploded into a dozen pieces and the second missile homed on to the debris as it fell into the sea. 'Splash one Canberra!'

Meanwhile, Mike Broadwater had acquired and fired at the trailing Canberra. His first missile fell short and he fired a second. As far as he could make out, it appeared to proximity-fuse under the target aircraft, but he wasn't sure. And by that time both remaining Canberras had commenced full evasion and disappeared into the cloud.

As I sat listening to it all on deck I could hear some indecision in the two fighter pilots' voices as they joined up after the fight and prepared to recover to the ship. They were obviously still wound up with excitement, and couldn't concentrate their minds on simple things like deciding at what height to fly. Both were concerned about their fuel states, for night was approaching fast and they had 70 miles to run. I transmitted what they needed to know.

'Full power climb to 15,000 feet. 330 knots. Cruise descent. Your fuel is fine. Well done!'

A day of mounting frustration had ended on a really high note. Two, possibly three Mirages accounted for, and one, possibly two Canberras. And, most important of all, there had been no Sea Harrier losses. It was just the start that I had been hoping for.

At the Command Briefing that night, the day's events were discussed in some detail. Wings and the Captain were very pleased with the end results and were keen to hear the squadron's views on lessons learned from the engagements.

'It was a pretty frustrating day to begin with, Sir. The Mirages were on site but didn't seem to want to play. They would make as if to attack and then at the last minute would turn away from the CAP and use their speed advantage to shoot off home. It seems as though they spoofed E-J and Paul

Barton into following them over anti-aircraft guns on the island to the north-west of Stanley. That was a bit of a shock to the system, but the boys took it well.

'The strange thing is that whenever it looked as though an engagement was on, we'd find these "missiles" winging their way towards us and the Mirages would disappear. We know that they probably have a French-made head-on missile, but if that's what we have been seeing then they were certainly fired without the enemy getting an acquisition first. As you know, the Mirage III only has a pretty simple radar — its nowhere near as capable as the Blue Fox. And looking down with it would not give them much information. So my best guess at present is that they are firing ordnance at us without any real hope or belief that they will hit us — and they must be releasing the "missile" on ranges given by their ground controllers. It's all a bit of a hope and a prayer on their side, as far as I can make out. But the ground control radar that they have is excellent, and somehow that needs to be knocked out or they will continue to plot our aircraft movements for the duration.

'Briefly on the action, we failed to shoot down the T-34s but did stop them getting at the Anti-Submarine Group to the north of Stanley. Thomas and Barton did a tremendous job on the two Mirage IIIs. It was a classic engagement making full use of the radar and of the tactics that we've planned and trained for. And it will certainly give the enemy a lot to think about! It was the only time that they committed to the fight and they were well beaten. Curtis and Broadwater did an equally impressive job on the Canberras. Full marks to our "D" for spotting the contact in the first place. What really pleased me though was the fact that the intercept was completely autonomous by the CAP pair; and it was against low-level targets. You don't get many better radar pick-ups than that against the Canberra because it has quite a low radar signature. I'd love to hear what the surviving Canberra crews reported when they got home.

'In summary, Sir, I believe we have given them a good lesson today. It was what we all hoped for and now we have to wait and see how it affects their style of operation. Of course a lot of credit must go to the "D" in *Glamorgan*. He did an excellent job all day long. And a lot of credit must also go to the way the boys handled the Blue Fox radar under operational conditions. Let's hope we have heard the last of *Hermes*'s doubts on that issue... Do you have any news from *Hermes* or the Flag, Sir?'

'No, I don't, surprisingly, Sharkey.' JJ replied. 'Not directly anyway. But we have intercepted a press release which says that a *Hermes* Sea Harrier aircraft shot down the first enemy fighter today. That's wrong, of course! Barton got the first kill, but that's water under the bridge now. What we haven't had is anything at all from the Flag to say "Bravo Zulu". And that disappoints me more than a little.' 'Bravo Zulu' is a senior officer's formal way of saying well done. The Admiral's staff had not even acknowledged the 801 kills, and that was very bad form. 'But I'm delighted with the results and I want to say so to your pilots in the bar later on this evening. OK?'

'Thank you, Sir.'

Wings, on the ball as usual, chipped in: 'Actually, I've had a chat with SAVO on the secure line, Sir, and have some news on the results of this morning's airfield attack. And some news of Bertie Penfold.

'It appears that the Vulcan's bombs all fell just over the target. The first bomb's crater clipped the edge of the runway and the remainder carved a path through a tent site to the east of the tower. Not quite what was hoped for! I think it was Neil Thomas who had drawn the short straw for the final run over the target after the *Hermes* effort, and he believes that the 800 attack certainly destroyed one light aircraft on the ground, possibly an Islander. And at Goose Green they think they destroyed a Pucara on the ground. No casualties, but a couple of the SHAR came back with some bullet-holes in the fuselage. Quite successful, I should say, particularly as the 800 attack was not intended to hole the runway. We'll get some high-level photographs taken soon to confirm the damage. Sharkey, can you see to that, please? What is important, I think, is that the runway is still usable.'

He had hit the main point on the head. Runway interdiction with simple iron bombs is not easy, and even if you do get the bombs on target, crater damage can usually be repaired within hours.

'Thanks, Dusty. I understand that the Vulcan will be having another go in a couple of days.' The Captain wasn't impressed with the runway denial results. 'Anything to add before we hear more from Wings, CO 801?'

'This might not be the best time to go into it, Sir, but I have a few figures here which will definitely be of interest to you concerning the Vulcan effort.'

'Do go on, Sharkey. I'd like to hear about that.'

'Well, Alan Curtis used to fly the Vulcan and knows a fair bit about its capabilities and what can be done with air-to-air refuelling. We have estimated that in order to get the aircraft over the target with twenty-one bombs it would have taken not less than ten AAR Victor tankers each loaded with 100,000 lbs of fuel to support the mission. Not counting the spare Vulcan that would undoubtedly have been airborne, that makes a total fuel usage in the air of something like 1.1 million pounds; that is 137,000 gallons. In Sea Harrier terms and in the five-bomb configuration with a land-on allowance of 800 lbs, that equates to 260 sorties delivering 1300 bombs. Or, with five aircraft in card formation over the target we could have dropped twenty-five bombs.'

JJ was busily taking notes on the figures, 'How very, very interesting,' he said.

'How would you drop those from high level, Sharkey?' Wings had already been briefed on the work that Mortimer had done. 'The Vulcan was designed for high-level work, wasn't it? But not the Sea Harrier.'

'Yes it was, Sir. But we believe our avionics package is a lot more advanced and just as capable as that of the Vulcan. The AWI has done the sums for a bombing release from 10,000, 15,000 and 20,000 feet. We use the radar and Navhars combined to time the release from an accurate radar fix. It has all been worked out and we'd like to try it soon on the airfield. But we're not thinking of runway interdiction — that requires a lot of bombing effort and is a thankless task when you find that any damage is repaired within twenty-four hours. What we propose is damaging thin-skinned targets and keeping the enemy awake, not knowing when the next bomb will fall. And we would stick to VT-fuse bombs for greater carnage over a bigger area.'

'Fascinating,' JJ enthused. 'Let me know when we are going to try it. Now, what's the other news from the Flagship, Wings?'

'Apparently, there is a bit of nausea going on over there because Bertie Penfold has reacted rather badly to his Mirage kill. I believe that the sight of the Mirage going up in a ball of flame in front of him — and presumably burning the pilot — got to him.'

I knew Bertie extremely well. 'I can't see that that is worth making a fuss about,' I interrupted. 'Bertie did all that could be asked of anybody. He shot the opposition down and should get a pat on the back.'

'I don't think that's the way they see it,' Wings responded. 'They are already talking about "lack of moral fibre" over there.'

'Good God!' I was amazed. 'That just wouldn't be right to call the man a coward. If he does nothing more, he has earned his keep.'

'I tend to agree.' The Captain drew the briefing to a close with the news that the night-tasking signal for the Sea Harrier alert had arrived from the Flag. 'You won't believe this, Sharkey. Your squadron is tasked with doing all tonight's alert. That is all night long — no alert for 800. I'm very angry and will be speaking to the Admiral personally about it as soon as this briefing is over. I really am getting fed up with the Staff!'

It took quite a long call to resolve the problem, but eventually it was agreed that 801 would only have to take the first half of the night's alert; two on deck and two in the crewroom.

'Shall we do it our way, Sir?' I asked hopefully.

'Affirmative.'

That evening, Wings escorted the Captain to the bar for a celebration drink with the squadron. It was a real pleasure for the squadron and the rest of the Wardroom to entertain the Old Man, and he made a point of personally congratulating the heroes of the hour: Paul Barton, Steve Thomas, Alan Curtis and Mike Broadwater.

The night alert Sea Harrier crews left early to prepare for their vigil on deck, and once the Captain had departed I invited Robin Kent to my cabin for a nightcap and to discuss the day's events.

Both of us were feeling pretty jaded, and not a little angry about the thoughtless and provocative tasking signals that kept on coming to the squadron from *Hermes*. It also appeared that the tasking anomalies hadn't all been confined to 801 and *Invincible*.

Neither of us had understood the wisdom of sending *Glamorgan* and *Arrow* inshore by day to continue the naval gunfire bombardment of the airfield. It had been reasonable as a surprise action by night, but to repeat the treatment by day was asking for trouble. And trouble had come in the form of three Mirage V Daggers. They had attacked and caused minor strafing damage to both ships, although the sailor in *Arrow* who received shell splinters in the chest might not have agreed with the description 'minor damage'. It was one of these Mirages that had been shot down by Bertie. Was it a worthwhile risk to hazard the warships when little was likely to be achieved by their gunfire? Robin and I thought not.

Robin brought the conversation closer to home. 'I know we are all feeling the pace already, Boss, but I have a strong feeling it is going to get worse. You and I are used to sleeping under any conditions, but some of the youngsters didn't get any sleep at all last night.'

'Oh? Why not?'

'It's all this bloody vibration down aft when the ship has got a lot of revs on. They can't shut their minds to it — particularly Charlie and Steve Thomas.'

The vibration was indeed a menace. *Invincible* had been built by Vickers, and when they were given the plans for the ship by the naval architects at Bath they insisted that with the proposed design there would be very high vibration levels in the ship at particular speeds; especially in the aft section (where all the officers slept). The naval architects apparently told Vickers to mind their own business and build the ship. After the *Invincible* had been launched, on her first high-speed trials, the heavy vibration set in, just as the builders had predicted. And now, in a war situation, with the ship regularly having to manoeuvre at high speed, the problem had come home to roost. My cabin was no better than anyone else's. Anything at all left on the desk would be removed by the vibration in less than 30 seconds — it was that bad.

'We had better keep a close watch on them. If anyone is out on his feet, I'll take him off flying for forty-eight hours and get the Doc to dose him up with sleeping tablets.' Robin was right about my own ability to sleep. The vibration didn't bother me — I'd slept in all sorts of uncomfortable places before. But on the night of 1 May I did find it difficult.

I couldn't take my mind off my encounter with the T34s and the Mirages.

I blamed myself for missing the snap shot and wasn't in the mood to be rational about it — otherwise I would have realised that with a snap shot you have to be more than lucky to hit anything. And I was quite intrigued by the Mirage tactics. There was something that kept nagging at my brain concerning the Mirage's 'missiles' and I could not fathom it out. After the war and when back in Whitehall, it finally registered with me that they weren't missiles at all. They were the centre-line fuel drop-tanks from the enemy fighters, which had been designed to be dropped in combat to make it easier for the Mirage to manoeuvre when it went into action. On each of the intercepts during which 'missiles' had been reported, the Argentines had decided to jettison their tanks and make a clean getaway. The trailing smoke was obviously not missile exhaust but unspent fuel.

Without the tanks, and it was a good bet that there were no spares available in Argentina, the Mirage IIIs would not have the range to get out to the Carrier Group and back. And although I couldn't know it then as I lay in my bunk, that was why no further Mirage IIIs were to be seen over the Falklands until much later in the conflict, and then they were limited to flights only as far as the Falkland Sound.

My mind drifted to my friend, Bertie Penfold, in *Hermes*. I hoped that the man would be treated sensibly and with compassion, but in the event I hoped in vain. Bertie didn't fly again and was sent home to the UK. For an officer who had served the Sea Harrier world so well and who had done what was asked of him in combat, it seemed a very poor thank you. When I eventually heard the full story I was simply disgusted.

I finally dropped off to sleep with happy thoughts about the Blue Fox radar and its performance on the day. Sadly, however, few ever appreciated or acknowledged that the 801 kills of 1 May could not have been achieved without the radar. Nor would the anti-submarine frigates have been saved from attack. There was only one further kill during the war resulting from full use of the SHAR radar and weapon system, and that also fell to 801. All the remaining kills were at low level and close to or over land in defence of San Carlos and other ground troop locations — where there was no chance for anyone to use the aircraft's full weapon system.

19

There was neither sight nor sound of the enemy air effort on 2 May 1982. Some reaction to their previous day's losses had been expected and so the Flag had moved the Carrier Group further to seaward in anticipation of retaliation. Exocet represented the most thought-provoking above-water threat, and my Planning Team were more than interested to find out whether the squadron threat-reduction exercise had come up with the right answer. The outer ring of air-defence pickets was now well outside the calculated 425-nautical-mile safety range from Argentine airfields. No one was taking any chances.

Airborne CAP stations were manned throughout daylight hours, and additional alert Sea Jets were ranged on deck. The previous day's activities had put an edge on the squadron's appetite for action but the hours of searching the skies with radar and with the Mark I eyeball bore no fruit. There was no sign of the enemy.

My days were becoming distinctly blurred. Alert, airborne, alert, airborne, night alert, airborne; although being on alert on deck was more often than not followed by a return to the crewroom. In between came the Command Briefings, squadron updates, a bite to eat, an occasional beer, and intermittent sleep.

By the evening of the 2nd I was pooped. At the Command Briefing I learned that the Argentine fleet had put to sea. To the south of the Falklands a group of warships led by the Exocet armed-cruiser *General Belgrano* was being shadowed by the nuclear submarine HMS *Conqueror*. This knowledge gave rise to the natural question in the Task Group: where was the Argentine carrier? Nobody knew. Logically, it should be to the north if the enemy was planning a fleet action against the Task Group. I put my thoughts to the Captain.

'If there is some sort of pincer move on against us, Sir, we can soon verify it. Why don't we send one Sea Harrier out to the north-west for 200 or 300 miles? It would be a radar-silent outbound mission with a letdown to low level at the far end. Having cruised for, say, 40 miles at low level, the SHAR would transmit on radar and see what he can find. If there is no contact at low level he can climb up and sanitise the ocean for contacts for over 300 miles across a 70-mile arc. And he can cover more sea area by returning on a different inbound bearing.'

'Remind me how far away you can pick up a frigate on your little radars — 100 miles, isn't it?'

'Correct, Sir. And the sea is very calm tonight — perfect radar conditions.'

JJ was interested. 'What do you think, Wings? Sounds a good plan to me.'

'Agreed. Who is going to fly the mission, Sharkey? You or Morts?'

'It will have to be Morts, Sir. I feel buggered, as the saying goes, and I know he feels fairly fresh.'

'All right,' said the Captain. 'Make it so please, Wings. And you'd better tell the Flag what we are doing. Don't want our boys being shot down by our own forces, do we?'

It didn't take much time to brief Mortimer. He had already discussed the idea with me and was as keen as mustard.

'What do I do if I find a bunch of ships, Boss?'

'Well, if they fire at you, get the hell out of there fast — but only after you have counted them! Seriously, I'll leave that in your capable hands, Morts. Do what you think is best, but make sure you come back in one piece.'

Mortimer launched into the dark on what must have been a very lonely flight. He was on his own miles away from his only sanctuary, *Invincible*'s deck, in a single engined-jet above an inhospitable sea and searching for an enemy carrier group that was very well defended. And if the enemy group was where we thought it might be and at full alert, then the AWI could be standing into real trouble.

It was nail-biting stuff waiting in the crewroom for the AWI to return from the reconnaissance mission. When he did, he was quite excited. Wings listened in on the debrief.

'I went out high-level as briefed, Boss; radar-silent. Let down at 200 miles and covered the next 40 miles at 200 feet. There wasn't a sound from the radar warner and not a light to be seen anywhere. At that point I thought we'd got it wrong. Then I switched my radar to transmit and, as we expected it might, all hell broke loose! The next thing I knew I was being illuminated by all sorts of radar including Sea Dart fire-control, and I counted four ship contacts less than 25 miles away. They obviously had at least one Type 42 out there.'

'What did you do?'

Morts gave me that old-fashioned look and then laughed — with feeling. 'I switched off the radar and fucked off, Boss! But not before I had got an accurate position of the threat on the Navhars, and here it is. I couldn't say whether the carrier was there or not.' The radar could not discriminate between types of ships but it was a fair bet that if a Type 42 was there, then so was the *Veinticinco de Mayo*.

Wings was delighted. 'Well done, Morts! That is excellent! Go and brief the Captain in the Ops Room. He'll be tickled pink and will want that position information to send to the Flag. First class!'

And so it was deduced that a pincer move against the Carrier Group was more than a possibility — with the recorded disposition of enemy forces it looked a reality: a surface battle group to the south-west and a carrier group to the north-west. After Morts had left for the Ops Room to brief the Captain, Wings observed that with the little natural wind of that night the Argentine carrier would have great difficulty launching its Sky Hawks. It was known that the old steam catapult on the carrier *Veinticinco de Mayo* was in poor repair and underpowered, and the Sky Hawks couldn't get off the deck carrying a war load without a strong wind to launch into. 'But we had better be on our guard...'

The enemy fleet was definitely manoeuvring for an assault on the Carrier Group and it would probably come at the same time as an air attack. Something had to be done, and quickly. The next day, the *Belgrano* was sunk by HMS *Conqueror* to the south of the islands, and that put paid to any planned pincer movement. It was learned later that the Argentine carrier group had failed to find wind for a launch and had returned to the safety of the mainland shore, never to venture seawards again during the rest of the conflict. If the *Belgrano* had not been sunk it could have been a different story.

I wondered whether it had yet dawned on the Flag and *Hermes* that the Sea Harrier's radar was more than earning its keep and should be trusted to do a good job. Without Mortimer's mission, which relied solely on the Blue Fox for its success, the carrier group would not have been found. A purely visual search at night by 800 Squadron was not feasible and if it had been attempted would have found bugger all — except possibly a missile up the chuff! Indeed, why did *Invincible* have to initiate and carry out the search to the north-east? Up to now all the reconnaissance flights around the Group had been programmed by *Hermes* and flown by her squadron. Why not this one? Was the answer that it needed special skills? There were lots of questions in my mind, but no answers coming from the Flagship.

During 4 May, it became more than obvious that you couldn't teach the old dogs new tricks. At the Command Briefing on the evening of the 3rd the Captain had broken the news that further attacks were going to be made against the airfield at Stanley. By night there would be a naval gunfire bombardment followed by a second Vulcan attack, followed by a second dawn raid by 800 Squadron. Where was the imagination of the modern military mind?

'My, my,' quoth Wings. 'That is really going to surprise everybody, isn't it?'

The predictability of it all was completely contrary to the principles of war. What on earth was the Command trying to achieve or prove? Before the Captain could give me the usual bad news about night alert, I saved him the trouble.

'Don't tell me, Sir,' I offered, '801 is to carry out all the night deck-alert tonight.'

'Absolutely correct. How did you guess?' JJ joked about it, then said in a slightly tired and resigned voice, 'Do you want me to have a word?'

'No, Sir. I think we'll have to manage tonight, and perhaps we can do it our way?' I meant a reduced alert state, otherwise no one would be fit to fly on the morrow.

'Of course.'

As on the previous occasion, 801 put up a Sea Harrier CAP to protect the Vulcan during its raid. The Vulcan came and dropped its bombs, and went. This time the V-bomber released its weapon load from a greater height than the first run of 12,000 feet, and the twenty-one bombs were off target to the west of the runway — but that mattered little. After 3500 miles en route to the target somebody in the aircraft forgot to make the switch to arm the bombs, and so they couldn't and didn't explode. Bearing in mind the doubtful operational benefit to be gained from the whole exercise, this error by the Vulcan crew was a cause for some amusement in *Invincible*. Another 137,000 gallons of fuel down the drain. And nothing to show for it.

What happened during the rest of the day, however, was neither amusing nor tactically sound.

800 Squadron had been tasked with precisely the same mission as on 1 May. The majority of their Sea Jets would plaster Stanley airfield and the balance would attack Goose Green. Come the time for launch, the Carrier Group had moved in towards the islands (with the SHARs carrying full under-wing ordnance they had to sacrifice the external fuel tanks and so their range was reduced). It was then realised that the weather over the target was not suitable for the planned attack — there was very low cloud and possible fog. The decision was immediately taken to move the Group back out to the east and away from the threat of enemy air attack. That was sensible, for by approaching the islands for the air strike the Group had closed the mainland to within Etendard/Exocet range.

But no sooner had the ships set off to put distance between themselves and the islands than the decision was reversed. The Group was to return to 'loiter' off the islands until the weather improved. The important criteria appeared to be that the Flagship wished to remain close to Stanley — within attack range of a fully bombed-up Sea Harrier. I didn't agree with this. Little had been achieved during the first attack on Stanley and it was unlikely that better results could be achieved now when the enemy was prepared. Why risk our valuable air-defence assets and our ships in the slight hope of knocking out a couple more light aircraft?

As had been agreed with the Flag, *Invincible* officially held the responsibility of Anti-Air Warfare Control ship; or so she had been led to believe. It was therefore her job to arrange, control and co-ordinate CAP and other air movements within and around the force. It was a job that the *Invincible* Ops Team were well practised at and very capable of doing efficiently − if they were allowed to get on with it.

Having spent all night on alert duties and because 800 were still being held by *Hermes* in readiness for their attack, 801 initially provided all of the CAP aircraft to protect the force. The calm sea conditions were ideal for low-level air interception work and with assistance from the radar pickets' Direction Officers it was probable that a robust anti-Etendard defence could be maintained. But that probability depended on the CAP and the AAWC being allowed to get on with their job. There was no room for mistakes.

As the morning progressed, I was not sure that I could believe what was going on. Sea Harriers from 800 were being launched from the Flagship to carry out visual searches of the surrounding seas, and no one was telling the AAWC who they were, when they planned to launch and recover, or where they were going. Short-range visual searches were even being tasked to the north-east, away from the threat direction. It was clear that the Flag were still not convinced that the entire sea area surrounding the two carriers was being regularly sanitised for surface intruders by Blue Fox radar whenever an 801 CAP pair was outbound or inbound. That included the 100 nautical miles to the north-east, east and south-east. The 'visual search' SHAR missions were therefore a waste of energy and resources.

On their own, these unannounced missions from *Hermes* were hard enough for the AAWC to cope with, but it didn't end there.

Steve Thomas and I were airborne on CAP at 100 miles west of the Carrier Group, searching above the relatively smooth sea surface for air targets to the west. The Port Stanley peninsula was about 40 miles away to the north-north-west, still covered in low cloud − the same carpet of cloud that covered the sea below us. We were under the firm control of *Invincible*. Suddenly the Flagship, *Hermes,* came up on the CAP frequency.

'Trident Leader and Two. We have trade for you on 090° at 90 miles. Vector 090.'

I, as Trident Leader, thought there must be some mistake. 090° was to the east, where *Invincible*, *Hermes* and the rest of the main body of the Carrier Group were gathered.

'This is Trident Leader. Confirm your last. What is bogey's heading?'

'Two bogeys heading 270° now at 85 miles. Vector starboard onto 090.'

This could not be right. The 'bogeys' just had to be friendly aircraft coming out to a CAP station or for some other task. Their position as reported by *Hermes* put them directly over the centre of the Task Group. I did not want to leave a significant gap in the outer ring of defence by leaving my CAP station vacant — especially to chase friendly forces that were already well within missile range of the main body of ships.

'Negative. Please check your identification of the pair outbound.' This produced an angry and indignant response from the Flagship.

'Trident Leader. From the Flag. Vector starboard 090 for trade!'

Flag or no Flag, I was not the type of brainwashed individual who would obey illogical orders without question. I would have none of it. It was my turn to be angry. 'I say again, negative. Check who has just taken off from your deck.'

There was a lengthy pause before the RT crackled again. The heavy silence was broken, and this time there was no pomposity. 'Roger, Trident Leader. That is Red Section from *Hermes*. Continue your CAP.' As I had guessed, *Hermes* had been seeking to use us to engage their own aircraft. What if we had taken them out head-on?

Where Red Section were going, I never found out. Nor did the AAWC. I, like many others in the force, was getting frustrated and confused. One of the CAP's most important jobs is to know where all friendly aircraft are, and because of the nature of the Sea Harrier — single-seat — the position of friendly forces has to be stored in the pilot's brain as a mental plot. No pilot could possibly keep a plot of where all friendly aircraft were with such interference and lack of co-ordination. And I wondered how all the escorts and pickets were getting on trying to keep track of the situation.

The sailors on board each ship were well briefed on Exocet. They had to work under direction as members of a team and, as individuals, they had no real direct control over their own destinies. Being a fighter pilot on CAP was a very different situation. You wanted to get to grips with the enemy in the air because it was you against the other man and you knew you could beat him. If you failed, then it was down to you and there was no one else to blame. An Etendard was no physical threat to us; it was just a target that had to be intercepted at all costs — and although there was pride rather than someone else's control of your personal security at stake, the resulting endeavour to get it right was always present.

But the sailors in the warships below had to grin and bear it. For most of them there was nothing they could do to influence the outcome of an attack other than do their best as members of their teams. They relied on those in command to get it right. So when the skies were saturated with unannounced aircraft movements on the 4th, confusion must have been the order of the day in most Ops Rooms. The lads wouldn't have had a clue what was going on around them.

All ships were able to listen to the different radar transmissions around them with their sophisticated electronic warfare devices. A transmission identified as that of an enemy, whether aircraft or missile, was nearly as useful as a radar contact on the same enemy unit. In each Ops Room, therefore, a constant watch was kept for the tell-tale transmissions of Etendard and the Exocet. Unfortunately, it was possible to confuse the different transmissions, especially those in the same band of frequencies. Sea Harrier, Etendard, Mirage III and Exocet radars were all in the same band as some of the ships' radars, so if you did not know where all friendly forces were you could not match transmissions to platforms and confusion could easily reign. And confusion leads to slow reaction to an identified threat.

Later that day, Robin Kent and Brian Haig were on CAP when they were sent to investigate an intermittent fast-moving contact at low level. *Invincible* had given control of the pair to a radar picket close to the CAP station and it was the picket that achieved the intermittent radar contact. It was a very similar situation to Alan Curtis's successful intercept of the Canberras on 1 May.

The two SHAR fighters immediately set off towards the west, as directed. 'An intermittent fast-moving contact' was a sure-fire indicator that an enemy fast jet was in the area at low level; and was probably an Etendard. Then, from just over 100 nautical miles away behind them *Hermes* called the pair back to their CAP station.

'Resume CAP. Contact assessed as spurious.' How in hell's name could the Flagship assess anything at that range? It wasn't their contact.

Having fewer maverick qualities than their Boss, the pair obeyed the order. Shortly after that one had 'got away', the *Invincible* CAP pair to the south of Kent and Haig were taken off CAP by a controller in *Hermes*. 'You are to proceed 120 miles to the south-west and carry out a visual surface search for enemy surface units.'

'Roger.' E-J and Barton did not argue. Did the Flag have information about enemy units in that area? Why not just fly south-west about 20 miles and sanitise the target area with radar? That would appear to be the logical thing to do, rather than leave a gap in the Carrier Group's defences. Although these questions passed through their minds, they did as they were told and departed to the south-westwards.

This removal of the CAP left a large hole in the outer ring of defence of the Group. And behind the 'hole' lay the destroyer *Sheffield* in company with the frigates *Arrow* and *Yarmouth*. It was not long before the 'hole' was penetrated by the enemy. The Etendards came straight through the gap and prosecuted their Exocet attack on the *Sheffield* from fairly short range. There was little time for the destroyer to react and by the time the missile was detected it was too late. The Exocet impacted amidships, destroying the Ops Room and setting ablaze the ship.

Was it actually the same Etendard that Kent and Haig had been sent to look for and had then been called off? That has to be questionable, but in my mind there was no question about the end result of removing E-J's CAP pair from their station. This had left the garden gate wide open, and the boys in *Sheffield* paid for the mistake.

At the time of the attack, I was in Flyco with Wings. News flashed through that *Sheffield* had been torpedoed. As a result, every anti-submarine helicopter in the vicinity converged on the stricken vessel to find and attack the submarine. HMS *Arrow* attended the destroyer, having been narrowly missed herself by a missile, and put rubber zodiacs in the water to survey the damage. Underwater and on sonar, the noise from the zodiacs' outboard engines sounded just like torpedoes. Everything pointed to a submarine attack.

Having only just listened to Robin Kent's experience on CAP, I didn't believe it, however. I grabbed the radio and called up Mortimer, who had just taken up CAP.

'Morts. This is the Boss. Go and look at *Sheffield* and let us know what the damage to her is above or below the waterline. And hurry!'

After a couple of minutes, Morts called back to the ship. 'She's holed above the waterline, Boss. Either a very clever torpedo or Exocet — and the hole is exactly at Exocet height.'

'Roger.' Problem solved.

It was then that the second piece of tragic news came through from *Hermes*. The weather over East Falkland had cleared and the Flag had launched the 800 attack on Goose Green.

Not surprisingly after the Vulcan strike and all the hiatus offshore, there were no aircraft waiting to be shot at or bombed at either location. Instead, the defences were ready, and at Goose Green the Sea Harrier world suffered its first war casualty. A radar-controlled 30-mm AAA cannon shot down Lieutenant Nick Taylor as he passed over the target at low level. He didn't stand a chance of surviving the hit. Flight Lieutenant Ted Ball later told me that he had also been running in to Goose Green and had watched, horrified, as the AAA shell exploded by Nick's cockpit.

When a member of the Staff was questioned later on that day ('What have you got to say about that?') the answer he gave was as thoughtless as the tasking which, in my opinion, had generated the loss: 'You have to expect casualties in war'.

Of course you expect casualties, but you don't invite them. Waiting inshore till the weather cleared over the land had now cost us the *Sheffield* and a Sea Jet — with nothing gained at the end of the day.

Immediately, morale sagged in both SHAR squadrons — especially when the press release from *Hermes* listed Nick as 'Flight Lieutenant'. When would the public at large learn that the Fleet Air Arm *did* exist and that it was this Naval service, and not the RAF, who were fighting in the Falklands?

There were those of us who were understandably beginning to wonder

173

when we would be allowed to get on with our jobs unhindered. To me the 4th had been a day of errors, a sad day of miscalculation resulting in interference with the AAWC's tasking; despatching aircraft from *Hermes* without informing the AAWC; employing Sea Harrier sorties on pointless visual searches of local waters; attempting to use the CAP to intercept aircraft that had just launched from the Flagship; aborting the CAP prosecution of a possible Etendard; taking a CAP pair off station to look for mythical surface targets which left a hole in the defences of the Carrier Group and arguably allowed the attack on the *Sheffield* to take place; and, last but not least, remaining within Exocet-delivery range to allow for a short-range Sea Harrier attack on relatively low-value airfield targets — resulting in the loss of one aircraft and the death of its pilot.

Later I heard that a signal arrived from the Flag expressing concern over *Invincible*'s lack of control and co-ordination on the 4th. If such a signal was indeed sent, then in the light of the actual events of that day it strikes me as most inappropriate, and little more than an attempt to rewrite history. And that is putting it extremely mildly.

HMS *Coventry* at the moment of her demise. Three 1000 pound bombs impact her simultaneously and tear out her bottom. A better understanding by the Staff of the Task Force's air assets might have saved her from this agony.

HMS *Coventry* capsizing seconds after being bombed by Argentine A-4 Sky Hawks on 25 May; *Broadsword*, on picket duty with her, was also damaged.

801 Squadron Sea Harrier returning from CAP off Fanning Head, near San Carlos, after the ground forces had landed.

Teal Inlet, West Falkland, during the war, terrain typical of much of the islands. The SHAR's Blue Fox radar could not 'look down' over land, which made Sharkey's advice, as principal Sea Harrier adviser to the Command during the campaign, about its use on CAP all the more important—advice that was largely ignored or overruled.

The runway at Port Stanley airfield after the third RAF Vulcan bombing raid, photographed by Charlie Cantan of 801 Squadron. Sixty-three bombs were dropped and several Shrike missiles were fired by Vulcans, at a cost of millions of gallons of fuel, and one bomber forced to divert to Brazil. One bomb clipped the runway—damage easily repaired—the rest missed; the twenty-one bombs dropped on the second mission were not fused, through an oversight, and so did not explode. Three 'swept-wing shapes' are clearly visible at the end of the runway (bottom of photo).

The Task Force relaxing after the end of Operation 'Corporate' and the recovery of the Falkland Islands. *Invincible* is the third ship. On their return to this country they received a joyous welcome. No such welcome greeted Sharkey Ward on his return to Britain, nor a number of other senior naval officers.

20

After the *Sheffield* incident, which had occurred well within the Exocet safety range that had been advised to the Command by 801, the Task Group was moved further to the east by day and even further by night. There had been no evidence of any active air threat at all by night, and with the much increased range from the mainland it was well-nigh impossible for the Argentine Air Force to menace the Group during the dark hours.

But there was still no respite for *Invincible* and 801 Squadron. The Flag continued to programme two alerts on deck and two in the crewroom by night, besides significant tasking by day. Throughout daylight hours up to three CAP pairs were stationed to the west of the Group and alerts were held on deck as well, in spite of our being well beyond the realistic range of possible air attack from the mainland.

And there was still no recognition of the disparity in size between the two Sea Harrier squadrons; every night 801 were given at least half the alerts. The Captain and Wings both spent much wasted time on the secure-voice facility, trying to persuade the Command to adapt to more sensible tasking rates. It was frustrating and annoying in the extreme, especially as the Staff wouldn't budge an inch.

What all this did achieve was an erosion of trust and a major but unnecessary increment in the cumulative fatigue affecting all the pilots in my squadron.

On 6 May, the squadron suffered a tragic and unaccountable loss. I was in my cabin, asleep after completing my stint at night alert, when the phone rang. It was Morts. He was in the crewroom.

'Boss, you'd better get up here... we have two aircraft overdue.' I didn't want to believe my ears.

'How long? And who's in them?'

'About forty minutes, I'm afraid. Its Al and E-J.'

As I made my way to the crewroom at the rush, I couldn't imagine what could have happened. They were two of the best and most experienced pilots in the force, but forty minutes overdue was too long. If they weren't on another deck, they must be in the water. Ian Mortimer and Mike Broadwater were waiting to brief me. Mike was Alan's Number

Two, and together they had worked up a very good relationship and understanding in the air. Both of them were QFIs and had all the various safety aspects of operational flying well sorted out between them. Mike had been on the same CAP mission as Alan when the two pilots had disappeared and he related what he knew.

'I can't tell you very much about it, Boss, because there isn't that much to tell. We were on CAP on the 290° station at medium to low level. The weather was fine; blue skies above, but there was a layer of cloud topping 2000 feet and the met. man had briefed us that it might go all the way down to the deck. Our controller called us up to say he had a small surface contact that he wanted us to investigate and gave us its range and bearing.

'As you know, Alan and I had a strict routine for penetrating cloud at low level when looking for a contact. First, one of us would go down through the clag and then, when visual below, would call the other one down to join up. This catered for the target popping up out of the cloud and getting away.

'So Alan descended into the cloud-tops, and that was the last I saw or heard of him.' Mike was obviously devastated by what had happened. His face was drained of energy as he went on: 'The only relevant call that I received after he entered cloud was one from E-J, who was on CAP to the south of us. He had obviously heard our controller telling us we had possible trade and I'm sure he wanted to give us a hand and get in on the action. He called that he was in descent and heading to the north-west.'

Morts interrupted. 'It seems from what I can gather, Boss, that although E-J thought he was about 20 miles to the south of Mike and Alan, his actual position at the time of his descent was less than 10 miles away. That's what the "Ds" reckon.'

'Is that all we've got?' I asked, and began questioning the pair on all the points that might be relevant. But both had already been over the same ground themselves.

'So,' I summarised, before going up to report to Wings, 'after the descent into cloud on converging headings, Alan heading west and E-J north-west, there was not a dicky-bird heard out of either of them. No radio call; no ejection-seat tone indicating that they had jumped out; no SARBE tone — just nothing [SARBE was a pilot's personal Search-And-Rescue Beacon]. Both of them were locked on to their radar screens heads-down in cloud, searching for a possible enemy contact and, although it's a million-to-one chance, they must have been converging in a manner which did not allow either radar to pick up the other aircraft. Each was outside the lateral coverage of the other aircraft's radar beam. Because of their experience as all-weather pilots, I'm sure that we can safely assume that there is no way that both could have flown into the sea independently and at the same time. Nor is there any evidence of any enemy action that could have led to their simultaneous disappearance. No. Our best judgement then is that they collided without seeing each other, were killed instantly by the impact — hence no RT — and went down with their aircraft.'

'That's about it, Boss.'

'OK. You two get some coffee and see if you can work out any other possible explanation. I'll go and brief Wings and the Captain.' I left the crewroom and climbed the ladders to Flyco.

Dusty and JJ listened carefully to the squadron theory about the missing pilots. Both were very understanding and helpful. 'What an absolute tragedy, Sharkey. Do tell the boys how very sorry I am for you all.' The Captain's eyes were filled with sadness.

There wasn't much more to be said. Helicopters from 820 Squadron were already scouring the seas hoping to find the downed aviators, but to no avail. Only some aircraft debris was recovered.

One of my pilots volunteered to sort out each of the dead pilots' personal belongings. I organised the incident signal that had to be sent, knowing that later in the day I would have to write to the two wives. The squadron aircrew had naturally taken it badly and there was absolute silence in the crewroom. There was a sense of loss throughout the ship. Ralph Wykes-Snead, 'H' and many other thoughtful friends dropped in to offer their comfort.

I was due on deck for alert and wondered how I could get morale back up from where it now lay — at rock bottom. I called the Chief Steward in the Wardroom. 'Chief, do me a favour would you? The boys are a bit down at the moment, for obvious reasons. Could you fill a rubbish bag with some cans of beer and have it sent up to the crewroom? That's jolly decent of you. Thanks.' And I went to sit in my jet.

After a quiet watch on deck I found that the aircrew were still getting used to the tragedy and were in no mood to be cheered up. So I grabbed a couple of cans of beer and went aft to my cabin to try to compose two of the most difficult letters I had ever written. Alan and E-J had put everything into the fight and it was heartbreaking that they should have died in such a way. After his success against the Canberras, I decided there and then to put a recommendation in for the Distinguished Service Cross to be posthumously awarded to Alan. In the event, Their Lordships preferred to honour Alan with a Mention in Despatches.

By the time I went to the Command Briefing that evening I had turned my mind away from the tragedy and back to operations. We were 'enjoying' a definite lull in hostilities. We all presumed that this had come about partly because the Task Group had been kept well out of harm's way since the 4th, and partly because the Argentine Air Force were licking their wounds and preparing themselves for the moment when the British troops landed in the islands.

There was only one thing in my mind now for every waking hour of the day, and that was how best to overcome the opposition. And I was convinced that the Flag could easily do more to harass the enemy at Stanley without undue risk to participating units.

There could be regular night gunfire bombardment of the airfield, with ships closing the target and departing under cover of darkness. Our own suggestion of high-level bombing could also be adopted, as a means of keeping the Argentines' heads up by day and night. I decided to make appropriate noises to the Captain.

At the briefing, my request to commence high-level bombing was agreed in principle. Wings would talk to SAVO and *Hermes* about it. But before leaving the subject of Sea Harriers, the Captain said that there were a couple of things which had astonished him.

'The first thing, Sharkey, is that we have had no communication at all from either the Flag or *Hermes* concerning the loss of E-J and Alan Curtis. Not one word of sympathy. Nothing.' JJ was quietly furious. 'And the second thing really does make me wonder what's going on over there. Tonight's tasking signal has come in and it makes absolutely no allowance for the fact that we have lost two pilots and two jets! It's the same tasking as before: two plus two for half the night. I really don't know what to say.'

'Nor me, Sir. But we'll manage it somehow.' I too was depressed, and very angry indeed. I now had six jets and nine pilots. *Hermes* had eleven jets and double the number of pilots. In anyone's book that meant we should bear about one-third of the alert task; not more. My pilots were going to be dropping like flies soon from fatigue. But there was no point in going through the figures with Wings or the Captain — they both knew them as well as I did, and they continued the fight to try to get a more rational level of tasking.

I went to the bar with Ralph, found Robin and some of the boys, and related the bad news. And, strangely, it was the Flag's approach to overnight tasking that provided the ladder for the recovery of squadron morale. A few beers and a lot of mutual commiseration brought back the aggression that I was used to seeing in my pilots. They were raring to go again, happy that Wings and the Captain were backing them to the hilt.

There was little need for aggression in the air over the next couple of days. Either out at sea or on the mainland, or in both locations, the foggy, wet weather reduced flying to a minimum. More alerts than usual were scheduled, but the brief spell of low-intensity flying gave most of the pilots some time to rest. But if confrontation with the enemy in the air was not on the cards, new orders and tasking proposals definitely were.

At the *Hermes* conference in April, I had mentioned an attack on the Stanley water-purification plant to SAVO. The reaction had definitely been unfavourable: 'You can't do that sort of thing! What would the public think? What about the Geneva Convention?' Now, suddenly, the Staff had decided that they liked the idea and suggested to *Invincible* that 801 should mount a night low-level attack on the facility. In my view they hadn't done their homework and balanced the benefits and costs of such an attack against the preservation of the diminished 801 Sea Harrier assets.

Unlike Stanley airfield, the only approach to the purification plant by night at low level would be directly past the airfield and the town, with all their associated defences: other avenues of approach were barred by hills. The night attack on the airfield planned for 1 May had relied on the element of surprise. There could be no certainty of surprise this far into the war, particularly after all the bombardment that had taken place to date. Also, the purification plant represented a point target which was quite hard to destroy even by day, and therefore a lot of weapons might be needed to ensure success. That meant a lot of aircraft having to pass through the target area, giving a higher risk of loss.

Balancing the value of the target against the value of our limited Sea Harrier resources, and not forgetting the lesson learned at Goose Green, I simply ruled out the possibility of a night low-level attack on the plant. I approached Wings with my arguments against the Flag's idea, proposed the alternative of high level-bombing as a possibility, and received strong support. The Flag's idea was shelved.

It was then that the Flag turned their attention to the use of the Blue Fox radar by Sea Harriers on CAP. A signal arrived in *Invincible* which stated that 'CAP aircraft should not transmit on the Blue Fox radar until ship's controllers had directed them to within 10 miles of their target. And in no circumstances should Blue Fox be used in the look-down mode, that is searching for targets approaching the force at low level – because it doesn't work.'

I was given the news and a copy of the signal by JJ. There was a twinkle in his eye as he said, 'I think you'll like this one, CO 801!' He paused and grinned. 'Now go away and put together your thoughts before we decide what to do about it.'

I felt like butting my head against the side of the ship. I wanted to scream with frustration as I sat down in my cabin to prepare the right brief for the Captain. It would be best if I marshalled my thoughts on paper, listing all that needed to be said, and then edited the result; no point in rocking the boat too much.

Having completed my written brief for the Captain and presented it, I just hoped that it would indeed find its way to the Admiral's desk. I would have to wait and see. Meanwhile I was planned for alert on deck.

The previous night-alert programme had left Steve Thomas snookered, so I was to carry out the alert with Brian Haig as my Number Two. It had been confirmed at the pre-flight briefing that the ship was stuck in a fog bank that had already persisted for several hours. The fog was set to remain over the Carrier Group for at least the remainder of the day. I had already been up to the bridge to discuss the weather with the Captain and we had agreed that if an enemy air raid was detected or suspected, then, fog or no fog, the CAP would get airborne. Getting back on board without getting wet would be a secondary consideration.

On deck, the ski-jump was just visible from the cockpits of our two alert aircraft as we received the order from Flyco, '004, 008, scramble for trade 260°, 140 miles.' The game was on. Adrenalin started to flow. The ship's internal broadcast system called all personnel to go to 'Exocet Stations'.

In both cockpits feverish activity followed the order to scramble and within two and a half minutes both aircraft roared off the deck into the swirling grey mist. It was certainly 'pea soup' weather, I thought, as I cleaned up the aircraft and climbed. At 900 feet the Sea Jet burst through the ceiling of the fog into brilliant sunshine and I was very quickly joined by 008. We headed 260°, but before we had time to switch to our briefed control frequency, Flyco came up on the air. 'Trade assessed as a Neptune with fighter escort. It has now departed to the west. Hold your position.'

Brian and I went into a race-track holding pattern under the blue sky and waited for further tasking.

The ship had to do a clever bit of mental balancing with its priorities now. Chasing the shadower from that range was quite impossible, but the two jets airborne could be used as CAP in case an Exocet raid was planned. On the other hand, the Group was beyond the maximum suggested range of Exocet delivery, and in that weather it was going to be difficult and time-consuming getting the SHARs back down on to the deck. First, the ship had to find a gap in the fog bank, and if one was found they had to take immediate advantage of it. There might not be a second chance, and we couldn't afford to lose two more jets.

'Sharkey, we're looking for a gap in order to try to recover you on board. Switch to Stud 3 and we'll call you down when we've found one.' Wings sounded confident but he had used my name on the air, which was a bad sign; usually he sounded either sleepy or cheesed off. No doubt he was hoping to keep us happy.

'Roger, Flyco. 008, Stud 3, go!'

We waited on the homing frequency and flew in a race-track pattern to the west of the ship. Still at relatively low level and without fear of enemy EW intercept, I turned my radar on to keep my own tabs on Mother.

'What do you make of it, Sharkey?' Brian's voice sounded a bit nervous.

'If they don't find a gap, what we'll do is for you to come down on my wing in close formation until we can see the water or until we hit 100 feet on the radio altimeter. Make sure yours is set now to that height. The CCA team will bring us down the slope early so that we can be in stable level flight at 100 feet before we have to go down further or decelerate to the hover. Provided we see the ship, at half a mile I'll wave goodbye and take myself round again while you commence transition, monitoring your own range until you're alongside the ship. If there is enough visibility, I'll stay down with you, we'll both decelerate to the hover and air-taxi onboard. OK?'

'Roger.' Brian sounded resigned, but relaxed.

It shouldn't be any harder than a night deck approach without ship's lights.

After about twenty minutes the ship found the gap it had been looking for. '004, 008. We are in a small gap now like an air bubble under the fog. Its not very big; half a mile wide and clear up to about 100 feet. The Captain wants you down fast while he tries to keep station with the gap.' Gaps in fog were notorious for their habit of disappearing without trace; it was usually the case that if you steamed out of a gap then there was no way you would find a way back into it again. The Captain had a job on his hands.

'Roger. Feed us down the slope early, please. I want to be level at 100 feet before we hit the gap.'

'Roger, 004. Vector 120° and prepare for descent.'

It was Tony Walker's voice. That was good. If anyone could get us down safely, he could.

With Brian's jet tucked in close formation on my wing, we let down into the fog. There was nothing to see outside the cockpit — we were in a complete white-out. Would we be able to see the ship and recover on board? We'd have to wait and see. Fortunately we had plenty of fuel in reserve.

Soon we were down near to the base-height that I had selected. 150 feet, 120 feet, 100 feet; radalt light on. Still no sea surface. But we were stable and level.

'Taking it down further, Brian, to 80 feet.'

At 90 feet the sea surface appeared below, and in quick time we were in the gap and visual the ship. *Invincible* was ahead of us beam-on to our approach — but there was no wind and therefore no handling problems to face. I looked round at Brian. He had already moved out of 'close' and was starting his 'decel'. Good lad. I selected nozzles to the hover stop and glided noisily towards the carrier. We rounded the stern, became visual with Flyco, and landed on deck. It was a relief to be home.

Slowly but surely the weather improved and the troublesome fog banks disappeared. We were flying again, and although the mainland airfields had also cleared of fog there was still no sign of fighter-to-fighter confrontation. But the Etendard threat was ever-present in our minds and this helped us to concentrate on our radar screens when on CAP. The Admiral hadn't responded, and didn't respond, to my paper on the Blue Fox, and so my squadron continued to search for the threat on every sortie with our radars looking down. It wasn't boring, but it was long, slow work with no contacts other than our own surface ships or helicopters from one hour to the next. But the *Invincible* boys stuck with it.

A day or so after our launch in the fog, I was again sitting on deck at alert. I was monitoring the CAP control frequencies when I heard some very strange calls from the *Hermes* CAP pair that had just got airborne. I recognised the voices of the two pilots: 'Right, this time we'll do a loop with a roll off the top.'

Aerobatics training! On CAP! When we are all sitting here relying on some form of air defence from them. I waited. Eventually Blisset called again, 'Getting a bit short of fuel now; I'm at about "two-eight". Let's do one last loop then go home early.' 'Two-eight' was verbal shorthand for 2,800 pounds of fuel, and in 801's book that was sufficient for at least another twenty minutes on task before having to return to the deck.

There was no question about it. The 800 Squadron pilots were supposed to be searching sky and sea to intercept any intruders that might be inbound to attack the Carrier Group, but instead had chosen to carry out a practice session of formation aerobatics, neglecting their operational task in war and running their fuel down unnecessarily quickly. 'Going home early' also meant that some other pair, guess where from? — *Invincible* of course — would have to launch early to do their job for them. It made a farce of the whole idea of holding a CAP station.

I finished my alert, then went to Flyco and told Wings what I had heard. 'If I or any of my team neglected their duty like that I am certain that the Flag would insist on a field court martial.' I was more than a little wound up and left the problem in Wings' tender care.

I felt pretty disgusted about the whole episode. It appeared that 800 were not taking the operation seriously.

Keeping busy was the only way to take my mind off the antics and tactical ineptitude of the other ship, and 9 May allowed me to do just that. Two very interesting operational missions awaited me.

21

The 801 Squadron recommendations for high-level bombing against Port Stanley airfield had been accepted somewhat reluctantly by the Flag. This reluctance was not really surprising, bearing in mind that the attack relied completely on the capabilities of the radar and the Navhars for its success; bearing in mind, too, what the Flag thought of such things.

In reply to our recommendations and after due deliberation, SAVO put forward several fully anticipated questions: how were the pilots going to ensure that they missed the town with their bombs? would the line of attack take them over the town? and so on. Finally, realising that my team had no intention whatsoever of risking the lives of the Falkland Islands community, and after having been briefed in detail about the profile to be flown by attacking aircraft, the Staff agreed to the proposal. But 801, having generated and recommended the new delivery, were not the first to be tasked with trying it out. That didn't matter very much to me. The main thing was that now we could do our bit to keep the enemy awake and on the alert; the less rest the Argentines ashore got before our amphibious troops landed, the better.

To that end — denying the enemy some sleep — we decided in *Invincible* to set up a mission that would give the opposition more than a little to think about in the middle of the night. There were two major detachments and airstrips away from Stanley. On East Falkland there was Goose Green, close to the settlement of Darwin. On West Falkland there was Fox Bay. With the Task Group well to the east, the distance to Fox Bay was about 225 nautical miles as the crow flies. The plan was very simple. I was to get airborne on my own in the small hours of the night and deliver a Lepus flare attack against each defended airstrip. It was hoped that this would give the troops on the ground the false impression that a Task Force landing was under way — the flares apparently providing illumination prior to an assault.

The mission was very straightforward. All I needed to do was enter the attack co-ordinates for each target into my navigation computer, follow the resultant HUD directions to the target areas, check the accuracy of the navigation using my radar, and drop the flares. Outbound to the targets I would fly direct to Goose Green from the climb-out point, which would take me close to Stanley. On the return leg I would approach the Carrier Group from 240°, that is, well clear of the islands, let down to low level and then run in to *Invincible* for recovery on board.

JJ was pleased with the idea of the planned mission: 'Anything we have missed, Sharkey? You know that the weather isn't too brilliant out there?' The weather round the Task Group was certainly not very sharp, with high winds, towering cumulo-nimbus, and snow showers. But over the islands the forecast was for much fairer conditions.. The mission would therefore present no problems and it hurt my pride even to think that I might have a problem getting back on board. I shut my mind to snow showers and thought only of dropping the flares.

'No, thank you, Sir. I'm very happy with all that. Can we just make sure that the Flag lets all our surface units know exactly what's going on? One lone aircraft approaching the force at night from the south-west is just asking for a "blue on blue".' ('Blue on blue' means own forces shooting down own aircraft.)

'Don't worry, we'll ensure that they let all units know.'

There was practically no self-briefing required for the mission. It was a question of kicking the tyres, lighting the fires, and getting airborne.

I arrested my rate of climb after launch at 500 feet, settled the aircraft down to a height of 200 feet above the waves, set 420 knots and departed the ship on a north-westerly heading for 70 miles. As my eyes became fully attuned to the darkness the sea surface became visible, with the healthy wind kicking up a lot of spray and phosphorescence and clouds towering around and ahead of me like huge cliffs. Inside the cockpit, I had dimmed the lighting almost to extinction, including the geometrical patterns on the HUD. Arming missiles and guns, just in case, I reached the climb-out point and headed for the stars, turning to port as I did so to get on track for the first destination.

The aircraft climbed at a cool 30° nose up for the first 15,000 feet and very quickly I was throttling back at Mach 0.85 and 35,000 feet, enjoying the view. Under the black, star-speckled sky and towards East Falkland, the cloud thinned and dissipated. Although it was the middle of the night, Stanley was well-lit and could easily be seen from the top of the climb.

Dick Goodenough had given me the jet with the most sought-after radar and Navhars, 004. The engineers kept full records of the performance, accuracy and reliability of each radar and Navhars system. This attention to detail, which included comprehensive post-flight debriefs, paid excellent dividends, but although all the aircraft performed well, 004 seemed to be the pick of the bunch. The avionics were functioning perfectly. Before passing just to the south of Stanley, I checked the navigation system accuracy with my radar and, until commencing descent for Goose Green, used the radar in its air-to-air mode to check the skies to the west for enemy fighters. There were none, nor did I expect any. I was enjoying being alone, and thought of my lads back at home — they would have given anything to have been on this flight.

I chose to run into Goose Green up Choiseul Sound and had an excellent surface radar picture to confirm the accuracy of my desired flare-drop position. Having checked the Lepus selector switches and pylon, I monitored the Navhars readout, which was telling me time-to-go to release, and the HUD, which was guiding me unerringly to the target. Pickling the bomb button, I felt the flare body leave the aircraft, applied power and commenced the second climb of the night to high level.

After about 20 seconds I rolled the Sea Jet inverted in order to see the flare ignite. Goose Green lies on a narrow isthmus of land which separates Choiseul Sound from Grantham Sound. When the flare went off it seemed to be in the right place — right on target. Now for Fox Bay.

The second target was well-covered in thick cloud, but that made no difference to the attack profile. My radar confirmed what the Navhars was telling me and I had no doubt at all when I pickled the bomb-release button that the Lepus was again bang on target. It was easy as riding a bike. Having seen the glow from the flare through the cloud, I turned to the east in the climb and set off on the long dog-leg home.

At 140 miles to go to the deck I was suddenly illuminated with fire-control radar from a ship below. The relative silence of the cockpit was shattered by the radar warning receiver alarm. I had detected a vessel on radar earlier and had presumed it was on detachment from the Task Group.

Thoughts of the Argentine Navy firing Sea Dart at me flashed through my mind. I broke hard to starboard and descended to the south-west away from the contact, which was only 20 miles to the north. But I was still locked up by the fire-control radar, and having taken initial avoiding action I started to analyse the threat. It certainly wasn't Sea Dart — the noise in my earphones didn't have the right characteristics — and so I was pretty safe now, 30 miles south. I turned port onto east, arresting my descent as I did so, and climbed back up to 30,000. I would circumnavigate the ship that had shown such an unhealthy interest in me. At the same time I would interrogate it on radio.

I found the culprit on the pre-briefed Task Group surface/air frequency. 'Warship illuminating lone Sea Harrier, come in.'

The warship had obviously not been briefed on the SHAR mission and was unwilling to believe I was who I said I was. Being now a little short of fuel after three and a half climbs to high level, I left my personal signature encoded in terms of four-letter words and bid them goodnight. If I had been on a slightly different track and hadn't had my radar information to tell me where to evade to, I could have been engaged by own forces. So much for the promise to pass information to all ships.

By the time I began my final descent towards the Carrier Group I was back amongst the clouds. They were massive and very turbulent. After I had descended to low level and was running in to the expected position of the ship via the safety lane, I called, '004, on the way in. Estimating 280°, 25 miles. Over.'

Tony was immediately on the air.

'Roger, 004. Read you loud and clear. I have no contact on you, repeat no contact. Clutter from snow clouds too intense.' He was concerned. Good old Tony; there's a man you can really trust. He'd do anything to get his pilots down safely.

'Roger. I'll conduct my own approach and call out my ranges to go.' I was feeling confident thanks to two important facts. Firstly, when *Invincible* gave a ship's estimated position for the recovery of aircraft, you could bet your pension on her being in that position when you returned from your flight; especially in bad weather. So I was very sure in my mind that I could find the deck using my Navhars information. The second fact was that I had practised self-homing to the deck on many occasions, and we had also carried out the trials on the software for self-homing when ashore in the Trials Unit. It was no higher work load for the pilot than following instructions from the ship's precision approach controller.

On my radar screen, the *Invincible* 'position destination marker' that I had selected on my nav computer sat less than 2 miles from one of the ship contacts in view. I had already programmed the 'marker' with the ship's pre-briefed recovery course and speed and was happy to see it was holding good formation on the contact nearest to it. That had got to be *Invincible* — I hadn't enough fuel left to make mistakes. There was enough for one approach only.

It was a simple matter to update the radar marker's position by fixing the radar onto the contact. The 'Self-Controlled Approach' programme in the Navhars computer software was provided so that pilots could safely carry out their own precision approach to a chosen destination. My chosen destination was the ship, and as I lined up 5 miles astern of what I thought was *Invincible*, I selected the precision approach mode on the HUD. I also locked the radar onto the ship to keep the 'destination' information as accurate as possible. Now I was all prepared for recovery to the ship.

'Five miles on the approach.' I called.

'Roger, still no contact.' Tony must be sweating buckets down there.

I was at 800 feet and the world outside was black. Approaching 3 miles I prepared to commence descent. The radar was firmly locked on to the contact ahead.

'Three miles.'

'Still no contact.'

Was I on the right ship? I began to wonder as I started down the slope. My jet was being tossed around a bit by turbulence from heavy clouds, which would certainly account for the clutter Tony had mentioned. There was no other course but to wait and see. I cleared the doubts from my mind.

'Have you now at 1½ miles. On the glide slope.' Tony sounded relieved. I was relieved.

Tony continued with his calls all the way to half a mile. He had passed the wind over the deck as 40 knots gusting 50. It felt like it in the cockpit, too. The buffeting increased as I got lower.

'Half a mile.' My head-up information said the same. I delayed selecting hover stop for a few seconds because of the strong head-wind, then nozzles down, power going on. At a quarter of a mile I called 'Lights.' And there, behind the radar cross in the HUD, appeared the ship's island. As usual the cross was just about on Flyco. Radar off and concentrate on controlling the jet. As I was moving sideways over the deck from alongside the wind backed through 30°. I ruddered the nose into it before settling onto the deck with an uncharacteristic thud.

'That's my excitement over for the night,' I thought. It was 0400 hours, and a long day lay ahead.

That same morning, news came through on civilian world radio that the Argentine government had announced the invasion of the Falkland Islands by British troops at Darwin and Fox Bay. The mission had produced the right results. There must have been chaos and panic inshore for a few hours.

It was also on that morning that *Hermes* tasked two of its pilots to carry out the first high-level bombing sortie over Stanley airfield. The mission was, however, abandoned over the target when the pair found the airfield to be hidden by cloud, which made good sense, since in this first attempt at the new delivery profile it was important to see where the bombs landed. But the flight wasn't wasted. Under the control of HMS *Coventry*, the 800 pair investigated a surface contact about 70 miles to the south-west of Stanley. They found the trawler *Narwal* under the Argentine flag and were instructed to attack it. It was in the Exclusion Zone and was probably a spy ship.

The bombs that the aircraft were loaded with would not fuse at low level and the pilots knew that − the fuses had been set for a high-level delivery − but they dropped them on the trawler anyway from close range and did well to achieve a single hit. The unexploded bomb caused considerable damage, immobilising the trawler's engine room. The two then strafed the vessel with 30-mm cannon-fire before returning to *Hermes*.

At about midday, two further *Hermes* aircraft were tasked with flying over the *Narwal* to check her position and condition. They were instructed not to attack the vessel.

The Special Boat Squadron (SBS) unit in *Invincible* was then tasked with boarding the trawler by helicopter. It was to be a two-helicopter operation supported by one Sea Harrier riding 'shotgun' in case of enemy air intervention. The brief was held in the 801 crewroom and was led by a young Royal Marine lieutenant. His men looked very tough and on the ball, and each had a selection of personalised weapons including garottes, daggers and specialist machine-pistols. They definitely meant business and the lieutenant was very precise as to what he wanted.

The Sea Jet would launch after the helicopters were en route, act as a communication link between them and *Invincible*, and arrive at the *Narwal* first. When the helicopters arrived on scene, the rope descent by the SBS marines onto the after-deck of the trawler would be conducted in two phases. One 'helo' would disgorge its special troops first, while the other strafed the forward deck with light machine-gun fire to keep any enemy heads down. Then the helos would swap places and repeat the evolution.

When the trawler was safely in the hands of the SBS, I — the SHAR 'shotgun' — would be free to leave the scene and inform the ship that all was well. Prisoners would be airlifted by the helos back to *Invincible*. The brief was concise, to the point and professional. I was most impressed.

Finding the stricken *Narwal* was straightforward. I descended through the thin, broken cloud to find no sign of life on the upper deck but with a sea boat lying off the trawler's stern and the remains of some life-rafts alongside the vessel. I called up the helos to bring them up to date.

'The sea boat has a green canvas cover on it and I expect at any moment to see a little head popping out. What did I say? Someone just had a quick peek, then disappeared under cover again. There is no sign of any armament or personnel on the trawler's deck.'

I continued, 'En route to here, the Command instructed me to pass a message to the boarding party. Are you ready to copy?'

'Affirmative.'

'From the Flag. You are to use minimum force, I repeat, minimum force to achieve the aim of taking over the *Narwal*. Is that understood? Message ends.'

'Roger. We'll brief the boys.'

It wasn't long before the two 820 Squadron Sea King helos arrived on the scene, and as one hovered by the bow of the trawler, giving covering fire, the other rapidly disgorged its Commandos onto the after-deck. There was no opposition. In fact, as I heard from the SBS lieutenant later, in the bar, the first Marine down found an aged fisherman at the other end steadying the rope for him!

I returned to the ship, recovered to the deck, and by the time the helos arrived with their prisoners I was already back at alert on deck in another Sea Harrier. I watched the SBS boys disembark from the choppers, each one leading either one or two fishermen by the arm up the deck towards the island. The prisoners looked haggard and some of them appeared to be well past the fifty mark. The exception appeared to be in his mid-thirties and had an air of authority about him. Practically all the fishermen were unsteady on their feet and needed assistance walking. I wondered if there had been some resistance by these old men of the sea.

On boarding the vessel, the SBS team found that the crew of about thirty had given up hope of getting out alive. The first attack by the pair of 800 'bombers' had inflicted enough damage to ensure that the small ship would eventually sink. According to the fishermen, it had been decided to abandon ship in the sea boat and rubber dinghies. This was under way when the second pair of jets arrived on the scene. The Argentine crew were adamant that the second pair had strafed the vessel with cannon whilst they were attempting to abandon ship, resulting in the death of one man and injury to two or three others. An investigation was under way in *Hermes* to get to the bottom of this allegation which, if true, said little for the integrity or humanitarian qualities of the pilots involved. With not enough rubber life-rafts left serviceable after the air attack and, knowing that any hope of rescue was out of the question, the fishermen had quite sensibly turned to drink. They had already consumed an unhealthy quantity before the SBS arrived; it was inebriation, not assault, that had caused them to stagger down the deck of *Invincible* after landing on board.

All but one of the trawlermen were found to be genuine fishermen. It was the younger-looking man who turned out to be an Argentine Naval Intelligence officer.

The prisoners were provided with one of the sailors' messdecks as living accommodation, where they had showers, clean clothes, sheets and bedding. Some had reached the age of seventy, and it wasn't long before the *Invincible* sailors started to send gifts to them to make their stay on board a memorable one. 801 contributed 3000 cigarettes and some of Charlie Cantan's girlie magazines. Although undoubtedly grateful as guests on board, the fishermen would not accept that they were in HMS *Invincible*. According to Argentinian news, *Invincible* had been struck at least three times and was definitely at the bottom of the ocean. Nothing would change their view, and so everyone gave up trying to do so.

In parallel with treating the captured fishermen like kings, *Invincible* also looked after the Lieutenant-Commander of Argentine Naval Intelligence in a manner befitting an officer. He was not particularly interested in whether his host ship was *Invincible* or not because he had more pressing things on his mind. He was convinced that, having been captured in a war zone in a spy ship and not in uniform, he was destined to be taken to the quarterdeck and there shot as a spy. He asked for permission to write a last letter home to his wife and children and, to keep him happy, his request was granted.

The Captain wondered how he was going to convince the man that he was not for the chop. Then he had a brainwave. 'I know what... We'll send the Roman Catholic Padre down to see him. He's sure to believe a man of the cloth.'

One sight of the Padre, however, convinced the Lieutenant-Commander that he was about to die. It took him several days of needless worry to realise that he was actually in civilised hands and would continue to be treated properly.

The day after the boarding of the *Narwal*, the fisherman who had been killed by the strafing was formally buried at sea in the presence of his shipmates.

22

The *Narwal* incident provided a welcome diversion from the routine of CAP missions that had to be flown each day. Warnings of possible Exocet attacks were frequent and always exciting, and the young lions on board took these as seriously as we took our CAP duties. The difference was that we pilots had variety and freedom in our task, whereas the lads in the Ops Room were now settled into a mind-boggling routine of four hours on duty in front of their radar screens, four hours off duty, four on, four off, and so on. One thing we did have in common, though, apart from a desire to protect the ship, was our wish to get the main show on the road — we all looked forward to the amphibious landing that would put our ground forces ashore. Where and when that would be we could only guess, but it was certainly still some way off.

There had been no air-to-air action since 1 May and, taking advantage of the relative lull in activities, I asked the Captain for permission to invite Desmond Hughes and Neil Thomas over to the ship for a chin-wag. Permission was readily granted and on the 11th the two ex-899 aviators arrived by helicopter from the Flagship.

I welcomed them on board, took them up to Flyco to say hello to Wings and the Captain, and then briefed them on the state of the art in *Invincible*. It was then their turn to brief me fully on how things were progressing in *Hermes*. Had their Blue Fox radars improved since the Ferranti expert's visit? And how were SAVO and the Staff responding to their own and to *Invincible*'s inputs?

I soon gathered that little had changed since I had last spoken with them. There were still several problems with the aircraft weapons system, one of which was water ingress into the radar nose-cone while the aircraft was standing on deck. The South Atlantic weather had exacerbated this but, as I explained to them, there had been a solution to that problem available for at least four months.

'When we were off the north of Scotland during "Alloy Express" it was just as wet as it is here and we had the identical problem with our own Blue Fox radars. But the lads in the hangar came up with a "fix" which has worked well ever since. Dick Goodenough published a formal AEO's

191

Memorandum on the problem giving precise technical instructions as to how to fix it — that was his job in relation to the Operational Trials that we were officially carrying out. A copy of the memo was definitely sent to 800 as well as 899. We'll have to let you have another copy before you go back.'

'That will be useful, but it ain't going to solve the main problem over there,' Desmond replied. 'The nub of the matter is that the majority of pilots in 800 Squadron proper have relatively little idea of how to use the radar/Navhars combination. They openly admit that they don't trust the Navhars at all and refuse even to contemplate using the radar when on low-level CAP. They will sit at anywhere between 2,000 and 5,000 feet and pretend to do a visual search for intruders. They won't even switch the radar to transmit when on patrol. How you can do a visual search for Etendards and the like when there is cloud below you from horizon to horizon beats me.'

Neil and Desmond returned to their ship no happier than when they had arrived. There was little that we in *Invincible* could do to ease their concerns.

Bouts of bad weather ashore and afloat continued and had an adverse effect on Carrier Group air operations. Inshore, close to the islands, it was a different story, however, with *Coventry* shooting down a Puma helicopter near Port Stanley airfield and *Brilliant* and *Glasgow* successfully defending themselves against attack from Sky Hawks.

The Sea Wolf weapon system fitted in the Type 22 proved itself in action by knocking down three of the attacking Sky Hawk aircraft in quick succession. *Glasgow* took a bomb through the ship but it didn't explode. Indeed, many of the bombs delivered against the British warships did not go off and, later, both the Argentines and some of the less well-educated legions of British journalism claimed that the Argentines suffered an 'unfair' disadvantage because of this. When this extraordinary claim came to my ears, I didn't know whether to laugh or cry; it represented more irresponsible comment in the media based on only half the story and even less actual knowledge. The simple reason why a lot of the Argentine bombs did not explode when they hit the ships was that they were not delivered correctly.

When attacking our well-armed warships with bombs at low level the AAF pilots had a simple choice: either fly at the correct minimum height for the effective release of the bombs and stand a greater chance of being shot down; or skim the water in very low-level flight and deliver the bombs from well below the required release height. Chances of pilot and aircraft survival were higher if you stayed low. Many AAF pilots took the latter course of action (quite sensibly), and therefore the bombs they released did not have enough time to go 'live' before hitting their targets. If all the attackers had come in at the correct bomb-release altitude, more of them would have been shot down but bombs that reached their targets would have exploded. The silly notion of what was 'fair' or 'unfair' was not part of the equation either for the pilots or for the ships' companies. If you don't release your weapons within the design parameters, you can't expect them to work properly.

By 14 May, the 801 Squadron AWIs and engineers had between them resolved a similar problem affecting our own pilots' survival. The AAA radar-directed guns ashore represented a very real threat to overflying aircraft, and it was therefore important to adapt our aircraft to carry chaff. 'Chaff' is the name for bundles of aluminium-coated plastic strips, some only the size of a household pin, which have been cut to special lengths to match the frequency characteristics of fire-control radars. Ships' rockets fire out large bundles of chaff when they are under attack and the chaff 'blooms' out into large radar targets, the purpose of which is to decoy incoming missiles. In the air it is just as important to be able to decoy missiles or gun-control radars that are threatening the aircraft.

The chaff and flare dispensers destined for Sea Harrier had not been procured prior to the Task Force being mobilised, so we did not enjoy the protection of this very useful form of self-defence (the flares are used to decoy heat-seeking, rather than radar-guided, missiles). Early in the conflict a supply of dispensers did reach the Task Group, that is, *Hermes*, but none were ever delivered by *Hermes* to *Invincible* until the war was practically over. The only answer therefore was self-help.

Two options were adopted. The first allowed chaff to be carried on every flight. The squadron engineers rigged a system that we had tried before where the chaff bundles were carried in the airbrake – and only dispensed when that brake was fully extended. The second option depended on the aircraft being in the bombing role. Chaff bundles were placed between the bomb and the aircraft pylon, so that when the bomb left the aircraft, the chaff would automatically be dispensed — with luck any fire-control radar tracking the bomber would be decoyed by the chaff. Both of these 'fixes' worked well.

On the night of the 14th I got airborne for my first high-level bombing run against Stanley airfield. The main flight mission was CAP, but first I was to overfly the airfield and wake everybody up. Mortimer had already conducted the first trial by day. He and his Number Two, Charlie Cantan, had both witnessed their bombs fusing (going off) about 200 feet from their aiming point, the aircraft hard-standing or parking area between the runway and the control tower. It was a very encouraging result and the credit for those bombs and all the others that were to follow belonged firmly with the AWI (who had thought up the idea and done all the calculations) and with the SHAR avionics package.

Provided you knew how to use the radar and the Navhars, and

provided the wind forecast over the target was reasonably accurate, there was no reason why every bomb dropped should not be 'on target'.

I approached the vicinity of the airfield at low level and took a radar navigation update fix on the local terrain before climbing to my planned release height, 10,000 feet. My target co-ordinates were already programmed into a Navhars destination and, once at the right height, all I had to do was follow the guidance commands in the HUD. I had already fed the wind factor into the computer. Now all that was left to do was 'pickle' on time – and the time was given to me by the Navhars. It was very simple. When the time to go hit 'zero', I pickled, turned away from the target and waited for the VT fuse to set the bomb off at 50 feet. As it exploded, I could see that the flash of the bomb was directly over the runway by the hard-standing. Slightly short of the aim point, but good enough for Government work!

Back on board, Wings and the Captain were both well pleased with the idea of the composite CAP-and-bombing sortie, and it was to become a regular occurrence. The accuracy of the attack was very much better than that displayed by the Vulcan, which altogether dropped three strings each of twenty-one bombs. The length of each string on the ground was of the order of at least 300 yards and, of course, the aiming point for the string would be to put the centre bomb on target. Of the three strings dropped, only one was close to the runway and the centre bomb of that string was something like 150 yards beyond the aiming point, with only the first of the sixty-three bombs delivered actually cratering the edge of the runway.

After the third Vulcan bombing attempt, the Captain was naturally keen to count up the cost of what we now referred to as 'One Bomb Beetham's finest hour'. He asked me to work it all out for him, and at an evening Command Briefing I read out my calculations.

'The first point, Sir, is that we don't know for sure exactly how many tankers were used to support each V-bomber attack, and so the figures that I'm about to give you are quite conservative. At minimum, the bomb on the edge of the runway cost the tax payer 3,300,000 pounds of aviation fuel. That is over 400,000 gallons. The same fuel would support 785 bombing sorties from the Carrier Group and allow for the delivery of 2357 bombs.'

JJ was rapidly copying the figures down onto the back of a photograph of the airfield. It was a squadron aerial photograph of the runway and the forty-two bomb craters – twenty-one bombs having fallen unarmed.

'Good. Thank you, Sharkey. That will all be very useful for after-dinner speeches in the future!'

What neither JJ nor I knew at the time was that, having realised that their bombing wasn't getting them many bouquets, the RAF were soon to send Vulcans armed with Shrike anti-radar missiles to try to silence some of the gunnery-control radars around Port Stanley. About four of these missions were flown, with about as much effect as the bombing sorties. Post-war inspection of ground-based radars by myself and others showed that, at best, one 30-mm AAA radar was put out of action by the attacks.

Of course, not all of the tanker-supported bombing raids that took off from Ascension reached the islands. An Air Force friend of mine later told me about one of the raids that was called off after it had got airborne. After take-off and when approaching high level, the Vulcan came up on the air and reported a cabin pressurisation failure. That meant it couldn't continue its mission as there would not be enough oxygen for the pilots. After all the aircraft had ditched fuel down to land-on weights (thirteen tankers throwing away about 80,000 pounds each) it was found that the 'pressurisation failure' had been caused by one of the cockpit windows being left open.

In total, educated guesswork indicates that the Vulcan attack effort during the campaign consumed not less than 13,000,000 pounds of fuel, or 1,625,000 gallons. That doesn't count the deployment costs to Ascension, either. And what was achieved? A half crater at the side of a runway that was filled in within twenty-four hours, and possibly a 30-mm gun radar knocked out. When air marshals talk of the tanker force as a Force Multiplier, do they not really mean a Cost Multiplier?

Propaganda was, of course, used later to try to justify these missions: 'The Mirage IIIs were withdrawn from Southern Argentina to Buenos Aires to add to the defences there following the Vulcan raids on the islands.' Apparently the logic behind this statement was that if the Vulcan could hit Port Stanley, then Buenos Aires was well within range as well and was vulnerable to similar attacks. I never went along with that baloney. A lone Vulcan or two running in to attack Buenos Aires without fighter support would have been shot to hell in quick time.

The real truth of the matter was that the Mirage IIIs and other aircraft had been outclassed by the Sea Harrier on day one of air combat and, as a result, all Argentine pilots were instructed to keep out of the way when Sea Harrier was around (this was confirmed in Argentina following the war). Jets sent out from the mainland to bomb or strafe Task Force targets had orders to the effect that if a Sea Harrier CAP got in their way en route to the target, they were to jettison their ordnance and return home. One Argentine attack pilot confirmed after the war that he was turned away by Sea Harrier CAPs on four missions before eventually getting through to his target. It was also the case that the majority of Mirage IIIs had 'lost' their centre-line fuel tanks on the first day of combat and could not therefore sustain CAP over the Falklands for any length of time.

Mirage IIIs were in evidence near the islands on several occasions during the conflict, either escorting the Neptune reconnaissance missions or on 'interference' flights that attempted to draw CAP attention away from air-to-ground attacks. But more of that later. Suffice it to say that you didn't need more than one or two Mirage IIIs to intercept a Vulcan attack on Buenos Aires, and that city was already used to ordnance flying around in the air when disputes between their Air Force and Navy got overheated. It would have taken much more than a lone Vulcan raid to upset Buenos Aires, and it was being rumoured around the fleet that if things went badly for us then the city would indeed be attacked. Maggie would send a Polaris missile without a warhead — and if the Argentines didn't toe the line after that, she would send one with a warhead.

Whatever rumours or 'Light-Blue fantasies' were flying around was not really our concern in the Task Group. There was much more to occupy the mind and, in *Invincible*, 14 May was a day to remember. It was the day on which *Hermes* at last provided her sister carrier with some light entertainment. The night before, the Flagship had planned covertly to approach within helicopter range of Pebble Island and insert an SAS team to knock out the light aircraft situated on the grass airfield there. *Glamorgan* and a Type 22 Sea Wolf frigate were to accompany her.

The SAS boys had parachuted into the sea alongside the carriers courtesy of a Hercules and were ready to go to war. It was a flamboyant arrival and the sailors in each ship were agog with excitement. In the 820 Squadron ready room, one of the dripping wet 'killers' dropped his parachute in a heap in the corner and said, 'Don't anyone touch that!' Three days later and after the man had left the ship it was still there — who was going to argue with the SAS?

The Pebble Island raid was planned for the early hours of the 14th, and so the Flagship and escorts had set off inshore shortly after dark. We in 801 would of course be responsible for all CAP duties that night. Later that evening, the three vessels reappeared within the Task Group, their mission aborted for twenty-four hours. Had someone had forgotten to ensure that all the equipment the SAS needed for their task was on board?.. Needless to say, 801 was still to do all the alert duties that night.

The actual raid on Pebble Island took place in the early hours of 15 May and was a great success. All the light aircraft were destroyed or disabled and the SAS suffered no casualties.

As time passed, the main talking-point on the ships of the Carrier Group concerned the landing of our troops on East Falkland Island. When would it take place, and where? Already the SAS and SBS had been put ashore in several locations to spy on enemy activity and to provide the command with intelligence that would assist the decision-making process. The Royal Marines knew the Falklands well, and so it was only appropriate that Major-General Jeremy Moore, OBE, MC and Bar, should be given command of the land operation.

In advance of his arrival the 3 Commando Brigade commander, Brigadier Julian Thompson, Royal Marines, worked closely with the Naval Commander of Amphibious Forces, Commodore Mike Clapp. It was their job to plan all aspects of the landing and follow-up activities, including the defence of the beach-head. Whilst this planning was progressing, the special forces inshore kept up a steady flow of useful intelligence. This included information on enemy air and ground movements, and all of it was collected by the Staff in *Hermes*, digested, and then used to their own complete satisfaction. No useful intelligence on any of the ground-to-air defences was passed to *Invincible*; instead, on the morning of 19 May, a tasking signal arrived in the ship for 801 Squadron.

I was asleep in my cabin when the signal arrived. A few hours earlier I had been conducting a second night Lepus 'wake-up' operation over Darwin and Fox Bay. The telephone rang.

'Boss, you'd better get up here fast. There is a row blowing up with the Flag and we are at the centre of it!' Within minutes I was in the crewroom and reading the signal, which went roughly as follows:

801 Squadron is to attack and destroy four helicopters known to be stationed at [reference position] on the slopes of Mount Kent. The attack is to take place at dawn. Aircraft armed with 1000-pound retard bombs will approach the target area at low level via Teal Inlet, deliver their ordnance and then depart the target area at low level on a northerly heading.

Target defences: there are at least three radar-laid 30-mm guns in the area of the target.

I digested the contents of the missive. The first and most obvious problem with the signal was that it had just arrived in the ship and that dawn had passed half an hour ago. All six 801 aircraft were available for the task, but not in the ground-attack configuration (how could they be when they were flying their backsides off on CAP missions and alerts by day and night?). That meant that they had to be role-changed, which takes time — although not the twelve hours apparently needed for the *Hermes* attack on the airfield.

I decided on my course of action without hesitation.

'Morts, get four cabs prepared for air-to-ground bombing. Three bombs per cab. I want retard and VT fuse free-fall bombs available. I'll decide which ones to load onto the aircraft later, after I've had a chat with Wings. Robin, Morts and I will fly on this one with two others. You arrange it. Duty boy, get in touch with the Met. Office and tell them I'll be down to see them in about twenty minutes.'

I then raced up the ladders to Flyco, to find Wings in a serious confab with the Captain. As I entered, he turned sharply on me: 'Why hasn't this been actioned, Ward? You should have taken off ages ago!' Wings was

probably more tired than the rest of us and not fully in the picture —
but I felt there was no need for the 'Ward' bit.

I looked at my watch. 'The tasking signal arrived in the squadron ten
minutes ago, Sir. We are now preparing the aircraft for the task as
quickly as possible.' Wings backed off but, like myself, was annoyed at
the impossible fast ball we had received.

'How soon can you get airborne, Sharkey?' The Captain intervened.

'It won't be less than an hour, Sir; but I am very unhappy with the
signal content.'

'Oh, why is that? Enlighten me.'

'Well, Sir, it describes the enemy defences but doesn't tell us where
they are. That is critical to our chosen track over the ground. I want
that information from the Flag. If we can't get it, then I want to do a
high-level delivery — four aircraft in card formation rippling three
VT-fused bombs each. That will saturate the target area with shrapnel
and should see to the helicopters — if they are still there, that is.' The
chances of them still being there were remote.

'But the signal clearly indicates low-level laydown bombing,'
interrupted Wings. 'Those are your orders and that is what you are to
do.'

Dusty had obviously not slept well, if he had slept at all, but I wasn't
giving up that easily.

'With the greatest of respect, Sir, the Staff should not tell us HOW to
do the job. They should give us a target and *all* appropriate intelligence
information and say "get on with it". I say that, Sir, because they want
us to use laydown bombs on the side of a bloody mountain! We should
have been tasked with rockets or guns. The rocket is the ideal area
weapon to use against thin-skinned targets such as helicopters. Nor is it
right for them to tell us exactly what route to fly — that's my AWI's
responsibility.'

Wings couldn't argue with the logic, but quite understandably didn't
like his Squadron Commander getting uppity.

'I'll be down in thirty minutes for the brief. And it will be low-level
laydown. Understood?'

'Aye, aye, Sir!' But before I could storm out of Flyco the Captain
poured some water on the gathering flames.

'Wings, get in touch with SAVO and get Sharkey the intelligence he
needs. That's the least we can do. And tell the Staff that their tasking
signal was not received until after dawn. Also check if they want the
sortie to go ahead — those choppers are probably miles away by now.'

I was definitely not satisfied with the answers I had had. Leaving
Flyco at the rush, I headed straight for the Met. Office. Bob Young was
there and waiting. I explained the bones of the problem, then continued,

'Now, Bob, what is the weather likely to be around the target area?'

'A lot of medium cloud and some at low level. You might be able to get through it, though.'

'OK. This is the met. brief I want from you: "Considerable chance of low-level cloud on the deck near Mount Kent. Doubtful if you would get through to the target." Can do?'

'Anything for you, Sharkey,' chuckled the tall Geordie. He loved a bit of intrigue.

Then it was back to the crewroom. The AWI had already prepared the low-level brief. 'Right, Ian. You will lead this sortie at low level. I will be your Number Two.' The AWI was definitely the expert down on the deck over land. 'We shall also brief an alternate sortie of high-level bombing. If we go high-level, then I will lead.'

Wings attended the rapid briefing, the main body of which concentrated on the low-level run-in to the target and the attack. It was going to be difficult if not impossible for the last two aircraft to avoid shrapnel from the lead aircraft bombs. The helo disposition on the ground was the trouble. And Mortimer was distinctly unhappy about the lack of real intelligence. 'If we don't know the position of those guns, Sir, we could start losing aircraft.' High-value Sea Harriers being used just to have a crack at relatively low-value helicopters; you could sense it in his voice — it wasn't a good exchange!

'I'm sorry about that,' said Wings. 'We are still trying to get the appropriate information from the Flag.'

I then gave the short brief on the high-level alternative before the Met. Officer arrived. Bob Young was as good as his word. He emphasised the probability of clag on the way in to the target at low level. That was enough for Wings. He got up. 'Carry on with the high-level alternative, Sharkey. Let me know how you get on.'

The Flag never came back with the much-needed intelligence.

I was flying 004 again and led the division of four aircraft to our turn-in point near Cape Dolphin. Much to my surprise, my Navhars was playing up a little and as accuracy of position was the key to the attack I handed the lead of the formation over to the AWI. Ian's system was good and all in the division knew that there was a very good chance of getting the bombs right on target — whether the helos were there or not. The formation was a loose box, the same dimension as the reported disposition of helicopters on the ground.

'Standby, standby, standby — now!' We all pickled at the same time and watched as the twelve bombs dropped away through the layers of cloud towards Mount Kent.

I rolled over on my back, pulled hard and followed the bombs down. I wanted to see where they landed, having studied the large-scale map of the target area hard before getting airborne. There were some paths on the side of the mountain bordering the target site and as I started to pull out of the near vertical dive at about 8,000 feet I saw the site through a gap in the cloud. The explosions in card formation were well placed inside the pattern of paths. I continued my pull-out and climbed away towards Stanley to join the rest of the team on the way home.

23

Returning towards the Task Group from Mount Kent, I climbed and caught up with the other three SHARs over Stanley airfield at 20,000 feet. For five days we had been delivering our single bombs there before taking up CAP stations, and on each occasion a moderate amount of flak had been put into the air against us. The ground fire was not very sophisticated and the only shell bursts that we saw were astern of the attacking aircraft. However, just to be on the safe side I had moved up the height of bomb release in stages from 10,000 feet, finally settling on the Vulcan release height of 20,000 feet. As I closed with the other three aircraft I was mildly amused to note that shells were still bursting slightly below and astern of the three. One thing was certain; the Argentines never gave up trying.

Very soon, thoughts of bombing Stanley were to be put aside for over a week. The amphibious landing date had been chosen as 21 May, and from that date the main effort of air defence was to be concentrated inshore around San Carlos Water at the head of Falkland Sound. This, plus the arrival on station of the *Atlantic Conveyor* with eight Sea Harriers, six Ground-Attack Harriers (GR 3s) and several helicopters, marked a change in lifestyle for all on board *Invincible*.

The main war effort was switching from over the Carrier Group to inshore, and naval aspects of the Amphibious Force tactics and control were vested in Commodore Mike Clapp. The Flag and his Staff were pretty well sidelined, and this was to mean far less frustration and hassle for *Invincible* and 801. The Commodore and his staff understood and respected the air element of their defences; suddenly everyone was pulling in the same direction.

The much-needed Sea Harrier reinforcements were split equally between *Hermes* and *Invincible*, bringing the 801 strength to ten aircraft and 800 Squadron up to fifteen jets.

The No 1 Squadron GR Mk 3 Harriers from the Royal Air Force were indeed a welcome sight as they perched on the deck of the container ship. Initially they had been despatched south with the additional eight Sea Harriers to support the air defence need, and it had been planned to operate them in the CAP role armed with Sidewinders. They would have worked extremely efficiently in mixed CAP pairs with the Sea Jet. But the SHAR losses that had been anticipated by the prophets of doom had not materialised and it was now more than likely that the GR 3s would be used for the job they were designed to do, ground attack and reconnaissance. They were a good squadron and a fine bunch of aircrew; they were also very professional ground-attack artists.

The two marks of VSTOL jet had to take off vertically from the *Atlantic Conveyor* (there was no runway available on the container ship) and then make the short air transit to the carriers. We received our four aircraft with delight and Dick Goodenough's team immediately went to work on them in the hangar. They were in good condition after their long sea transit and so the engineers were able to concentrate their efforts on the avionics; modifying, tuning and generally bringing them up to standard. There were only four extra pilots allocated to 801, Tim Gedge, Dave Braithwaite, Dave Austin and Alasdair Craig, giving a total strength of thirteen. *Hermes* now had twenty-one.

Before their arrival on board, Wings asked me to drop in to his cabin for a chat.

'Sharkey, do sit down. I want to have a word about the new pilots we are getting and, in particular, Tim Gedge. I know that you respect him as an officer and a gentleman but it is no secret that you have some doubts about whether he has the right temperament for a fighter pilot. Now I don't want any trouble between you two and that is why I asked you to come and discuss the matter with me.'

'Thank you, Sir, I appreciate that. I can't see any problems arising as long as he pulls his weight like the rest of the squadron.'

'Ah, well that's my point. He was CO of 800 before and for the transit down was appointed as CO 809 Squadron. So I am thinking of granting him CO status in this ship as well.'

He continued: 'You of course would remain as CO 801, but with an 809 detachment working for you on relatively equal terms. Then Tim would be seen to have the right status.'

'I'm sorry, Sir, I'm afraid I can't agree to that. There is only one Sea Harrier squadron in this ship. That is 801, and it belongs to me. We have never let this ship down; in fact quite the contrary. We have set very high standards and I intend to see that they are maintained. I can't see that that would be possible if it were under joint control. All I can promise you is that off-duty he will be accorded the prestige of a CO's standing. But on duty and in the air, he is an 801 pilot — no more, no less.'

'Hmm... I knew that was going to be your response! I have of course discussed it with the Captain and he tends to think like you do. All right — have it your way, but I'll be keeping an eye on you to make sure you treat him fairly.'

I grinned with relief. 'Thank you, Sir. I'll speak to Tim and let him know the score. I'm sure he will understand.'

Tim Gedge did understand, and hadn't expected anything else.

Robin Kent and Ian Mortimer set up twenty-four hours of intensive briefing for the four newcomers and I crossed my fingers that all would go well for them. They were all delighted to be on board *Invincible* and I was especially pleased to have my old friends Dave Braithwaite and Alastair Craig in the 801 team.

'Robin, you'd better pair up Dave the Brave with Tim Gedge. They've been flying together recently and so should complement each other well in the air. And though Dave is the AWI, Tim had better lead the section.'

Over in *Hermes*, the Harrier GR Mk 3 aircraft landed-on just before dark. The Squadron CO, Peter Squire, and two others were immediately instructed to remain in their cockpits by the Captain. It was their first visit to a carrier at sea and they were not quite certain what this delay in getting out of the cockpit meant. It wasn't quite what they had expected after their long journey. Activity around their aircraft was soon intense and it slowly dawned on the No 1 Squadron Boss that they were being prepared for launch — and with weapons. It was dusk and soon it would be dark; and a black night, to boot.

In anybody's book the very idea of launching the three newcomers without a proper briefing on their first deck sortie by night was absolutely incredible. But it nearly happened. Only intense pressure from Squire in the cockpit and the team in Flyco eventually persuaded the Command to see reason. They didn't get launched, but neither did they forget their welcome on board. It seemed that all the hassle that had been directed towards 801 in the past few weeks was now going to be centred on the RAF Harrier boys. When would the command in the flagship start directing their venom against the enemy, instead of our own forces?

The leadership of the land forces was more akin to what one would have expected in a war situation. In advance of the imminent arrival of Major-General Jeremy Moore, Brigadier Julian Thompson was busy briefing all his troops personally and getting to know his unit commanders or, in the case of the Royal Marines, renewing acquaintances with old friends.

The Brigadier knew what he was doing. He was short but tough as blazes, and had the respect of all who knew him. Those who didn't were soon taken by his genuine concern for their welfare in the field. At the end of one of his major. briefing sessions to his troops he covered a bit of air warfare advice: 'If you are sitting in your dug-out and an aircraft comes towards you at low level, shoot the bloody thing down!' His comment went down well with the lads, and when I heard about it I made sure that all my pilots knew the ground rules.

The beach-head had now been chosen by Brigadier Thompson and Commodore Clapp, and well before the landings on the enclosed beaches of San Carlos Water took place Admiral Woodward had to take one of many difficult decisions. No one knew for sure whether Falkland Sound had been mined by the enemy or not, and the Task Force had no minesweepers or hunters available. He couldn't risk the *Canberra*, for example, being immobilised or sunk by a mine in the entrance to the Sound; not with thousands of soldiers on board. So he had to use a guinea pig for the 'minesweeping' task, and the ship to draw the short straw was HMS *Alacrity*.

The frigate was seen entering the Sound at its southern end under cover of darkness by three interested observers ashore, a unit of the SAS that had already been inserted by another frigate. Their job was monitoring enemy sea movements in the Sound and they were able to inform *Alacrity* that a cargo vessel had recently preceded her heading northwards in covert fashion. It had probably been a stores supply vessel. That meant that the southern end of the Sound must be clear of mines, so *Alacrity* proceeded to chase, find and attack the stores ship with her gun. The vessel blew up when one of the first 4.5 inch shells hit her. She had obviously been delivering fuel or ammunition.

Good for the *Alacrity* and good for the boys ashore! The latter's morale had been slightly dented earlier that night. A bright moon was casting long clear shadows all round their hiding place when suddenly they heard movement up the beach close to them. About twenty tall shadows were approaching their nest and, for a short moment, they thought that the enemy had detected them and was moving in. If so, it would be Argentine commandos. Would it be a fight to the death or surrender? As the shadows came into full view, the 'enemy' turned out to be a gaggle (or penguinire) of penguins.

Alacrity proceeded with her sweep of the Sound and was able to report that all was clear. On the grey and overcast morning of 21 May, the Amphibious Group passed White Rock Bay, entered the Sound and then steamed into San Carlos Water. Seven of Her Majesty's Ships were ordered to remain in the Sound outside the protection of San Carlos to present a ring of steel against enemy air attack. The Commodore knew that the seven frigates and destroyers were in for a lot of unfriendly attention and that their weapon systems had not been designed for use in land-locked waterways. But the priority had to be getting the troops ashore. It was a brilliant move by the Commodore and led to the safe and almost casualty-free disembarkation of over 4000 men and their equipment.

Mike Clapp also knew his business about air-to-air warfare, and he was relying on having three CAP stations up-threat of San Carlos, each filled by a pair of Sea Harriers throughout daylight hours. He didn't think he needed to tell the CAPs what height to fly at, or so he thought. He trusted that the Sea Harrier boys would achieve the best possible results using their own initiative.

On board *Invincible*, I was briefing my pilots as to exactly what I wanted.

'Gentlemen, as you know, the Amphibious Force is right at this minute setting up the beach-head for landing in San Carlos Water. With any luck, by now the first part of the operation, that is, getting into the area unscathed, has been completed successfully. We have had no indications to the contrary. But pretty soon the shit is going to hit the fan, and the only things standing between our disembarking troops and disaster are seven of Her Majesty's Ships and the Sea Harrier.

'The Commodore Amphibious Forces has got his "wings" and knows what he can and can't expect from us. We are going to give him all we've got.

'There are three CAP stations established for us to the north-west, west and south-west of San Carlos. Take down the co-ordinates from the board. The plan is to keep all three stations filled with two Sea Jets throughout daylight hours. Even with a total of twenty-five Sea Harriers, that means a lot of flying because you are actually going to spend more time in transit than on task. We are now 150 nautical miles from the beach-head, and that distance could get greater.

'The defensive ring of frigates in the Sound will be close to San Carlos, and very soon we hope that a T-33 Rapier battery from the Army will be set up and giving some protection to both the amphibious shipping and the encircling defences. So at no time are you to enter the Rapier missile zone around San Carlos without being given clearance by the Local Air Defence Control Ship. If you do have to go and land in San Carlos on one of the assault vessels, then get clearance first and come in at less than 250 knots with your gear down and landing lights on. No mistakes, please.

'Up until now, our task has been over the 'oggin. Our weapon systems have worked well — witness 1 May. We are now going into a very different environment which is, in the main, over land. We all realise that the Blue Fox cannot operate when looking down over the land, but I want you all to understand that it will continue to have considerable deterrence value against the enemy. You are to keep the radar transmitting in the air-to-air mode at all times on CAP, whatever your height.

'From the attacks on our ships to date it is clear that the enemy are no slouches at low-level flying and, when they run in to attack San Carlos, that is where they will be; on the deck. So there is no point at all in you being up at 2000 feet or more thinking what a nice day it is. Your patrol height will be no more than 250 feet above sea or ground. In that way you will have a good chance of a visual detection of incoming raids. I don't want any missed chances because you were too high.

'Now, patrol speed when on task. Because of the distance from the ship and because we shall be operating at low level, fuel will be at a premium. But those boys sitting on the water are depending on us being there for their lives. And although it is contrary to normal fighter policy, I want you to fly the CAP at endurance speed. Yes — I know that will give the opposition an advantage when they come horning in at attack speed, but you are all big enough and good enough to allow for that — or you should be. The point is that you have to remain on station for as long as possible so that the attackers have to get round you. Rest assured, they will already be afraid of you. And your presence plus their fear means deterrence. If you can turn them away then you have achieved the main goal. Shooting them down will be a nice bonus.

'While still on the subject of fuel, let's talk about recovery fuel states. You've all heard 800 returning from CAP at sea with 2000 pounds of fuel or more. That is a disgrace. And anyone landing back on board this ship after a CAP at San Carlos with more than 800 pounds will get my boot up his arse. Understood?

'En route to and from the CAP you will continue to sanitise the sea areas around the force for surface contacts with your radars. And use your radars also to assist in deconfliction against CAPs coming or going the other way.

'Finally, two points. Most of you have been flying together now in pairs since day one. Continue to keep the RT to a minimum until you have to use it. There should be no need for any radio transmission post-launch until contacting the Control Ship in San Carlos. Second point: I'll leave it to your judgement about briefing each mission. Seems pretty bog standard to me, apart from checking the weather and checking which CAP station you have to take up. You shouldn't need to brief anything else.

'Any questions? No? Then carry on, and good luck!'

Before getting airborne for my first mission of the day I had to provide a relatively comprehensive brief because Alasdair Craig was joining my section as a Number Three. It was his first time airborne since arriving from *Atlantic Conveyor* and he was keen to get into the swing of things. We knew each other well from the *Ark Royal* days when Alasdair was flying the Buccaneer.

There were two ways to approach the CAP stations, transiting north or south of the missile zone, and on this first mission we had been given the southerly CAP station. The early morning clag had abated a little but there were still extensive layers of medium to low cloud partially covering the islands, especially to the north of Falkland Sound. We descended in battle formation past Darwin and took up the CAP station, with Alasdair sticking to Steve's wing. In the morning sun the Sound was a beautiful sight with an amazing mixture of startlingly clear blues, greens and shades of turquoise. Banks of yellowish kelp seaweed took their form from the currents and the colour of the water, in sharp contrast to the muddy browns and greens of the surrounding landscape.

It was initially a quiet mission with no trade until we had commenced our climb-out after 45 minutes at low level. As we were passing about 10,000 feet the *Antrim* controller came up on the air. 'I have two slow-moving contacts over the land to the south of you. Possibly helicopters or ground-attack aircraft. Do you wish to investigate?'

As soon as the controller had said the word 'south', I had rolled hard to starboard and down. Steve Thomas and Alasdair followed suit.

'Affirmative. Now in descent heading 160°. Do you still hold the contacts?'

'Affirmative. 10 miles, very low.'

Steve spotted them first. It was a good sighting against the indistinct colours of the gently undulating terrain. 'Got them, Sharkey! Looks like two Pucaras on the deck. About 15° right of the nose.'

'Not visual. You attack first.' Then, as I spoke, I saw one of the Pucaras. Steve was closing in on the aircraft from its high right, 4 o'clock. I decided to attack the same aircraft from astern as I couldn't see the second target. 'Got one visual now. Same one you are going for. I'll attack from his 6.'

My Numbers Two and Three opened fire in unison against the target, their cannon shells ripping up the ground beyond the Pucara. I had a little more time for tracking and closed in astern of the enemy aircraft, which was hugging the ground and weaving gently — with any more bank its wing tip would have been in the dirt. I had a lot of overtake, centred the Pucara at the end of my hotline gunsight in the HUD, and squeezed the trigger. The aircraft gave its familiar shudder as the 30-mm cannon shells left the two barrels. They were on target.

The Pucara's right engine burst into flames and then the shells impacted the left aileron, nearly sawing off the wing tip as they did so. I was very close, and pulled off my target.

Meanwhile, Steve had reversed to the left of the Pucara and was turning in for a second shot from a beam position. I had throttled back, jinked hard right and left, and prepared for a second stern shot. As the ground to the right of the enemy took the full weight of Steve and Alasdair's cannon fire, I dropped half flap. I wanted to get as low as possible behind the Pucara and dropping the flap brought my nose and gun axis down relative to the wing-line. Aiming... hotline on... firing! The left engine of the Pucara now erupted into flame and part of the rear cockpit canopy shattered. My radio altimeter readout in the HUD told me I was firing from as low as 10 and not higher than 60 feet above the ground.

I pulled off a second time, fully expecting the pilot to have ejected. Must be a very brave bloke in there because he was still trying to evade the fighters. Steve's section attacked again from the right, but it just wasn't his day – the ground erupted in pain once more. I was amazed that the Pucara was still flying as I started my third and final run. Sight on — and this time you're going down. Pieces of fuselage, wing and canopy were torn from the doomed aircraft. The fuselage caught fire. I ceased firing at the last minute and as I raised my nose off the target, the pilot ejected. The aircraft had ploughed into the soft earth in a gentle skid by the time the pilot's feet hit the ground. He only had one swing in his parachute.

Later, I was to find out that the pilot's name was Major Tomba. He managed to hoof it back to his base at Goose Green after his ejection; before the war was over the man's bravery was to prove useful to both sides.

Our division of three SHARs then resumed the climb and returned to the ship. Needless to say, we were pretty short of fuel.

Everyone was keen to hear the gory details when I got to the crewroom.

Steve and I flew the next mission as a pair. There was no trade for us under the now clear blue skies, but we could see that to the south of the Sound HMS *Ardent* had seen more than enough action for the day. She was limping northwards and smoke was definitely coming from more places than her funnel. We were to see more of her on our third and final sortie of the day.

For this final 'hop' we were given the station to the west of San Carlos over the land. We descended from the north-east and set up a low-level race-track patrol in a wide shallow valley. As always, we flew in battle formation — side-by-side and about half a mile apart. When we turned at the end of the race-track pattern, we always turned towards each other in order to ensure that no enemy fighter could approach our partner's 6 o'clock undetected. I had just flown through Steve in the middle of a turn at the southerly end of the race-track when I spotted two triangular shapes approaching down the far side of the valley under the hills from the west. They were moving fast and were definitely Mirages, probably Daggers. I levelled out of the turn and pointed directly at them, increasing power to full throttle as I did so.

'Two Mirages! Head-on to me now, Steve. 1 mile.'

'Passing between them now!' I was lower than the leader and higher than the Number Two as they flashed past each side of my cockpit. They were only about 50 yards apart and at about 100 feet above the deck. As I passed them I pulled hard to the right, slightly nose-high, expecting them still to try to make it through to their target by going left and resuming their track. I craned my neck over my right shoulder but they didn't appear. Instead I could see Steve chasing across the skyline towards the west. My heart suddenly leapt. They are going to stay and fight! Must have turned the other way.

They had turned the other way, but not to fight. They were running for home and hadn't seen Steve at all because their turn placed him squarely in their 6 o'clock. Steve's first missile streaked from under the Sea Harrier's wing. It curved over the tail of the Mirage leaving its characteristic white smoke trail and impacted the spine of the jet behind the cockpit. The pilot must have seen it coming because he had already jettisoned the canopy before the missile arrived; when it did, he ejected. The back half of the delta-winged fighter-bomber disappeared in a great gout of flame before the jet exploded.

I checked Steve's tail was clear but he was far too busy to think of checking my own 6 o'clock. Otherwise he would have seen the third Mirage closing fast on my tail.

Steve was concentrating on tracking the second jet in his sights and he released his second Sidewinder. The missile had a long chase after its target, which was accelerating hard in full burner towards the sanctuary of the west. At missile burn-out the Mirage started to pull up for some clouds. The lethal dot of white continued to track the fighter-bomber and as the jet entered cloud, I clearly saw the missile proximity-fuse under the wing. It was an amazing spectacle.

Adrenalin running high, I glanced round to check the sky about me. Flashing underneath me and just to my right was the beautiful green and brown camouflage of the third Dagger. I broke right and down towards the aircraft's tail, acquired the jet exhaust with the Sidewinder, and released the missile. It reached its target in very quick time and the Dagger disappeared in a ball of flame. Out of the flame ball exploded the broken pieces of the jet, some of which cartwheeled along the ground before coming to rest, no longer recognisable as parts of an aircraft.

Later I was to discover that the third Mirage Dagger had entered the fight from the north and found me in his sights. As he turned towards the west and home he had been firing his guns at me in the turn, but had missed. It was the closest shave that I was to experience.

We were euphorically excited as we found each other visually and joined up as a pair to continue our CAP duties. We had moved a few miles west during the short engagement and now steadied on east for some seconds to regain the correct patrol position. As I was looking towards San Carlos, about 10 miles distant behind the hills, I noticed three seagulls in the sunlight ahead. Were they seagulls?

I called *Brilliant*, 'Do you have any friendlies close to you?'

'Wait!' It was a sharper than usual reply.

A second or two later, *Brilliant* was back on the air. 'Sorry, we've just been strafed by a Mirage. Hit in the Ops Room. Man opposite me is hurt and I think I'm hit in the arm. No, no friendlies close to us.'

Full power again. 'Steve, those aren't seagulls ahead, they're Sky Hawks!' What had looked like white birds were actually attack aircraft that had paused to choose a target. As I spoke the three 'seagulls' stopped orbiting, headed towards the south and descended behind the line of hills. And from my morning flight I knew where they were going.

'They're going for *Ardent*!' I headed flat-out to the south-east, passing over the settlement of Port Howard at over 600 knots and 100 feet.

In quick time I cleared the line of hills to my left and was suddenly over the water of the Sound. Ahead and to the left were the Sky Hawks. To the right was the stricken *Ardent*, billowing smoke like a beacon as she attempted to make her way to San Carlos. I wasn't going to get there in time but I knew that Red Section from *Hermes* should be on CAP on the other side of the water. 'Red Section! Three Sky Hawks, north to south towards *Ardent*! I'm out of range to the west!'

Red Section got the message and appeared as if by magic from above the other bank of the Sound. I saw the smoke of a Sidewinder and the trailing A-4 exploded. The middle aircraft then blew up (a guns kill, so I heard later) and the third jet delivered its bombs into *Ardent* before seeming to clip the mast with its fuselage.

I looked around to see where my Number Two had got to.

'Steve, where are you?' He should have been in battle formation on the beam. No reply. My heart missed several beats. There was only one answer, he must have gone down!

I called *Brilliant*. 'Believe I've lost my Number Two to ground fire. Retracing my track back to the CAP position to make a visual search.' I didn't feel good. My visual search resulted in nothing. But I did hear the tell-tale sound of a pilot's SARBE rescue beacon. Maybe that was Steve? '*Brilliant*, I can't locate my Number Two but have picked up a SARBE signal. Could be him or one of the Mirage pilots. Can you send a helicopter to have a look, please? I'm very short of fuel and must recover to Mother immediately.'

I felt infinitely depressed as I climbed to high level. Losing Steve was a real shock to my system. At 80 miles to run, I called the ship.

'Be advised I am *very* short of fuel. I believe my Number Two has been lost over West Falkland. Commencing cruise descent.'

'Roger, Leader. Copy you are short of fuel. Your Number Two is about to land on. He's been hit but he's OK. Over.'

'Roger, Mother. That is good news. Out'.

Invincible could be clearly seen at 60 miles. She was arrowing her way through the water towards me like a speedboat, leaving a great foaming wake. Good for JJ — doesn't want to lose a Sea Jet just for a few pounds of fuel. My spirits had suddenly soared and it felt great to be alive.

I throttled back and didn't need to touch the power again until I was approaching the decel to the hover. On landing with 200 pounds of fuel remaining, I couldn't help thinking what a remarkable little jet the Sea

Harrier was. The fuel was right on the button. I had calculated 200 pounds at land-on before leaving San Carlos.

On board, I heard from Steve that he had been hit in the avionics bay by 20-mm machine-gun fire from Port Howard. He had lost his radio, couldn't communicate with me, and thought he might just as well go home. I was too pleased to see him to be angry.

'What was I supposed to think, then?'

'Oh, you were hightailing it after those Sky Hawks, Boss. You can look after yourself and as I didn't have any missiles left I thought the best thing was to get the aircraft back and get it fixed.'

'Steve, that is definitely worth a beer!'

It struck me later that if Red section from *Hermes* had been capping at low level over the sound (where any 801 CAP would have been) instead of at altitude, the Sky Hawks would have had to get through them to get at *Ardent*. The A-4s would not have tangled with the SHARs so *Ardent* would not have been hit again and mortally wounded.

24

On the whole it had been a very good day, especially for the San Carlos beach-head landings. The main priority of the Task Force had been to ensure the safe disembarkation of General Moore's men, and in spite of the loss of the fighting *Ardent* (she was abandoned and later went down) this had been achieved at relatively little cost. The Argentine forces had been taken by surprise by the chosen location of the beach-head. They had probably expected a traditional head-on confrontation on the shores of the peninsula at Port Stanley; that had been the style of the Royal Marines in the past. But they had been mistaken, and were soon to be made to pay dear for that mistake.

Commodore Mike Clapp's tactics for the air defence of San Carlos had proved very effective. Defence in depth had worked. The outer layer of Sea Harriers on CAP had shot down a mixture of nine enemy aircraft, mainly Mirage V Daggers and Sky Hawks. (Steve Thomas's second Dagger, against which the Sidewinder had proximity-fused, was never to get home and Steve was later credited with it as a confirmed kill.) But although the air-to-air confrontations had been exciting in the extreme, it was already clear that the Argentine pilots were not going to mix it with us; knocking them down had become a question of being in the right place at the right time.

That did not mean that confrontations between Sea Harrier and attack aircraft relied just on chance. Although the Argentine jets had to face the tedium of long transits from their bases to the beach-head, they had the enormous advantage of being able to choose their time of attack and of being able to adjust their attack runs to bypass CAP aircraft. The Argentine area surveillance radars on West Falkland were well-placed to advise attack aircraft of CAP positions and CAP changeover times. Further, and of immense tactical significance to the success of the CAP, attack aircraft were instructed that if confrontation with the Sea Harrier seemed inevitable then they were to jettison their attack ordnance and return to base. This happened on many occasions.

Each of the attack aircraft had equipment enabling them to detect Sea Harrier Blue Fox radars, and this represented a major element of CAP deterrence. And it was deterrence that was the most important factor in reducing the number and intensity of attacks on the beach-head, and indeed on the Task Group at sea. For example, there was not one occasion when an enemy attack on the Carrier Group passed through or close to a CAP station that was physically manned by Sea Harrier.

It is clear now that a very high percentage of the Argentine attack missions never got through to their targets, and all the credit for this deterrence must fall to the outer ring of defence, that is, the three CAP pairs. (See Epilogue for further comment.)

Nevertheless, the gallant perseverence of the Argentine attack pilots ensured that some of them did get through. Why was this? The principle reasons were: the bravery of their pilots; the topography of West Falkland, which allowed an almost limitless choice of attack routes; the fact that the Blue Fox radar could not detect targets at low level over the land; and the fact that the Argentines planned co-ordinated attacks from different directions; and the Flag's policy of keeping *Hermes'* CAPs at high level.

The CAP success in turning away air raids was significantly enhanced by the results of any opportunity for the Sea Harrier to engage the enemy in combat. Sea Harriers knocked down more enemy aircraft than any other Task Force weapon system, and not one SHAR was lost in air-to-air combat. Without the jump-jet's extraordinary deterrence factor and its combat results in defence of San Carlos, the amphibious landings would probably have realised insupportable casualties.

Although *Invincible*'s aircraft were patrolling at very low level, other reports written after the war clearly state that the *Hermes* CAP aircraft patrolled at about 8000 feet and sometimes higher, and that they remained on CAP for as little as ten minutes at a time. The result of being at this height was that they achieved very little deterrence value against incoming strikes and, critically, were normally only able to engage enemy attack aircraft after the latter had been through their target (San Carlos) and when they, the CAP, were directed down on to the tails of the escaping Argentine aircraft by the ships under attack.

I now understand that this arguably misguided use of CAP assets was based on instructions from the Staff. As such, it was a tactical error. Would it not have been far better for our ships in San Carlos and in the Sound if the *Hermes* CAP had joined the 801 air-defence barrier at low level? After all, the latter was later judged to have been successful by the Argentine airmen themselves. More CAPs at low level would have increased the deterrence factor and turned more attackers away.

On the waters of Falkland Sound, the ring of steel represented by Her Majesty's seven warships was also highly effective and was successful in taking the brunt of enemy attack intentions from those attack aircraft that did get through the CAP barrier. *Plymouth* and *Argonaut* brought down a

Dagger between them and watched it crash into the sea. This in itself was almost a bonus when compared with the inestimable value of the warships' physical presence, which was soaking up the firepower and attention of such attack aircraft as had succeeded in bypassing the CAP. It must have been a terrifying experience for the young sailors on board. Five of the seven ships suffered varying degrees of damage from bombing and strafing, but the barrage of gunfire that the ships put up into the air had forced the pilots to release their bombs at too low a level and none exploded on impact.

In spite of the effectiveness of these two outer layers of defence, it could hardly have been described as a peaceful day in San Carlos Water itself. But the site had been chosen well. Steep hills ringed the inlet on all sides and so attacking aircraft, having run the gauntlet of the CAP and the 'lions' in the Sound, had very little time to acquire and fire at their targets when at last they crested the hills and looked down on the amphibious force. After the war, we heard that the first target usually seen by the pilots in the enclosed waterway was the *Canberra*. By chance, she was painted white, which was taken by the attackers to mean that she was a hospital ship. Without exception, the Argentine pilots were honourable men, and not one attacked what they thought was a sanctuary for the injured. And from their angle, the mental process of having noticed *Canberra* first, decided she was a 'no-go' target and then looked for a secondary target, cost their attack effort its impetus. The seconds lost in deciding which ship to attack were irreplaceable. By the time they had chosen another target it was often too late to turn towards it, track it and release their ordnance.

The three declared British hospital ships were stationed to the north of the islands and were never threatened by the enemy in any way. So, not only were the Argentine flyboys brave, as Major Tomba had shown, they were also gentlemen and lacked nothing in guts and moral fibre.

What made things worse for them in San Carlos Water was the barrage of tracer bullets being fired into the air from various, but not all, ships' decks. Records later showed that the tracer acted as a very real deterrent to the attacking pilots; they generally went for the ships that were not using it.

Tracer was something very close to my heart. I had argued long and hard in the MOD for the supply of this type of ammunition for Sea Harrier. Tracer bullets and shells indicate to the firer whether his aim is good or not, so it is, in my view, essential for air-to-air as well as surface-to-air guns. Not only does it tell you whether your aim is correct by showing you where your bullets or shells are going, it also frightens the hell out of the opposition. Hence, the ships firing tracer were attacked less.

My biggest opponents in the fight for tracer for Sea Harrier were the RAF: 'they didn't use it because they didn't believe in it'. And the Civil

Servant masters of the MOD purse-strings couldn't see why the Navy should need tracer if the RAF didn't. The truth of the matter was that the RAF view was wrong. Their experts who vetoed my procurement of tracer had probably never fired air-to-air guns in their lives and didn't have the imagination to see how helpful tracer could be in combat. And so the Task Force went south without tracer rounds for their fighters. It was fortunate for the ships in San Carlos that the Army had viewed the need for tracer more professionally.

On board *Invincible* that evening, I had eventually wound down from the euphoria of the day's combat and was trying to analyse the tactics and limitations of the enemy air effort. In a curious way I had been disappointed that my head-on pass and initial turn against the Daggers had not developed into a real dog-fight. Logically, the Daggers could have made a decent fight of it because it had been at least a three-to-two situation. Perhaps there had actually been four Mirages running in to the beach-head, and when the third had a go at my aircraft with guns, the fourth, unseen by us, had peeled off and attacked *Antrim*. Whatever the actual truth behind that thought, one thing was definite: the enemy were not going to stay and chance their luck in a dog-fight.

On the passage south, it had seemed logical and tactically sound to me that the enemy would place the highest priority on shooting down as many Sea Harriers as they could. We had very limited assets and any losses would be bound to hurt us badly. Why had they not really had a good go at it? Probably they had used 1 May as a testing ground to see what truth there was in the claimed combat track-record of the SHAR in peacetime. Had it really out-performed the F-15 and other superiority fighters? Why was CO 801 so confident in his press releases?

Photographs in the press of Argentine Air Force crewrooms certainly later showed that the AAF studied the Sea Harrier and its capabilities most carefully. And the 'jousting' on 1 May also indicated that their initial fighter policy was to conduct slashing attacks against the SHAR CAP — a 'hit-and-run' philosophy. That gave credence to my theory that they already had a great respect for the Sea Jet's close-combat capability. The results of 1 May obviously underlined that respect; presumably it had been decided after their losses on that day that it was not worth mixing it with the British fighter. That had to be the answer. But still I could not fully understand why they had chosen this policy — 'don't tangle with the SHAR'. If I had been running the AAF, and in spite of early losses on day one, the policy would have been 'get the SHAR at any cost — then mop up the operation on land and at sea'. They would have lost a lot of jets in combat, but eventually the weight of numbers would have told and the Task Force would have been finished; no air defence meant no operation.

It later became open knowledge that the Argentine pilots had indeed been instructed to avoid the Sea Harrier at all costs. It was a fatal staff error and prevented Argentine aspirations of holding on to the islands from coming to fruition. How strange, I thought, that some of our senior officers failed to demonstrate a real understanding of or respect for the SHAR's capabilities, whereas the enemy high command were willing to give the British fighter the kudos it deserved.

All now seemed set for a cat-and-mouse game with the enemy air-attack effort. If the cat (the Sea Jet) was around then the mouse would run for its hole. Because of the over-land location of most of the meetings between the airborne protagonists, the SHAR was denied use of its full weapon system, but still maintained the upper hand. And in the coming weeks, the tactics adopted by attack aircraft against the CAP proved to be suicidal. To turn tail and run as a first move presented the Sea Harrier pilots with a very easy task – acquire the heat source and fire the missile. It was money for old rope, and suited the Carrier Group pilots well; not only 800 Squadron, who did not need to take full advantage of the aircraft's superior avionics and weapon system, but also ourselves in 801 — the easier it was, the better. In general it was now time and place that decided which Sea Harrier would shoot down which attacker, not weapon-system expertise. But it was professional expertise that had provided the foundation for the SHAR's success in the first instance. Without the pre-war combat sessions against the best that the West could provide, there would have been no reputation to take to the South Atlantic. Then the Argentine policy might have been the correct one – get the Sea Harrier and win the day.

. The only Harrier loss of the day had been the RAF Harrier GR 3 of Flight Lieutenant Glover as he penetrated the north of Falkland Sound at low level. His aircraft sustained hits from 20-mm fire and forced him to eject over the water close to West Falkland. Badly injured during the high-speed ejection, he could do nothing to help himself in the near-freezing water. His life was saved by an Argentine soldier who dived into the icy Sound to pull him to the shore. He survived the war as a prisoner, was well treated by his captors and later returned home.

Although San Carlos was now the main focus of attention for friend and foe, Argentina still pursued its aim of attacking and disabling one or both of the British carriers. The Argentine staff had got that right, for without the carriers there would be no air defence for the ground forces, and the AAF would have had a field day.

On the night of 21/22 May, the Task Group came under observation by a reconnaissance aircraft in the small hours. It was the only time of day or night that it was 'safe' for the enemy to attempt to gather information on the Group position for targeting purposes. By day shadowers would have been intercepted by CAP on the way to or from San Carlos – and they knew it. And so quite sensibly they only chanced their luck by night.

I was the night alert pilot with the job of dissuading such intrusions by shadowers and, on first radar contact by ships in the Group, was scrambled from my cabin. I received no brief for getting airborne, nor did I need one. The only information I had to have was the range and bearing to the target's present position; 'Three contacts 280°, 120 miles. Looks like a Neptune plus two Mirages.'

There was very little chance that the shadower would remain above the radar horizon for long enough for me to get out to it and prosecute it. The important thing was to ensure that it was sent packing in quick time. That meant a high-speed low-level dash outbound on 280° with radar silent, and then a zoom climb with radar on and a rapid search to attempt to make contact. I never had the luck to get to close quarters with the enemy surveillance platforms, but the sortie was always an enjoyable one and made me feel I was doing one of the most important tasks − denying the enemy information.

It was a lonely ride on the outbound leg. One small jet beetling along at 500 knots-plus and 200 feet − and the weather in the early hours of the 22nd was clamped. But there was quite enough to think about in the cockpit already without wondering whether the recovery to the deck would be testing. I would take out at least one of the Mirages first with a Sidewinder, and then make the decision as to whether it was the Neptune next or the other Mirage; probably the Neptune, although that could be taken out with the Aden cannon. For the Mirages at night it would have to be missiles. The computations weren't so difficult and they kept the adrenalin running while I was progressing to the pull-up point.

On pull-up, I switched the radar to transmit and called the ship for 'more help'. The contacts, as expected, had disappeared. I didn't get the chance to use my weapons but *Invincible* had given another message to the enemy: they could not take liberties at night. And to reinforce the message, the Sea Jet remained on CAP to dissuade and deter any attempt by the enemy to take advantage of information that might have been gained by the Neptune.

Having reached the hoped-for intercept point and found no trade waiting, there was still the opportunity to sanitise the sea surface for any approaching surface threat over a considerable area; more than 35,000 square miles. This figure by itself may mean little in isolation, but when compared with the type of visual area surveillance favoured by the Flag it meant quite a lot in terms of energy and resources saved. Four aircraft fanning out over 45° for 80 miles would cover only about 4000 square miles, allowing a target visibility of 10 miles. That is 1000 square miles per aircraft. or 1/35th of the CAP area coverage for a single aircraft using the Blue Fox radar correctly.

I just wished for of a modern and sophisticated Airborne Early Warning system. That would have given the over-the-horizon low-level cover needed against the Super Etendard. After the war I read in certain misguided journalistic records of the air fighting that such AEW was indeed provided by the Nimrod with 'regular patrols over the Task Force and Falklands sea areas', and other patrols which 'paralleled the Argentinian coastline and surveyed it from only 60 miles' range'. This was, of course, absolute poppycock. The Nimrod was never once in evidence over the Task Group or in adjoining areas. If it had been it would, like the Vulcan, have been clamouring for fighter cover. And as for it approaching the mainland to within 60 miles, that has to be fantasy. The nearest the Nimrod came to the scene of action during the fighting was 600 miles to the north – and that was a one-off occasion.

So the only means we had of preventing the Exocet threat were, firstly, to keep out of range and, secondly, if you had to come within the threat range, keep the Sea Harrier CAPs airborne and transmitting on the Blue Fox radar. That way there was the chance of radar contact over a calm sea and, without question, the radar emissions would deter an attacking Etendard.

The problem for the Task Group after 21 May was that, by day, 100 per cent of the SHAR effort had to be devoted to defending San Carlos Water. This meant that the transit distance to low-level CAP for the SHAR had to be balanced against the distance of the Task Group from mainland Etendard-capable airfields. The further the Group was to the east the safer it would be, but any increase in range from San Carlos would entail a corresponding reduction in on-CAP time for Sea Harriers.

Every high-level movement of CAP aircraft to and from San Carlos was monitored by the Argentine radars stationed at various locations in East and West Falkland. This information must have been a tremendous help to the AAF planners for timing their raids on the beach-head and they appeared to have used it to good effect during the days following the 21st. Any confrontation with the SHAR was avoided where possible, and although this 'avoidance' often meant that the attackers had to return to base without delivering ordnance, some did get through.

As a result of one of these raids, HMS *Antelope* took two unexploded bombs inboard, one of which later exploded when being defused. *Antelope* sank, but although the bomb-disposal expert was killed, the crew of the ship survived to fight another day.

The limited opportunities that did present themselves for SHAR to engage the AAF attackers were taken with relish. One Dagger went down to Sidewinder on 23 May and a formation of three Daggers succumbed to the same fate on the 24th when *Coventry* controlled two 800 jets on to the tails of the enemy fighter-bombers. None of the Daggers saw their opponents coming.

Task Force morale blossomed with the successful landings in San Carlos and the air-to-air successes of the Sea Jet. But on the evening of 24 May that morale was dented when the night sky was lit up with a huge explosion close to the Task Group. The *Hermes* Sea Harrier team had been tasked with a night-bombing effort, presumably high-level bombing of Stanley airfield. It was not possible for the Harrier GR 3s to do this sort of task by day or night because they lacked both radar and the Navhars.

Why, after a heavy day's flying on CAP, the *Hermes* Sea Harrier crews should have had to turn their minds to a four-aircraft night-bombing mission was beyond me. Especially as they were definitely lacking in night deck experience and had certainly not been able to practise any form of co-ordinated attack in the dark. They also lacked radar expertise, according to our recent visitors and, following some educated guesswork, I believed that this was the root cause of the accident which lit up the night sky and killed Lieutenant-Commander Gordie Batt.

Invincible were informed in the briefest terms that Gordie had flown into the sea when attempting to join up visually in formation with the other three aircraft. It seemed probable that the join-up was being conducted without making full use of the Blue Fox radar — the Staff having attempted to ban the latter's use and the command of 800 squadron having little faith in their aircraft's avionics package. I had already listened with dismay to one join-up by night by two pairs of 800 jets preparing to go on CAP. I and Steve had launched at the same time as the *Hermes* team and set off silently for the briefed climb-out point, checking our weapon systems out on each other as we did so, and climbing to high level for transit to the CAP station. We were already 120 miles en route to CAP before the two *Hermes* pairs at last managed to join up with each other. They were still overhead their carrier.

It was with that background in mind that I tried to imagine what post-launch join-up instructions had been given during the briefing for the bombing mission. It sounded as though it had been left to individuals to join their leader visually, and on a black night it was not surprising that one pilot would become slightly disorientated and forget how close he was to the water. It was even easier to lose track of your position in the sky if you were tired. And after a reported three days of CAP missions plus alerts, Gordie was very tired. But he was also game, and his untimely death was a great loss to the Task Force and to the Navy.

The next day, 25 May, was probably the worst of the war as far as Task Force losses were concerned. In overcast conditions the Carrier Group was supporting the San Carlos CAP effort from roughly 100 miles to the north-east of Stanley. This was just within the threat radius of the Super Etendard as calculated by my team prior to action commencing.

Although there was no air-to-air action for the SHARs to enjoy over Falkland Sound, their presence was undoubtedly frustrating the ingressing

AAF attackers. They referred to the Sea Harrier on Argentine national radio as 'the Black Death' (*La Muerte Negra*), and when advised of this at a Command Briefing I implemented a policy amongst my pilots to take psychological advantage of this flattering pseudonym. On all overt missions, my pilots were to call out on the Argentine air-safety frequency, 'La Muerte Negra ees-a-coming!' The calls were heard by the enemy pilots and can have done nothing to bolster their already dented morale. But if they were avoiding the Sea Jet, they were certainly not avoiding their surface attack responsibilities. Every day some got through to San Carlos, where they were met by a sustained barrage from small arms, ships' guns and missiles, Rapier and Blowpipe (the infantry's hand-held surface-to-air missile). And when an opportunity arose to attack ships outside Falkland Sound they were quick to exploit it.

Commodore Clapp had noted that most of the attackers that penetrated the CAP barrier were doing so to the north of the Sound on a route that took them close to Pebble Island. This northerly CAP station was usually filled by 800 Squadron SHARs from *Hermes* - flying at medium or high level. And so in order to reinforce this CAP station's reduced effectiveness, he picketed the noted avenue of attack with two ships, the Type 42 *Coventry* armed with Sea Dart, and the Type 22 *Broadsword* armed with Sea Wolf. The combination of the two types, known compositely as a 'Type 64', should have been a lethal deterrent to the attackers. But instead, the Argentines took it as an invitation they couldn't refuse. On the morning of the 25th, a Lear Jet reconnaissance aircraft overflew the Amphibious Operating Area early in the day at very high level and its photographs revealed the position of the two warships.

During the first part of that day — which was an Argentine national holiday and also the day that their soccer team was contesting the World Cup — attacks against San Carlos were less than had been the norm. Had the enemy taken enough losses? With all the claims of kills from within San Carlos Water it would not have been surprising, though those claims didn't actually match up to post-war examination. Very few aircraft were shot down in San Carlos. The lull in the action was more a result of all the Argentine pilots wanting to watch their football team on television. Then it was back to business as usual.

The 'business' began with four Sky Hawks approaching the two ships lying off Pebble Island at low level and high speed from over the land. They were armed with 1000-pound bombs. There was little time to react to their covert approach-and-attack route, but the CAP section of Neil Thomas was on hand and was vectored in to intercept the A-4s. The Sea Harriers had contact and were almost at Sidewinder-release range in the attackers' 6 o'clock when they were called off by their controller. *Coventry* and *Broadsword* had acquired their targets and the Sea Harriers were forbidden to follow their prey into the ships' missile engagement zone. Tragedy then struck. *Coventry*'s weapon system failed to produce the goods and, just when *Broadsword* was about to open fire, her view of the attackers was cut off by the superstructure of *Coventry*. The attacking aircraft were having the luck of the devil, and they made the most of it!

One bomb richocheted off the water through *Broadsword*'s stern and wrote off her Lynx helicopter. Three bombs, which for a change were released at the correct altitude, impacted the luckless *Coventry*, exploded, and blew her bottom out. Within about 45 seconds she had capsized. The A-4s got clean away.

Out at sea a further tragedy was to befall the Task Force. Two Etendards had, with the aid of air-to-air refuelling, come within Exocet range of the main body of ships. They had circled the Falklands well to the north to avoid the SHAR CAPs and set up their attack from the north-west.

I had already flown two CAP missions during the day and when the alarms sounded in *Invincible* I was in my cabin. It was an Exocet alarm. I reached the crewroom in less than two minutes to find that there was only one aircraft still left unmanned. Two were airborne on CAP, two en route to CAP, and two had been about to launch when the alarm sounded. Of the remaining four jets, three had already been manned, leaving just one for me to take. As I emerged on deck with the Petty Officer of the Watch, Bob Cummins, all flight-deck personnel were lying flat out with hands over heads and anti-flash gear donned – preparing for missile impact. One by one, the remaining SHARs went roaring down the centre-line and launched into the sky.

As I rapidly strapped in I slowly realised that there was little chance of getting my jet airborne. It had recently been moved by a flight-deck tractor and the machine was still attached to the aircraft nose-wheel. I patted Cummins on the shoulder and pointed to the deck – 'lie down and take cover'. The Chief Petty Officer of the Flight-Deck then took his place by the aircraft, ready to give me the signal to start up. As he looked up to the cockpit, the ship's chaff rockets began firing from above his head. They made a tremendous noise, but nothing like what was to come. I signalled to the Chief to relax and take cover, and then sat back to enjoy the scene of action. There was nothing else that I could do.

On the port bow of the ship about 10 miles distant, a dark, thick column of smoke was rising above one of the ships on the screen. That was obviously where at least one of the Exocets had struck. *Hermes* was about a mile ahead of *Invincible* and heading down towards us at high speed. She was going to pass close down the port side. Suddenly the Sea Dart mounting, which was less than 30 yards from my aircraft, came to life. JJ was about to engage the enemy — it was to be the most impressive sight of the war for me, better even than watching Mirages blow up in the sky.

When the first Sea Dart missile was fired it was like an explosion on deck. The grey-white exhaust was deflected upwards by the blast deflectors as the missile departed with astonishing acceleration towards the flat grey layer of stratus cloud. As it disappeared incredibly quickly into the cloud, the second missile fired. The force behind each launch was mind-boggling. More missiles swiftly emerged from their below-decks magazine, took their places automatically on the launcher rails, and the whole exercise was repeated.

The sky was full of smoke trails from chaff rockets and missiles. Exocet-decoy helicopters had launched from both carriers, and all ships were manoeuvring at high speed. It was a magnificent sight, one always to be remembered.

As the action subsided I remained in the cockpit and wondered which unfortunate vessel it was that was now burning uncontrollably on the horizon. It turned out to be the *Atlantic Conveyor*. Rescue helicopters, one of them flown by 'H', were already on the scene and managed to save all but twelve of the crew. Sadly, the Master, who had come out of retirement to drive his ship to the Falklands, was lost.

Meanwhile, 801 had nine out of its ten aircraft airborne, some of which would by now be very short of fuel, especially the pair due to return from CAP. As soon as the all-clear to approach the deck was given by ship's controllers, the Sea Harriers appeared and, without any fuss and from all directions, landed wherever there was space to do so.

Shortly afterwards, I got airborne to provide the last hour's CAP cover over Pebble Island and *Broadsword*, before returning to the deck in the dark. It had not been a good day.

25

On the morning of the 26th, HMS *Broadsword* continued her overnight search for possible survivors from *Coventry*. As dawn started to lighten the eastern sky, Steve Thomas and I arrived on CAP station to provide cover for the rescue operation. Casualties from the bombing attack had mercifully been few, which said a lot for the *Coventry's* crew discipline when under fire.

It wasn't a comfortable feeling for Sea Harriers on CAP to witness the onslaught by the AAF attackers against the warships in Falkland Sound. A terrific team spirit had grown up between the sailors in the ships and the jet-jockeys, and this could be sensed in the cockpit in all communications with the ships' controllers. Most of the ships in the thick of the action were commanded by aviators, with one or two notable exceptions.

Alan West, the Captain of *Ardent*, was a fish-head (seaman officer), but from the way he conducted himself in peace and war I guessed he would have made an excellent fighter pilot. When under attack he did all the right things with his frigate, such as putting maximum wind over the deck to give the attacking aircraft a bigger aiming problem with their bombs. He knew his business without having to refer to any of the war-fighting manuals that were like a Bible to most seamen officers. In my book he was of the same ilk as J.J. Black — to all in *Invincible* there could be no higher accolade than that.

Within the Senior Service there had been intense rivalry for many years between the Seaman and Aviation Branches. This was mainly based on the seaman officers' jealousy of the flying pay received by the aviators, but there was also a ludicrous gripe on the lips of almost every fish-head: 'Aviators can command squadrons of aircraft as well as ships at sea. That's not fair because we aren't allowed to command squadrons! Therefore aviators shouldn't be allowed to command ships!' It was kid's stuff, but they believed in it.

To me, there were two fundamental differences between the two branches of the service. Firstly, fish-heads were never marked or graded on their war-fighting knowledge or ability (whereas on every aviator's confidential report such things were stressed). One result was that you would sometimes get a certain type of seaman officer who appeared to concentrate on presenting 'officer-like qualities' to his superiors, and to cultivate the demeanour of an upright but obsequious yes-man. Their main intent in life was to 'keep a clean sheet' and get regular high marks in the keenly contested race for promotion. The second difference followed on from the first; few fish-heads seem to know very much about other branches of the service, or about fighting their ship as a weapon system in war.

Because of their 'trade', aviators were generally aggressive, confident and extrovert, and they had to remember all the tactics involved in war-fighting in their heads. There was no space in a cockpit for books on tactical doctrine or information about threat capabilities. What better expertise could be found for commanding warships in action? Arguably none, and, in most cases, so it proved down south.

One of the major problems facing us, as aviators commanding aeroplanes, was fatigue. Gordie Batt, E-J and Alan Curtis were all suffering from varying levels of fatigue when they died, and in Gordie's case tiredness could have been a definite contributory factory to his disorientation. And the rate of day flying and alerts had now reached a peak. The aircrew were shattered, as was everyone else in the air department.

Already, I had had to take certain of the younger pilots off flying for forty-eight hours, including my Number Two. One morning, Steve Thomas had arrived in the crewroom for his CAP mission looking like a zombie. He was totally drained and wasn't coping with the night-long vibration of his cabin down aft.

'What do you think, Robin?'

The Senior Pilot had no hesitation. 'He can't fly like that, Boss. It's just asking for trouble.'

'OK, Steve, go to the Sick Bay and get dosed-up with sleeping-tablets. You're off the programme for forty-eight hours.'

'But I'm fine, Boss. Really! I haven't complained, have I? I don't need a break.' He was as game as anyone could wish and really did not want to take an enforced rest.

'Yes you do, and that's final. Go and get some rest. You deserve it.'

The 26th was as long a day as any other. I flew three missions, and was having more than a little trouble in the air with lung problems. Every time I pulled any G on the aircraft I lapsed into uncontrollable heavy coughing for several seconds, unable to fly the aircraft proficiently or talk on the radio. The problem had been there for several days and so when I landed in the evening I approached Bob Clark's Number Two, 'Baby Doc', and explained the problem again (I'd seen him a few days earlier).

'Those pills you gave me the other day just aren't working, Doc. I want some more, but this time the strongest antibiotics that you have on board. OK?'

'OK, Sharkey, but you'll have to come off flying while you take them.'

'Horseshit! I'm sleeping well and just have this problem in the air. Give me the tablets and let me decide how they affect me. If I pile in, just don't tell anyone.'

Baby Doc couldn't say no, and the treatment swiftly worked.

It was on the 26th that Dave Braithwaite provided all in the squadron with some much-needed light entertainment. He was tasked with a mission to go and sink the upturned hull of the *Coventry*. She was slowly going down offshore, but until she had actually gone down she has to be watched carefully — nobody wanted the Argentines going through her. This extra patrol work was an unnecessary drain on resources, and so Dave was despatched to open up her nearly submerged belly with cannon fire. He was given an accurate position by the command in San Carlos, and off he went.

On his return, all were keen to know how it had gone.

'Perfect! And I have pioneered a new attack, Boss.'

'Really, Dave? What is that?'

Dave looked as pleased as punch with himself; but there was also devilment in his eyes. 'Well, I got to the briefed position but there was no *Coventry* to be seen. So I thought "orders are orders" and carried out a strafing attack on the Navhars position that I had been given. It worked a treat.'

'What do you mean, "worked a treat"?'

'I got a Delta Hotel on the piece of sea where the target should have been!'

It was a hilarious idea, and no harm had been done.

It also reminded me of a recently aborted attack of my own. When in descent for CAP to the north of the islands in calm weather I had picked up a surface radar contact on the Blue Fox. The contact was intermittent at 22 miles and obviously very small. Could it be a patrol boat? There were no friendly forces in the area. I continued the descent and at 17 miles was getting an intermittent radar lock on the contact, though the lock wouldn't hold. At 7 miles to go the lock still wouldn't hold and behind the acquisition marker in the Head-Up Display I could see no sign of a boat. But the calm waters were being disturbed by something and the radar could see it. Could it be a submarine periscope? That must be the answer! I checked my guns were armed and ready and continued down towards the 'target'.

At 3 miles I started to realise what my target was. A school of killer whales were cavorting about, breaking the sea surface. It was a great sight, and yet another indicator of the value of the Blue Fox against targets on or above a calm sea.

During the next few days the weather played its part in limiting flying operations, but on the 28th the squadron resumed the high-level bombing of Port Stanley when en route to CAP stations. It was also a period in which the force lost two Sea Harriers and two Harrier GR Mk 3s within six days.

The first Harrier loss came near Goose Green on the 27th. Squadron Leader Tubby Iveson had been tasked with providing close support for the Paras. He and his Number Two were to attack Argentine ground forces and Tubby entered into the mission with enthusiasm. The chances of being hit by ground fire were higher on each run, and on the third he was hit and had to leave his aircraft. There was no gain involved, only loss, and now the GR 3 numbers had dwindled to four.

He remained on the ground and on the loose for three days until he was eventually picked up by an Amphibious Force helicopter on the 30th. Although he had not exactly covered himself with glory, he did merit every effort to rescue him. Over-enthusiasm on an operational mission is certainly no crime (although throwing the aircraft away for no return is verging on gross negligence). When Tubby managed to make contact with Harriers and Sea Harriers from the Task Group using his SARBE radio facility, he felt that rescue must be on the way. And so it should have been. But the Flag suspected that his radio calls for help were a 'set-up' by the Argentine forces, that he must have been captured and was being used to drag an unsuspecting rescue helicopter to its destruction.

This conclusion was never accepted by those who had spoken to Tubby from their cockpits in the air. Eventually, it was the Amphibious Force that sent a chopper to retrieve the downed pilot. Without their help he would still probably be yomping round the Falklands, making like a penguin.

Although the 28th saw no losses or claims in the fighter war, I was able to get airborne with the AWI, Morts, for our first CAP mission together. Steve Thomas was still enduring his mandatory rest cure, and it turned out to be fortunate for me that Morts was with me. We each dropped a 1000-pound bomb on Stanley airfield en route to our allotted station. The CAP brought us no trade and so when our fuel state dictated a return to Mother we commenced the climb-out from over the centre of Falkland Sound. As we were going through about 12,000 feet Morts transmitted 'Three bogeys, swept-wing, left 9 o'clock low!'

Morts was to the right and was looking left through his leader. 'Very low, passing underneath us now.'

I inverted my jet and pulled. I levelled the wings in a steep descent and spotted the three bogeys. 'Got them, Morts. Acquiring with Sidewinder.' But for some reason the missiles wouldn't lock.

'Wait, Boss! I think they're GR 3s!'

I had convinced myself that the three were enemy aircraft. But I also knew that Morts, more than anybody, should be able to recognise a GR 3 even from this height and range. I called the control ship, HMS *Minerva*.

'Do you have any friendlies in the area at low level?' If there were any, *Minerva* would know about it.

'Negative. No friendlies in the Sound.'

Just at that moment of distraction, I lost sight of the three swept-wing shapes below. They just disappeared into the multi-coloured background of the water.

'I've lost the fucking things, Morts. Do you hold them?'

'Negative. But I'm sure they were GR 3s.'

I was mad as a hatter, and wasn't thinking straight. I was tired, and 'missing' the enemy jets seemed to drain me of all energy. If I hadn't been so tired I might have considered the line 'better safe than sorry', but I was in no mood for that when I landed on board. The debrief was short and to the point: 'GR 3s, my arse!'

The AWI could see that his Boss was in no state for a constructive discussion and sensibly buttoned his lip. But he was naturally upset at being doubted by the CO, and set to work with the Ops Team to establish exactly what the three jets were. Logically they were not the enemy or they would have attacked something in San Carlos, and they had flown straight past the beach-head. In the early evening he approached me.

'Sir, may I have a word, please?'

I was no longer angry, but was still fretting over the missed 'chance'.

'Yes, Morts, of course. What is it?'

'I've confirmed with *Hermes* that three Harriers did transit Falkland Sound, north to south, at low level at the time of our sighting. They were definitely No 1 Squadron cabs!'

I was shattered. 'Well bugger my old boots! I owe you an apology.' And after a pause, 'I and the Harrier boys owe you our thanks too, Morts. Well done. And please accept my apologies.'

But for Morts's eyesight and aircraft recognition, the Task Group could have been down to one Harrier. No wonder I couldn't get a tone on the Sidewinder. From above, the unannounced Harriers' wings were hiding the hottest part of the jets, the efflux from the nozzles.

'Come on down to the bar. I definitely owe you a beer, and I need a drink too.'

That night I began to realise how tired I was and how tired all those around me were. Wings was almost out on his feet too, but refused to rest. The only man who seemed to be weathering the storm well was JJ. And JJ always slept from midnight to 0600 hours. Only in the event of action stations was he to be disturbed. During the silent hours, his second-in-command, Tony Provest, took the helm. It was good thinking by the Captain, and one reason why he was always able to retain his sense of humour and sense of proportion.

The next day, 29 May, was full of incident, and a costly one for 801 Squadron. The weather over the Task Group was stormy, with 40-knot winds and a heavy sea. Day by day the Flag was moving the Group further east and the transits to CAP stations were becoming longer; approximately 200 miles by this stage.

After the previous day's near-miss and the usual night alert stint, I was no better for wear. I was to fly three CAP missions during the day, and on the first I made a somewhat basic though fortunately uncharacteristic error. Steve Thomas was back on the programme flying as my Number Two, and we launched to bomb Stanley airfield and then take up CAP.

As we ran in towards the airfield target, I carried out the update on my Navhars with a radar fix and prepared to give the drop signal to Steve, who was just behind my wing-line about 20 yards away. It was a beautiful day at altitude; blue sky and hot sun, with the town of Stanley laid out like a model below.

'Now, now, NOW!' I gave the signal and Steve's bomb dropped away towards the target. But there was no characteristic thump from my own aircraft. Suddenly, I realised why. With a great whoosh, my port missile left its rails, searching for a non-existent target and leaving a long trail of white smoke over the airfield and the town. I had failed to switch the armament mode selector from the air-to-air to the air-to-surface mode.

'Oh, fuck, Steve! I've fired a Sidewinder!'

'I can see that, Boss. Glad I'm behind you!' Steve had a very strong, if dry, sense of humour.

We went round again and delivered the second bomb. It seemed to matter little to me that it was on target.

Back on board Wings and the Captain managed to see the funny side of it and I was allowed to get on with the rest of the day's flying without too much ribbing. Between my second and third flight, I was sitting at my desk in my cabin when the phone rang. It was Robin Kent. 'Boss, you'd better get up here. I'm afraid we've just lost another Sea Jet — this time over the side.'

'Is the pilot OK?'

'Affirmative. It's Mike Broadwater and we've got him back on board. He's a bit shaken, that's all.'

Up in the crewroom, I listened while Robin explained what had taken place.

'Mike was sitting on deck behind Paul's jet down aft. Both were burning and turning, on the centre-line and ready for launch — so the deck chains had been taken off. It's wet on the deck and you know how slippery it has become recently — like a bloody ice-rink. The ship was in a hard turn to starboard at fairly high speed and so she was heeling to port quite markedly. There was also a 40-knot wind over the deck from starboard, and the deck was heaving up and down badly in the heavy sea. The ship lurched strongly against the sea when without warning the nose of Mike's aircraft swung to the left through 90 degrees and, in spite of the brakes, slid gracefully over the side. He could do absolutely nothing about it and ejected as the nose dropped. He was picked up by the SAR helicopter in less than two minutes!'

Dick Goodenough was on hand to give the final bit of information as to why it had happened. 'The nose-wheel steering is designed so that if too great an outside side-force is put on it, it will give rather than break. For example, a tractor on the nose-wheel might apply such a force with the nose-wheel steering inadvertently engaged. So it looks as though a combination of the strong wind, the heel of the ship in the turn, and a sudden heave of the deck from the heavy sea took charge of the nose of the aircraft and pointed it at the point of least resistance.'

'Thanks Robin. Thanks Dick. Better get the incident signal drafted while I go and brief Wings. At least they didn't both go over the side.'

It was a pretty unexciting way to lose an aircraft in war, but neither Wings nor the Captain were perturbed about it. We all regretted the loss, but there was nothing more to be said or done about it on board.

I went off to fly my third CAP mission and returned to the ship just in time to attend the evening Command Briefing.

When the briefing was over, we invited JJ to the Wardroom for a quick drink with the boys and he accepted with pleasure. Robin Kent, Ralph Wykes-Snead and others welcomed the Captain and we all relaxed and discussed the events of the day. JJ was obviously enjoying his short break from the bridge and the Ops Room when Dave Braithwaite sauntered over from the bar. At that moment we were chatting about the SHAR going over the side. Suddenly Dave came out with one of the classic lines of the war. Without a by your leave, he looked JJ square in the eye and, in totally inappropriate AWI fashion, bullishly said, 'That'll teach you to treat this ship like a fucking speedboat, eh, Sir?' He was rapidly removed by the Senior Pilot, and when he had gone the Captain had a good laugh.

26

After I had returned from another uneventful CAP mission over the islands on 30 May, I was laying aft to my cabin when I was joined by Robin Kent.

'Boss, do you mind if we have a chat about Mike Broadwater?'

'Of course not, Robin. Come in and make yourself comfortable.' I took off my life-saving waistcoat, ditched my helmet and gloves in the corner, and asked, 'How is the ejectee today? Coming up smiling?'

'Well, he's putting a brave face on it, Sharks, but things aren't quite right and he certainly isn't smiling.'

'How's that?'

'This morning I asked him to come up to the crewroom for a chat just to see how he's feeling. He didn't look all that sharp and although he had a few pains in the back he wasn't actually complaining at all. But then I suggested that we went through to the flight-deck Ready Room together to grab a spot of fresh air and for him to sign off the lost cab's A700 sheets. He came along, but was visibly trembling as we stood there looking out on the flight-deck. He just couldn't control it. He didn't stop until we got back down to the crewroom. We then chatted some more and the bottom line, as far as I can see it, is that he isn't going to be much use anywhere near an aircraft for some time to come. I reckon he's been badly twitched by what's happened and needs a good rest.' Robin knew a lot more about the trauma of ejection than I did. He was looking very concerned indeed.

'Are you sure about that? It's a little early to tell yet, isn't it? Wouldn't a couple of days off flying do the trick?'

'I agree it's early days in one sense, but this is Mike's second ejection and I'm sure as eggs is eggs that it has got to him. You'd better have a chat with him yourself, but I'm betting that you come to the same conclusion.'

'If you're right, what do you recommend?'

'If I'm right, then he won't be much use here, will he? He'd better go home to the UK on one of the supply ships.' Robin obviously had no doubts at all about it.

'OK. Thanks for that input. Get him to come down to see me before my next trip.'

Robin didn't seem to miss a trick. He was flying as much as anyone, had to run the daily flying programme, and was dog-tired, but he still had plenty of time to worry about the welfare of his pilots.

It meant a lot to me to have a second opinion up my sleeve when I saw Mike. He had done an excellent job on board under very trying circumstances and I had already decided that there was no way that I was going to put him on the spot unnecessarily. When he came into the cabin, he was a very different man from the one I had seen getting airborne the day before. His chirpy confidence had disappeared and he was very cagey about when he thought he would be able to get airborne again. Robin's assessment was right, and I made the decision on the spot.

'Mike, to be honest,' I lied fluently, 'I've already had a word with Bob Clark about your back and we both agree that risking a third ejection without a proper hospital examination and period of convalescence could be dangerous for you. So, together, we've decided to pack you off to the UK for examination. How does that grab you?'

He was unable to say anything at all initially. The idea was obviously a welcome one because I could see the relief on his face. But there was also concern.

'How are you going to manage with one less pilot, Sharkey? Everyone is shattered already and if I go it will only make things worse.' With Tim Gedge having just left us unexpectedly for a shore-based job and now Mike leaving us, we were again down to eleven pilots.

'That's true, but I'd rather have a little extra hassle on my conscience than a permanently disabled Command QFI. I'm afraid I've made up my mind; you are on your way home, you lucky sod. And I am very sorry that you're going. I couldn't have asked for more from you — you've done an excellent job in the air and I'm very grateful. We'll have a beer or two together before you go.'

It was a simple matter to gain the approval of Bob Clark for our plans and, after leaving the Surgeon Commander, I went up to Flyco to brief Wings and the Captain. As always they were sympathetic, and having heard the diagnosis both agreed the way ahead. Broadwater would be disembarked at the first opportunity.

During my next sortie, I listened in as another mini-drama unfolded in the air. Squadron Leader Jerry Pook's GR 3 Harrier had been hit with ground fire and was losing fuel rapidly. According to his wingman his jet was leaking like a sieve. He was definitely not going to make it back to *Hermes* and had to make a planned ejection from his aircraft when well on his way back to the Flagship. From all accounts he didn't enjoy his short spell in the sea, which was very rough, but he was picked up after only ten minutes in the water by the helicopter boys.

That left only three RAF Harrier GR 3s for the Flag to play with. And very soon two of the three were being tasked to follow up some intelligence from *Invincible*.

Back on board the ship, I was shown some high-level aerial photos of Port Stanley airfield. Charlie Cantan had taken the shots earlier and they clearly showed two swept-wing 'shapes' at the end of the runway. The shapes were parked on the perimeter track facing the runway, as though in an alert posture. JJ had already been briefed on the photos and had ordered a second set to be taken before talking to the Flag. The second shots showed the same 'shapes', which appeared to us to be A-4s. It was only then that the photos were despatched to *Hermes* by helicopter and delivered to the Flag Captain.

By chance, when the photos arrived in *Hermes*'s bridge, Peter Squire and his Number Two were preparing for take-off on one of their routine ground-attack missions. Based on what he could make out from the photos, Lyn Middleton not unreasonably changed the tasking of the pair of Harriers. Their original mission was cancelled. Instead they were to carry out an armed reconnaissance of the airfield, their targets being two swept-wing jets on the eastern end of the runway. They were told that the intelligence had come from 801 Squadron.

Peter Squire's pair launched and conducted their mission. But all they got for their effort were some bullet-holes in their aircraft, two of which penetrated Squire's cockpit, and there had definitely been no sign of swept-wing aircraft on the airfield. When he landed, Peter Squire was not a happy man, and complained about being sent on what proved to be a fruitless yet very dangerous mission. No one showed him the photographs from *Invincible* and eventually his complaints reached the Admiral himself.

That evening *Invincible* received an open signal from the Flag. It stated that the Admiral would wish to know whether the 801 pilot responsible for passing duff intelligence had any antecedents and if so, would they have approved of this irresponsible reporting which resulted in the hazarding of two other pilots' lives, namely the CO of No 1 Squadron and his wingman?

The signal was passed to me at the Command Briefing by an obviously tired, if undaunted, Captain. 'What would you like to do about that, CO 801?'

I read it carefully, twice.

'Well, its a pretty heavy signal, Sir, and I can't imagine that Peter Squire knows the full story. What I plan to do is to write a note to Peter straight away explaining where we stand on this, and send him copies of the photos that already went to *Hermes*. I would also like to have a chat with my Senior Pilot and aircrew because this signal has been copied to all and sundry and I feel our reputation is at stake. When I've done that I'd like to report back to you, Sir, if I may?'

'Very good. I'll be waiting. You'd better get on with it straight away.' JJ didn't need this; none of us did.

Robin Kent was absolutely horrified when he read the signal. He was a stickler for etiquette and good manners, and couldn't believe the pale blue print. I attempted to cool him down, but to no avail. Finally he said: 'I want to talk to Charlie and the other guys to see what they have to say, then I'll come back to you.'

'OK, Robin, but please make it quick, will you?'

He left the cabin a quite furious and indignant officer. Nor was it long before he returned with Charlie Cantan in tow. Both were of the same view. They wished to see a retraction in signal form, and a public apology.

'For Christ's sake, fellers! How in hell is the Captain going to get that?' I knew I was on a loser but, without showing it, was pleased with the strength of reaction. It had been just as I expected. What I didn't relish about the situation was forcing a head-on clash between JJ and the Flag.

Charlie was keen to see the Captain himself.

'No, Charlie. That won't be necessary. Please leave this with me now. But what you can do is go to the bar for me and get a flagon of Glenfiddich malt whisky on my Mess number. Take it with this letter [I had already written a note to Peter], plus copies of the appropriate photographs, and ask 820 to deliver it to *Hermes* tonight: to be handed personally to Peter Squire from CO 801. OK?'

'Leave that to me, Boss. It will be done.'

I then returned to the Ops Room and the Captain. I wasn't going to water down the reaction from Charlie. Nor did I.

'I'm afraid Charlie is standing on pretty firm ground, Sir. And frankly I don't blame him. I know its not very helpful, but what I have to ask of you, Sir, is for an apology, and a public one at that. I've already written to Squire explaining how it all happened, and sent him a large bottle of Scotch. No doubt that will clear the air on his side.'

JJ didn't argue. 'I'll try my best, Sharkey. Let's see how I get on.'

On the following day, *Invincible* received a surprise visit from the CO of No 1 Squadron, Peter Squire. He had had no idea that aerial photographs were available and that *Invincible* had taken a second lot of shots to confirm the first. It was a very generous gesture of his to take the trouble to come across and calm troubled waters. He was happy to reassure Charlie about his ancestors and related that the professional Photographic Interpreters (PIs) in *Hermes* had now assessed the 'swept-wing shapes' to be 'spoof targets' — nothing more than cardboard shapes. In his view, the armed recce mission should never have been sent before the PIs had had their say. We had no PIs in *Invincible*.

Later that day JJ again called for me.

'It's not quite what you asked for, Sharkey, but it's more than I expected to get.'

It was a hand-written letter from the Admiral, saying that he had reacted too quickly to the situation and without being in receipt of all the relevant facts. He apologised.

'You may show that to Robin Kent, Charlie, and your aircrew, but it is then to be returned to me.'

'Thank you very much indeed, Sir.'

Charlie was not altogether satisfied, but I had had enough of it by now.

'You've got your apology, Charlie. No, you can't take it further. This episode is closed. Understood?'

'OK, Boss. And tell the Captain thanks from me, will you?'

I relaxed and went back to thinking about fighting the war.

On the 30th the enemy had launched what was to prove their last Exocet-armed Etendard raid, and they had obviously planned their attack against a position that related to the climb-out point for the Sea Harriers. The simple subterfuge of flying low-level to some distance from the carriers before climbing out had worked. By coincidence and at the time of the raid, Her Majesty's warships *Exeter* and *Avenger* were proceeding inshore from the Task Group and were passing through the SHAR climb-out point.

The engagement was a text book demonstration by the two ships of how to deal with the attack. They launched their chaff rockets early, on first detection of the attackers' radars. *Exeter* successfully engaged two aircraft with Sea Dart, knocking down two A-4 Sky Hawks (it had been a composite raid of Sky Hawks and the Etendard), and *Avenger*, having acquired the Exocet on its inbound track, opened up with her 4.5-inch gun. The missile was destroyed and the ships escaped unscathed from a bombing attack by the two surviving A-4 attackers. These pilots returned to their base and were convinced that they had attacked *Invincible* successfully, though their ship-recognition training must have been pretty poor. *Invincible* and the Task Group were many miles away to the north-east.

After this action, the Argentine stocks of air-launched Exocet were exhausted. Al Curtis and *Jane's* had been correct in their assessment that only five missiles were available, but the Group at sea could not rely on that and had to remain well to the east.

Having virtually run out of steam against the main body of the British force at sea, the AAF now added a new emphasis to their attacks. In addition to continuing their daylight assaults on San Carlos and other targets, they once again introduced the Canberra into the action, but this time only by night. They remembered the lesson of 1 May too well, and did not wish to confront the Sea Harrier by day. Instead, they began to conduct high-level bombing raids over the islands in an attempt to interdict the progress of Jeremy Moore's men towards Stanley.

The whole exercise could only be viewed as a last-ditch effort to demoralise the British ground forces, and it failed pathetically. Presumably the Argentine troops at Port Stanley airfield had complained about the accuracy of the Sea Harrier high-level bomb deliveries. At least, the 801 bombs had all fallen on target.

I had listened to some 800 Squadron attempts to use the same high-level attack profile, and had heard calls of '1 mile short', '2 miles over', from the *Hermes* boys. If only they had done their homework on the radar and Navhars, they too could have produced good results. As it was, the 801 effort was enough to persuade the Argentinians to try their hand at the same sort of game.

But the Canberras did not have any easy targets to aim at. There was no runway, just black open spaces below them, and they certainly couldn't mark the fall of their bombs. Nevertheless, they continued to conduct night bombing missions, so the Carrier Group began to launch CAP aircraft to dissuade them from their activities. As a result only one of my next eight missions was flown by day, and that exception was on 1 June. But before that there was more Vulcan activity.

Having delivered their last sixty-two bombs off target, the Vulcans had switched to using the Shrike anti-radar missile. They could, of course, have tried their bombing missions by day in an attempt to get better results, but this was deemed 'too risky.' It actually would have made no difference at all in terms of risk if it had been planned correctly.

On 31 May about thirteen Victor tankers and one Vulcan carrying two Shrike missiles launched from Ascension with an embarked fuel load in excess of 220,000 gallons. It was a colossal effort that was extremely well-stage-managed, and its aim was to deliver the two missiles against fire-control radars in the Stanley airfield area.

In order for the missiles to work, the enemy had to transmit on their radars and continue transmitting until the missile impacted. A near-miss was not going to be good enough as the missile relied on direct contact to achieve its damage. It was therefore a huge and enormously expensive effort that had little chance of any significant success, and had no chance at all of affecting the course or outcome of the war. But it did allow the boys in light blue to have some fun.

801 was inevitably tasked with waking up the airfield defences for just before the Vulcan arrived on the scene. I got airborne with three 1000-pound bombs, and at the pre-briefed time delivered them on target. Then, as briefed, I continued to fly around the target area to attract the attention of the ground radars. The Vulcan arrived on scene, was quickly detected by the alerted ground radars, and when it fired its missiles the Argentines switched their radars off. The operators on the ground had already proved to be bright and professional, and had cottoned on to what was happening pretty quickly.

The Vulcan returned home with 220,000 gallons of aviation fuel down the drain and no result. They would try again.

I returned to the deck wondering how long the V-bomber pantomime was going to continue.

27

By the time June arrived we had grown well-used to operating in the unpredictable South Atlantic weather, and to our routine air transits to and from the islands for CAP. Combat opportunities against the Argentine Air Force and Navy pilots were becoming less and less frequent. But there was never a moment to relax vigilance on CAP because the enemy had not given up. On the contrary, they still held all the strategic points on the islands, and although Jeremy Moore's men had landed they were not yet in a position to displace the occupation forces.

Intelligence gleaned from various sources indicated that Port Stanley was still being supplied by air on a nightly basis by AAF Hercules aircraft, and the same aircraft were making regular use of the landing-strip at Fox Bay to support their logistic resupply efforts. Without a radar look-down-over-land capability, there was little that we could do to intercept these night resupply flights, especially with the Task Group positioned between 200 and 230 nautical miles to the east of San Carlos Water. The majority of the Sea Harrier effort by day continued to be spent on maintaining CAP stations around the beach-head and, at that range from the carriers, our on-task time had come down to about 25 minutes over the Sound (and that was pushing it). It was nevertheless effort well spent, and the SHAR's continuous presence to the west of the Amphibious Operating Area continued to deter and disrupt enemy air attacks.

On 1 June, my section had launched after daybreak and we had carried out our CAP duty over Falkland Sound without any sign of trade. Everything appeared quiet in the skies to the east as our two jets commenced the climb-out to the north of San Carlos en route to the ship. Our transit home would be at 35,000 feet and, in the climb, Steve kept his Sea Jet in neat battle formation on my starboard beam.

HMS *Minerva* was the Local Area Control Ship and we had not yet switched from her radio frequency. The craggy north coast of East Falkland Island was well below us when my helmet headphones crackled as *Minerva* called us up.

'I just had a "pop-up" contact to the north-west of you at 40 miles. Only had three sweeps on the contact and it has now disappeared. Do you

237

wish to investigate? Over.' I could tell from the controller's voice that he really felt he had something but didn't want us to waste our time if he was wrong. After all, 40 nautical miles was a long way in the wrong direction when our aircraft could be running low on fuel.

He needn't have worried; neither I nor Steve would dream of turning down the slimmest chance of engaging the enemy. Before he had finished his call I had already started a hard turn to port with Steve following in my wake. I was flying aircraft side number 006 and its radar was on top line.

In the turn and using the radar hand-controller thumb-wheel, I wound the radar antenna down to just below the horizon, and as we steadied on a north-westerly heading there was the target. The green radar blip stood out as bold as brass in the centre of my screen at just less than 40 miles.

'Judy! Contact at 38 miles. Investigating.' This was a chance we couldn't miss.

I decided to try to lock the radar to the target to get some accurate height information on it. The radar locked easily, telling me as it did so that the target had to be a large one at that range, and gave me what I wanted to know, a height difference of 4000 feet. I was at 12,000; that made the target at 8,000. I broke the lock so as not to alert the target (he would be listening out on his radar warning receiver) and wound our speed up to 500 knots in a shallow descent. Target range decreased rapidly to 34 miles, 30 miles — then it seemed to hold. There was only one possible reason for that.

'Steve, I think he's turning away. He's now at right 10° at 28 miles. 4000 below.'

'Roger. Contact.' Good! Steve also had contact.

I locked the radar again. Still about 4000 feet below, but we had already come down to 10,000 in descent.

'He's definitely turned away and he's descending. Must have seen us.' The shore control radars of the Argentine forces must have monitored the start of our intercept and then passed the information to the target.

It was now a race against time and fuel. *Invincible* was over 200 miles away and we should have been heading home. But there was an easy alternative. I called *Minerva* on the radio.

''We may be too short of fuel to get back to Mother after this. Can you ask the assault ships to prepare to take us on board in San Carlos?'

A short pause before *Minerva* came back. 'We have decks ready to take you if you need it.'

'Roger. Please check that weapons will be "tight" in the missile zone if we pay you a visit.' I knew it wasn't necessary to remind *Minerva* of that, but it was better to be safe than sorry.

'Roger. No problem.' The ship-borne controller then settled down to monitor the chase — if we destroyed the target it would all be as a result of his sharp radar pick-up and concentration.

Having sorted the fuel problem out in my mind, I could give my full attention to tracking the target, which was now heading west and had descended to low level below the cloud. We were still cracking along above the cloud in brilliant sunshine. I checked my missile and gun switches; safety flaps were up and everything was live and ready to go.

The sea state was markedly rough and as we continued to close the fleeing target from above, I wished that the Flag and all his Staff could have been in the cockpit with me to witness the radar's performance in these look-down conditions. The radar was holding contact with the target on every sweep.

We were now approaching the cloud-tops at 6000 feet and catching the fleeing aircraft fast. To stand any chance at all of survival, the slower target ahead would need to stay in the cloud layer and try to evade us with hard manoeuvring. But there was little chance of that being successful either, since I had had a lot of practice against large evading targets in cloud by day and night.

'Steve, you'd better stay above the cloud until I am visual with the target below.' If he popped up through the cloud layer, Steve would get him.

'Roger. Still good contact at 9 miles.'

I descended steeply into the cloud layer, breaking through the bottoms at 1800 feet. I still had the enemy on my radar screen; a fat blip at 6 miles and closing fast. I looked up from the radar and flight instruments and there it was, at 20° left, a Hercules heading for the mainland as fast as it could go. It was at a height of about 300 feet above the waves.

'Tally ho, one Herky-bird! Come and join me down here, Steve.'

I closed the four-engined transport fairly quickly and when I felt I was just within missile range and had a good growl from the seeker-head I fired my first Sidewinder. As usual it seemed an eternity before it came off the rails and sped towards its target. I had locked the missile to the left-hand pair of engines. The thick white smoke trail terminated after motor burn-out and the missile continued to track towards the Hercules' left wing. I was sure it was going to get there, but at the last minute it hung tantalisingly short and low on its target and fell away, proximity-fusing on the sea surface below.

There was no mistake with the second missile. I locked up the Sidewinder on the target's starboard engines, listened to its growling acquisition tone, and fired from well under 1¼ miles. It left the rails with its characteristic muffled roar and tracked inevitably towards the right wing of the Hercules, impacting between the engines. Immediately, both engines and the wing surface between them burst into flames.

Our fuel state was now getting marginal, to say the least. The job had to be finished, and quickly. Otherwise the Argentine aircraft might still limp home and escape. I knew the Hercules had an excellent fire suppression system in the wings and we couldn't let it escape now.

I still had more than 100 knots' overtake as I closed to guns range and pulled the trigger. My hot-line aiming point was the rear door and tailplane and all of the 240 rounds of 30-mm high-explosive ammunition hit their mark. There were no splashes in the sea below.

As I finished firing, and with its elevator and rudder controls shot away, the large transport aircraft banked gracefully to the right and nose-dived into the sea. There could have been no survivors.

Pulling off the target hard to port, I called *Minerva*.

'Splash one Hercules! Well done on spotting it!'

As the controller's excited voice came back on the air, I could hear the cheers of the Ops Room staff in the background. They also knew that the Hercules force had been running supplies in to Stanley on a daily basis, usually at night and always at very low level. To our ground forces they were a high-priority target. This Hercules had shown some complacency by popping up to 8000 feet, and had paid the price.

'Nice one.' It was the *Minerva* controller. 'Do you wish to land in San Carlos? We'd all like to see you both.'

'Roger. Wait. Steve, check fuel.'

'21 hundred,' came the reply.

I had a couple of hundred less and the ship was 230 miles away. We couldn't rearm my aircraft on board the assault ships and as I thought we could just squeeze home to *Invincible*, I decided to turn down *Minerva*'s kind invitation.

'Sorry, we can just make it back to Mother, so we'd better do that. Thanks anyway for standing by.'

We were already in the climb and in less than half an hour were touching down on deck. There had been a tail-wind so we ended up with about 400 pounds of gas in the tanks — more than I had expected.

During preceding weeks there had been much talk in our crewroom about knocking down a Hercules or similar large transport. Given the chance, everyone favoured flying up alongside the cockpit and signalling to the crew to jump out. We felt no animosity towards the Argentine pilots; they were just doing what they had to do, and if their lives could be spared then they would be. Sadly there had been no time for such chivalry on this occasion. The choice was chivalry, thus possibly giving the enemy aircraft the opportunity to survive and maybe running our Sea Jets out of fuel, or a quick kill. Circumstances and, in particular, fuel states dictated that it had to be the latter choice. I didn't lose any sleep over it, but wished that we had had more time to play with.

The Hercules intercept turned out to be the last kill of the air war in which the Sea Harrier weapon system was able to play its full part. There should have been one further full weapon-system kill by Sea Harrier, and that was when there was a close contact with the enemy at night. It took place on the night of 1 June when an 800 Squadron pilot was sent from the deck of *Hermes* to intercept Canberras over the Port Stanley peninsula.

The Sea Harrier was vectored to within 4 miles of one of the enemy bombers as it tried to escape to the west. The story goes that it was dropping chaff and flare decoys and 'taking violent evasive action'. If the latter was the case, then the Sea Harrier should have easily closed into firing range, provided that the pilot was able to handle his radar at all adequately. That appeared not to have been the case, and the night kill opportunity was missed.

I remember sitting on the tail of a violently evading Vulcan at very high level during 'Alloy Express'. The Vulcan had used a full year's allowance of chaff to try to 'lose' my Sea Harrier from its 6 o'clock. But by staying in the search mode on the Blue Fox radar, it had been relatively easy to stay 'tied' on to the bomber's tail for about 45 minutes, even at ranges of less than half a mile.

It seemed that the 1st was certainly not the day to demonstrate the efficacy of the Flag's Blue Fox radar policy...

The month had started well for us but our good fortune was not to continue. On the same afternoon, Ian Mortimer and Charlie Cantan were launched for a CAP mission that was to be split between Falkland Sound and Port Stanley. Once airborne, Charlie found that his missile system was defective and decided to recover on board while the AWI proceeded on his own to the CAP station. Charlie's logic was that without missiles he would be less than half effective, but he was not popular with me when he landed.

'You should have stayed as a pair with your leader, Charlie, to give mutual support. Don't let it happen again!'

The AWI flew out to the Sound, where all was quiet. The incidence of attacks on San Carlos had dropped almost to zero and so he decided to transfer his CAP station to the Port Stanley area. He passed his intentions to *Minerva* and set off via Darwin and Goose Green to take up his patrol to the south of the airfield at Stanley. *Invincible* was not in radio contact with him — the range was too great — and so we were not aware of his precise movements after he had left Falkland Sound.

As he sat at about 15,000 feet and 4 miles to the south of the airstrip, he could see some Pucara aircraft practising circuits on the airfield. While he remained where he was the Pucaras could not leave the circuit and attack British ground forces, so he stayed put. He was hoping to see an Argentine pilot make a dash for it, but that never occurred.

Instead, he observed what looked like the launch of a missile from the race-track on the southern edge of Stanley town. The smoke trail soon confirmed that it was a missile — and that it was coming for him. He turned away to the south and climbed, confident that the missile, which was probably a Roland, would run out of steam before it got to him. It didn't. It impacted his Sea Harrier astern of the wing and blew the tail off.

To say that it was a violent shock in the cockpit is an understatement. The AWI suddenly found himself upside-down, then tumbling violently seawards with no control over the jet. He ejected.

Although the remains of the jet fell to the south of the peninsula, the strong prevailing winds blew Mortimer north-east in his parachute and finally deposited him in the sea about 5 miles off the end of Stanley runway. Suffering not a little from shock but unwilling to admit it to himself, he was surprised at how difficult it was to divest himself of the parachute and climb into his rubber dinghy (the dinghy is installed in the pilot's seat-cushion which stays attached to him during ejection). No doubt the iciness of the water and the weeks of cumulative fatigue on board contributed to his lack of apparent physical strength, but he eventually pulled himself aboard the tiny rubber raft.

Once in the dinghy his problems were far from over. He immediately put out a 'Mayday' call on his SARBE, saying that he had been shot down by a Roland missile off Stanley airfield. Then he switched the SARBE beacon off because he had seen two aircraft getting airborne from the airfield. One was a helicopter and one looked like a Pucara. They had just one mission in mind, and that was to find him and pick him up.

He risked another call on the SARBE and broadcast the information that there were two Argentine aircraft airborne 5 miles to the south of Stanley (which is where he thought he had landed). What he didn't know was that his SARBE radio was only working intermittently. By pure coincidence, two SHARs were at that moment transiting from the Carrier Group towards where Morts had come down. They were bound for CAP duty but the Argentines didn't know that and were obviously not happy. They presumed that their aircraft were at risk and recalled the helicopter and the Pucara to the airfield, leaving Mortimer to stew.

On board *Invincible*, the first Mayday call (or a rather garbled version of it) was received. I was called and briefed that Mortimer had gone down and 'was in the water' somewhere. It wasn't a lot to go on. Ralph Wykes-Snead and the 820 team immediately volunteered their help to rescue the AWI.

'What can you tell us, Sharkey?'

'Not one hell of a lot at the moment, Ralph. Morts was supposed to have taken up his CAP station in the Sound, and did so. Then he told *Minerva* that he was going to look for trade at Port Stanley. That was the last thing on him that is positive. A Mayday call was heard but it was garbled and seemed to indicate that he was in the water somewhere.

Logically that could be anywhere between San Carlos and Stanley. But *Minerva* is sure he departed via Goose Green. So that cuts the options down a little as to where he could be. It looks like we need to search all the water between Choiseul Sound and Stanley.'

'Don't worry, Sharks. We'll get straight on to it now and if he's there we'll find him.'

That signalled the start of a 9-hour search-and-rescue mission by the 820 Squadron helicopters. They took enormous risks by going close inshore before nightfall to scour more than 50 miles of inlets, waterways and sea areas. At any time they could have been attacked by ground fire or the Argentine Pucaras — but Morts was as popular with them as one of their own and they disregarded all the dangers.

By mid-evening they had still had no luck. A message from the Flagship indicated that the search might have to be abandoned, but Ralph wouldn't take no for an answer.

'Sharkey, don't worry, we are going to continue looking for Morts till we find him. I promise you that.'

It was good to have such friends. I was probably closer to Morts than anyone in the squadron and was desolated by his disappearance. We'd had three years of good flying and hard work together and the squadron couldn't be the same without him.

But the war effort had to go on, and while the search continued I attended the evening Command Briefing as usual. After it had finished, JJ called me to one side for a private word.

'Sharkey, I'm really sorry that Mortimer has gone missing. We'll do everything possible to get him back for you. Something else has come up, although it is not very apposite in the present circumstances. But I want to let you know formally that you have been awarded the Air Force Cross. Many congratulations. But I suggest that this is not the time to make any announcements on board. Let's save that till later, shall we? Anyway, well done from me — it is a well-deserved gong.'

I was pleased and glad that the Captain wanted to keep the good news quiet for a bit. I retired to my cabin in the depths of despair, but clutching at the straw offered by 820. While I slept, the 'ring-bolt' squadron were really going to town on the search, but for several hours they got nowhere. By midnight their Senior Pilot, Keith Dudley, was getting frustrated and decided it was time to play some hunches. He, too, was a close friend of the downed pilot. Now he remembered a conversation with Morts in the bar.

Keith had said, 'If I've ever got to come looking for you, Morts, the first place I'll look is off Stanley runway!' It was worth a try, and so away he went with his Sea King and crew.

By now, Morts had been tossed around in his dinghy for nearly 9 hours and was suffering the early symptoms of exposure; he was bloody frozen! He had kept switching on his SARBE beacon every half hour to assist any search for him, but he didn't know that the transmissions weren't going out. Even so, and in spite of the cold, bouts of sea-sickness and considerable apprehension, he was still very alert. Through the noise of the wind and the sea, his ears picked up the regular beat of the helicopter rotor as the darkened aircraft approached his position.

Friend or foe, it was time for him to get out of the 'oggin. He switched on his aircrew strobe light. The bright flashes were picked up straight away by the 820 crew and soon he was being dazzled by the Sea King's searchlight. Without hesitation or ceremony, the helicopter observer jumped into the waves next to Mortimer, assisted him out of the dinghy, and he was winched aboard.

820 had done it.

When the phone rang in my cabin in the small hours and I heard the news, I was very close to tears. Funny, I thought, the pressure must be getting to me. I raced up to the flight-deck in time to greet the AWI as he arrived back on board, shivering uncontrollably but smiling.

'Hiya, Boss. How's things? I'm sorry about all this...'

'You don't need to say a dickie-bird, Morts,' I interrupted. 'Just welcome back — and, turning to Keith Dudley and his crew, 'thank you, 820!'

The Sick Bay was all prepared for Morts's arrival. Bob Clark had a hot bath and a large brandy ready for him there, and later I returned to my cabin a very happy man. I had lost yet another Sea Harrier but had regained a pilot, and an important one at that.

Not all on board or in the Staff were content to leave the incident there, though.

On the following day, when the Task Force and the Falklands were shrouded in fog and there was little chance of flying, I detected signs of a 'get Mortimer' campaign building up. My first clue was when the Captain raised the issue with me in a fairly oblique way.

'You know, CO 801, that if Morts had been the captain of a ship and had lost it in similar circumstances, he could be court-martialled. What is your view on that?' Was JJ giving me a warning of some sort? Did he really take the view that Morts had hazarded his aircraft unnecessarily?

I laughed. It was a genuine laugh, but I somehow felt a little uneasy. 'You can't court-martial a pilot every time he loses an aircraft, Sir. That wouldn't be cricket. And we'd end up like the RAF, with no one wanting the responsibility of squadron or air station command. I'd hate to see that in the Fleet Air Arm, and so would my pilots.'

'Yes, but there may be some circumstances where a court martial is appropriate, don't you think?' We were talking on common ground. JJ had been court-martialled when off Borneo in command of a minesweeper.

One of his officers had not kept the books correctly. JJ's defending officer had been none other than Henry Leach, now Admiral Sir Henry Leach, the First Sea Lord. During the case for the defence, the then Captain Leach had been able to announce to the court that JJ had been awarded the MBE for his meritorious service during the campaign. He was acquitted of some pretty frivolous charges.

My court martial had been as a result of low flying up the coast of Devon and Cornwall in a Sea Vixen. I had frightened a lot of grockles, had pleaded guilty, been found guilty, and been reprimanded. But that was very different from court-martialling a man for doing his job in war and trying to get it right.

'Yes, Sir, I most certainly do. When you do something particularly stupid and against the rules of common sense and flight safety, then you can expect to be smacked on the bottom. But I wouldn't put Morts's loss in that category. He was doing his job and attempting to get to grips with the enemy.'

'But he misjudged the situation didn't he?'

'There's no question about that. He got too close to the airfield and received a missile up the chuff. But I believe what is critical here is that he did not intentionally get too close. His presence near Port Stanley was keeping the Pucaras from prosecuting our troops and that was very useful, I think. He genuinely thought that he was at a safe distance and a safe height.'

We discussed the subject some more before I left the bridge. I wasn't very concerned about the discussion and dismissed it from my mind. Later in the day, however, the Captain raised it again.

'Rod O'Connor doesn't take the same view as you do, Sharkey. He believes there is probably a case against Mortimer. I'm not sure what I think, yet.' Wings was present but remained silent.

JJ was perhaps expecting to hear some mitigating circumstances from me. Although I didn't think in terms of mitigation (Morts had not been negligent, in my view) I did try to put some balance into the discussion.

'There would be a lot of higher priority cases than Morts if we were looking for someone to hang, Sir. I believe Rod is over-reacting and I'm quite surprised that we are even having this conversation. If they court-martial Mortimer they will have to do me as well — and I would relish putting my views across in such a forum.'

'I'm sure you would, I'm sure you would. I'll note what you say and think on.'

One thing didn't worry me. I knew my Captain and, whatever the man decided, it would be after a lot of honest and fair thought. And the implications of a court martial for Mortimer were far-reaching. If he was to be blamed for getting too close to the enemy then there were several other cases that needed to be examined in court as well. There was the officer responsible for tasking the second attack on Goose Green which led to the predictable loss of Nick Taylor. There was the officer who took away the CAP protection from *Sheffield* and let in the Etendard. There was *Sheffield* itself, which could have been better prepared. There was Tubby Iveson, who broke the rules about re-attack and lost his aircraft. There were too many to contemplate, and when balanced against any of those incidents, Morts's actions paled into insignificance. 'Balance' was the critical word, and in my mind it would not be a balanced decision to take this matter further.

After a few days, the rumblings about courts martial and the like stopped. There was still a war to be fought and, after three days of dreadful weather, flying had started again in earnest.

On 3 June, before the weather abated, another of the Vulcan Shrike missions took place. A further quarter of a million gallons of high-octane fuel enabled the V-bomber crew to fire two of the four Shrike missiles it carried against the Stanley airfield ground radars. Why the second two were not fired remained a mystery to those of us on board *Invincible*.

On its long flight back to Ascension Island the Vulcan was reported to have lost one of its four engines; or at least that was the first message that was received on board. This meant, according to the RAF peacetime rule-book, that it had to divert to 'the nearest available airfield', which happened to be Rio de Janeiro in Brazil. Our educated guesswork suggested that it would still probably have had sufficient fuel to get to Ascension on three engines. If this was the case, then it was a dubious decision by the aircrew to invoke peacetime rules and embarrass the Government by landing in Brazil — where British machines of war were not welcome. Another, later, story indicated that the Vulcan had broken its refuelling probe when trying to take a suck from a Victor and was short of fuel. Indeed, one public account indicates that its tanks were almost dry when it reached its diversion airfield.

Nevertheless, the aircraft did land in Rio and, according to the media, still retained the two Shrike missiles under its wing. I and my team couldn't help wondering why the remaining missiles hadn't been jettisoned to save political embarrassment, and whether the total cost of these ineffective missions was getting slightly out of proportion. Still, it was a good talking-point on board!

Operational matters soon took our minds off the Vulcan saga and, over the next thirty-six hours, caused a most regrettable rift in the relationship between Wings and myself.

28

5 June was my mother's birthday. It started well. The weather had improved, and at the Command Briefing that morning the assembled HODs were briefed by the Captain that it was time to tweak the tail of the opposition. The plan was for *Invincible* to steam under cover of darkness to a position south of Cape Meredith at the south-western tip of West Falkland and virtually challenge the enemy fighters to come out and play. This would be achieved by putting Sea Harrier CAPs up within 80 miles of the Argentine mainland coast; well within range of the enemy's air surveillance radars. *Invincible* would not be alone in her one-night stand. She would be accompanied by a 'Type 64' combination of missile warships, a Type 22 and a Type 42.

After the briefing I got hold of Wings and asked him what needed to be done from the squadron angle.

'How can we help with planning this mission, Sir?'

'You don't need to do anything, Sharkey. I and the Air Ops team will do all the planning necessary. We shall probably launch three single aircraft on a rotational CAP; so you had better choose your pilots and get your heads down to prepare yourselves properly.' By 'get your heads down' he meant grab some Egyptian PT — or in other words, get some sleep.

I did as I was bid, and with the help of the Senior Pilot decided that Steve Thomas and Charlie Cantan should be second and third on CAP. I would be first.

Having achieved a respectable dose of shut-eye during the day, I grabbed a bite to eat and then went in search of Wings to see how things were progressing.

'Anything that we can do, Sir?'

'No thanks, Sharkey. It's all planned. Do you want a quick run through it?'

'Yes please. I'd be grateful.'

Wings outlined the plan, which was very straightforward. 'As we approach the furthest point west for the three ships, we shall launch the first CAP. Who is that to be, by the way?'

'That will be me, Sir.'

'Good. You will proceed on CAP to a point 150 nautical miles from the ship to the west, where you will remain until relieved by the second aircraft. Same again for the third. In order for the ships to get back to a safe area by daylight we shall commence steaming to the east during the second CAP cycle.'

Whilst listening I was rapidly doing my mental arithmetic. If the CAP station was 150 miles to the west then the Sea Kings couldn't conduct search-and-rescue operations there if the ships were steaming to the east. They would be out of range for getting back on board.

'What search-and-rescue arrangements have been made, Sir?'

'SAR? What do you mean?'

'Well, we are asking the enemy to come out and play and there must be some chance that one of us could end up in the drink. If that happens, who is going to pull us out?' I fully expected to hear from Wings that the submarine *Conqueror* or a sister vessel had been tasked with SAR responsibilities. Instead I got a very frosty response.

'It's no use you being in your sack all day and then coming up with new ideas at the last minute. If you wanted special SAR arrangements you should have said so earlier!'

I only just resisted telling him that he had twice refused squadron help in planning the mission. And, I thought to myself, for 'special' missions you obviously need 'special' SAR arrangements. Instead, I tried a bit of tact: 'If there is going to be no SAR capability at the chosen CAP position then the CAP station will have to be placed further to the east. That isn't much to ask. I can't have my pilots going down in the water with no hope of rescue, can I?'

'You will do exactly as you are told to. Do you understand?' Wings was in no mood for discussion. He was grey with fatigue and wanted things done his way.

I was a bit bombed-out too, in spite of having got some rest during the day, and I wasn't going to let him and his 'planning team' off the hook that easily.

'I understand what you say, Sir, but I am very unhappy about it. If the plan isn't changed to accommodate sensible SAR arrangements then I won't fly the sortie. Nor will my pilots.'

'We shall see about that.' Wings was not amused. He turned on his heel and left me in open ground. Sadly, both of us were tired and on short fuses.

I went off to the crewroom, found Robin Kent and sounded out his opinion. It was the same as my own. The boys deserved to have SAR options open to them and the mission should cater for that. The fact that the ship's air planners had totally forgotten about SAR was their problem, not ours. We were both fed up with irresponsible tasking from the Flag and didn't need the same from our own ship. The CAP stations would have to change.

Before the main briefing for the mission, I again approached Wings. 'What have you decided about SAR, Sir?'

'Nothing has changed, CO 801. You just get airborne and do as you are told.'

If Wings can stand his ground, then so can I, I thought. This is ridiculous! You don't risk losing aircrew when you are short of them already. That lesson was learned the hard way in World War II. By the end of the war, no one went on a mission without a chance of being picked out of the water. And nor were my pilots going to.

'If there is going to be no SAR available, Sir, the CAP stations will have to be changed to a range that makes SAR possible.'

'No chance.'

'Then I must tell you that if you brief the mission without including a proper SAR content I will go over your head and see the Captain. I will not risk my aircrew unnecessarily.'

'Sharkey, just you dare! The Captain is not, repeat not, to be disturbed between midnight and 0600.'

Right or wrong, if he didn't accommodate the squadron's wish for SAR availability then I would do as I threatened — even though I hated the thought of it. I couldn't put out of my mind the thought of a lone pilot sitting in his dinghy with no hope of rescue, slowly freezing to death. No joke.

I and my aircrew attended the mission briefing just after midnight. There was no mention of SAR. At the end, the Air Ops Staff presenter said, 'Any questions?'

I stood up, turned to where Wings was sitting, and said, 'Yes, I have an important question. What are the SAR arrangements going to be for downed CAP aircrew?'

Wings answered. 'There are none.'

Without pausing, I replied, 'In that case, Sir, I must discuss this matter with the Captain.'

I left the stunned meeting and made my way down to the cabin off the Ops Room Annexe, where the Captain was asleep. I knocked on the door, entered, and shook J.J. Black by the shoulder.

'Hullo, Sharkey. What on earth is it?' He was very sleepy, but showed no sign of annoyance.

'It's about these CAP sorties tonight, Sir. No provision has been made for SAR and I wish to adjust the planned position of the CAP stations to ensure a proper SAR service by our Sea Kings. That's all.'

At that moment Wings burst through the door like an avenging angel.

He was almost blue with rage. He gave a short but not very sweet recital about 801, and an even less sweet assessment of the 801 CO.

'Hang on, you two!' The Captain took charge. 'What is it exactly that you want, CO 801?'

'I want to adjust the CAP stations for tonight's missions to ensure a decent SAR back-up for my pilots, Sir.'

'Is that all? Where do you want the CAP stations to be?'

'120 miles west instead of 150 miles west, Sir. And then remaining that distance from the ship as the ship proceeds east.'

'Anything else?'

'No, Sir.'

'Well, make it so – and now let me get some sleep.'

The ruling had been given.

I launched, flew to the west of Cape Meredith at low level, and then climbed to high level for the transit west. When I reached the newly agreed CAP station I called, 'Trident Leader, on CAP.'

Once there my Navhars platform toppled and I was left with no Head-Up Display references, no navigation assistance, and no radar stabilisation. This is certainly not my night, I thought, and began the routine for the airborne realignment of the Navhars system. If it wouldn't realign then the recovery on board would definitely not be easy; nor would any night combat.

The Navhars realignment worked fine and I settled down to the task of searching for contacts on the radar that would indicate to me that I had 'company'. The Argentine coastline was clearly visible on radar, and as I ran towards it from my CAP station I looked up and saw three red orbs in the blackness ahead. Were they after-burner plumes from Mirages? There was no contact at all on the radar, and I was too far from the ship for any control. Shit! Better watch them to see how they manoeuvre.

They didn't manoeuvre, and slowly I realised that I was looking at gas-burning waste-pipes on the coastline, the bright flames condensed by distance to dots in the sky.

The Argentine pilots didn't want to play. No one launched from the shore bases and at the end of my planned cycle on patrol I turned to the east and waited to hear Steve Thomas's check-in call. 'Trident Two, top of climb, en route CAP.'

'Evening, Steve. Nothing doing up here at the moment. See you when you get down.'

I was in descent towards West Falkland before I was able to make contact with the ship. 'Loud and clear, Trident Leader.'

'Roger, likewise.'

I was just updating my Navhars system on Cape Meredith with the radar when adrenalin started to flow. I had picked up a large slow-moving target ahead at low level. Could it be a Hercules on a night supply run?

I decreased height rapidly and throttled back.

'Do you have any friendlies in my area? Over.'

'Negative. But we do have one Sea King out of contact to the north-west. Probably south of you.'

'Roger.' I couldn't take any risks by firing at an unknown target. Maybe it was the Sea King. I was now in thick cloud and approaching to within 2 miles of the contact. It was very slow. I tracked it down to quarter of a mile and then flew past to starboard, very close. Whoever it was, they would know that they had had company.

The remainder of the flight was uneventful. A low-level transit to the ship and a simple recovery to the deck. Charlie Cantan was preparing to get airborne as I grabbed a coffee and went aft to my cabin. My confrontation with Wings had depressed me more than a little, but I tried to put it out of my mind.

Nothing had changed; there was still a war to be fought and that took priority over everything else. I was asleep as my head hit the pillow, unaware of the drama that had just begun in the air.

Charlie had been launched and Steve Thomas had recovered. But the low cloud was getting lower, and fog was a strong possibility. Wings called Robin Kent to Flyco, but before he arrived there the fog had set in. Charlie was en route to the CAP station at high level when he was recalled. Flyco was lucky that he was still within radio range.

But, having steamed into the fog bank, *Invincible* was unable to get clear of it. Areas that had been clear a few minutes before were totally socked in. Even the far side of the flight-deck was not visible from Flyco. The fog was as thick as you could get.

Charlie returned to the ship with plenty of fuel and set off down the slope for his first recovery attempt. He entered the fog bank at a little over 200 feet and from that point was able to see nothing outside the cockpit. He started his transition to the hover but had to throw it away and accelerate past the ship. He was very close because in Flyco they heard the roar of the Pegasus pass down the deck — but they didn't see him at all.

As he climbed out through the black murk and into the still moonlight above the cloud, Charlie knew that if he didn't come up with something he was going to get his feet wet. Picking him out of the water might not be so easy either. But he had been a Sea King helicopter pilot before training for the SHAR and decided to adopt the last-ditch profile for getting a helo back on board in fog.

'Flyco, will you put on a searchlight, please, and shine it vertically through the fog. I'm going to find it above the clag, hover alongside and then descend down to the deck.'

'Roger. Wilco.'

The searchlight was soon doing its work and Charlie found the diffused glow easily above the fog layer. The next bit wasn't going to be so easy, but it was his best bet. He transitioned to the hover, steadied next to the searchlight's glow, and then carefully selected a moderate rate of descent down into the gloom. It was a totally disorientating experience and he flew it brilliantly.

In Flyco, they first heard the noise of the jet, and then out of the clag above the deck appeared the Sea Harrier with the rear nozzles glowing red-hot in the night. Charlie touched down and relaxed into a ball of sweat. It was a marvellous demonstration of airmanship and aircraft control. His skill had definitely saved the aircraft and the whole evolution was undoubtedly Air Force Cross material.

The three ships sped eastward and before dawn were within spitting range of the Task Group. Perhaps the AAF had taken some message from the exercise, because within forty-eight hours the Mirage IIIs started showing themselves again by day over West Falkland.

In the morning I awaited the telephone call that I knew would come from Wings. When it came I made my way to the Commander Air's sea cabin. I knocked on the door.

'Come in!' There was no invitation to sit down, nor did I expect one. 'I'm trying to make up my mind what action I should take after your behaviour last night. I am not going to tolerate anyone, including you, going over my head.' He was still furious, but I was resigned by then to whatever he threw at me.

'Dusty, I'm here to fight a war and to get the best out of my Sea Harriers. When anything threatens the safety of my team I shall react, and nothing that you can do or say will stop me. Will there be anything else?'

'No!' I left the cabin without another word being spoken.

From that moment the two of us spoke only on professional matters, but in spite of 'getting on with the war' I strongly regretted losing a good friend. On Wings's side, he was fair but distant in his treatment of the CO 801.

That night in the bar I stood close to a fairly animated group of Sea King aircrew from 820 Squadron. Toby, one of their tallest and most affable pilots, was letting off steam about his experience the night before, when 'whilst in cloud at low level some lunatic jet-jockey passed by too close for comfort.' He and his crew 'could hear the roar of the jet engine as it passed' and 'he would dearly like to get his hands on the pilot!' His Sea King was obviously the unidentified contact that I had been preparing to take out with guns. But in view of Toby's feelings, and his stature, I decided not to discuss the matter with him. Instead, I retired to my cabin and slept the sleep of the dead.

As the weather continued to restrain air activity on both sides, the squadron caught up on some sleep between the alerts on deck. Ashore in San Carlos Water a portable Harrier landing-pad and take-off strip had been laid to act as a forward operating base for the jets. It would have been available earlier but for the loss of the *Atlantic Conveyor*. In *Hermes*, the Harrier GR 3 strength had been brought up to five with the arrival of two jets from Ascension. At last the Victor tankers were being used to provide the Task Force with something useful. On the 8th, a further two jets were due to arrive.

I didn't fly again until the night of the 7th, when I conducted two CAP missions over East Falkland and Choiseul Sound. On the first sortie I was vectored for trade against a Canberra strike, but the enemy aircraft turned away to the west before I could get within 20 miles. Although there was no other action for me, it was hardly a boring flight. The night sky was clear to the stars, and down on the ground there were signs of sporadic but intense activity, with shell-fire and tracer lighting up the map. Our ground forces were doing their stuff and slowly closing in on Port Stanley.

My second sortie was equally pleasing to the eye, though this time I was stationed further south over the approaches to Choiseul Sound.

The night was still very clear, and when I picked up a surface contact on radar I vectored towards it. It wasn't long before I was able to see the ship visually from my CAP height of 20,000 feet. The Ops Briefing on board had made no mention of friendly naval forces to the south of the island so I called my controller.

'This is Trident Leader. I have a large surface contact 10 miles to the south. Do we have any friendlies in this area?' It would be fun to strafe an Argentine supply ship. There hadn't been many of those around.

'Trident Leader. Not according to our information. But it is possible that the contact could be from San Carlos and we haven't been told about it.' It was a very sensible answer.

'Roger. I'll leave well alone.'

It wasn't until the following day that I found out the identity of the vessel. The two LSLs *Sir Galahad* and *Sir Tristram* had made a covert night passage from San Carlos and were to offload their charges at Fitzroy Settlement, close to Bluff Cove. It must have been one of these ships that I had seen from my CAP.

I was not on the flying programme again until the last daylight launch, when I got airborne to take up the CAP station to the south of Choiseul Sound. The two landing-ships had been badly hit during the morning by A-4s, with *Sir Galahad* suffering the greatest loss of life. She was carrying the Welsh Guards and it sounded as though they hadn't stood a chance. There were many casualties.

The two vessels were still gushing smoke when I and Steve arrived on station. To the north of us and directly over the stricken vessels were a pair of Sea Harriers from *Hermes*. Ashore, the Rapier batteries of the RAF Regiment had been unloaded and set up. Initially they had been too far from the water and could do nothing about the first attack on the ships. They were then hurriedly relocated and were able to fire at a second Sky Hawk attack in the middle of the day. They definitely frightened the attackers off, but achieved no kills. Nor were they to achieve any kills at all during the conflict – that pleasure fell to T-33 Battery from the Army. But their presence was not wasted. Their deterrence value was high and prevented enemy air attacks being conducted against the troops gathering at Bluff Cove for the final offensive on Stanley.

As the light was failing, four Sky Hawks suddenly came off the land and attacked the burning ships again. They weren't detected until they had delivered their weapons, but must have known that directly above them were two Sea Harriers ready and waiting. The *Hermes* pair dropped straight into the 6 o'clock of the A-4s and knocked three of them down with Sidewinder. The fourth headed west at low level, jettisoning its tanks on an island at the eastern end of the Sound. Steve and I had a bird's eye view of the action as we closed the Sound at full chat from the south, and were about to give chase to the sole survivor of the attack when we were vectored for trade at high level.

'Trident Leader. I have trade for you to the west at 40 miles, high level. Three bogeys at high speed.'

There, in the distance over Falkland Sound, were three con-trails in the sky. Two were heading directly towards our CAP station and one was paralleling their track to the north. They had to be Mirage IIIs.

'Roger, I'm visual with three trails. Keep calling ranges.'

At full power we started the long climb up to meet the threat, concentrating on our radar screens. There was no chance of a detection until about 15 miles, but we were closing each other very quickly.

'Contact at 14 miles. Stand by to go round the back, Steve.'

At that moment, and as soon as I had gained contact, the Mirages turned hard away to the north-west and were soon well beyond reach of our Sea Harriers. They might not have known it but their intervention had prevented any pursuit of the lone A-4.

Back on board after the mission, I caught up with the day's events. Inshore at San Carlos, Peter Squire had strayed to the edge of the VSTOL pad when in the hover and his engine exhaust had lifted a large plank of metal sheeting. The 'metal plank' was blown around like tissue paper before being ingested into Peter's engine. He crashed in a heap in the mud, fortunately escaping injury. The RAF Harrier force had received two more reinforcements from Ascension in the afternoon and so they were now back to six in number. News also came through from San Carlos that the *Exeter* had shot down another aircraft, this time a Lear Jet at high level.

The Sea Harriers' main CAP task continued to be shared between defending the San Carlos beach-head and the troops to the south-west of Stanley, but all in *Invincible* thought it was time to get another Hercules. Supplies were still reaching Fox Bay and Port Stanley, and they had to be stopped.

29

There was no doubt by now that the Sea Harriers of the Task Force enjoyed command of the skies over the islands. In the air-to-air confrontations to date there had been no SHAR losses in air combat, and even the re-emergence on the scene of the Mirage III could not change the established status quo. The Argentine fighters still refused to chance their arm in combat against the Sea Jet, and we could go virtually where we liked and when we liked without feeling threatened.

In spite of the air supremacy established by the Task Force fighters, it was still not possible for us to achieve airspace denial for twenty-four hours a day. Our carriers were stationed too far to the east for that. Pilots of the AAF attack aircraft had continued to display tremendous courage, and in spite of heavy and regular losses never stopped pressing their cause. They could not be denied access to the islands at low level. It would have been a different story had the Blue Fox radar been able to look down over land.

As it could not do so, we in the *Invincible* team decided to expend some air effort on extending the SHAR's influence further to the west without hazarding the ship. Hercules transports continued to fly daily missions to Fox Bay, bringing in much-needed stores and provisions for the Argentine ground forces. They had become masters of low-level flying over the sea between the mainland and West Falkland, and once over the land they remained at low level by day and night. Some intelligence from the troops ashore indicated that there was often a post-dawn 'milk run' by the Hercules, and it was decided to attempt to intercept these missions. The only place where contact on the large airborne target at low level might be assured was over the sea, west of West Falkland.

This presented several problems. The first was the distance between the Task Group and the western approaches to the Islands. The Jason Islands to the north-west of West Falkland lay approximately 300 nautical miles from where *Invincible* was stationed. That was equivalent to 345 statute miles, or the distance between London and Edinburgh as the crow flies. Such distances demanded high-level transit, where fuel consumption per air nautical mile was much less than at low level. But a simple high-level transit was not going to help achieve the aim of assuring an intercept on the Hercules, thanks to the second major problem: the Argentinian radar sites on West Falkland. These could and would detect the Sea Harrier transit and would be able to warn the enemy transport aircraft of the approach of 'La Muerte Negra'. Deterrence might be achieved, but not intercept. A further problem was that the SHARs were still constrained to carrying out a low-level leg of about 70 miles away from the Task Group before climbing to high level.

The initial low-level leg could not be sacrificed. Therefore some way of disguising the SHAR's high-level transit towards the west had to be sorted out because there simply was not enough fuel in a Sea Harrier to conduct the whole of the planned mission at low level.

The solution that we hit on was for the designated Sea Harrier interceptor to fly out to the San Carlos area in close formation with an aircraft destined for CAP, and then to detach and proceed further west when at low level. In that way the Argentine radars would detect only one contact, and might be deceived. The whole of the return leg to the ship could, of course, be conducted at high level.

We attempted to fool the enemy in this way on 10 June, but by the time I arrived south-west of the Jason Islands my fuel state decreed an almost immediate return to *Invincible*. This allowed no time for searching or waiting for the Hercules.

There was only one other choice, and that was to use the Forward Operating Base in San Carlos Water as a staging-post. On the 11th, I repeated the mission, and this time had over 15 minutes at low level to the west of the islands, hoping to trap an incoming transport. But although I was flying the same aircraft as on 1 June to bring me luck, the enemy did not appear.

The chances of 'catching' prey in such a limited time-slot were small, especially if the Argentine radar on Mount Robinson had an unobstructed view of the sea surface to the west. If so they would have detected the SHAR, and once again the enemy would have been warned off. It was possible that this was the case. Perhaps deterrence had been achieved. We would never know. But a bonus from the mission was a most enjoyable sightseeing tour around the islands.

It also gave me the opportunity to land at San Carlos, which in itself was a fascinating experience. I was able to picture better the scene when the beach-head was under attack, with tracer and missiles filling the sky and bouncing off the protective hills.

I entered the Rapier Missile Engagement Zone at low speed and with my undercarriage down, and landed vertically on the metal pad. The support team ashore were very efficient and their morale was very high. None were unduly concerned about air attack. They were hardened to it, and all were pleased to welcome a visitor from *Invincible*. They took only half an hour to turn the aircraft round and soon I was launching off the well-laid metal strip to take up a further CAP station for 35 minutes before returning to Mother. It had been an enjoyable mission, albeit disappointing as far as tangible results were concerned.

Although the air war appeared to be over bar the shouting, the task of providing CAP defence for our ground forces remained as important to us as on day one of the landings. By now the boys ashore had completed their memorable and heroic forced marches from the beach-head and were tightening their noose on Stanley. But the Argentine land forces still had the odd surprise up their sleeve.

For some time it had been known that a land-based Exocet launcher was sited close to the airfield, but it had not been fired in anger — until 12 June. Had the 'missile helicopter' from Pebble Island been destroyed by a timely attack, there might have been no Exocets to launch. But there were some on the 12th, and HMS *Glamorgan*, lying close inshore to provide gunfire support for our troops, was the recipient of one of these 'smoking telegraph poles'. The guided-missile destroyer had to withdraw from inshore with a gaping hole in her side and a black scar where her helicopter hangar had been.

This was to prove to be my last day of intensive operational flying. My three missions culminated in another night scramble from the deck to try to intercept a shadower with its two Mirage escorts. The shadower disappeared into the night and I spent the majority of the flight deterring Canberras from overflying East Falkland. On the ground below, the pyrotechnics continued as the Royal Marines moved through the Mount Kent defences.

The final action in the air war occurred on the 13th, when the sharp shooting of HMS *Cardiff* downed another enemy aircraft with her Sea Dart — this time a Canberra.

It was on my second mission on 14 June and when outbound for CAP that I received a special call from the controller in *Invincible*.

'Trident Leader, weapons tight.'

By this stage in the proceedings all the aircrew were more than a little punch-drunk. I didn't register the implications of the message.

'Say again your last.'

'I say again, weapons tight.'

Was this another special rule for yet another Vulcan sortie? I still didn't register.

'What on earth for?'

There was a long pause.

'Stanley has fallen, Sharkey. The war is over.'

Part IV

AFTERMATH

30

There was jubilation ashore and afloat as Jeremy Moore accepted the surrender of the Argentine forces in Port Stanley. Actually getting the General to Stanley from his location in the field had been no easy task. With winter setting in, the weather had deteriorated from just cold to abysmal. Visibility was near zero and the RAF Chinook helicopter did not want to risk flying in the prevailing conditions. But one of the Fleet Air Arm Sea King helicopters from 820 Squadron decided to brave the fog and the sleet. After all, this was a pretty important occasion! It airlifted the Commander British Land Forces to the centre of Port Stanley, thus ending the war as it had begun — courtesy of the Dark Blue.

On board *Invincible* we found ourselves in a strange sort of limbo. As far as reoccupation of the islands was concerned the air task had been completed most satisfactorily, but now there were new objectives for the ships and aircraft of the Carrier Group. The air and sea around the islands had to be policed and a selection of the ships in the Group had to remain on task until relief vessels could be found. It was decided that *Invincible* would remain on station and that *Hermes* would return to the UK early. The Flag would hand over his responsibilities to a new admiral, and many of the redoubtable frigates and destroyers that had fought so well and were crewed by so many young lions would remain until their replacements arrived.

I was not to fly again for more than two weeks. For me the end of the conflict had spelt the end to the most satisfying and rewarding phase of my naval career and, probably more than was the case with many others, I needed time to be able to revert to the bureaucracy of 'peacetime rules and regulations'. Since we had left Portsmouth I had had two battles to fight, one against the enemy and one against the Flag, and the frustration that had resulted from the latter battle had left me drained, mentally and physically. I was suffering from the effects of long-term fatigue and recognised that I should try to relax, now that the ultimate test of operational expertise was over.

My 'wind-down' period was initiated in style by kind invitation of Ralph Wykes-Snead and, later, J.J. Black. I had already told the Senior Pilot to leave me off the flying programme for a few days. I was going to get down to writing my official Report of Proceedings and sample a few well-earned jars in the bar. But this plan of action was temporarily sidelined when the CO of 820 collared me.

'Sharkey, how about a trip inshore tomorrow? I'm taking "H" with me for walkabouts, and I reckon a few hours on dry land would do you good, too.'

'Delighted, Ralph. Nothing would please me more.' It was a heaven-sent opportunity to get a feel for the town of Stanley and to see the results of all our endeavours over the past weeks.

We flew in to land between the race-track and Government House on a large square patch of vividly green grass. The feel of the turf under foot was good, and first impressions were that the town buildings had suffered little from either occupation or action. But we three 'tourists' soon began to realise that the Argentines had definitely not disappeared without leaving their mark.

The detail of all that confronted us soon took on the appearance of a spectacular Hollywood movie between takes. It was as though the film director had ordered a quick tea-break. Wherever we walked we found countless rounds of unspent ammunition littering our path. It was everywhere, but represented no hazard. What did present a hazard, though, was that the occupying forces had not had the common decency (or sense) to dig themselves latrines, and had used all the open spaces in and around the town as one large toilet.

The capitulating forces had also 'downed tools' as soon as word of the surrender had reached them, hurriedly divesting themselves of all materials of war. Handguns of all descriptions from machine-pistols to shotguns were piled in disorganised heaps. There were also the bodies of dead Argentine soldiers lying about at random, particularly in the outskirts of the town. They lay where they had fallen, mostly as a result of Task Force shelling, and were preserved grotesquely in the near-zero temperature. Their faces were waxen images of their former selves with lifeless eyes, skin tinged a yellowish brown and lips a stronger slate blue. They lay stiff and deserted, awaiting the attention of the overworked British bomb-disposal teams.

Each corpse represented the threat of a booby trap; perhaps a grenade placed under the armpit with the safety pin withdrawn. There were many such 'nasties' left behind by the defeated army, either hidden about corpses or under discarded helmets. It was not safe to touch anything without expert supervision.

Nor was it safe to stray outside the town limits. Beyond the houses, in the featureless brown countryside close to the town, the Argentines had laid minefields. They were unmarked and uncharted. Each little anti-personnel device was about 4 inches across, intermediate grey in colour, and constructed entirely from plastic. They could not be located by conventional mine-detectors, nor could they be exploded by the passage of heavy vehicles. They lay virtually invisible to the naked eye amidst the mud and tough grasses of the terrain. In the panic to prevent the UK Land Forces from reaching their goal, the Argentine command had ordered Hercules aircraft to dispense thousands of the mines at random from the air. During the coming weeks many a soldier was to lose a foot or a hand to these evil devices, and many local cows, sheep and penguins were to suffer untimely deaths.

At various locations in the town, queues of disillusioned Argentine prisoners stood in line awaiting 'processing'. It was a major task to care for and repatriate each one. When the luckless souls had arrived in Stanley in April they had expected a tumultuous welcome from the inhabitants. They had been led to believe that the Falkland people had suffered deprivation under British rule and yearned for Argentinian sovereignty. It was a shock for them when they were met with a cold and unwelcoming hostility.

During the day, I chatted to a Royal Marine major and his sergeant, who were discussing bomb-disposal.

'Major, would it be possible for your experts to check out some of the Pucara aircraft standing on the airfield? A couple look serviceable to me and my pilots would like to see how they fly.'

The major was in no mood to be either helpful or considerate. 'Our bomb-disposal man is the recipient of two Queen's Gallantry Medals for his work. I wouldn't dream of asking him to risk his life to check out aircraft just so that you and your flyboys can have some fun. His life is worth more than that.'

'Touchy bastard,' I thought. The job would have to be done sooner or later, and when the major got off his high horse he would realise that. By the time the aircraft were eventually checked out the RAF had arrived at Stanley in strength and the valuable prizes of war were claimed by the junior service for all their museums in the UK. This was part of the great propaganda campaign to demonstrate how significant a part had been played by the Light Blue in reclaiming the islands.

Jeremy Moore had set up his headquarters at Government House and it was there that I met up once more with John Witherow of *The Times*. He had been ashore with the rest of the journalists since 21 May and was in great spirits. He happily lent us the Mercedes jeep that he had managed to commandeer so that we could drive out to the airfield.

It was a short drive along a narrow road lined with columns of prisoners en route to 'processing' in the town. There was neither interest nor humour in any of the faces that flashed past the windscreen of the jeep. The airfield approaches looked more like a moonscape than anything else, with craters from bombs and shells covering the ground. Massive piles of small arms lay by the side of the road and from these we selected a few mementoes to take back on board the ship. I claimed a couple of pistols and a Carl Gustav rocket-launcher.

The only building evident on the airfield was the control tower. It had seen better days and was covered with the scars of bomb fragments, shell splinters and Aden cannon fire. It was a mess. By comparison, the runway was in pristine condition. The Vulcan bombing effort had no more than shaved the edge of it, and the slight damage had long since been repaired. But the area surrounding the runway could only be described as a mud bath; thick, clinging, uncompromising mud that was soon to be the home of Task Force Shore Alert aircraft – three Sea Harriers and six GR 3s.

Back in town 'our' jeep was stolen, along with its souvenirs, from outside Government House. It seemed that anything in enemy colours was up for grabs, and the loss did not bother John Witherow.

I was interviewed by the local radio station and was pleased to be able to chat to one or two of the stalwart locals. They were absolutely thrilled to be back under the British flag and had already renamed the local hostelry in honour of the Royal Marines. The pub now enjoyed the name 'The Globe and Laurel'.

One senior citizen was keen to get news of his nephew. 'My nephew, young James, is in the Navy. You *must* know him. Is he down here with you?' There were only 70,000 men in the service, and 15,000 were in the South Atlantic! But I had a guess.

'Do they call him Jimmy James? Because we have a four-ring captain onboard the QE2 and I know him well. He'll soon be ashore here, I believe.' It turned out to be the right nephew.

Before returning to the ship, I heard from the Royal Marine major we had met earlier a story which typified the ordeal suffered by the townspeople during the brief occupation. The major and his man had just been billeted with an elderly couple in their small house on the outskirts of the town.

'I am really sorry to have to ask if we can stay with you temporarily,' he had explained to his hosts, 'but we shall really try hard not to get in your way, and will do everything possible to fit in with your wishes. And of course, we shall supply our own food.'

The lady and her husband were very pleased to have the two to stay and invited them in for a cup of tea. As they sat in the small lounge overlooking the bleak low hills to the south, it began to rain. Soon a steady drip of water was passing through a crack in the ceiling and collecting in a bucket below.

'Oh, one of your shells fell in the back garden and caused a bit of damage to the roof,' the lady explained without rancour. The major held his hand under the drip.

'But this water is pink!'

'Yes,' she replied, 'that's because one of our five recent Argentine guests was in the garden at the time of the shelling. Half of him is still in the garden. The other half is on the roof.' And she carried on with her tea unperturbed.

The five Argentine officers had arrived demanding a full hotel service five weeks before the fall of the town. When the owners refused to cook for them, the 'officers' said, 'Until you start cooking for us and looking after our needs properly we shall use your bath as our toilet.' And for five weeks they had been as good as their word, defecating in the bath each day. It was little wonder that the townspeople had no love for the force of occupation.

Armed with such anecdotes, I returned to the ship, only to find that another opportunity had arisen for me to go ashore. JJ had been invited by the CO of the 2nd Battalion, Scots Guards to join him for his 'hot debrief' on the battle for Tumbledown Mountain, which his men had fought. 'I'm afraid I really can't make it, Sharkey. Would you like to go tomorrow in my place?'

'I certainly would, Sir. Thank you very much indeed.'

And so the next day I was airlifted ashore again by 820. This time I was deposited at the western end of Tumbledown amidst the rocks and tufted grasses of the shelving mountain slope. The Scots Guards officers and senior NCOs were already gathered on site.

I listened in awe as I heard what it had been like to be a Guardsman in battle. Tumbledown is a rocky ridge stretching from west to east, where its highest point overlooks the town and harbour. It was the last stronghold for the British troops to overcome before the planned final assault on Stanley's defences. The helicopters had deposited us all at the point where the action had started. I was looked after personally by a Major Smith, and was privileged to hear the blow-by-blow account of how each of the battalion's three rifle companies had conquered the opposition.

The Scots Guards colonel listened with a mixture of pride and sadness as he heard details of the night advance against strong, well-dug-in Argentine commandos. The defenders had had the best available night-vision sights for their rifles and had laid booby-traps everywhere on the mountain. Some of the thousands of boulders littering the route of advance were the size of houses, and the whole assault was conducted in the dark with the temperature below zero, a fair wind blowing, and a smattering of snow on the ground. It was a most moving story of bravery, determination and loss of life. The battle lasted for several hours and culminated with the survivors of Major John Kizley's company taking the peak. During the action, the battalion's cooks and bandsmen acted as stretcher-bearers, ably assisted in the thick of the fighting by one A.J.McIlroy of the *Daily Telegraph*.

On the way to the summit, Major Smith kept a close eye on my every move. There were trip-wires and booby-traps everywhere, and to the untrained eye they were very difficult to detect. I was relieved that my host knew his business.

When the story had been told, Pipe-Major James Riddell stood alone on the crags overlooking the town and played the pipes for his colonel. During the battle he had composed a new ballad on the back of a fag packet; it was called 'The Crags of Tumbledown Mountain'. It was a moment to remember for life as the accumulated stress and the grief for fallen comrades was churned up by the pipes in the hearts and in the throats of all present.

Around the peak lay the bodies of the fallen enemy, some with letters from loved ones lying in disarray by their sides. There were also many rosaries littering the ground and, embarrassed by intruding on the private grief of the battalion, I bent down to pick one up. My host put a hand on my shoulder and said, 'That wouldn't be right, would it? Come back with us now to Port Howard on West Falkland and share a glass or three of whisky with us.' As I looked up at him I realised that my protector from all the booby-traps was none other than the battalion padre.

We crossed the familiar terrain to Port Howard by helicopter, and as I sat enjoying the major's Scotch in the spartan farmhouse I felt especially privileged to have been able to share such a day with the Guards. Later, a lieutenant from the battalion visited the ship for a good bath and forty-eight hours' relaxation. I treated him as my personal guest, and together we got as drunk as lords!

31

Invincible remained far out to sea, and at last I got down to some of the tasks awaiting me, the most pleasurable of which was reading the backlog of mail newly arrived from home. They were very special moments as I savoured the news about my boys, my wife, my parents, and many other friends and well-wishers. I then had to send back the news that the ship would not be returning home until September. That would inevitably go down like a lead balloon with the family, but there seemed to be no way round it. One of the carriers had to show the flag down south, and we had drawn the short straw.

Perhaps, with hindsight, that was a good thing. It gave us all time to remember that there were other things in life besides war.

After having dedicated my body and soul to the defence of *Invincible* and the Task Group for the previous three months, it was time for me to start thinking of my future. Now that the war was over, the Officers' Appointer in London was busy deciding where I was to be appointed next. A Staff College course was scheduled for the beginning of September and, much against my wishes at the time, I was to be on it. That meant leaving the ship and the squadron before they returned to the UK in order to be able to carry out the mandatory pre-Staff College work. In his inimitable style, JJ invited me to his cabin to discuss what the future held for me — and broke open a bottle of champagne for the two of us to drink.

'It's back to the peacetime Navy now, Sharkey, and I'm sure it's going to be very difficult for you, in particular, to decide what you want to do next, after Staff College and the MOD. You have achieved everything anyone could wish for as "Mr Sea Harrier", and now the question is will you take your Ship Command exams and join the mainstream of the surface Navy, or what?' He was really saying, 'Could I knuckle down to playing the promotion game like everyone else?'

'Well, Sir,' I replied, fully at ease, 'I didn't take Squadron Command exams and I think I showed that I didn't need them. No. I won't take Ship Command, at least not yet. You know that I'm not a star at Naval Rules and Regulations... Nor can I see the pertinence of knowing what code-number a particular stores requisition form has been given. To me that is nothing to do with leadership or command. But, having said that, I will consider it carefully while I am at Staff College and when I go to the MOD.'

The Captain understood my loathing for bureaucracy and for the Appointers' habit of ticking boxes on a wall-chart. 'Yes, I should go and relax at the Staff College, then raise some hell in the MOD. You'll be going as the Air Weapons Adviser, won't you?'

'Yes, Sir.' We chatted about my future for some time. JJ knew full well that I was too much of a maverick to toe the party line for long, and he was hinting that, if I couldn't change my spots, then I should consider the challenge of a new career out of uniform. His main point was that without Ship Command exams under my belt the system would not appoint me to a command at sea; and if I couldn't enjoy that pleasure, then my talents (for what they were worth) would be wasted.

He filled my glass with more bubbly before returning to the question of decorations to be awarded. Wings had already asked me for my list of recommendations and had forwarded these to the Flag. The list was returned swiftly from the Flagship with the comment that there were too many. I was to reduce the list by half in order to show a 'fair comparison' with the *Hermes* air group. And Charlie Cantan's Air Force Cross recommendation was 'simply not on'.

'This really gets my goat!' I explained to JJ. 'An officer gets a bloody DSO for a helicopter rescue flight in bad weather off South Georgia, and most of my boys with sixty war missions under their belts look as though they will get nothing. The pilots I have recommended for decoration definitely deserve gongs, and Charlie really must have an AFC for his night landing in that thick fog.'

JJ was very patient and very frank. 'Sharkey, I can't fight this one through for you, I'm afraid. I've already tried but have had to face a stone wall. As for Charlie's AFC, you can easily follow that up when you get home. I agree that he deserves it.'

I was sharing the private hospitality of the man I most admired, and I didn't wish to rock the boat when there was no chance of a result. The sailors on board loved their Captain too, and, to a man, would go through the whole conflict again just to be with him. They had already made up their *Invincible* T-shirts: 'There and back with J.J.Black'. Some men hadn't seen the light of a day since before the war began. It had gone on for eight weeks now without a break and without a single complaint. None of these young lions would get gongs. Nor would Dusty Milner, though he definitely deserved one.

'OK, Sir. I know you're right and so I won't be a bloody nuisance any more. But for the record, I bet you that the RAF will look after their own better than our system will look after us.'

The gongs themselves didn't matter that much to me. Each man knew what he had achieved and how he had conducted himself. But when the Falklands Honours List came out in the *London Gazette* later in the year the imbalance of it all struck home. For one flight in a Vulcan in highly protected conditions and for dropping poorly aimed bombs, RAF pilots were awarded the Distinguished Flying Cross. Sixty Sea Harrier missions over enemy territory and under enemy fire obviously counted for less. Or did it?

The real causes of any imbalance rested with the manner in which the hierarchy of the three services pressed their individual claims. I was to find out that the list submitted by the RAF was bigger than that of the Army and the Navy combined — and they had hardly taken part in the action. The only Light Blues that had been in the thick of it down south were the Harrier GR 3 pilots, some pilots flying with the Sea Harrier squadrons such as Paul Barton, some brave bomb-disposal boys, and the RAF Regiment team. Yet, later on still, after the publication of the Honours List, when the Memorial Service to those lost in the war was held in St Paul's Cathedral early in 1983, it was obvious that the RAF had taken pride of place. Light blue uniforms were not just a majority, they dominated the service, and one of the lessons was even read by Squadron Leader Tubby Iveson. It was not, in everyone's book, a 'balanced' representation of the air war over the Falklands. Neither I nor any member of my squadron was even invited to attend.

Nevertheless, it was a sound lesson in public relations. The RAF propaganda machine was teaching the Navy how to look after their own, and was apparently stealing all the glory. How they had the gall to do this was beyond me. But they were masters at twisting fictional achievement into 'fact'.

A schools survey was conducted by the Director of Public Relations, Navy, at the end of 1982. The question asked of boys who were about to leave school was, 'If you wanted a military career, which of the services would you wish to join, in what order, and why?' The vast majority of answers put the RAF first, with the Army second and the Navy last. The reason behind this response was that 'The RAF won the air war, the Army won the land war, and the Navy didn't really take part.' Obviously the Navy and the press had failed to get the right message across. The RAF bullshit machine had done its work well, but it wasn't just a question of fooling the public.

I heard of dinners being held commemorating up to thirty Rapier kills by the RAF Regiment — when the statistics showed that they didn't actually score a single one. At RAF Linton-on-Ouse, near York, Robin Kent became the senior naval officer overseeing the basic training of naval fixed-wing pilots. He had sixty war missions under his belt flying from the deck of *Invincible*, and his RAF hosts knew it. But there was also a Vulcan aircrew officer at Linton who had flown just one mission to the Falklands from Ascension. He was fêted at every opportunity and frequently asked to tell his 'war stories', whereas Robin Kent's vastly superior experience of the war was never mentioned once. It was purposely ignored.

Even in the MOD, formal staff papers were generated by RAF rising stars who had never even set foot down south. These reflected a make-believe world, inferring many impressive and heroic deeds in the Falklands. Even the Nimrod with its Sidewinder fit was passed off as a genuine threat to Argentine fighters, and the papers were written in a manner which suggested that the Nimrod had actually appeared in the skies over the Task Force and the islands — which it did not.

Nevertheless, back on board *Invincible* I accepted my Captain's advice, resigned myself to the fact that the Flag would have his way in the end without regard to performance in the field, and settled down to apply myself to my Report of Proceedings. All commanding officers had to submit a detailed account of their unit's participation in the conflict.

As 'Mr Sea Harrier', I hoped and anticipated that my comments on the air war would prove useful, and in my introduction to the report I covered several SHAR-relevant issues, including the *Sheffield* incident. On my signature, the report became an official document which no one, including the Flag, had the right to alter. I submitted the report and forgot about it; until the following year in the MOD when it landed on my desk along with all the other reports from Squadron COs. Opening it up for old time's sake, I was more than a little surprised to find that some pages from the introduction were missing, including comment on the *Sheffield*. They had been removed by somebody up the chain and, try as I did, I was unable to have them reinstated. So much for honesty and obeying the rules. Perhaps this book will help remind those who need it that covering up incompetence in the field does not help the nation's defences.

It had been decided by the Appointers in London that I should leave the ship by the end of July, and there were to be many rewarding days on board before I finally disembarked. Relief destroyers and frigates began arriving on station, and with the departure of Admiral Woodward and his Staff by Hercules from Stanley a new Flag arrived. The new Staff were a breath of fresh air and the new SAVO did much to erase the frustrating memories of the old administration. Geoff Cavalier had a helicopter background and was more than willing to listen to the advice and recommendations of 801 regarding all SHAR operations. He had known me for some time and was a good friend. His and the new Flag's attitude went a long way towards ensuring that the task of preparing the freshly arrived ships for action was an effective and relatively painless one.

801 Sea Harriers had three primary tasks after *Hermes* had left the South Atlantic theatre: defend the Carrier Group; work up the new ships; defend

the airfield at Port Stanley. The first two tasks fitted nicely together and were inter-dependent. Our aircraft still flew in a fully armed condition (except for the pilot's personal pistol) and we used some of our airborne time to simulate Exocet attacks on the Group. It was exciting flying and in spite of 'peacetime rules', which normally prohibited flight over the sea below 50 feet, 801 were allowed to go lower to achieve a more realistic missile simulation.

The initial approach to the force would be made from an unannounced direction at about 450 knots and 100 feet. At about 40 miles the SHAR would pop up to about 300 feet to simulate the Etendard releasing its Exocet, and then descend to 30 feet and 550 knots for the run-in to the ships.

There were two main hazards attached to the flight profile. The first was losing concentration and hitting the sea. The second was hitting one of the many albatrosses that cruised above the South Atlantic waters at about the same altitude. The radar altimeter helped with the first problem; the size of the birds helped with the second. They could be seen relatively easily and at good range, so serious mishaps were avoided. The fish-heads in the newly arrived ships soon learned to respect the fast low-level target — especially when at first they failed to detect it until the attack was all over. But it wasn't long before they were fairly well up to speed and were detecting the low-level SHARs on radar at good range.

Inshore on the airfield, the flying task was less demanding but undeniably boring. Three of *Invincible*'s eight aircraft were detached ashore to provide fighter alerts. A total of nine maintenance personnel also went inshore to support the aircraft. This was balanced nicely by the support for the six RAF Harrier GR 3s from *Hermes*: 400 maintenance ratings, four wing commanders and a group captain! RAF Stanley had come into being and a new empire was born.

The chosen changeover rate for the RAF ground-support staff represented a very considerable and very expensive challenge — on a level with the abortive Vulcan sorties. Each man's tour of duty was just three weeks! This meant a return trip for up to three Hercules each day from Ascension and very soon the boys who had been fighting the war were forgotten by the new branch of the Light Blue club: Transport Command of the RAF had taken over.

When the SAS team moved out of the only hotel accommodation in Stanley, it was the Hercules boys who moved in. The pub had already donated two cases of beer to the Sea Harrier community to say 'thank you' for the war effort; this too was taken over by the RAF and consumed without a by-your-leave. But the prize demonstration of Light Blue arrogance occurred one evening when Robin Kent, Soapy Watson and Brian Haig visited the bar in their flying kit. Whilst on alert duties, the Navy fighter pilots lived in a tent on Stanley airfield alongside the GR 3 boys.

Having just spent three months preparing for a war and then fighting it, they were happy to be ashore and thoroughly enjoyed the odd evening with the locals in the pub.

On this particular and memorable evening, down the stairs of the pub sauntered a young Hercules pilot immaculately dressed in sports jacket, beautifully ironed cavalry twill trousers, cravat, and shiny brogues. He stretched himself, chose a comfortable armchair, and sat down with his pint amidst the war veterans. The pantomime began.

'Phew!' sighed the hard-working taxi-driver. 'I don't know about you guys, but I'm bushed!'

I had given my pilots inshore strict instructions: 'Don't piss off the crabs! Be nice to them!' So the three fighter pilots just sat and listened, giving just the odd prompting remark to help the conversation along.

'Do any of you gents have a green pen I can borrow?' asked the Hercules driver.

'Why is that?' asked Soapy, innocently.

'Oh, you know. Filling in the old log-book. Has to be done in green for wartime sorties, doesn't it?' No one had told him that the war had finished weeks ago — or was this just one facet of the propaganda game? The SHAR pilots almost choked on their beer.

'No, sorry, I don't have one on me. But I must say you do look a trifle pooped.' Soapy was baiting the hook, and the fish was happy to rise to the occasion. 'What has it been like for you fellows in the transport world?' The whizz-kid took the bait.

'Oh, awful. When the balloon went up at the beginning of May we were all called in to work at Brize Norton. You've never seen anything like it on the roads; every roundabout was chock-a-block with traffic.' Presumably it wasn't normal for everyone to go to work in the morning.

'My goodness!'

'Yes, and then the Boss said to us that the big time had arrived and we were in for some heavy training. We worked flat-out for two weeks and then the Boss said we had all worked so hard that we had better take a week off. We deserved it.' He visibly pushed out his chest with pride when he added, 'But I said to the Boss, "No thanks, we're at war now and we can stand the pace!" '

There was a pause for applause (which didn't materialise), then he went on. 'Oh yes! We've been practising our fighter-evasion counter-measures. They are going very well and we reckon we can hold off a fighter and prevent it shooting us down for at least five minutes by manoeuvring hard against it. That will run the fighter out of fuel and he'll have to leave us alone!' He was very pleased with himself.

'That's interesting,' came Soapy's sarcastic reply, 'It only took my Boss 20 seconds to shoot down a Hercules the other day.'

The young transport pilot's face went white. It was at that moment that the small figure of A. J. McIlroy of the *Telegraph* took over. He had been sitting in the corner of the bar listening to the conversation and had had quite enough of the young Walter Mitty. He grabbed him by the shirt, pushed him against the wall, and tore verbal strips off him for a good five minutes. The gracious air of the king of the skies left him and he began to realise what a wally he had been.

It wasn't until I was at Greenwich on the Staff Course that I had any personal contact with the Hercules boys. One day a young flight lieutenant phoned me and asked if he could come and 'bend my ear' about Hercules flying and fighter evasion. 'I'd like to learn everything you can tell me about your kill, if you would, Sir.'

I was very happy to oblige anyone who was trying to help himself. 'Of course, how about joining me for dinner here at the College tomorrow night and we can chat as much as you like?'

The flight lieutenant sounded most grateful and promised to be at the College gates by 1900. But he didn't arrive; nor did he call to apologise. I guessed that his peers had found out about the initiative and had forbidden the visit — they wouldn't want to be seen learning anything about air warfare from the Navy.

As the time drew near for my departure from the ship an horrific accident took place on the airfield. The shore-based Harrier GR 3s had been fitted with Sidewinder missiles and there was a new switch in the cockpit to arm the missiles in flight. It had to be wired to the 'OFF' position, where it was to stay until action was taking place. A young pilot who had recently arrived on the islands was getting airborne for his first sortie with the new missile configuration when disaster struck. We heard later that there was a wiring fault in the missile arming circuit, for as the aircraft left the runway the main armament safety lock in the undercarriage was made 'live' and both missiles fired.

At the far end of the runway a detachment of Welsh Guards who had survived the *Sir Galahad* disaster were assisting with snow-clearing duties. The Guardsmen were unaware of the danger until the missiles tore through them. The result was mayhem. Dreadful injuries were sustained and the hospital ships were back in business. It was the last air incident associated with the confrontation, a very sad one with which to end.

When I was discussing the tragedy later with Surgeon-Commander Rick Jolly, I learned some interesting news. After the fall of Goose Green to the Paras, Rick's field hospital was working flat-out trying to treat both British and Argentine casualties. But there was a language barrier and his staff were unable to understand anything that the foreign patients said, which made the task of emergency surgery very difficult. Then Rick was informed that Major Tomba, a Pucara pilot and now a prisoner, spoke good English and he asked for his help. Initially Tomba appeared to think that there was some catch and refused. Rick pressed his case.

'Aren't you the same Major Tomba who was shot down by Sharkey Ward?'

'Yes, I am.'

'Sharkey has told everyone in the fleet what a brave man you are, sticking with your aircraft until the very last minute. Why won't you help these wounded men? It doesn't sound right for a man with your guts.'

Realising that he was a hero in the eyes of the Sea Harrier community did the trick for Tomba. He volunteered his services as interpreter for the wounded and helped save lives and limbs.

As the time approached for me to leave the ship, arranging a Hercules ride to Ascension for the CO 801 was more difficult than it sounded. Signals reference Commander Ward were sent daily from the ship requesting a seat. Each day a negative reply was received from ashore, and each day the signals staff at RAF Stanley referred to the prospective passenger as lower and lower in rank. Eventually their replies referred to Sub-Lieutenant Ward — it was obvious then that they were playing silly games. It can only have been a calculated insult. In the end it was decided that I should disembark to the airfield anyway on 29 July. Steve Thomas and Dave Braithwaite asked to go along to keep me company inshore.

In advance of leaving the ship, Dick Goodenough collared me and asked for a private word on deck. We went out onto 'goofers' and in the gale-force winds under grey skies all eight 801 Sea Harriers flew past in formation to say goodbye. It was a terrific moment for me and, thanks to that and many more generous goodbyes from my squadron ratings, by the time I climbed into the helicopter to go ashore with my two companions I was a bit of an emotional wreck.

On landing at Stanley the three of us entered the patched-up control tower and spoke to the pilot officer standing behind the passenger check-in desk.

'Hullo, I'm Commander Ward. I'm due to fly to Ascension today and then onwards to the UK.'

'Oh, I'm sorry, Sir,' the pilot officer chirped, with that 'I'm the power round here' gleam in his eye, 'we have three Hercules coming in today but they are all fully booked for Ascension. I don't think we can get you on.'

Dave Braithwaite could see the explosion coming. He grabbed me by the arm and dragged me away from the desk. 'Let me sort this out for you, Boss.' He went back to the desk to provide a few good reasons why Task Group personnel including Squadron COs should be given seats. The reply that he brought back to me was amazing.

'The crabs now say that it doesn't matter how long you have been down here or what you have been doing. Their new rules are that scheduled bookings come first. All the RAF ground crew who arrived here only three weeks ago are due to fly out today, and they all booked their return seats before they flew out from the UK. That's why you can't get a seat.'

That was enough for me. I was very sad to be leaving *Invincible*, my nerves were completely on edge, and I'd had enough of being messed around. I stormed over to the desk.

'Listen to me very carefully, laddie! You are to go and find your group captain and four wing commanders now, this minute! I wish to speak to them all and we shall soon see if there is a seat available for me. When you have got them here find me and let me know. That is a direct order and if you don't do what I ask I shall definitely have your miserable guts for garters! Get on with it!'

The pilot officer no longer saw the funny side of keeping a senior naval officer waiting. He fled like a scalded cat. I, Steve and Dave disappeared to the air-direction hut, where we were invited in for a beer (not all crabs necessarily hated the Navy). We sat down and waited. Before long a very harrassed looking flight lieutenant entered the hut at the rush. 'Are you Commander Ward, Sir?'

'Of course I am! How many other dark blue brass-hats do you have on the airfield?' I wasn't in the mood for pleasantries.

'Group Captain's compliments, Sir. The first Hercules is about to land and you have been given a seat on it.'

I paused to think of how the lesser-ranked young lions of the Task Group would be treated by these donkeys. They simply wouldn't have a prayer of getting a seat. I also wanted to have a half-hour chat with Tony Ogilvy, who was due in on the first aircraft. Tony was taking command of 801.

'Go and tell the Group Captain that I don't want to travel on the first aircraft. I'll travel at my choice on the second or third.'

The flight lieutenant's eyes bulged. But he could see no point in arguing the toss. Ten minutes later he was back.

'From the Group Captain, Sir. You may have a seat in whichever aircraft you wish.' The bewildered young officer then disappeared as he had come — at the double. When the first aircraft landed, we went out to greet Tony Ogilvy and my squadron hand-over was conducted on the windswept tarmac.

'Tony, this might seem like a fast ball to you, but whether on board or here in this fucking gale my hand-over would be very brief. The first thing I have to say is that there are no skeletons in the cupboard and my paperwork In Tray is clear. Second, all eight aircraft are in pristine condition and you have the best team of air engineers in the Navy working for you. Dick Goodenough is a splendid AEO, the best there is, and you can trust him to get it right all of the time. That leaves the aircrew; they know their job and are a very loyal and professional team. You'll have no worries there.

'On the ship side, J.J.Black is the best Captain that I've ever served. He understands the SHAR, too. You already know Dusty Milner. He's a good hand and a good Boss. He's looking forward to seeing you.

'I hate to have to leave the ship and the squadron and I envy you taking over. Anything you'd like to ask me?

'No? Well, good luck and goodbye.' We shook hands and, after reluctantly bidding farewell to Steve and to Dave, I watched them all board the 820 helicopter and disappear towards *Invincible*.

I boarded the Hercules and spent the next fourteen hours thinking of home. En route to Ascension the aircraft crew enjoyed thick, juicy fillet steaks cooked in the aircraft microwave. The Commander and the two wounded stretcher-cases down aft enjoyed dried-up sandwiches from a bagged meal.

In Ascension, I signalled to the air station at Yeovilton that I would be arriving at Brize Norton on the morrow by VC10 and requested a car to meet me. My new rank entitled me to that privilege and I fully expected that the Navy would do the right thing and drive my family up to meet the aircraft.

The VC10 flight passed without incident and the closer I got to the UK the more difficult it became to control my emotions. I was drained of energy and permanently tired, and couldn't take my mind off seeing my young boys again.

By all tradition and service etiquette, I, as the senior officer on board the aircraft, should have been the first to be invited to disembark. But because I was Navy I was totally ignored. Without any reference to me the cabin staff announced the order for disembarkation: two stretcher-cases; followed by non-commissioned Welsh Guards personnel; followed by Falkland Islanders; followed by 'any other party'. It was another calculated insult, but I didn't have the will to cause à fuss. I was too excited at the thought of seeing my wife and children again.

At last I was able to step ashore on to home soil and, carrying my own bags, walked the 200 yards in my full-dress uniform to where I could see my family waiting. There had been four generals to meet the Welsh Guardsmen. There was no sign of the Navy.

It was a wonderful welcome home from the family and friends. They met me and hugged me outside the VIP lounge, where all the other VC10 passengers were already enjoying a drink on the Crown. Clutching the hands of my two boys I said, 'Come on! Let's grab a quick drink before we hit the road.'

As we were about to enter the lounge, the entrance was suddenly blocked by an officious-looking flight-sergeant. He put his hand up in front of my chest and said, 'Sorry, Sir. You can't come in here. Falkland VIPs only.'

It was another planned insult, and after the bad manners on board the VC10, I had had enough. Welsh Guardsmen were welcome, but the Navy wasn't.

'Get me the Station Commander. NOW!'

As if by magic, a dapper group captain appeared. He was rubbing his hands together nervously and seemed to know that his staff had overstepped the mark.

'Hullo, Commander. Is there a problem?'

I was as mad as a hatter. 'Yes, there fucking well is! I've been insulted in your aircraft and now I've been insulted here in front of my family. I have just returned from fighting a real war and I don't need your sergeant telling me that your VIP bar is for Falklands VIPs only. Your team lacks courtesy and good manners!'

'I'm really very sorry. Please do come in and have a drink. Is there anything else I can do?'

'Yes. I and my family will have a drink. But only while these two wing commanders of yours collect my wife's car and that of my father-in-law.' The two wingcos received the car keys and disappeared.

As soon as the cars arrived, I thanked the Station Commander for his hospitality in a very icy tone, and my party left for Wincanton and home.

In the car en route to Somerset I asked my wife, Alison, the question that had been bothering me. 'Why didn't you let the Navy drive you up here, darling?'

She didn't want to say anything, but I pressed her. She replied:

'Commander Air was very crafty. He rang me up yesterday and said "Your husband will be coming home tomorrow; arriving at Brize Norton. Are you going to meet him?" So I said, "Of course!" Then Wings said "Oh, in that case you won't need a car from us, will you?".'

So much for good manners in the Navy as well. I wondered what on earth was going on at Yeovilton.

Later I was to hear that the much more eminent figure of Commodore Mike Clapp was also unattended when he arrived in the UK. Not a soul met him. It slowly dawned on me that jealousy of those who went South was rampant in the Service.

Epilogue

The ill-mannered treatment of myself and other Task Group personnel at Port Stanley and Brize Norton represented just one facet of the orchestrated attempts by the modern RAF to isolate the achievements of the Royal Navy, and the Fleet Air Arm in particular, from possible public recognition. It can not be said that a propaganda war took place between the two services because you need two parties to generate a war. Being the Silent Service, the Royal Navy was never keen to blow its own trumpet, preferring that its reputation should stand on results. This sadly anachronistic attitude failed to take account of the power of the press and broadcasting media. How else could school-leavers be left with the impression that the Royal Navy didn't really take part in the Falklands conflict?

I was soon to find that the discourteous attitude of the Captain of Yeovilton was not widespread within the Service. The majority of the personnel who had had to remain in the UK were generous in their praise of the Task Group's achievements, and initially the part played by the Sea Harrier was also well recognised. Sir Henry Leach, the First Sea Lord, summed up the contribution of the VSTOL fighter: 'Without the Sea Harrier, there could have been no Task Force.'

However, it turned out that the anti-Fleet Air Arm faction within the Navy again held full sway within a year. The official Navy Presentation Team touring the country and providing the public with an insight into the service soon gave scant attention to the Sea Harrier or the importance of organic air power at sea. It was as if the air war in the Falklands had never taken place. The very officers who had relied on the Sea Harrier for the outer ring of defence at sea and in San Carlos, and who had been terrified of the Exocet threat, again shut their minds to the real needs of a war-fighting navy.

New warships were designed with grossly limited over-the-horizon hitting power. Instead of arming new ships' helicopters with Exocet-style missiles, it was decided that such missiles were to be fired from launchers bolted to the deck! The Etendard air-delivery flexibility was forgotten. Fish-heads in the Ministry preferred to limit their options in war rather than give the Fleet Air Arm a further string to its bow. Enemy ships would now have to be closely approached by the new RN frigates before the latter could engage them; instead of preserving the safety of the ship by sending missile-armed helicopters to meet the threat at long range.

I did my best to influence the choice of weapon-delivery systems for the future Royal Navy, but mine was a lone voice in the corridors of power. It was as though no one was interested in operational expertise − JJ had often said that the further you were away from the rank of lieutenant-commander, the less competent you became. He seemed to have got it right.

The logical needs of a fleet at war were again sidelined and priority was given to 'not rocking the boat'. This head-in-the-sand phrase was used time and time again to confound the professionalism of the Fleet Air Arm desk officers. It sickened me to hear it from senior admirals who appeared to be more interested in their personal careers than the good of the service and the country. The reluctance to see things were they are and to fight hard for the proper needs of the service was creating a recipe for ill-spent or wasted Defence Vote monies.

Opponents of my strongly held views were content to close their eyes to reality. 'Yes, the Navy could have three Invincible Class carriers, but no, the Navy can not have three full air groups to go with them.' It was ludicrous in the extreme; three carriers but not enough aircraft to equip them for war. Had everyone forgotten the limited air resources that we had had to work with in the South Atlantic?

'Why can't we have three air groups?' I would ask.

'Because of the cost of modern aircraft, dear boy!' There was always the inference of naivety when very senior officers spoke down to me on these matters. But, of course, the naivety lay with Their Lordships and their unwillingness to argue for adequate funding for the Fleet Air Arm.

'But why won't you accept the hard facts about such costs, Sir? May I remind you that these are:

a. The Sea Harrier Mark II costs about half of one Tornado and much less than the new European Fighter Aircraft [EFA].

b. Neither the Tornado nor the EFA have the legs to get out over the ocean to protect the fleet at sea, even with tanker support.

c. A tanker, Tristar-style, costs the equivalent of at least five Sea Harriers.

d. To put twenty-four-hour fighter cover over the fleet at just a few hundred miles would take up all the tanker resources of the RAF and most of the fighters.

e. The RAF say they will defend the fleet at sea and justify part of their planned slice of the Defence Vote on that requirement. In the practical, real world at sea, it is a mathematical fact and proven by experience that it is impossible for them to do what they say they can do.

f. The money theoretically allotted to the RAF's wish to defend the fleet at sea should therefore be spent on a realistic level of organic air power.

g. The country would save money and increase its ability to protect its interests on the high seas by buying more Sea Harriers and shipborne AEW aircraft and fewer Tornadoes and EFA.'

There was no substantial or logical counter-argument to my theme. The only things preventing the Navy maintaining a sensible and functional level of organic air power were the RAF saying, 'We can do it for you,' and Their Lordships being unwilling to say, 'Bullshit! Demonstrate your claims'.

The RAF have never demonstrated an ability to provide twenty-four-hour fighter cover over the fleet, and could not do so at any realistic range from land.

The sickness in Whitehall had been reflected in the Flag's attitude to the Sea Harrier during the Falklands War, and neither the Flag, his Staff, nor most other observers seemed to have learned from the experience.

Long after the war was finished, and having completed the manuscript of this book, I found myself with the opportunity to read Admiral Woodward's rather different account of the same war. *One Hundred Days* (1992) documents the Admiral's views, policies and reactions to events, and in doing so provides considerable substance to my own views and deductions concerning 'what happened down south'. In the light of his commentary as well as my own experience on site as 'Mr Sea Harrier', I have no hesitation in presenting the following as the most important lessons of the Falklands air war.

The two main lessons must be:

Know your weapons platforms, their systems and their operational capabilities;

then employ them accordingly and to best effect.

The reader will have already gathered from my story that I felt that the Admiral and his Staff neither appreciated nor trusted in the value of the Sea Harrier as the Task Group's first line of defence against air attack. *One Hundred Days* confirms this; the Admiral clearly infers that in his view Sea Dart represented the first line of defence against the Etendard/Exocet combination, and he does not even acknowledge the presence of the outer ring of CAP aircraft that were defending the Task Group.

Defence in Depth is the foundation of the modern Navy's equipment and tactical philosophy. It relies on each separate layer of defence acting as a deterrent and, it is hoped, causing some attrition to the enemy attack effort. On the open admission of the Argentine attack pilots after the war, the Sea Harrier 'Black Death' represented the single most effective deterrent to their attack plans. Sea Dart, Sea Wolf, and other systems were also feared, but the great question in my mind is, 'Why did the Flag recognise the importance of the inner layers of defence and yet fail to recognise the vital first layer — Sea Harrier?' The importance of the Sea Harrier weapon-system successes of 1 May were not recognised: if they had been, 4 May might have been a very different story.

On 4 May I was convinced that the removal of the CAP aircraft from their station up-threat of *Sheffield* contributed to that ship's demise. I am still of the same opinion.

That the Admiral should decide on the 8th that 'we were getting absolutely nowhere with aviation' and that he 'was going to have to get on with his war largely without it' is quite revealing. Did that sentiment govern his thoughts about defending San Carlos?

The air defence of the San Carlos beach-head was, in my opinion, less robust than it could have been thanks to the Flag's policy concerning the positioning of the *Hermes* Sea Harrier CAP aircraft. By keeping the 800 Squadron CAPs high above the Amphibious Operating Area and waiting for enemy aircraft to attack the ships in San Carlos before engaging them, the Flag did not take proper advantage of a significant level of extra deterrence. (This high CAP policy was akin to saying, 'Come and beat shit out of our ships but stand by because after you have done your business we shall try to knock you down.') It would appear now that the low-level 801 CAPs from *Invincible* were solely responsible for turning away the significant number of enemy air attacks that never penetrated through to San Carlos. Had the 800 CAPs been at low level as well, the options open to the enemy for getting through to their target would have been very much less. Fewer ships would then have been lost and damaged in San Carlos and Falkland Sound.

Had the Command in the Falklands understood the Sea Harrier and its capabilities better, the aircraft could undoubtedly have been used to greater effect and the war might well have been a less costly affair. In my view, it needn't have been 'A damned near-run thing'.

What it was decided to do down south as a direct result of the war takes us back into the world of Walt Disney and pantomime.

After the war, the RAF made the case to the Government for a major new airfield to be constructed south-west of Port Stanley. The argument used to justify this major project was that it could be used to defend the islands properly against any future possible aggression by Argentina. But the argument does not stand up to professional inspection.

Picture the scenario as it developed. The new airfield runway is capable of operating any aircraft type in the world. It is ideal for fighters, strike aircraft, tankers and transports. On construction it was protected by a moderate garrison of troops, surface-to-air missiles and fighters. The cost of maintaining these defences was found to be too high when compared with other defence priorities in the Northern Hemisphere, so now the defences have been markedly reduced and are totally inadequate. A surprise amphibious offensive over the local beaches by Argentine commandos supported by a sustained air attack would rapidly result in the new group captain's married quarter being occupied by a grateful Argentine general.

The RAF will always claim that they can rapidly reinforce the airfield in times of trouble. But how? And with what? A surprise offensive would secure the airfield within hours, and then there would be no airfield for the reinforcements to land on.

Instead, the airfield would be the ritzy new base of the Argentine Air Force. Squadrons of Mirages, Etendards and Sky Hawks would be stationed on site very rapidly, and these aircraft would enable the Argentine government to establish their own total exclusion zone around the islands. As sure as eggs is eggs, and as happened during the war, the RAF would then say, 'Oh, we can't possibly attack the airfield without fighter cover. That fighter cover must be in place before any attack by our bombers — we can't risk having any of them shot down.' The next step, as in the 1982 conflict, would be for the RAF conveniently to forget their responsibilities of providing fighter cover over the oceans and say, 'The Navy must send a task force to secure air superiority for us before we do anything.'

So the Fleet Air Arm would be asked to do the dirty work again, and again they would have inadequate resources for the job, thanks to the RAF promises that they can protect the fleet at sea. Unlike 1982, the might of the Argentine Air Force's hitting power would now be based on the islands, not on the mainland. They would be well-backed-up by a short logistic supply route. Any task force from the UK would then have a very different fight on its hands. The Sea Harrier Mk II resources are no greater in number than those of the earlier mark, and although they can definitely provide a more robust outer ring of defence for the fleet, they could not possibly support another San Carlos from, ranges of 400 nautical miles and greater. And any carrier group steaming closer to the islands than this would stand to suffer heavy casualties from air, sea and submarine attack.

In other words, the new airfield is a white elephant. It cannot be defended from a serious assault by Argentine forces, and could not be retaken by British forces without the Fleet Air Arm and the Navy being given the proper tools for the job. The RAF and Their Lordships combined have failed to make proper provision for this.

What was the sensible alternative to the new airfield?

Port Stanley airfield runway is not long enough to support the operation of conventional fixed-wing fighters and fighter/ground-attack aircraft. The Phantom and Tornado cannot be operated from there. But it is ideal for the operation of VSTOL fighters such as the Sea Harrier Mk I and Mk II. A relatively small amount of money could have been spent on the airfield to provide adequate ground-support facilities. Forward operating strips with fuel and air ordnance dumps could have been strategically placed on West Falkland for the SHAR and the ground-attack Harriers to use. Realistic defences for airfield and satellite strips could have been provided at relatively low cost. And, most important of all, the runway at Stanley would *never* have been extended. This would deny the Argentine the possibility of ever operating fighters from the islands, and would inevitably dissuade any further attempts by them to take the Falklands by force.

The Sea Harrier Mk II is armed with the Advanced Medium-Range Air-to-Air Missile (AMRAAM) and a new sophisticated radar that can look down over land and rough sea. It also has the Sea Eagle air-to-surface sea-skimming missile in its inventory for long-range shipping strikes. With its new hitting power it could assure air superiority over the islands *and* effective policing of the surrounding sea areas. And all this at a cost of much less than half the money spent on the new airfield. The Falklands would remain very securely in British hands.

But now, who can tell? For the moment it appears that the RAF propaganda machine had the last laugh about the Falklands conflict of 1982. But will they accept the blame if the islands and the expensive new airfield are retaken for good? I doubt it. Their PR machine has coped with worse problems.

I could only sit and watch helplessly as the manner in which the Falklands were reclaimed for Britain in 1982 was forgotten and the credit for the successful conclusion of the conflict was misplaced in terms of Defence Vote money.

I was awarded the Distinguished Service Cross in the Falklands Honours List and proudly received this and the Air Force Cross from the Queen at Buckingham Palace. I emerged from the Staff College at the top of the course and became the Air Warfare Adviser to the Naval Staff and the First Sea Lord. But the brotherhood of fish-heads denied me the opportunity of ever commanding a carrier, and the brotherhood of crabs continued to deny the Senior Service adequate organic air resources at sea. I, and many other fighter pilots, became tired of fighting donkeys and soon decided to leave Her Majesty's Service.

I retired with fond memories of the young lions of the Navy putting their lives on the line in Falkland Sound for the benefit of others. I also retained one of the battle ensigns flown by *Invincible* during the war. But my proudest memento of it all was the comment made by J.J.Black on my post-Falklands report: 'He made a significant personal contribution to the defeat of the enemy.'

It wasn't bad for a maverick.

Postscript: after the war, the then Chief of the Defence Staff, Admiral Lord Lewin, met me and said, 'Sharkey, you should write a book about it all.'

This is that book.

Appendix I

Air Combat Diagrams

MAY 1st, 1982 — THE FIRST AIR-TO-AIR CONFRONTATION

(NOT TO SCALE)

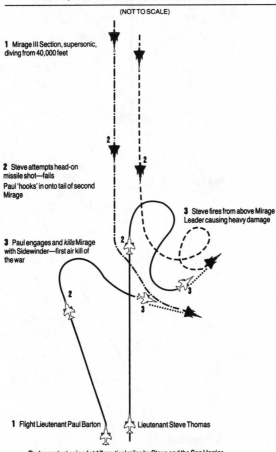

1 Mirage III Section, supersonic, diving from 40,000 feet

2 Steve attempts head-on missile shot—fails
Paul 'hooks' in onto tail of second Mirage

3 Paul engages and *kills* Mirage with Sidewinder—first air kill of the war

3 Steve fires from above Mirage Leader causing heavy damage

1 Flight Lieutenant Paul Barton   Lieutenant Steve Thomas

Radar contact gained at 17 nautical miles by Steve and the Sea Harrier
Section start to climb from 12,000 feet

MAY 1st, 1982 — SEA HARRIERS INTERCEPT CANBERRAS AT LOW LEVEL

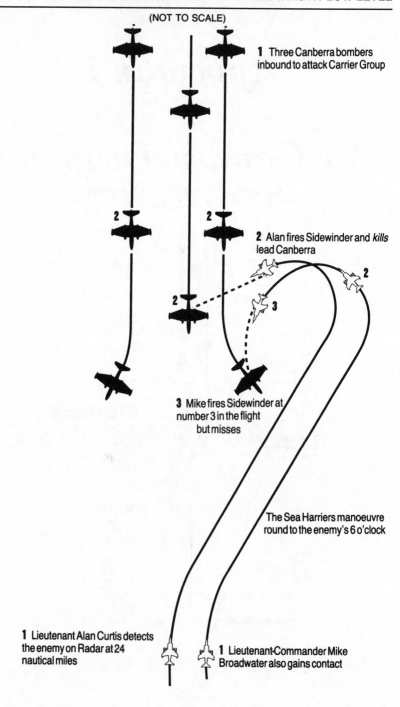

(NOT TO SCALE)

1 Three Canberra bombers inbound to attack Carrier Group

2 Alan fires Sidewinder and *kills* lead Canberra

3 Mike fires Sidewinder at number 3 in the flight but misses

The Sea Harriers manoeuvre round to the enemy's 6 o'clock

1 Lieutenant Alan Curtis detects the enemy on Radar at 24 nautical miles

1 Lieutenant-Commander Mike Broadwater also gains contact

MAY 21st, 1982 — SHARKEY'S SECTION DOWNS 3 MIRAGE V DAGGERS

(NOT TO SCALE)

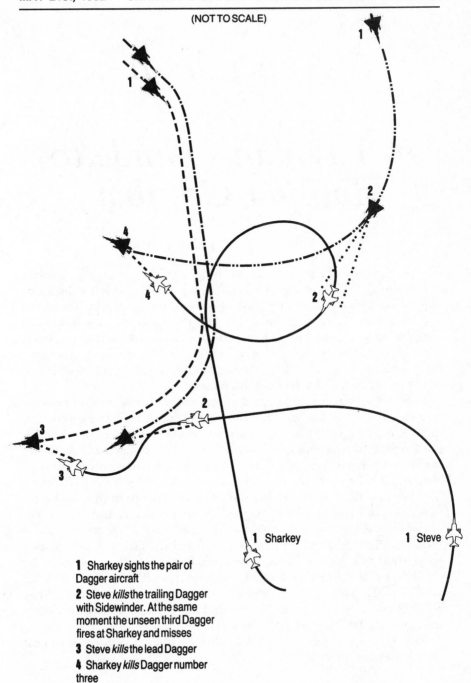

1 Sharkey sights the pair of Dagger aircraft

2 Steve *kills* the trailing Dagger with Sidewinder. At the same moment the unseen third Dagger fires at Sharkey and misses

3 Steve *kills* the lead Dagger

4 Sharkey *kills* Dagger number three

Appendix II

A Layman's Guide to Fighter Combat

'Fighter Combat' is also referred to, in military jargon, as Air Combat Manoeuvring (ACM) or Air Combat Training (ACT) and is not dissimilar in principle to two cowboys of the Wild West having a gunfight. The easiest and safest way of shooting down the opposition is in the back from close range when he isn't looking! The majority of the air kills in the two World Wars were achieved this way but, unlike the 'one-on-one' gunfighter confrontations in the Wild West, there is nothing unchivalrous about taking advantage of an enemy aircraft in this manner.

There are two generally accepted, supporting reasons for this statement. The first is that in any air combat scenario things tend to happen very quickly and all fighter pilots are trained to know and understand the basic ground rule: 'Watch your 6 o'clock!' The 6 o'clock is that area behind you that you can not normally see from the cockpit without special effort or mutually supporting cover. It is where every fighter pilot hopes to end up – in the enemy's 6 o'clock; because it is easier to shoot from there and most of his weapons will have been designed to operate best from that position.

The second reason for disregarding the label 'lack of chivalry' is that a modern fighter aircraft is an expensive national resource and the taxpayer would not welcome the nation's fighter pilots giving the opposition the opportunity of the first shot. ('After you my friend!' 'Oh, No! Sir! After you!') It only takes one high-explosive (HE) 30-mm cannon shell or one missile to destroy a fast jet in flight: therefore, if you want to stay alive to fight another day, no quarter can be given.

What then is the fighter pilot's job when he is faced with an air combat situation against other fighters?

It is 'to use his aeroplane as a weapon system with which he can destroy any enemy aircraft that are menacing him or that are threatening the security of the resources that he is there to protect.' And he must do this without letting the enemy threaten him.

How does he carry out his task?

'By putting his aircraft into a position in the sky which allows him to bring his own weapons to bear on an enemy aircraft and to use those weapons to shoot the enemy down before the enemy can bring his weapons to bear.' That is more easily said than done if the opposition happens to be another capable fighter aircraft and, importantly, if the other aircraft is also manoeuvring to shoot down your own aircraft. Two aircraft manoeuvring against each other in this way constitutes a 'dog-fight'.

In this situation, the pilot who manoeuvres his jet 'better' should be able to bring his weapons to bear first and should win the fight by shooting down the opposition. 'Better' signifies manoeuvring successfully in a manner which suits the needs and/or limitations of his own aircraft and weapons. But, and it is a big 'BUT', with a dog-fight involving different weapons and dissimilar fighters, an inferior pilot may well be able to achieve a kill over a more talented fighter pilot. This could be, for example, because he has a sophisticated missile at his disposal and his opponent in the superior fighter only has a gun.

For any combat situation, therefore, there are certain logical rules that a fighter pilot must apply if he is to give himself and his aircraft the best chance of success. These do not cover all that the fighter pilot needs to know but are nevertheless basic essentials, particularly when up against good opposition.

Rule 1.

The first rule for the fighter pilot is to know his aircraft and weapon system backwards. He must be able to fly his aircraft to its physical manoeuvrability limits; in a manner which best benefits his task of bringing his weapon system to bear on the enemy in the quickest possible time.

Rule 2.

The second rule develops naturally out of the first. He must know the weaknesses of his weapon system and the limitations of his aircraft (where, for example, within its flight envelope, it performs badly relative to any opposition).

Rule 3.

The third and most difficult 'rule' in practice is always to apply the better points of his weapon system and aircraft performance to a particular fight; that is, he must adopt the fighter tactics which best suit his own aircraft needs.

Rule 4.

The fourth rule is to know the detailed capabilities of the opposing fighter (and if possible of the opposing fighter pilot) and to avoid allowing the fight to develop in a manner which suits the opposition. For example, if your jet fights better at low level (or worse at high level) than the opposition then you must bring the fight down in altitude to your own best environment.

Rule 5.

The fifth rule is to approach every fight in a *totally* aggressive manner but without ignoring Rules 1 to 4. Under-confidence and a half-hearted approach never won any battle, either in the air or on the ground. The pilot's motto should always be 'You can if you think you can!'

Rule 6

The sixth rule is continuously to predict where it is physically possible for the opposing fighter to move to next and to fly your own aircraft to take advantage of that predicted information. All aircraft have to obey the laws of physics and aerodynamics and therefore the flight-path options of the opposition fighter will be limited at any particular moment in a fight. But he can still do a variety of different things with his jet from most positions in the sky, and the sixth rule demands that you must be continuously aware of all such options and know how to take advantage of them or counter them.

Rule 7.

If Rules 1 to 6 are obeyed then compliance with rule seven should ensure that the fight will be won. Rule 7 is to sight the opposition before he sights you and then never lose sight of him until you have achieved the kill.

Rule 8.

There is always the possibility of a further enemy fighter that you haven't seen. Rule 8 is to keep looking for the unseen 'bogey' and, if there is one, apply Rules 1 to 7 to him as well as to the guy you are already fighting. (The 'unseen bogey' may appear on the scene at any time, not just during a fight, and that is why pilots fly in 'battle' pairs. 'Battle' formation may be defined as aircraft flying side by side and far enough from each other to be able to keep a close watch on their partner's vulnerable '6 o'clock' area.)

Obedience of these rules represents the basic minimum discipline that a fighter pilot must apply in combat. And successful obedience of these rules means that the fighter pilot has to think of many things at the same time and take appropriate action at the right time. For a fight between professionals, one small mistake by either party will usually mean victory for the other man. This could be something as simple as applying G (pulling back on the stick or control column) one second later than it should have been applied. A reasonable parallel to the importance of a minor error in judgement or application would be a frame of top-class snooker. Everything can be lost on one mistake. And in a fighter aircraft in a dog-fight in war, 'everything' means your life, and so obeying the ground rules is vital to survival.

If these are the basic rules that the fighter pilot abides by in combat, what is it that he actually does with his aircraft, and why?

First of all, let us define the type of combat that we want to discuss: two jet fighters that are visual with each other in the sky and each one is trying to shoot the other one down.

Modern fighters are often equipped with head-on capable weapons but fighters approaching each other head-on have a very high relative airspeed (closing speeds in excess of 1,000 knots — more than 550 yards per second). With such closure speeds coupled with the limitations of some head-on weapon systems, the opportunity for the head-on release of a weapon can be fleeting at best. Whether in the head-on situation or with any other relative aspect between aircraft (e.g. side-on), the pilot is always trying to point his weapon system at the other jet. But he has to do this at a range which suits the parameters of his weapons. Air-to-air missiles in particular have maximum and minimum effective ranges for release, and these must be obeyed and recognised in a fight. (Firing a weapon out of range is not always a bad thing — it will always worry the hell out of the opposition until it is seen to miss! And the distraction of being fired at by missile or tracer ammunition from cannon can upset the opposition's control of his own aircraft and allow you to gain an advantage.)

Because of the high closing rates of fighters when head-on and the limitations of maximum and minimum weapon release ranges, it is logical that the best position for a pilot to be in is behind the enemy aircraft, and that is where he normally attempts to get to in a dog-fight. (He will obviously fire his weapons from any angle if they are going to be effective, but life isn't always that simple in the cockpit.)

If he hasn't been seen by the other aircraft he can take 'all day' to get into the 6 o'clock and ensure that his weapon release parameters are correct. But if he has been seen then the opposition will be trying to get into his own 6 o'clock and that is where the tactical manoeuvring of the aircraft comes in. (There is still no such weapon system as depicted in James Bond-style movies, where a pilot can fire successfully at anything he sees around him in the skies without manoeuvre.)

Manoeuvrability in combat means 'turning the aircraft through pitch, roll and yaw to where you want it to point so that you end up with your aircraft positioned for the successful release of weapons'. Each aircraft has a particular wing design which provides it with lift. In straight and level flight that lift is equal to the force of gravity, i.e. 1 G. To get more lift you need to raise the nose of the aircraft relative to the airstream passing over the aircraft and its wing. The higher this 'angle of attack' of the wing relative to the airstream at any particular speed, the higher the G level —

but only up to the design limit of the wing. The higher the speed you go, the greater the lift or G that can be achieved from the airstream up to the design limit of the wing. Therefore fighters usually have wings designed to give as much lift or G as possible at any particular speed. This is because the quicker you can turn the aircraft through the application of G compared with the opposing fighter, the easier it will be to point at him before he points at you and the easier it should be for you to bring your weapons to bear and/or fly into his 6 o'clock.

When you create more lift or G by raising the nose of the aircraft relative to the airstream, you also create more drag on the aircraft. Drag tends to slow the aircraft down and any reduction in speed reduces the lift available. To maintain a certain level of G at a particular airspeed you require a specific level of thrust to be available to overcome the increased drag.

Every fighter therefore has a turning capability that is based on the wing design (lift/G). High levels of G may be available for short moments at particular airspeeds but it is the thrust of the aircraft which will decide how much sustained G is available, as opposed to instantaneous G. (The thrust is needed to compensate for drag and to maintain forward speed through the air.) Having high instantaneous and sustained G available is a marked advantage in combat against any fighter with a lower G capability.

But G in isolation is not the answer to the fighter pilot's prayer. Pulling the joy-stick hard back to get high G and feeling the blood drain from the upper body until blackout occurs may be fun but it is not the only aspect of manoeuvre that needs attention. At high speed and high G an aircraft will have a greater radius of turn than another jet pulling the same G at lower speed. Therefore G on its own is not the 'be all and end all' of combat. Turn radius is even more important because being able to turn 'inside' an opponent's turn assists you in pointing at the opposition, which is the main aim of the game. That is why you want to turn the aircraft in the first place: to bring your weapon system to bear on the opposition and fire at him successfully. It is no good blatting round the sky at high speed and high G if your opponent is able to point at you continuously while you are doing it. The end result will only be a missile homing in on you.

Now imagine two aircraft on the same heading and side by side in the air, each trying to get into the other's 6 o'clock or trying to point at their adversary. (This 'side-by-side' position often occurs in combat as a result of initial manoeuvres by the two aircraft.) One aircraft may get some advantage over the other (partially behind the other) but could have too much energy (speed); the other aircraft would then force a partial overshoot by throttling back and using the airbrake to reduce forward movement.

There are two options that need to be considered by each pilot in this situation: turning hard towards the point where you want to be behind the other aircraft (without hitting him); and slowing down relative to the other aircraft so as to reduce forward progress through the air. Combining the two options successfully means that you will end up in the right place provided that the opposition is not doing the same thing equally or more successfully. With aircraft of the same type (with the same G and thrust capability), the pilot who flies his aircraft best in manoeuvre should win. With dissimilar aircraft each with its own G and thrust characteristics but with equally capable pilots, the aircraft with the better manoeuvrability characteristics should win.

From the side-by-side position the aircraft will use roll and lift (G) to try to point towards each other's 6 o'clock and airbrake and throttle to slow the aircraft down and retard forward progress. This turning manoeuvre has then to be reversed when passing close to the other aircraft until one or other aircraft gradually falls behind the other and gains the advantage of a firing position. The fight is then over bar the shouting. The manoeuvre is known as a 'scissors'.

If aircraft have initially met head-on and they both want to fight, they will immediately turn back towards each other with the aim of pointing the other aircraft first. This 'turn' can be a looping manoeuvre, a flat turn, or anything in between. Whatever disposition there may be between opposing fighters in the air, the successful fighter pilot will balance the use of speed, G and rolling moment with the optimum chosen flight-path to point the adversary as quickly as possible. There is considerable skill required not only in handling the aircraft smoothly (albeit aggressively) but also in knowing which flight path to opt for to get the best results.

The term 'pointing the aircraft' is a subject alien to most fighter aircraft designers. They, like many of the less educated fighter jocks, believe that power/speed and high G will always produce the correct results in combat. Although speed and high G are undeniably most desirable qualities in a fighter, neither are as important as being able to point at the opposition quickly. This comment often appears to be a contradiction in terms to the uneducated and so let us examine it more closely.

In a fairly evenly matched combat, it is more often the case than not that the high-speed flight will degenerate into some form of 'scissors' manoeuvre and, as the aim of the game in a 'scissors' is to retard forward progress relative to the opposition, it is logical that both aircraft will end up at very low speed. At this point, whichever aircraft can point or turn better in the slow-speed environment will win the fight.

Pointing can either be achieved by rotating the nose in pitch in conventional fashion (by pulling back on the stick) or by slicing the nose left or right (using the rudder pedals) when the aircraft is slow and in a vertical position. In some aircraft, much higher rates of pointing can be achieved by slicing the nose than by using the conventional pitch (back stick) manoeuvre.

It is easy to see, therefore, that the aircraft that can decelerate most rapidly into its best pointing regime will often hold the advantage in one-against-one (1 v 1) combat – provided that the basic rules of combat continue to be obeyed.

It is in the slow-speed pointing regime that the Sea Harrier VSTOL aircraft is unmatched. Its ability to reduce forward speed with use of the aircraft's nozzles cannot be equalled by a conventional fighter and its slow-speed handling characteristics allow it to point faster and better than any other fighter in the slow-speed environment.

For 1 v 1 combat, therefore, the key characteristics of a successful fighter are:

a. The ability to point an adversary before he can point at you (so you can bring your weapons to bear).

To do this aircraft must have

b. Adequate G characteristics at medium and high speed;

c. Enough thrust to sustain adequate G at reasonable speeds;

d. Outstanding low-speed handling and pointing characteristics;

The successful fighter must also have

e. A good, flexible, easy-to-use weapons system;

f. A fighter pilot who knows what he is doing.

When multi-aircraft combat is considered, different priorities may be placed on each characteristic. Pilot expertise is essential in any combat and in the multi-aircraft environment tactical expertise and close co-ordination between friendly fighters becomes of paramount importance. Two good pilots in inferior jets will always have a good chance of beating two inferior pilots in theoretically better aircraft.

On the normally accepted statistics as interpreted by the 'greater unwashed' it could be assumed that the Mirage III is a much more capable fighter than the Sea Harrier. It is able to pull much more G at any chosen speed and has a top speed that is double that of the SHAR. The same is true of most of the 'acknowledged air superiority fighters' such as the F-15, F-16, F-18, etc. But the SHAR can and has regularly beaten all these fighters in closely monitored combat, which disproves the assumption that G and high speed are all important. (And the proof of the pudding as far as the Mirage III and the Mirage V are concerned was the Falklands confrontation. Although there was no fully developed 1 v 1 combat, some initial manoeuvring did take place and as the world now knows there were several Mirage losses and no Sea Harrier losses in combat.)

Fighter weapon systems play an increasingly important part in the air-to-air scenario and, with the advent of new aircraft radars and the Advanced Medium-Range and Short-Range Missiles, the much-vaunted high-speed and high-G characteristics will mean less and less. Pointing the fighter and firing the weapon system will be the key to air fighting.

294

Situations of developed close air combat between single fighters will still remain a possibility, and designers should therefore concentrate on the key characteristics needed for 1 v 1 combat rather than spending a fortune on extracting one more G or a few extra knots.

The last and most interesting characteristic that the modern fighter aircraft should enjoy is the ability to land vertically and operate from short airstrips. The inability of the Argentine fighters to do this cost Argentina the Falklands War. If they could have operated from the short runway at Port Stanley, the Task Force's job would have been vastly more difficult. As it was, the UK enjoyed the benefit of having the only fighter in the world with VSTOL attributes. The SHAR also points better than any other fighter, costs less than other fighters, operates from almost anywhere without reliance on long runways, uses less fuel and can beat all fighter opposition in combat.

What more can one ask for? And why do the world's air forces cling to old-fashioned jets that can only be operated safely from long and expensive runways?

The answer to the second question is commercial, national and inter-service rivalry — and an astonishing failure by the British Government to promote and market the unique British Sea Harrier fighter product.

Perhaps there is one disadvantage to the present generation of VSTOL jets; and this invokes the first question, 'What more could one ask for?' The Harrier family of jets are versatile and capable — but they need the best pilots to fly them. That is why the cream of RAF pilot capability gets channelled into the Harrier world. One might therefore ask for a VSTOL jet (with the Sea Harrier's unique combat performance) that can be flown successfully by 'an average pilot' rather than just the best pilots!

Appendix III

The Fleet Air Arm Toast

Here's to us in our sober moods
When we ramble, sit and think!
And here's to us in our drunken moods
When we gamble, sin and drink!
And when our flying days are over
And from this world we pass
May the fish-heads bury us upside down
So the world can kiss our arse!

INDEX